American Isolationists

American Isolationists

Pro-Japan Anti-interventionists and the FBI on the Eve of the Pacific War, 1939–1941

Roger B. Jeans

ROWMAN & LITTLEFIELD
Lanham • Boulder • New York • London

Published by Rowman & Littlefield
An imprint of The Rowman & Littlefield Publishing Group, Inc.
4501 Forbes Boulevard, Suite 200, Lanham, Maryland 20706
www.rowman.com

6 Tinworth Street, London SE11 5AL, United Kingdom

Copyright © 2021 by The Rowman & Littlefield Publishing Group, Inc.

All rights reserved. No part of this book may be reproduced in any form or by any electronic or mechanical means, including information storage and retrieval systems, without written permission from the publisher, except by a reviewer who may quote passages in a review.

British Library Cataloguing in Publication Information Available

Library of Congress Cataloging-in-Publication Data

Names: Jeans, Roger B., author.
Title: American isolationists : Pro-Japan anti-interventionists and the FBI on the eve of the Pacific War, 1939–1941 / Roger B. Jeans.
Other titles: Pro-Japan anti-interventionists and the FBI on the eve of the Pacific War, 1939–1941
Description: Lanham : Rowman & Littlefield, [2020] | Includes bibliographical references and index.
Identifiers: LCCN 2020040161 (print) | LCCN 2020040162 (ebook) | ISBN 9781538143087 (cloth) | ISBN 9781538143094 (epub) | ISBN 9781538171172 (pbk)
Subjects: LCSH: World War, 1939–1945—United States. | Isolationism—United States—History—20th century. | America First Committee—History. | Neutrality—United States—History—20th century. | Japan—Foreign public opinion, American. | World War, 1939–1945—Causes.
Classification: LCC D753 .J43 2020 (print) | LCC D753 (ebook) | DDC 940.53/2273—dc23
LC record available at https://lccn.loc.gov/2020040161
LC ebook record available at https://lccn.loc.gov/2020040162

Contents

List of Illustrations	vii
Acknowledgments	ix
Introduction: Isolationism, Japan, and the FBI, 1939–1941	1
1 O. K. Armstrong and the Pro-Japan Isolationists in Prewar America	13
2 Businessmen and Generals	35
3 The Professoriat	53
4 Pacifists and Former Missionaries	91
5 Journalists	105
6 "We Plan to Prevent War, if Possible, with Japan": The Committee on Pacific Relations	117
7 The FBI and Pro-Japan Isolationists	163
Conclusion	189
Epilogue: The Afterlife of an Isolationist	199
Bibliography	205
Index	213
About the Author	225

List of Illustrations

Photographs follow p. 104.

　　Figure 1: O.K. Armstrong election poster, ca. 1930s.
　　Figure 2: O.K. Armstrong, ca. 1940.
　　Figure 3: William J. Baxter Sr., 1956.
　　Figure 4: Frederick J. Libby, ca. 1930s.
　　Figure 5: Payson J. Treat, 1935.
　　Figure 6: Elizabeth Boody Schumpeter, n.d.
　　Figure 7: William Henry Chamberlin, n.d.
　　Figure 8: Mark Revell Shaw, n.d.
　　Figure 9: Ralph Townsend, 1934.

Acknowledgments

This book is, in a sense, a continuation of my 2009 work, *Terasaki Hidenari, Pearl Harbor, and Occupied Japan*. While that study told the story of the activities of a Japanese intelligence agent, propaganda chief, and diplomat in Washington on the eve of war, this book examines more closely the Americans who sympathized with Japan right up to the Japanese attack on Pearl Harbor.

In preparing this volume, I have incurred many intellectual debts. As usual, several staff members in Washington and Lee's Leyburn Library proved indispensable. Professor Elizabeth A. Teaff, access services manager, efficiently, cheerfully, and faithfully helped in numerous ways, including filling interlibrary loan requests. John White, help desk and shared services manager, Information Technology Services, cheerfully and efficiently solved my computer problems. Brandon Bucy, senior academic technologist, made time to electronically send the book manuscript and photographs to the publisher, despite the press of his own work. Richard F. Grefe, senior reference librarian, proved a good listener, advisor, and understanding friend when, all too frequently, I showed up in his office needing to talk to someone about this project. On numerous occasions, Laura Hewlett has cheerfully and swiftly provided badly needed assistance, especially during the pandemic, when I was unable to enter the library for several months at a crucial stage in preparation of this book.

Susan McEachern, editorial director at Rowman & Littlefield, is a wonder. She has cheerfully and efficiently served as editor for two of my earlier books but has been much more than that. Over the years, whenever I had an idea for a new book, including this one, I could depend on swift and wise advice from her. It has always been a pleasure working with her on a new project. My longtime friend Edward J. Drea was extremely helpful and encouraging with the manuscript of this book (as with earlier scholarly projects), and for that and over a half century of friendship, I thank him.

In the course of searching for photographs for this book, I found ready and willing assistance from several archives and their archivists. James Zobel, archivist at the MacArthur Memorial Archives, went far beyond the usual scope of his profession to assist me in revisiting the Terasaki Hidenari papers I donated to the MacArthur Memorial a decade ago. Jonathan Konzal, now archivist at the State Historical Society of Missouri, located and sent a pair of photographs of O. K. Armstrong, the "spark plug" of the pro-Japan Committee on Pacific Relations. Sarah Patton, archivist at the Hoover Institution, located a photograph of Professor Payson Treat receiving a Japanese imperial award. Damon Hart, director of operations at Baxter Investment Management, helped me obtain permission from William J. Baxter Jr. to include a photograph of his grandfather, William J. Baxter Sr., in my book. Bryn Keytanjian, technical services specialist, Swarthmore College Peace Collection, located and ably steered me through the process of obtaining a photograph of Frederick J. Libby. Robin Rancourt, archives assistant in the Special and Archival Collections at Providence College, cheerfully and efficiently identified and sent a photograph of William Henry Chamberlin. Harvard University Archives and the Bentley Historical Library at the University of Michigan very kindly provided photographs of Elizabeth B. Schumpeter and Mark R. Shaw, respectively. Melissa Davis, director of library and archives at the Marshall Foundation, offered several helpful suggestions regarding photographs.

An unexpected benefit of being shifted nearly five years ago from a locked study to a student carrell was the friendship made with the two successive students, Philip Harmon and David Shook, who sat at the desk across from me.

Finally, my wife, Sylvia A. Fesperman, has been a pillar of support throughout the preparation of this book. She has patiently listened to my grumblings about various scholarly undertakings for over fifty years, for which she surely deserves some sort of medal.

Introduction

Isolationism, Japan, and the FBI, 1939–1941

I thought I was finished with pro-Japan American isolationists on the eve of World War II when I published a book a decade ago on the connections between these groups and Japanese intelligence.[1] However, our current president's single-minded focus on U.S. interests at the expense of its traditional alliances and constructive engagement with the international community rekindled my interest in the isolationists of an earlier time. His repeated references to "America First" reminded me of the isolationist America First Committee (1940–1941), which attracted hundreds of thousands of members in a concerted effort to keep the United States out of the war in Europe. Finally, the FBI's investigation of Russian influence on Donald Trump's election campaign in 2016 was reminiscent of the bureau's investigation of pro-Japan isolationists just before the Pacific War.

This is a study of American isolationists (also known as anti-interventionists) and the coming of the Pacific War with Japan during the late 1930s and early 1940s. Some years ago, a scholar asserted, "When it comes to Japan, there is enough material concerning the anti-interventionist response to make a small book."[2] In my earlier study, I plumbed the cooperation between a relatively unknown isolationist, Missouri conservative activist Orland Kay ("O. K.") Armstrong, and a Japanese diplomat and propaganda chief, Terasaki Hidenari, whose mission was to cultivate antiwar isolationists and pacifists in the United States in an effort to keep America out of war in the Pacific. Here, I focus on Armstrong's attempted creation of a pro-Japan isolationist organization, the Committee on Pacific Relations, which portrayed itself as a rival of the America First Committee for the allegiance of anti-interventionists. Whereas America First primarily focused on opposing U.S. involvement in the European conflict, however, the mission of Armstrong's committee was to oppose war with Japan. In doing so, its members were frequently critical of U.S. policy while sympathetic to Japan. Although they were willing to abide by the 1937 Neutrality Act, which banned the export of arms to all belligerents and refused to sell American aviation fuel and scrap iron to Japan, "Most anti-interventionists did not want to confront Japan."[3]

Next to nothing has been written about the pro-Japan isolationists' sympathetic views of the Japan in the late 1930s and early 1940s, while the story of the America First Committee's mobilization of numerous Americans in 1940 and 1941 in opposition to American involvement in yet another European conflict has been extensively covered, especially by historians of an earlier generation, such as the masterful Wayne S. Cole (see the bibliography for his writings). More recent studies of isolationism as well as of individual isolationists, such as Lynne Olson's *Those Angry Days* in 2013 and Susan Dunn's *1940: F.D.R., Willkie, Lindbergh, and Hitler* also in 2013, have continued to focus on their opposition to the European war (1939–1945)[4] while largely ignoring the small group of pro-Japan anti-interventionists.

Historians have paid far less attention—if any—to the opposition of the latter to expansion of the Sino-Japanese War (1937–1945) into a conflict between Japan and the United States. This conflict had roiled international politics for years prior to the "Great Debate" of 1939–1941. In September 1931, the Japanese manufactured a pretext to attack Chinese forces in Manchuria and annex that huge territory. During the 1930s, they expanded southward into the provinces of North China. In contrast to the invasion and occupation of Manchuria, this time they did not create a pretext for further expansion. The Marco Polo Bridge Incident occurred as a result of miscalculations on both sides. The resultant clashes between Chinese and Japanese troops were followed by Japanese expansion of the fighting to Shanghai in central China. Eventually, the trials of strength led to fighting throughout eastern China, with the Chinese government withdrawing in 1938 to southwest China, where it remained for the rest of the war.

In this study, I have tried to fill the historical void surrounding the pro-Japan isolationists by examining the correspondence, books, and articles and FBI dossiers of a dozen or so members of Armstrong's committee during the years and months before Pearl Harbor. This study pays particular attention to such committee members as Armstrong, Vassar economics professor Elizabeth Boody Schumpeter, journalist Ralph Townsend (who ended up in prison), and former Japan missionary John Cole McKim, among others, who were suspected of "collusion" with a foreign power (Japan) and investigated by the FBI.

The committee's handful of distinguished members ran the gamut from university professors to New York businessmen to Christian leaders and former missionaries to journalists to professional pacifists. The few soldiers

Armstrong approached declined to participate; they took seriously their duty as officers to defend the nation rather than engage in debate and form committees. As became clear on the eve of Pearl Harbor, the committee was never formally constituted but remained an informal group of like-minded people who had signed Armstrong's May 1941 policy statement opposing war with Japan.

Two members were especially important because of their connections with several other members. As founder of the group, Armstrong was most important. Dr. Elizabeth B. Schumpeter was perhaps the most supportive member after Armstrong. After being contacted by the Missourian, she in turn reached out to other actual and potential members, such as historians Professor A. Whitney Griswold (Yale) and Professor Payson J. Treat (Stanford). During the brief lifespan of the committee, she was one of the most committed members. She, along with Treat and journalist and author William Henry Chamberlin, represented a dissident voice in the debate over U.S. policy toward the Sino-Japanese War in the late 1930s and early 1940s. They felt alienated from the Far Eastern studies field because their attempts to see the Japan side of the war resulted in them being ostracized as pro-Japanese. Those were fraught times for Far Eastern studies, just as the 1950s were ugly times for the field because of the anticommunist zealotry fueled by such infamous figures as Senator Joseph McCarthy and their largely baseless accusations.

HISTORICAL SETTING

During its earlier history, the United States had traditionally hewed to isolationism, keen to stay out of entanglements in other countries' (especially Europe's) wars. With the beginning of the European conflict in September 1939 with Germany's invasion and conquest of Poland, a "Great Debate" was launched in the United States between interventionists, who wanted to aid nations resisting Germany and Italy (mainly Britain), and anti-interventionists, who, drawing on traditional American isolationism reinforced by what they viewed as America's disastrous involvement in World War I, believed their country should remain aloof from European struggles. This debate involved a series of fiery clashes between interventionists and anti-interventionists during the period from 1939 to 1941.

During those years, the isolationists met with a string of defeats. Following the outbreak of war in September 1939, many people called for amendment of the 1937 Neutrality Act to allow the United States to sell arms to the Allies (Britain and France). Because of fears that the war would threaten the United States, in November 1941, despite opposition from the isolationists, the blanket embargo on arms was repealed and exports to belligerents approved on a cash-and-carry basis.[5]

Before the Germans' defeat of a string of European democracies in the spring of 1940, American isolationists vehemently opposed conscription. However, with western Europe effectively under the thumb of the Germans by the spring and summer of 1940, the isolationists' resistance to the draft collapsed. A few months before the German assault on western Europe, two-thirds of the nation had opposed conscription, but following that invasion, the opposite was true.[6] In September, Congress passed the Selective Service Act, which provided for registration of all males between twenty-one and thirty-six as well as training for a year of 1.2 million soldiers and 800,000 reserves.[7]

With Britain the only European democracy left standing after the German victories on the European continent in 1940, support mounted in the United States for aid to it. As a result, in March 1941, the Lend-Lease Act was passed by both the U.S. Senate and House and signed by President Roosevelt. It stipulated that any nation whose defense the president thought vital for the protection of the United States would be eligible for the receipt of war supplies through sale, transfer, exchange, or lease.[8] Despite America First's vehement opposition to lend-lease, which it dubbed the "war dictator bill," by this time the vast majority of Americans supported aiding Britain.[9]

Getting the supplies to the United Kingdom was another matter. Every day, ten thousand tons of goods were being sunk by German submarines. Thus, following the adoption of the lend-lease policy in March, a debate in the United States arose over whether to use American warships to convoy war supplies to Britain. The president was the only one who could approve a convoy policy, but he moved slowly with piece-meal measures, such as giving the British ten U.S. Coast Guard cutters for use in protecting lend-lease shipments over the Atlantic. As 1940 gave way to 1941, U.S. destroyers played an increasing role in protecting British convoys, which resulted in German attacks on those American warships. By June, a majority of the people favored the convoy policy, which marked yet another defeat for the anti-interventionists.[10]

These political victories over the isolationists were helped along by the creation, in the spring of 1940, of a new interventionist pressure group, the Committee to Defend America by Aiding the Allies, which has been described as "the first organization to combat isolationism on a national scale." Headed by famous newspaper editor William Allen White and including on its board luminaries such as Frank Knox (future secretary of the navy) and Henry Stimson (future secretary of state), it attracted the support of 60 percent of the country. By the end of October 1940, it had one million members with millions more supporting its petitions calling for aid to Britain. The issue that held them all together was their strong belief in helping that country.[11]

At the same time, a second interventionist group, the Century Group, entered the lists with the demand for a declaration of war against Germany. They were Eurocentric, with only one member, *Time-Life* impresario and child of China missionary parents Henry Luce, with eyes for Asia. In early 1941, the group metamorphized into the even more aggressively interventionist Fight for Freedom committee. It established hundreds of chapters, while six hundred small-town newspapers spread its message.[12]

Buoyed by the one-third of the nation that was anti-interventionist but unorganized, the isolationists fought back. In September 1940, they established a national isolationist organization, the America First Committee, with headquarters in Chicago. It expanded quickly into an organization with hundreds of thousands of members and 450 chapters. Although powerful in the Midwest, it was weak in the South (as Armstrong was to discover) and less than a success in New England.[13] From December 1940 to May 1941, the America First Committee was in the midst of its greatest period of expansion. By the time of the Japanese attack on Pearl Harbor in December, it boasted a membership of 800,00 to 850,000 and was supported almost entirely by voluntary contributions.[14] All this made it the main isolationist lobbying organization during the fifteen months before Pearl Harbor.[15]

Opposed to aid to Britain, it was considered the "ultimate spearhead of isolationism" in the United States. That did not mean that just because isolationists wanted to steer clear of the European war they were all pacifists (although some were, of course). In fact, the stance of some isolationists toward Japan was one of "extreme belligerency."[16] Much of America First's leadership was conservative and Republican, and the organization had a difficult time attracting liberals as members. The "isolationist fetish," one author argued, was "strong in the Republican hierarchy."[17] Interventionists went so far as to accuse America First of aiding fascists and Nazis. It was true, in fact, that the committee failed to block fascists and communists from joining its ranks.[18] Meanwhile, there was no question that the isolationists made it extraordinarily difficult for President Roosevelt to prepare the United States to defend itself.[19] At the same time, America First leaders worried that because the organization's raison d'être was opposition, it lacked the "positive ideology" that would keep it going over time.[20]

In April 1941, America First received a tremendous boost when Charles Lindbergh, who had earned everlasting fame by being been the first to fly solo over the Atlantic in 1927, joined America First's executive committee. The previous October, he had already delivered his first America First speech, at Yale University. It must have given comfort to Japanese who knew of that address that he indirectly dismissed any possibility of an aerial threat from their nation. "No nation in Asia," he declared, "has developed their [sic] aviation sufficiently to be a serious menace to the United States at this time." Over the following year, he proved America First's biggest attraction, giving thirteen speeches in cities nationwide.[21]

The European "Phony War" of the winter of 1939 and 1940, when Germany initially failed to follow up its victory in Poland with a full-scale assault on western Europe, proved to be what one writer dubbed the "heyday of isolationism" in the United States. The uneasy pause ended with the German conquest of the countries of western Europe in the spring of 1940. When the fighting was over in June, Britain stood alone (although it succeeded in evacuating a large part of its defeated expeditionary force from the French beaches at Dunkirk).[22]

During all those struggles, most isolationists, fixated on Europe, gave less thought to Japan, even though it had been steadily expanding its overseas empire since its conquest of China's Manchuria in the early 1930s (and even earlier with its swift victory in the first Sino-Japanese War, 1894–1995).[23]

JAPAN AND AMERICAN ISOLATIONISTS

Meanwhile, Americans were not the only ones interested in isolationist organizations. In January 1941, Japan's Foreign Ministry asked its Washington embassy for information on American organizations and prominent people opposed to U.S. entrance into the war in hopes of using them to gather intelligence. The following month, Foreign Minister Matsuoka Yosuke ordered the embassy to survey persons and organizations that publicly or secretly opposed U.S. participation in war, which largely meant isolationists and pacifists.[24] He "thought he knew America very well," according to a Japanese journalist, "better than anyone else." However, he "overestimated the influence of the isolationists in the United States."[25] He had grounds for believing he knew America and the Americans well, for he had worked his way through school in the United States and graduated from Oregon University.[26]

In Japan, the isolationists received a lot of favorable publicity. Referring to a December 1940 radio address by President Roosevelt, the Japanese newspaper *Chugai* optimistically claimed, "In view of the opposition to war participation by Charles A. Lindbergh and others, Roosevelt's broadcast can be regarded as merely a private opinion not necessarily representative of the American people." Commenting on this, the U.S. ambassador to Japan, Joseph Grew, wrote in his diary: "Opposition and isolationist utterances by well-known Americans are always prominently displayed here but seldom anything on the other side of the story. So, of course, the Japanese public gets an unbalanced and distorted impression."[27] According to Frederick Moore, Ambassador Nomura Kichisaburo's American adviser, many Japanese believed that because there were many peace societies in the United States, it would stay out of war. The Japanese press reinforced that impression by informing its readers of the United States' many weaknesses. Americans, it argued, were not united behind Roosevelt's foreign policy. Moreover, Gallup polls showed that a majority of Americans opposed entering the war in Europe. There also was opposition in Congress, it reported, including Democrats as well as Republicans. Opponents of Roosevelt's policies, it noted, drew mass audiences at rallies. In addition, there were numerous labor strikes. All this, Moore opined, "seemed to the Japanese incontrovertible evidence" of U.S. weakness.[28]

In June 1941, Japan's ambassador in Washington, Nomura Kichisaburo, made clear that keeping the United States out of war was the main objective of Japanese diplomatic policy. Writing exactly six months to the day before his countrymen's surprise attack on Pearl Harbor, he expressed confidence the United States was "not likely to enter the war so soon." Three weeks later, he cabled the Japanese foreign minister that if they could obtain an "understanding" between Japan and America, they could use diplomacy to keep America out of the war. Japan's "fundamental policy," he explained, was "to make the Tripartite Alliance [Germany, Italy, and Japan] our keynote and to avoid Japanese-American War."[29] In August, he informed the Italian ambassador that even though Japan did not want the United States to enter the war, it would remain loyal to the pact. A month before the Pearl Harbor attack, he assured U.S. Secretary of State Cordell Hull that the pact and peace between Japan and America were compatible.[30] Unfortunately, it seems that neither Nomura nor many of his countrymen grasped the contradiction between the two goals. A month before Pearl Harbor, Hull made plain American objections to this formula when he told Nomura of the "difficulty of readjusting Japanese-American diplomatic relations so long as Japan was tied up with Hitler by the Tripartite Alliance."[31]

Japan was not the only Axis power to cultivate the isolationists in hopes of keeping the United States out of the war. The "only real purpose," a journalist later asserted, of the German, Italian, and Vichy French diplomats in Washington was "to encourage, however they could, the America First and *other isolationist groups* [author's emphasis] trying to keep the United States out of the war." Thus, the FBI accused the Vichy ambassador of allowing German agents to use his embassy to spread "defeatism and isolationism."[32]

In deciding to approach antiwar Americans, though, the Japanese and other Axis diplomats were struggling against growing American support for helping Britain rather than staying clear of the war. It was true that many isolationists were vehemently anti-British.[33] Nevertheless, in January 1941, 60 percent of Americans questioned in a Gallup poll were willing to risk war by supporting Britain.[34] By late April, 81 percent of Americans opposed going to war, but support for fighting against Germany and Italy, if necessary, had risen to 68 percent.[35] Meanwhile, in a radio address in December 1940, Roosevelt made clear his disdain for the anti-interventionists. He anticipated the activities of O. K. Armstrong and his pro-Japan Committee on Pacific Relations when he declared, "There are . . . American citizens, many of them in high places, who, unwittingly in most cases, are aiding and abetting the work of these [foreign] agents." They were, he added, "appeasers" and "defeatists."[36]

There was evidence to support the president's charge of appeasement in the suggestion of America First's chairman, General Robert Wood, that the United States placate Hitler by giving him the lower half of South America—so much for America's Monroe Doctrine, which in 1823 warned European powers against encroachments in its hemisphere[37]—which was naturally the farthest portion from the United States. Hitler would thus add seventy million people and five million square miles to his growing empire. This arrangement was vastly better, Wood added, than a protracted war with Hitler. To appeasement, he blithely added imperialism, for he went on to advocate the United States seize the northern part of South America for itself. The general also was among those Americans who attempted to appease Japan by asking if Asia was worth a major conflict.[38]

ISOLATIONISTS FOCUS ON EUROPE OVER ASIA

Meanwhile, most isolationists (such as members of the America First Committee) did not pay as much attention to Asia as to Europe. In part, that was because they did not believe that a conflict in Asia would be a land war that called for a large-scale mobilization that might threaten U.S. democracy. The only possible foe was Japan and, unlike in Europe, in a conflict with Japan the United States would not be hampered by interference from strong allies. As anti-interventionist Senator Robert A. Taft put it, a Pacific war would not be as "dangerous" as a European conflict, although the isolationists did worry that even a Pacific conflict might turn into a larger war. They were concerned by the possibility of entanglement posed by Japan's actions in Manchuria in September 1931 and the appointment the following month of an American representative to the Council of the League of Nations.[39] Nevertheless, in 1939, one writer scoffed at the idea of war with Japan. The notion that war with Japan was "possible, that Japan may attack us, and we may fight in Japanese waters," he wrote, was the "worst" of the "defense impostures and delusions."[40]

At the same time, in the 1930s most isolationists opposed the Japanese attack on China. Some feared that if the president declared China and Japan to be at war (the Japanese called the conflict the "China Incident"), the Neutrality Act of 1937 would take effect and an arms embargo would deprive China of vital U.S. supplies. Most isolationists, however, disagreed with that position. In 1937, a group of congressmen urged the president to declare China and Japan to be at war and apply the Neutrality Act equally. On the other hand, some anti-interventionists adopted a hard-line position toward Japan. A congresswoman representing the isolationist National Council for the Prevention of War, founded in 1921, argued that if the Neutrality Act was not invoked, "we are definitely helping Japan." The isolationist Women's International League for Peace and Freedom urged Roosevelt to embargo the shipment of oil, scrap iron, and other materials to Japan. An isolationist senator, who in early 1941 shifted to an interventionist stance, called for a boycott of Japanese goods as well as application of the Neutrality Act.[41]

There also were isolationists who believed that tensions with Japan, following the September 1940 signing of the Tripartite Pact, constituted a "backdoor to war." Conflict with Japan, they believed, could result in the United States entering the European war. In addition—sounding like the famous American evangelist, missionary, and pacifist E. Stanley Jones—they argued that the Roosevelt government was using the "pretense of a Japanese threat" to support Western rule in Hong Kong, Singapore, French Indochina, and the Dutch East Indies (and, Jones would have added, India). Most anti-interventionists, wrote a leading scholar of isolationism, claimed Japan was not a military threat.[42]

In December 1940, an America First advertisement announced: "We have no real quarrel with Japan. We have no conceivable stake in Asia worth the terrific cost of a long-distant struggle with Japan." Sounding much like some members of Armstrong's future Committee on Pacific Relations, the advertisement declared that although America First "sympathized with China," the United States should not dive into war "across 6,000 miles of the Pacific for sentimental reasons." It should not become a "knight-errant in Asia." America First could not have been more wrong when it concluded, a year before the Japanese attack on Pearl Harbor, "There will be no 'emergencies' that necessitate war with Japan unless we make them ourselves."[43] As one writer later put it, the anti-interventionists did not consider the war in Asia the harbinger of the kind of "entanglement" they feared from a European war. As a result, they saw little reason to talk about the Far Eastern crisis. When it was discussed, they insisted that America had no "overriding interests" in the Far East. The Sino-Japanese War involved "boundaries and trade" and was none of the business of the United States.[44]

In August 1941, however, critics of America First pointed out that a national poll revealed that Americans favored stopping Japan "even at the risk of war." "Virtually all the America First Committee leaders and members," though, a scholar argued, "opposed American participation in a war in the Pacific before the Japanese attack on Pearl Harbor." America First's executive committee went on record as unanimously opposed to a Pacific war unless the United States was attacked. America First, a prominent historian wrote, "never mounted a major campaign to prevent war with Japan"—which left an opening for Armstrong and his Committee on Pacific Relations.

Trade with Japan, they believed, was an adequate basis for good relations with Japan. Some—sounding like the members of Armstrong's committee—argued that Japan had as much right to hegemony in the East as the United States had in the Western Hemisphere (the Monroe Doctrine). One writer played into the hands of Japanese expansionists and propagandists when he argued that "we want 'America for the Americans', so perhaps they want 'Asia for the Asiatics.'" Many, like E. Stanley Jones, believed war with Japan would be merely to protect British imperialism in Asia. Only a handful of America First spokesmen talked toughly about Japan. The star of the isolationist movement, Charles Lindbergh, did not seem to be opposed to war with Japan, if it did not involve Europe. The chairman of the Columbus, Ohio, chapter of America First favored war with Japan. However, those were "exceptions to the general views of America First supporters."[45]

The day before Pearl Harbor was attacked, the New York chapter of America First was still declaring the Roosevelt administration would be responsible for any "breakdown in relations with Japan." Despite this, America First never conducted a campaign to prevent war with Japan. It was still focused on Europe when Japanese bombers destroyed the committee's reason for existing.[46] It was Armstrong's Committee on Pacific Relations that undertook to prevent war with Japan.

NOTES

1. Roger B. Jeans, *Terasaki Hidenari, Pearl Harbor, and Occupied Japan* (Lanham, MD: Lexington Books, 2009).

2. See Justus D. Doenecke, "Explaining the Antiwar Movement, 1939–1941: The Next Assignment," *Journal of Libertarian Studies* 8, no. 1 (1986): 159, for a list of Japanese actions between 1939 and 1941 that could be studied for the isolationists' responses.

3. Doenecke, "Explaining the Antiwar Movement," 159.

4. Lynne Olson, *Those Angry Days: Roosevelt, Lindbergh, and America's Fight over World War II, 1939–1941* (New York: Random House, 2013); Susan Dunn, *1940: F.D.R., Willkie, Lindbergh, and Hitler—the Election amid the Storm* (New Haven, CT: Yale University, 2013).

5. Geoffrey Perrett, *Days of Sadness, Years of Triumph: The American People, 1939–1945* (New York: Coward, McCann & Geoghegan, 1973; Penguin Books, 1974), 17–18, 23–24, 58, 170–71, 192.

6. Perrett, *Days of Sadness*, 27.

7. William L. Langer, comp. and ed., *An Encyclopedia of World History* (Boston: Houghton Mifflin, 1952), 1155.

8. William Bridgewater, ed., *The Columbia-Viking Desk Encyclopedia*, 2nd ed. (New York: Columbia University Press, 1964), 1012; Perrett, *Days of Sadness*, 75–76.

9. Perrett, *Days of Sadness*, 157.

10. Perrett, *Days of Sadness*, 77–78, 170–71.

11. Perrett, *Days of Sadness*, 58–60, 155–56; Robert E. Sherwood, *Roosevelt and Hopkins: An Intimate History*, rev. ed. (New York: Universal Library, Grosset and Dunlap, 1950), 166–68.
12. Perrett, *Days of Sadness*, 58–60, 156–57.
13. Perrett, *Days of Sadness*, 60–61.
14. Wayne S. Cole, *America First: The Battle against Intervention in World War II* (Madison: University of Wisconsin Press, 1953), 30–31.
15. Cole, *America First*, ix.
16. Sherwood, *Roosevelt and Hopkins*, 123, 130–31, 142; Wayne S. Cole, *Roosevelt and the Isolationists* (Lincoln: University of Nebraska Press, 1983), 379.
17. Sherwood, *Roosevelt and Hopkins*, 173; Cole, *America First*, 71–72, 75, 167.
18. Cole, *America First*, 104; Perrett, *Days of Sadness*, 62.
19. Cole, *America First*, 197–99.
20. Doenecke, "Explaining the Antiwar Movement," 161.
21. A. Scott Berg, *Lindbergh* (New York: G.P. Putnam's Sons, 1998), 412–13. On his Yale speech, see also Wayne S. Cole, *Charles A. Lindbergh and the Battle against Intervention in World War II* (New York: Harcourt Brace Jovanovich, 1974), 108.
22. Sherwood, *Roosevelt and Hopkins*, 142.
23. Cole, *America First*, viii.
24. U.S. Department of Defense, *The "Magic" Background of Pearl Harbor*, 5 vols. (Washington, DC: Government Printing Office, 1978), 1:(113), (118), (119); Gerhard Krebs, "The Spy Activities of Diplomat Terasaki Hidenari in the USA and His Role in Japanese-American Relations," in *Leaders and Leadership in Japan*, ed. Ian Neary (Richmond, UK: Curzon Press, 1996), 191.
25. Kato Masuo, interviews by Roy L. Morgan, Worth McKinney, and Harold Nathan, 6, 7, and 8 February 1946, box 1, folder [IMTFE] (IPS), February–July 1946, Interrogations of Japanese Officials, Roy Leonard Morgan Papers (MSS 93-4), Special Collections, University of Virginia Law School.
26. Janet Hunter, comp., *Concise Dictionary of Modern Japanese History* (Berkeley: University of California Press, 1984), 124.
27. Joseph C. Grew, *Ten Years in Japan: A Contemporary Record Drawn from the Diaries and Private and Official Papers of Joseph C. Grew, United States Ambassador to Japan, 1932–1945* (New York: Simon and Schuster, 1944), 364.
28. Frederick Moore, *With Japan's Leaders: An Intimate Record of Fourteen Years as Counsellor to the Japanese Government* (New York: Charles Scribner's Sons, 1942), 151–53, 162.
29. Nomura Kichisaburo, "Diary of Kichisaburo Nomura, June–December 1941," in *The Pacific War Papers: Japanese Documents of World War II*, ed. Donald M. Goldstein and Katherine V. Dillon (Washington, DC: Potomac Books, 2004), 139, 146.
30. Nomura, "Diary," 175, 203.
31. Nomura, "Diary," 204.
32. David Brinkley, *Washington Goes to War* (New York: Knopf, 1988), 32–33.
33. Manfred Jonas, *Isolationism in America, 1935–1941* (Ithaca, NY: Cornell University Press, 1966), 227–32.
34. Kenneth S. Davis, *The Hero: Charles A. Lindbergh and the American Dream* (Garden City, NY: Doubleday & Company, 1959), 402.
35. Berg, *Lindbergh*, 421.
36. U.S. Department of State, *Foreign Relation of the United States, Japan: 1931–1941*, 2 vols. (Washington, DC: Government Printing Office, 1943), 2:173–81.
37. Langer, comp. and ed., *An Encyclopedia of World History*, 770–71.
38. Perrett, *Days of Sadness*, 163–64, 188.
39. Jonas, *Isolationism*, 23–24.
40. Jonas, *Isolationism*, 128–29.
41. Jonas, *Isolationism*, 200–202; "Historical Introduction," National Council for the Prevention of War, electronic finding aid, Swarthmore College Peace Collection.

42. Doenecke, "Explaining the Antiwar Movement," 160. For Jones's role in the frantic efforts to avert war on the eve of the Pearl Harbor attack, see Jeans, *Terasaki Hidenari*, especially chap. 4.
43. Cole, *America First*, 190.
44. Jonas, *Isolationism*, 104.
45. Cole, *America First*, 64, 189–92; Cole, *Charles A. Lindbergh*, 208.
46. Cole, *America First*, 192–93.

Chapter One

O. K. Armstrong and the Pro-Japan Isolationists in Prewar America

O. K. Armstrong, who hailed from Springfield, Missouri, and served on the Foreign Relations Committee of the American Legion, was one of many activists in the isolationist movement—although those so dubbed rejected the label of "isolationist"—before the war.[1] He was a journalist and author defined by his Baptist faith, which led him, periodically, to crusades to "clean up" the media and battle "obscenity," and, especially in the postwar period, to an ardent anticommunism.

During World War I, he served in the U.S. Army Air Corps.[2] He attended Drury College, a small liberal arts school in Springfield, Missouri, before going on to the School of Journalism at the University of Missouri. For many years, he served as president of the Missouri Writers Guild.[3] Following World War I, he established a journalism department at the University of Florida and served as its chairman through 1928. A Republican, he was elected to the Missouri legislature in 1932 and 1934 and again in 1942 and 1944. He ran for reelection in 1936 but was defeated.[4] In 1939, the governor of Kansas commissioned him to investigate "vice and gambling conditions" in that state.[5] In February of that year, Missouri Governor Lloyd C. Stark (1886–1972) appointed him a special investigator charged with looking into possible malfeasance in elections in Kansas City, Missouri.[6]

Armstrong was friends with prominent antiwar figure Charles Lindbergh as well as the famous Antarctic explorer Admiral Richard E. Byrd, a pacifist who in January 1937 proposed a "six-month moratorium on war."[7] Armstrong also had pacifist credentials. In 1937, he participated in the World Peace and Foreign Relations meeting as an American Legion delegate. In October of the same year, he was one of twelve U.S. representatives to the Federal Iterali des Ancient Combatants, a group of World War I veterans dedicated to world peace and amicable international relations, which convened in Paris. In contrast with its subsequent harder stance, in 1937 the American Legion endorsed these aims.[8] In June 1940, while still a member of the American Legion's Foreign Relations Committee, he spoke at an antiwar mobilization meeting, sponsored by seven peace groups, in Washington. The gathering opposed intervention in the European conflict and the "war trend" in American foreign policy. In his own address, Armstrong declared the legion had a policy that called for "urging the President and the Congress to keep us out of war, to combat propaganda, and to strive for the restoration of good faith and nonaggression among men and nations."[9]

A year later (1941), an FBI report noted, Armstrong was earning a living by writing for *American Legion Magazine* and other periodicals. He made, the bureau added, "considerable sums of money by writing newspaper articles."[10] He was a gifted magazine author, according to another account, whose "boundless energies and great enthusiasms often outdistanced his judgement and organizational talents."[11] The irony was that while Armstrong, as well as members of his Committee on Pacific Relations, were opposed to what they saw as domestic propaganda,[12] his main contact in the Japanese embassy in Washington (Terasaki Hidenari) was responsible for Japanese propaganda in the United States.

COLLABORATION WITH PACIFIST FREDERICK J. LIBBY AND SPLIT WITH THE AMERICAN LEGION

In June 1940, Armstrong issued a statement to Congress in which he asserted the "hour has struck for the American Legion to take a vigorous stand and assume leadership to keep this country from involvement in war." He had, according to a press report, "pledged his time and energy" to that policy.[13] The following month, however, many legion posts wrote to their congressmen in support of the Burke–Wadsworth Selective Service Act, which was passed in September. In late July, Frederick J. Libby, executive secretary of the isolationist National Council for the Prevention of War, a pacifist organization, wired Armstrong asking if he could "change all this through your commander and through letters to legion posts."[14]

Libby, a Maine native, played a major role in the establishment of the council in 1921 and, as its executive secretary, personified it until his retirement in 1954.[15] As time passed, he "*became* the NCPW in the minds of many Americans." Proof of this was the council's suspension of activities when he retired.[16] The *New York Times* and *Washington Post* frequently mentioned him during his years with the council. He also had a history of political activism regarding China policy before World War II. As early as 1934, he was asking, in a radio address, "Why should we try to police Asia?"[17] In

1936, he declared he could not "imagine a more unpopular cause to die for" than "for the sake of our investments in China."[18] In September of the following year, he accused the president of "nullification" of the Neutrality Act of 1937, which banned shipments of war supplies to all belligerents, by not applying it to the Sino-Japanese War, which had begun in July.[19] In 1938, in testimony before the House Naval Affairs Committee, he warned against going to war to defend British interests in Asia. He was, he added, "in favor of peace at any price if it involves a foreign war."[20] Six months before Pearl Harbor, he called for the "democratic right to a national referendum on peace or war."[21]

In December 1939, three months following the beginning of the war in Europe, he adopted an accusatory tone toward the Roosevelt administration, asking "how far the Administration is willing to go in protecting the massive interests of Great Britain and France in China" and insisted that American investments in China were "relatively unimportant." He dismissed the prospect of a Japanese attack on the West Coast as a "hoary bogey." He was opposed to United States threats of an embargo on Japanese goods and termination of the United States–Japan trade treaty in January 1940. "Diplomacy by bluff and threat," he argued, "is . . . poor diplomacy." Those who oppose the United States' entry into a foreign war, he concluded, "must now pay attention to our relations with Japan."[22]

In early 1940, he opposed the efforts of some China missionaries to persuade Congress to embargo shipments of war materials to Japan. His pacifism trumped all, and thus he argued that such an embargo would be a "long step towards war," and the National Council for the Prevention of War "emphatically" opposed it. "We hold unwaveringly," he asserted, "to the neutrality policy today." He was right, in the light of history, when he added that the Japanese would not take such an embargo "lying down." That, he argued, was a "very dangerous type of wishful thinking." Instead, he called on the president to practice "neutral mediation" toward the Chinese and Japanese. If the Japanese knew about it, it must have been music to their ears when he advocated a U.S. policy that acknowledged Japan had "special interests" (Libby's quotation marks) in China.[23] There is no evidence that he gave any thought to what the Chinese might think about his proposal. Later the same year, he insisted the United States could not win a war with Japan. The ultimate victors, he asserted, would be communism and Stalin.[24] Thus, his position was in line with that held by America First leaders, who believed interventionism would lead to the spread of communism.[25]

In July 1941, he opposed the idea of sending an American Expeditionary Force "anywhere in the world."[26] Speaking under the auspices of America First in August, he called for the impeachments of Secretary of the Navy Frank Knox and Secretary of War Henry Stimson.[27] That same month, though, he viewed the Atlantic Conference of Roosevelt and Churchill as paving the road to "genuine peace negotiations with the Axis powers."[28] In October, he opposed increasing the size of the U.S. Navy and accused Knox of pledging the American fleet for "imperialistic adventures in cooperation with the British Empire, all over the world."[29] That same month, he repeated his earlier call for a negotiated peace.[30]

At this time, Libby collaborated with both Armstrong and Lindbergh. In March 1940, Libby and the latter met for the first time. Lindbergh commented that Libby resembled a "New England preacher" characterized by "unusual understanding and intelligence (if one can apply the latter term to a pacifist)." According to the colonel's diary, the two men met four more times that year to coordinate their isolationist efforts.[31] The "great" pacifist saw eye to eye with Lindbergh, who also cherished high hopes for Armstrong's work with the American Legion. It must have impressed the colonel in their initial meeting when Libby told him the National Council for the Prevention of War had mailed out 140,000 copies of one of Lindbergh's anti-interventionist speeches. Unlike Libby, though, Lindbergh was no pacifist. In December, he declared, "I like him more as I know him better—much as I disagree with his ideas on pacifism."[32]

Lindbergh's wife was less taken with Libby. The "head of all peace organizations," she wrote, was "a round-faced, scrubbed little man, full of vigor and zeal, shining with sureness, compact, tidy, and in order." There was an "enamel quality" about people like that, she complained, "which is as hard as the enamel of a sophisticated worldly person. No crack to let you in. Bright and hard—like a button."[33]

America First shared Lindbergh's feelings about pacifists. It was not a pacifist organization and initially barred them from its ranks. That did not mean, though, that it had nothing to do with them. Pacifists supported America First (such as mailing out Lindbergh's speech), while it cooperated with pacifist organizations. Therefore, three weeks after barring them, it lifted the ban on pacifists as members. It also gave funds to two pacifist organizations, the isolationist Women's International League for Peace and Freedom and Ministers' No War Committee.[34]

In the meantime, Armstrong's worldview gradually diverged from that of most legionnaires. In October 1939, a month after the outbreak of the European war, the legion declared it was opposed to any actions that might involve the country in war. The following July, Armstrong mailed editors of religious presses in the United States copies of "Program of World Peace and Foreign Relations." Also called "The 1940 Program," it was drafted by the American Legion's Foreign Relations Committee, of which Armstrong was one of three members. It came with seven suggestions on how to "make this program known and effective," with Armstrong listed as the contact person. Unfortunately for the Missouri anti-interventionist, it presumed to speak for the entire legion when it declared, "we of the American Legion have pledged ourselves to seek and keep an honest neutrality."[35]

At its annual convention in September 1940 in Boston, the legion broke with its isolationist past. Armstrong joined with others to sponsor an amendment to the legion's strong foreign-relations resolution that called for the legion's membership to "reaffirm our policy of neutrality and peace." In calling for support, he argued that the legion had been a "bulwark of sanity in a world gone mad with war." Although for sixteen years the legion had followed a policy of neutrality toward foreign disputes, this time neutrality was "roared down" in a voice vote. In its place, the legion adopted a resolution condemning "aggressor nations and war parties."[36]

Two months later (November), Armstrong's term on the Foreign Relations Committee expired. Before it did, however, he was involved in a scandal. According to correspondence from the legion's headquarters in Indianapolis that an informant in Springfield shared with the FBI in February 1942, in the summer and fall of 1940, while still a member of the American Legion's Foreign Relations Committee, he was given desk space at the Ford Motor Company in Dearborn, Michigan. Moreover, the company paid his expenses during that summer, when he addressed ten or eleven department conventions of the legion. This support stemmed from Henry Ford's interest in isolationism. During World War I, Ford had been a pacifist, but in the 1930s that had turned into a pro-German isolationism. When Ford's views changed in the fall (Ford began to construct a gigantic plant to manufacture engines for a new Douglas bomber) and he was increasingly criticized for his isolationist position, he broke with Armstrong. What was even more offensive to legion leaders was Armstrong's speech at an antiwar rally in June while wearing his American Legion uniform and also his connection with prominent pacifist leaders such as Norman Thomas and Dorothy Detzer.[37]

Thomas, an American Socialist Party leader (he joined in 1917) dubbed "the political left's gadfly" during the 1930s, was a candidate for president six times from 1928 to 1948. With the onset of the worldwide depression in the 1930s, he rose to become one of the major spokesmen for isolationism on the left. After the U.S. Congress overwhelming approved the Lend-Lease Act in March 1941, he joined America First. He feared that if the United States entered the war in Europe, it would swiftly turn into a "capitalist-imperialist dictatorship."[38] Following Lindbergh's controversial Des Moines speech, in which he argued that Jews were one of the key stokers of war fever, Thomas was so angry that he cut all ties with America First.[39]

As national executive director of the U.S. Section of the Women's International League for Peace and Freedom with headquarters in Washington, DC, Dorothy Detzer argued for neutrality as World War II drew near.[40] She came by this position naturally. She had served at Hull House, the social welfare settlement in Chicago founded in 1899 by cowinner of the 1931

Nobel Peace Prize Jane Addams (1860–1935), who had been an activist in peace movements and in the struggle for women's suffrage. Detzer also had worked for the American Friends Service Committee in Russia and Austria. In 1935, she exhorted the United States not to interfere in Italy's invasion of Ethiopia and not to join with the other powers in levying sanctions on Italy. The current world order, she argued, was "unjust," and Americans should wait for "basic corrections" before defending it.[41]

Meanwhile, the legion expressed opposition to being represented at meetings convened by organizations (the National Council for the Prevention of War?) whose leadership contained "some of America's leading pacifist radicals." The legion tried to rein Armstrong in, instructing him not to participate in the Keep America Out of the War Congress, scheduled for Chicago, to inform it of "any such commitments," and to submit the text of his addresses in advance. Keep America Out of War was created in 1938 by Norman Thomas and liberal pacifist Oswald Garrison Villard, a former editor of the liberal journal *Nation*. They worried that if the United States entered the war, American democracy would be undermined.[42]

Many telegrams also were dispatched to Armstrong pointing out his "improprieties" in conveying the impression, in his appearances for the legion, that it endorsed his views. In the end, he was expelled from the American Legion post in Springfield. He also lost his position as a member of the "executive committee for the Americanization of the Legion." In June 1941, the FBI reported that he had been part of that committee "up to a short time ago."[43]

EMERGENCY PEACE CONFERENCE

He was no quitter, though; as a leading scholar of the isolationist movement put it, Armstrong was "a hard man to down." In October 1940, he called a two-day "Emergency Peace Conference" (21–22 October), which assembled in the nation's capital twenty organizations opposed to U.S. involvement in the war, such as the National Council for the Prevention of War, represented by Libby; the Women's International League for Peace and Freedom, whose delegate was its national executive director, Dorothy Detzer; and America First's national director, R. Douglas Stuart Jr. Perhaps the greatest coup by Armstrong, who was described in news reports as a "long-time friend" of Lindbergh's, was to persuade the latter to deliver a short dinner speech. At Armstrong's invitation, Stuart also spoke at the banquet. The conference created a No Foreign War Campaign, with Armstrong as temporary chairman. In theory, it was designed to coordinate the anti-interventionist activities of various pacifist and isolationist organizations. In fact, the campaign revolved around individuals, such as Armstrong and other conservative isolationists. Whereas many liberals and socialists were drawn to the Keep America Out of War Congress, founded two years earlier, many conservatives now backed the No Foreign War Committee.[44]

In Armstrong's opening address, he explained that he had called the meeting in response to nationwide requests. "Apparently," he declared, "the majority of . . . American people have begun to realize that they are being taken for a ride down the trail to another foreign war."[45] American military strength, he insisted, should be used only for defense. In the name of defense, though, he worried that the government had discarded some of "our cherished traditions of peacetime individual liberties." In return for that deprivation and the heavy burden of defense costs, he argued, the American people were entitled to demand that "no one responsible for a single item in our defense program use his position to create ill will, to suggest belligerency toward a neighbor nation, to participate in the intrigues of warring states, to betray the neutrality of the American people."[46]

NO FOREIGN WAR CAMPAIGN

The conference called for an immediate nationwide "No Foreign War Campaign" to stop America's "steady drift toward war." The meeting elected a committee of twelve to "expose and combat war propaganda." As temporary chairman of the campaign, which included Frederick Libby, Armstrong explained that it would use mass meetings, advertising, speeches, and "exposure of war propaganda" to keep the United States out of war in Europe and Asia.[47] Less than three months later (January 1941), keeping America out of war in Asia was exactly what Japanese Foreign Minister Matsuoka Yosuke instructed his diplomats in Washington to strive for.

The National Council for the Prevention of War might have felt threatened by the meeting and campaign, for in reporting on the conference in its magazine, it claimed, "No new organization is being set up," and called on officers and members of "existing organizations" to join in the campaign, the first stage of which would be a series of mass meetings. For more information, it urged people to write to Armstrong in Springfield.[48] Perhaps aware of possible anxiety on the part of Libby and the National Council, Armstrong tried to work with the latter and America First in developing the campaign. In November 1940, Libby asked Armstrong to send him a revised statement of purpose for the campaign, which he might use in the November issue of *Peace Action*, the council magazine, as well as a tentative list of cities where "mass meetings" should be convened between Thanksgiving and Christmas.[49]

A week later, Armstrong informed Libby he was going to meet with General Hanford MacNider—a committed isolationist, member of America

First's national committee, and, by September 1941, its national vice chairman—the following Monday. He hoped the general would accept the chairmanship of the No Foreign War Campaign, for that would help in fundraising efforts. He anticipated all-day discussions with MacNider and other America First members. He "confidently" expected, he added, to "agree upon some working arrangement. I think I have in mind a rather clear picture of the basis upon which any cooperative effort must be made."[50] However, MacNider, an Iowa businessman, veteran of World War I, former assistant secretary of war, past national commander of the American Legion, minister to Canada, and self-described "rabid Republican," wanted nothing to do with a pacifist like Libby, who also was a participant in the No Foreign War Campaign.[51]

Meanwhile, Libby was not encouraging. "You doubt the success of my efforts to set up meetings, etc.," Armstrong complained to Libby in early December 1940. He understood that America First wanted him to abandon the No Foreign War Campaign, but the only way he would do that, he told Libby, was if the America First Committee allowed the organization to continue its campaign as part of America First but "in no way hampered by their policies." "I want to cooperate," he added, "but I do not want to be sabotaged."[52] The result of the America First decision not to work with the campaign, however, led to the campaign's collapse.[53] It had possessed a friend in Lindbergh, though, who took an interest in the campaign from the beginning. In late November and early December, he participated in meetings to discuss its formation and tried to persuade MacNider to head it, while at the same time the campaign's organizers kept him informed.[54]

NO FOREIGN WAR COMMITTEE

Two months following the Emergency Peace Conference, Armstrong played a prominent role in founding yet another antiwar organization, the No Foreign War Committee. The arrangements were apparently made at a dinner at the University Club in New York hosted by Merwin K. Hart and attended by Armstrong; Lindbergh; Charles S. Payson, co-owner of *Scribner's Commentator*, and George T. Eggleston, editor of the magazine; as well as several other writers and editors.[55] This was, as can be seen below, an ultraconservative bunch with nary a liberal or socialist to be seen.

Head of the ultraconservative New York State Economic Council, Hart was later described by a biographer of Lindbergh as an "alleged promoter of an American Fascist movement . . . assumed to have ties with more reactionary fringe groups." This allegation might explain why the national director of the America First Committee declined to give Hart permission to organize a New York chapter of the committee.[56]

Connected to the Whitney family fortune through his marriage to Joan Whitney, Charles S. Payson was the president of the P & S Publishing Company, established in March 1940, which published *Scribner's Commentator*, an ultraconservative (rightist) anti-interventionist magazine with a circulation of thirty thousand that published from 1939 to 1942. A Yale graduate, financier, and lawyer in his midforties, in May 1939 he had purchased *Scribner's* magazine and, within four months, had invested three hundred thousand dollars in merging it with *Commentator*, a small magazine he had started in January 1937, to create *Scribner's Commentator*. Unfortunately for Payson and his collaborators, by the fall of 1941, the new magazine was losing six thousand dollars a month.[57]

Because it was fervently anti-interventionist, it was not surprising that *Scribner's Commentator* was closely associated with Charles Lindbergh and America First. Editor George Eggleston (beginning in mid-1940) and Douglas Stewart—naval veteran, conservative economist who opposed the New Deal, magazine part owner, and vice president of P & S Publishing—were well acquainted with Lindbergh. In a meeting with him in June 1940, Lindbergh recalled, they promised they were "one hundred per cent behind the stand I have taken."[58] During the months that followed, he met frequently with the two men.[59]

In December 1940, Lindbergh explained that the movement had begun as the No Foreign War Campaign, directed by Armstrong, but ended up as the No Foreign War Committee, headed by Verne Marshall.[60] A Pulitzer Prize–winning journalist, Marshall, like Armstrong, was a World War I veteran, having enlisted as a private in the French army in 1916 and served with the American Ambulance Field Service on the front lines at Verdun.[61] In September 1940, his name had been on the short list to head the newly created America First.[62]

In the beginning, isolationist Mark Shaw asked, "To what extent is the No Foreign War Committee in cooperation with the America First Committee"?[63] Armstrong's response was that the No Foreign War Committee would complement America First. It planned to concentrate on the eastern United States, while America First, with headquarters in Chicago, focused on the Midwest. The committee wanted to do better at contacting ordinary Americans than the more aloof America First.[64]

The No Foreign War Committee's fundamental purpose, obviously, was to keep the United States out of war. On 17 December 1940, several months following the Germans' series of victories in Europe, Armstrong joined Verne Marshall, at that time the group's treasurer, in announcing the committee's formation. It set out to counter the propaganda of William Allen White's Committee to Defend America by Aiding the Allies, which it accused of fostering the same public psychology that had preceded America's entry into World War I in 1917. One of the shared viewpoints of the anti-interventionists was that they feared the "recent tragic history of the Great War repeating itself," and thus the World War I example was frequently cited.[65]

Marshall sounded a defensive note when he explained, "Let no man accuse us of the No Foreign War Committee of being appeasers, fifth columnists, pro-Nazi, pro-British, pro-Fascist or of being anything save a group of determined pro-Americans." In retrospect, though, they were tragically naive about the Nazis. Arguments that Hitler would attack the United States after he took Britain, asserted Marshall, were "pure poppycock." Although Marshall seemed to do most of the talking at the press conference announcing the establishment of the new organization, Armstrong chimed in to claim that the committee had fifteen senators "ready to speak on the [committee's] program," while the committee anticipated "half the Senate" behind it. Twenty-five congressmen were "ready to speak and that is just a beginning." The committee, he added, would use all means to give voice to that "overwhelming majority of American citizens opposed to our direct physical involvement in the present war or any other war beyond the seas." "Eighty-three per cent of the population is against the war," claimed Marshall, "and we expect to enroll the majority of that percentage." "Public contributions," he added, would support the committee. Its temporary headquarters were in New York, but its permanent headquarters might be opened soon in Washington.[66]

Unfortunately for its organizers, in January 1941 Marshall sabotaged his own committee with a disastrous performance on a radio show called *Town Hall of the Air*. In what was billed as a debate over lend-lease, he rambled on about his background and Pulitzer Prize while appealing repeatedly for money. The studio audience became increasingly hostile until Marshall finally challenged them to step up and fight him "even though I'm twenty pounds under weight." He made such a laughingstock of himself with his "wild ideas on how to end the war" that he began to refer to himself as the "Wild Man from Borneo." Not long afterward, concluded a historian, the No Foreign War Committee collapsed, which left America First with "a near monopoly on what was left of isolationism."[67]

At the same time, the personal alliance between Armstrong and Marshall did not last. On 11 January 1941, less than a month following the establishment of the committee, it was reported that Armstrong, one of the organizers as well as the field director for the committee, planned to resign. When contacted in Washington, Armstrong did not deny that at a meeting of the governing council of what he now called the Keep America Out of War Congress, he had indicated his intention to leave. In doing so, he joined his hero, Lindbergh, on the sidelines. The latter had declined to assume an active role in the committee, and Marshall had omitted Lindbergh's name from a recent roster of supporters. It was not surprising the colonel was not a member, for he had expressed doubts about Marshall from the beginning. Devastatingly for the group, rumors circulated that it was anti-Semitic, antidemocratic, "haters of England," and "defeatist."[68]

Two days later (13 January), Armstrong resigned, giving as his reason that the committee was, according to a press report, "not being conducted along lines he considered basic for any movement trying to lead and influence public opinion." He was obviously angry. In a prepared statement distributed at the National Press Club, he wrote that he "heartily favored" a congressional investigation of the committee, for which he was willing to serve as a witness, as well as of all other organizations attempting to influence public opinion in the United States on important questions. He insisted the committee should accept only financial help "against which there can arise no public suspicion or mistrust." Coming from a man who a few months later was willing to accept partial Japanese financial support of his pro-Japan Committee on Pacific Relations (funds the committee never received), this seemed, in retrospect, a bit hypocritical. In resigning, he also explained that Lindbergh had authorized him to reveal that the colonel was not going to speak at the meeting in St. Louis scheduled by the committee. Perhaps aware of Lindbergh's displeasure at his tendency to speak for him,[69] Armstrong added that he was not qualified to comment on Lindbergh's reasons for declining to participate.[70]

Although Lindbergh's *Wartime Journals* alluded to personal differences between Armstrong and Marshall,[71] at this time the Missourian declined to respond to reporters' questions about his relationship with Marshall and whether he was resigning from the No Foreign War Committee because the latter had turned the group into a "one-man committee." Nevertheless, his press statement made clear his main problem was with Marshall as chairman. Although four months later, he began to organize his Committee on Pacific Relations, at this time he assured reporters he had no immediate intention of founding a new organization.[72] In a circular letter to friends written three days later to further explain his resignation, however, he declared he had been counseled by "numerous advisers" to immediately launch a "Peoples Campaign Against War."[73] Some months later, he lamented to pacifist, evangelist, and missionary E. Stanley Jones that after Marshall took charge of the No Foreign War Campaign (Committee), it "cracked up badly."[74]

At the same time Armstrong was quarreling with Marshall, he was attracting further press coverage for his opposition to the Lend-Lease Act. When, in early January 1941, congressional hearings set off a nationwide debate on the legislation,[75] he sided with its opponents. In mid-January, he charged that it would establish a military dictatorship (he lacked moderation, as his various positions in the 1950s were to confirm).[76] In testimony before the Senate Foreign Relations Committee in early February, he vehemently attacked the bill. Its purpose was to take the United States into war, he charged, which would be a "betrayal of the American people, the vast majority of whom desire to keep out of the wars now raging in the Old World." Thus, he urged that it be "overwhelmingly defeated."[77]

He also appeared in the press at that time in another context. Being an isolationist did not mean, of course, that one was a liberal. During the 1950s, Armstrong would make his mark on the public consciousness as an ultraconservative and rabid anticommunist. Before the war, he joined those conservatives—such as George Eggleston, editor of the "extreme and largely right-wing" isolationist magazine *Scribner's Commentator*—who attacked school textbooks and their authors.[78] In January 1941, an author of social science textbooks accused him of being one of the "self-appointed censors" and "persistent enemies of liberalism." In an article in the September 1940 issue of the *American Legion Magazine*, Armstrong criticized those he claimed wanted to debunk American heroes, replace the American constitution and government with "socialistic control," exchange private ownership for collectivism, and influence opinion against "tradition, religious faiths, and ideas of morality."[79] ("Plus ça change, plus c'est la même chose.")

The dispute was still raging the following February, when he took part in a roundtable discussion on "subversive textbooks" at the National Education Association's convention in Atlantic City, New Jersey, a debate that was broadcast on the *People's Platform* program on CBS. Predictably, he attacked the increase of "subversive" material in widely used textbooks. He believed that around 1932 or 1933—implicitly linking the debate to Roosevelt's administration and the New Deal—textbook authors began to include materials that tended to "deprecate our American ideals and institutions." "I think," he declared, "that when you destroy the faith in the fine work done by our founding fathers you do irreparable harm to the boys and girls of this country."[80] In a rejoinder, a textbook author wrote the editor of the *New York Times* that in a recent speech to the New York Association of History Teachers, he had enumerated and rebutted Armstrong's charges against him as well as other educators. In his talk, he criticized the "self-appointed censors of our schools," including Verne Marshall as well as Armstrong.[81]

ARMSTRONG, LINDBERGH, AND THE AMERICA FIRST COMMITTEE

While engaged in these antiwar and right-wing activities, Armstrong drew closer to Lindbergh. His first contact occurred when he wrote to the colonel in December 1939.[82] Between June 1940 and February 1941, he met frequently with Lindbergh concerning the isolationist movement.[83] Because of his prominent role in the American Legion, he was the catalyst for talks Lindbergh had, during the summer of 1940, with Missouri Democratic Senator Bennett Champ Clark, Congressman James E. Van Zandt, Theodore

Roosevelt Jr., and others associated with the legion.[84] In July, he briefly served as a go-between for Lindbergh and the founder and national director of the America First Committee, R. Douglas Stuart Jr.[85]

At first, Lindbergh was impressed with Armstrong and his American Legion connections and was interested in using the legion and other veterans' organizations in his campaign against war.[86] In June 1940, he praised the legion "mandate" Armstrong showed him as "excellent American defense—anti-war policy." The two men discussed plans for the legion to play a greater role in opposing U.S. entry into the war, and the famous aviator praised Armstrong as "full of action." Lindbergh promised to address the legion, which he believed could be "of tremendous value . . . in this situation." Later in the month, he again discussed "American Legion projects" with Armstrong.[87]

Until September 1940, it seemed possible the Missourian could throw the weight of the legion behind the isolationist movement. At that time, however, he suddenly became far less useful to Lindbergh and his associates. He had used his post on the legion's Foreign Relations Committee to plan a conference against the war. The legion's national commander immediately rejected Armstrong's plans and helped expel him from the committee. During 1940 and 1941, the legion switched from neutralism to interventionism, and thus its usefulness as an isolationist weapon disappeared.[88] By May 1941, it was supporting convoying lend-lease supplies going to Britain in the Atlantic, a policy rife with risk of war with Germany, which was using its submarine fleet to sink the ships carrying the war supplies.[89]

Despite this setback, Armstrong and Lindbergh met numerous more times during subsequent months. In September 1940, they talked about the legion's Boston convention and the abandonment of the organization's neutral stance. They also discussed Armstrong's work with the America First Committee in Chicago, where the organization had its headquarters.[90] Some in that committee worried that Armstrong was attempting to create a competing isolationist organization. His No Foreign War Campaign seemed too conservative to them, while Armstrong's associates thought the America First crowd exhibited New Dealer inclinations. Most pacifists thought the "conservative-nationalist tone" of Armstrong and his colleagues even less acceptable than America First. For his part, Lindbergh wanted to foster cooperation, so he promised an America First member that the No Foreign War Campaign would not clash with America First's work. Nevertheless, in December 1940, Armstrong was rejected for a second time (the first by the American Legion leadership in September 1940) when America First's leaders rejected cooperation with his No Foreign War Campaign. As a result, it collapsed.[91]

Until early 1941, the Japanese could be forgiven if they believed Armstrong represented a direct link to the famous Lindbergh, for the latter was not only close to Armstrong and other founders of the No Foreign War

Committee, he also had participated in the discussions that led to its establishment. Furthermore, initially he had agreed to speak at a December 1940 rally in St. Louis organized by Armstrong and sponsored by the No Foreign War Campaign. As early as November, though, Lindbergh had become worried that Armstrong was "a little impetuous at times," especially about making promises regarding Lindbergh's activities.[92] He was suspicious of Armstrong's tendency to use him for his own purposes. Thus, he agreed to address the St. Louis rally on the condition that Armstrong obtain his approval before making any commitments or announcements. When Armstrong and his colleague, Verne Marshall, made plans that Lindbergh found unacceptable, he canceled the St. Louis appearance. All would have gone well, he commented, "if Armstrong had not allowed his enthusiasm to push him quite so fast." In the end, Lindbergh did not formally join the No Foreign War Committee but preferred to maintain his independence.[93]

Lindbergh's wife, Anne, also knew Armstrong, toward whom she had mixed feelings. He was, she wrote,

> a dependable, earnest, hard-working, honest man humble and yet undaunted—none of this disease of the soul, this pessimistic fatalism that attacks intellectual Easterners. He is Middle Western, American Legion, and *very* American. His mind is clear and undivided. He is not, or does not seem to be, besieged by conflicts. But goes right to work, writes a speech in an afternoon, has six all ready to be put out on records and distributed throughout the Legion posts! He has done more work, C. [Charles] says, than anyone else, without help or money, by himself, in a quiet dogged way. I suppose if we pull through it will be due to people like that and yet when he leaves, I feel a terrible inexplicable longing for Europe and Europeans.[94]

In addition to Lindbergh's refusal to join the No Foreign War Committee, he also recognized the tensions between Armstrong and Marshall. Striving to smooth things over, Lindbergh suggested Armstrong be made director of field organization in the new committee. Armstrong, however, did not like Marshall's way of dealing with the press. That friction, Lindbergh commented, had a very bad effect on morale, and hence a break seemed inevitable. Consequently, in January 1941, Lindbergh and Armstrong discussed the latter founding another antiwar group and holding mass meetings around the country. In early February, the two men again consulted regarding Armstrong's proposal to hold some antiwar rallies.[95] Meanwhile, the committee's divisiveness was compounded when America First's leadership broke with Marshall and the committee. In a final blow, Lindbergh himself publicly disassociated himself from the committee, announcing he had no connection with it and had never been a member. He admitted he had attended meetings while the committee was being organized but declared he could not accept its "methods and policies." Abandoned by both Lindbergh and Armstrong and embarrassed by Marshall's radio disaster, in April the committee was dissolved.[96]

ARMSTRONG AS A FIELD ORGANIZER FOR AMERICA FIRST

Meanwhile, in June 1941, the FBI mistakenly credited Armstrong and others (names censored in the FBI reports) with being founders of an "American Peace Movement," which "reportedly has since adopted the name of the American First Committee [sic]."[97] Far from being a founder, though, he was simply an employee of America First from May through July.[98] It hired him to organize meetings of isolationists in the interventionist South, which was the most resistant region in the United States to America First's organizational efforts. A number of southern states lacked even a token chapter, which helps explain America First's failure there.[99]

America First's leaders knew about his hard-charging reputation and ordered him to tackle only projects they assigned him. Ironically, in view of his behind-the-scenes connection with the Japanese embassy as well as its decision to partly fund an antiwar organization led by him (the Committee on Pacific Relations), he enthusiastically assured an America First leader that he was "ready to be used anywhere, anytime, in any way, and you know that."[100]

Local organizing for America First was a demanding occupation, as the following exchange of telegrams and correspondence between Armstrong and the America First National Speakers Bureau reveals. On 22 May, while he was in Knoxville, Tennessee, Barbara McDonald, chairman of the Speakers Bureau, instructed him not to schedule a meeting in Louisville, Kentucky, yet, because America First's national chairman, General Robert E. Wood, hoped Lindbergh would speak at that rally, "although arrangements could not be made for this much before June 15." She also asked Armstrong to cable her the address of his Louisville headquarters so she could send him the names of contacts in that city. The first person to get in touch with, she instructed, was Judge Charles Dawson, which was to be expected because he was a fervent isolationist as well as an opponent of the New Deal. She also asked that Norman G. Moore of the Knoxville Peace Council let her know the name of the auditorium for the Monday evening meeting in that city.[101] Louisville may have been chosen as a target by America First, because it was what one historian termed a "militantly isolationist" city. On the other hand, its newspaper, the Louisville *Courier-Journal*, was one of a very small number of papers in the country that were agitating for the United States to enter the war in Europe to rescue Britain.[102] In short, it was a battleground in the "Great Debate" between interventionists and anti-interventionists.

Armstrong replied to the Speakers Bureau later the same day that members of the local group in Knoxville could not decide on the best meeting place. He was having dinner with them that evening to discuss plans. He would stay on the next day for a necessary "publicity drive." Responding to instructions not to set a date for a Louisville meeting because Wood wanted to arrange for Lindbergh to speak there, Armstrong replied he was "delighted" because Louisville was an "ideal spot for [the] colonel [Lindbergh]." Later, he reported the dinner in Knoxville that evening was successful. It was important, he wired, "to lift local group out of old peace council attitude to make mass meeting [a] success." He was preparing a "real publicity program" as well as the recruitment of prominent citizens for the meeting and their "future activities." Their total budget, including press advertisements, he reported, would be about $160. They had a "dingy" hall that would seat four hundred, but he advised reserving a theater that could accommodate a thousand. They were launching a fund-raising drive the following day, which should make it possible for them to break even, but he thought the America First Committee should help them. "Could we go fifty [percent] or could be [we] guarantee any deficit?" he inquired and added that he needed a reply by Friday's luncheon.[103]

The following day (23 May), he wired and asked America First's Speakers Bureau to arrange advertising copy, posters, handbills, radio announcements, and "[as] much news publicity as papers [newspapers] will give," and mail the publicity materials to Norman Moore in Knoxville. He had to return to Springfield on Monday to arrange his children's vacation, he wrote, but promised to be "right on [the] job" on Tuesday—which meant he would miss America First's Monday evening meeting in Knoxville. That same day, McDonald wired that she was sending one hundred dollars by air mail. "Shoot the works," she instructed Armstrong. "What about literature?" she asked. "Go full steam ahead," she added, for "Knoxville [is] important." Referring to the inquiry by the Speakers Bureau about the venue for Monday evening's meeting in Knoxville, he responded that it had definitely been decided to use the Lyric Theater.[104]

While he was working for America First in Tennessee and Kentucky, Armstrong pursued his own goals by keeping his "Japanese project" (the Committee on Pacific Relations) contacts apprised of his activities. On 24 May, he wrote New York financier and future member of his Committee on Pacific Relations William Baxter that he could not go to New York two days later because the America First Committee had sent him to Louisville to arrange a meeting at which Lindbergh would be the main speaker.[105] A week later, he forwarded the same report to Mark Shaw, regional secretary of the National Council for the Prevention of War and also a member of the future Committee on Pacific Relations. His passionate isolationist feelings were on full display. "This is the hot-bed [sic] of interventionism!" he wrote Shaw.

"They need some opposition," he added, "and we are going to give it to them."[106]

During a later trip to Missouri to visit his family, he also spearheaded the creation of an America First chapter in his hometown, Springfield, Missouri. On 7 June, he presided over its inaugural meeting at his home. According to the FBI, he told the attendees that the America First Committee planned to establish other chapters in southwest Missouri, and "at that time they did not have to worry about finances." The following month, he was the lead-off speaker at an America First meeting in Springfield, where, like a good isolationist, he criticized President Roosevelt and the British government. Around six hundred people attended the rally, which the anti-interventionist senator from Missouri, Democrat Bennett Champ Clark, also addressed.[107] In September, Clark was to deliver his sensational charge that Hollywood had turned "17,000 movie theaters into 17,000 nightly mass meetings for war."[108] In retrospect, Armstrong was right to criticize the British, whose intelligence operation (vaguely and awkwardly called British Security Coordination) in the United States had been ordered to do all it could to undermine American isolationists.[109]

Predictably, though, Armstrong's enthusiasm boiled over. Assigned to organize a meeting in Atlanta, he declared, "On to Atlanta! We'll take that town like Sherman never dreamed of." That rallying cry was hardly calculated, in light of U.S. General William Tecumseh Sherman's attack on the city during the Civil War, to appeal to the southern interventionists he was out to convert. As field representative of the America First Committee, he tried to book Atlanta's municipal auditorium for a speech by isolationist Burton K. Wheeler, a Democratic senator from Montana since 1923. In June and again in July, however, the city council refused to permit the auditorium to be used for the address (as in August, the city council in Oklahoma City refused to allow America First to use its municipal auditorium for a Lindbergh speech). Thus, the address was postponed indefinitely.

Armstrong "failed spectacularly," according to one assessment, to convene a meeting in Atlanta. The Missourian attributed the failure to "the stupendous difficulties thrown in our way by the interventionist south." At first, it seemed America First agreed with him. After the second denial of use of the auditorium, the assistant national director of America First issued a statement that accused Atlanta politicians of attempting to suppress free speech. Other leaders of America First, however, came to believe some of the problems lay with Armstrong himself, and they fired him after only two months.[110] Armstrong did not give up, though. Because Senator Wheeler wanted to appear in Atlanta later and might bring Lindbergh with him, Armstrong tried and failed a third time to procure the hall.[111]

Although America First dropped Armstrong from the payroll in July, he continued to be active on the committee's behalf. In early August, the FBI reported, he attended a meeting in Springfield to discuss ways to raise money for the committee. According to the bureau, he left the meeting early to travel to Chicago, where he planned to "take care of urgent business for the National Committee of the America First Committee in Washington, D.C." At this time, the FBI seemed a bit confused regarding his role in the committee. In a report just a few days prior to the Pearl Harbor attack, it stated that "further efforts are being made to establish the true status of the Subject's membership."[112]

In the meantime, Armstrong's connection with Lindbergh weakened. In February 1941, his name appeared for the last time in Lindbergh's wartime journal. Nevertheless, he continued to write to Lindbergh in the years that followed, with his last letter dated July 1956. He cherished strong feelings for "The Hero" (as author Kenneth Davis titled his biography of Lindbergh) and named his son Charles Lindbergh Armstrong.[113] In 1971, Marjorie Armstrong wrote in place of her elderly husband to ask the publisher of the colonel's *Wartime Journals* to let the Lindberghs know "we have enjoyed this book and consider it a highly significant record of some of this country's most painful experiences." By chance, she added, they had met Lindbergh's son and congratulated him on his father's "superb book." In her letter, she reminded the Lindberghs that their youngest son was his namesake.[114]

NOTES

1. Justus D. Doenecke, "Explaining the Antiwar Movement, 1939–1941: The Next Assignment," *Journal of Libertarian Studies* 8, no. 1 (1986): 145.
2. W. Forbes Webber, "Orland K. Armstrong alias O.K. Armstrong, Espionage-G[erman]," 1 December 1941, Orland Kay Armstrong, FBI File No. 62-45631-12, Freedom of Information Act (hereafter FOIA).
3. O. K. Armstrong to the Honorable Kaname Wakasugi, Minister Pleni-potentiary [sic], Washington, DC, 31 May 1941, box 42, Japanese Relations File, Orland Kay Armstrong (1893–1987) Papers, 1912–1987 (C4056), State Historical Society of Missouri, Manuscript Collection.
4. Armstrong to J. Edgar Hoover, 2 November 1936, FBI File No. 62-45631-5, FOIA.
5. Memo from Harry M. Kimball to D. M. Ladd, FBI, U.S. Department of Justice, Washington, DC, 31 October 1941, Terasaki Hidenari, FBI File No. 65-HQ-37232, FOIA.
6. Webber, "Orland K. Armstrong," 1 December 1941.
7. "War Moratorium Proposed by Byrd," *New York Times* (hereafter *NYT*), 22 January 1937, 1.
8. Webber, "Orland K. Armstrong," 1 December 1941.
9. "'War Trend' Is Hit at Peace Session," *NYT*, 8 June 1940, 16.
10. Webber, "Orland K. Armstrong," 1 December 1941.
11. Wayne S. Cole, *Charles A. Lindbergh and the Battle against Intervention in World War II* (New York: Harcourt Brace Jovanovich, 1974), 108.
12. Doenecke, "Explaining the Antiwar Movement," 150.
13. "Congress Is Facing Fight over Ending Session This Week," *NYT*, 17 June 1940, 1.
14. Frederick J. Libby, telegram to Armstrong, Springfield, MO, 27 July 1940, National Council for the Prevention of War (hereafter NCPW), reel 41:223 (box 280); Manfred Jonas, *Isolationism in America, 1935–1941* (Ithaca, NY: Cornell University Press, 1966), 32; David M. Kennedy, *Freedom from Fear: The American People in Depression and War* (New York:

Oxford University Press, 1999), 459. For an outline of Libby's life (1874–1970), see "Historical Introduction," NCPW electronic finding aid.

15. "Frederick Joseph Libby (Deceased)," *Marquis Who's Who on the Web* (accessed 12 August 2005); "Frederick Libby, Peace Crusader," *NYT*, 28 June 1970, 65; "Led Relief Effort," *NYT*, 28 June 1970, 65; "Frederick J. Libby, 95, Dies," *Washington Post* (hereafter *WP*), 28 June 1970, 32. His papers are in the NCPW archives.

16. "Historical Introduction," NCPW electronic finding aid.

17. "U.S. Gets Warning against Policing Asia," *WP*, 16 December 1934, 16.

18. "Congress Opens Drive to Build up All the Nation's Defenses," *WP*, 11 February 1936, 1.

19. "Scores Roosevelt on Neutrality Act," *NYT*, 7 September 1937, 11.

20. "Johnson Now Sees Hull at Sea on Foreign Policy; Wants 'Clear Definition,'" *NYT*, 11 February 1938, 1.

21. "Supreme Endeavor by Industry Seen," *NYT*, 28 May 1941, 1.

22. Libby, "You Won't Forget Japan," *Peace Action* 6, no. 4 (1939): 1–2.

23. Libby, "Time Approaches for Mediation in Far East," *Peace Action* 6, no. 6 (1940): 2.

24. Libby, "We Cannot Win a War with Japan," *Peace Action* 7, no. 2 (1940): 2.

25. Wayne S. Cole, *America First: The Battle against Intervention in World War II* (Madison: University of Wisconsin Press, 1953), 83.

26. Charles Hurd, "Urgent Need Cited," *NYT*, 4 July 1941, 1.

27. "Peace Group Head Would Impeach Knox, Stimson," *WP*, 14 August 1941, 7.

28. "Another Aid Bill Is Seen in the Capital," *NYT*, 15 August 1941, 1.

29. "Backs Bill to Get 400 Patrol Ships," *NYT*, 9 October 1941, 4.

30. "Foes of Ship Arming Demand President Make Peace Move," *NYT*, 15 October 1941, 1; "U.S. Envisioned as World Trustee," *WP*, 27 October 1941, 9.

31. Charles A. Lindbergh, *The Wartime Journals of Charles A. Lindbergh* (New York: Harcourt Brace Jovanovich, 1970), 320, 382, 392, 408–9, 430.

32. Lindbergh, *Wartime Journals*, 320, 430; for other meetings of the two men, see 382, 392, 408–9.

33. Anne Morrow Lindbergh, *War Within and Without: Diaries and Letters of Anne Morrow Lindbergh, 1939–1944* (New York: Harcourt Brace Jovanovich, 1980), 150.

34. Cole, *America First*, 89–90.

35. Armstrong, member, Foreign Relations Committee, American Legion, Springfield, MO, to Dear Editor, 29 July 1940, NCPW, reel 41: 223 (box 280), with enclosed programs.

36. "Legion Yells Down a Neutrality Call," *NYT*, 27 September 1940, 12; Jonas, *Isolationism*, 218–19.

37. W. Forbes Webber, FBI, Kansas City, MO, "Orland K. Armstrong alias O.K. Armstrong; Espionage—G[ermany]; Sedition Act," 16 March 1942, FBI File No. 62-45631-18, FOIA; Susan Dunn, *1940: FDR, Willkie, Lindbergh, Hitler—the Election amid the Storm* (New Haven, CT: Yale University Press, 2013), 60; Vincent Curcio, *Henry Ford* (New York: Oxford University Press, 2013), 252.

38. Geoffrey Perrett, *Days of Sadness, Years of Triumph: The American People, 1939–1945* (New York: Coward, McCann & Geoghegan, 1973; Penguin Books, 1974), 157–58; Jonas, *Isolationism*, 77–80; William Bridgewater, ed., *The Columbia-Viking Desk Encyclopedia*, 2nd ed. (New York: Columbia University Press, 1964), 1822.

39. Lynne Olson, *Those Angry Days: Roosevelt, Lindbergh, and America's Fight over World War II, 1939–1941* (New York: Random House, 2013), 388.

40. Dorothy Detzer Papers, 1913–81, Collection: DG 086, Swarthmore College Peace Collection, Swarthmore, PA.

41. Bridgewater, *Columbia-Viking Desk Encyclopedia*, 28; Jonas, *Isolationism*, 107.

42. Webber, "Orland K. Armstrong" 16 March 1942; Olson, *Those Angry Days*, 135–36, 227.

43. Webber, "Orland K. Armstrong," 16 March 1942; Webber, "Orland K. Armstrong," 1 December 1941.

44. Cole, *Charles A. Lindbergh*, 109–10, 118; Cole, *America First*, 71.

45. "Lindbergh Calls for Avoiding War," *NYT*, 22 October 1940, 12; Cole, *Charles A. Lindbergh*, 109–10, which includes an abbreviated list of attendees.

46. "Peace-Makers Meet as War Rages Abroad," *WP*, 22 October 1940, 12.

47. "'No Foreign War' Campaign Planned by Peace Conference," *WP*, 23 October 1940, 6; Cole, *Charles A. Lindbergh*, 109–11.

48. *Peace Action* 7, no. 3 (1940): 8.

49. Libby, executive secretary, NCPW, to Armstrong, [16] November 1940, NCPW, reel 41: 223 (box 280); Doenecke, "Explaining the Antiwar Movement," 144.

50. Armstrong, Springfield, MO, to Libby, 23 November 1940, NCPW, reel 41: 223 (box 280); Cole, *Charles A. Lindbergh*, 116, 161, 222; Jonas, *Isolationism*, 237; Lindbergh, *Wartime Journals*, 421; "MacNider, Hanford (2 Oct. 1889–17 February 1968)," in *American National Biography* (New York: Oxford University Press, 1999), 14:280–81. During World War II, MacNider served in the South Pacific. An ultraconservative, he supported right-wing zealot Senator Joseph McCarthy in the 1950s. On MacNider, see also Cole, *Roosevelt and the Isolationists*; Cole, *America First*.

51. Cole, *Charles A. Lindbergh*, 111; Cole, *America First*, 184.

52. Armstrong, Springfield, MO, to Libby, 8 December 1940, NCPW, reel 41: 223 (box 280). For a thorough discussion of the dispute between America First and Armstrong's No Foreign War Campaign, see Cole, *Charles A. Lindbergh*, 110–12.

53. Cole, *Charles A. Lindbergh*, 111–12.

54. Lindbergh, *Wartime Journals*, 421–22, 423–24, 426–68.

55. John Roy Carlson, *Under Cover: My Four Years in the Nazi Underworld of America* (New York: E.P. Dutton & Co., 1943), 247.

56. A. Scott Berg, *Lindbergh* (New York: G.P. Putnam's Sons, 1998), 409. See also Cole, *Lindbergh*, 105, 176; Cole, *America First*, 73, 118–19.

57. Justin Doenecke, "*Scribner's Commentator* (1939–1942)," in *The Conservative Press in Twentieth-Century America*, ed. Ronald Lora and William Henry Longton (Westport, CT: Greenwood Press, 1999), 273–74.

58. Lindbergh, *Wartime Journals*, 352; Doenecke, "*Scribner's Commentator*," 273–74.

59. Lindbergh, *Wartime Journals*, 378, 381, 391, 393, 394, 408–9, 415, 417, 421–22, 426, 428–31, 436, 445. For Eggleston's memories of his association with Lindbergh, see George T. Eggleston, *Roosevelt, Churchill, and the World War II Opposition* (Old Greenwich, CT: Devin-Adair, 1979), 74–76.

60. Lindbergh, *Wartime Journals*, 430.

61. Doenecke, "Explaining the Antiwar Movement," 145.

62. Cole, *America First*, 17.

63. Clayton D. Loughran, Mr. [Frederick] Libby's secretary, to Armstrong, 28 December 1940, NCPW, reel 41: 223 (box 280). This source contains a list of Shaw's criticisms and suggestions concerning the No Foreign War Committee, many of which concerned the relationship between the committee and America First.

64. Cole, *Charles A. Lindbergh*, 112; Lindbergh, *Wartime Journals*, 430.

65. Doenecke, "Explaining the Antiwar Movement," 145, 151; Lindbergh, *Wartime Journals*, 430. On the committee, see also Cole, *Charles A. Lindbergh*, 112–13.

66. "New Group Fights War Involvement," *NYT*, 18 December 1940, 12; "Editor Organizes Committee to 'Help Keep U.S. out of War,'" *WP*, 18 December 1940, 2; "A War Veteran Organizes a National Committee to 'Help Keep the Country out of War,'" *Peace Action* 7, no. 4 (1940): 8; Doenecke, "Explaining the Antiwar Movement," 145.

67. Perrett, *Days of Sadness*, 158.

68. "Dissension Seen in No-War Group," *NYT*, 12 January 1941, 14. See also "Marshall's Director to Quit; Lindbergh to Fight 'Whispers,'" *New York World-Telegram*, 11 January 1941, in NCPW, reel 41: 223 (box 280); Lindbergh, *Wartime Journals*, 427–32, 436, 438–40.

69. Lindbergh, *Wartime Journals*, 421.

70. Foster Hailey, "Aide of Marshall Quits Peace Group," *NYT*, 14 January 1941, 10; "No Foreign War Committee Director Quits," *WP*, 14 January 1941, 8.

71. Lindbergh, *Wartime Journals*, 431, 436.

72. Hailey, "Aide of Marshall Quits Peace Group," 10; "No Foreign War Committee Director Quits," 8.
73. Armstrong, Washington, DC, to Dear Friend, 16 January 1941, NCPW, reel 41: 223 (box 280).
74. Armstrong to Dr. E. Stanley Jones, Clifton Springs, NY, 16 September 1941, Armstrong Papers.
75. Kennedy, *Freedom from Fear*, 470.
76. Hailey, "Aide of Marshall Quits Peace Group," 10.
77. "[Walter] George Clears out Spectators," *NYT*, 7 February 1941, 7; "Flier Fears Aid Plan Will Lead to War on Losing Side; Calls U.S. Air Force Weak," *WP*, 7 February 1941, 1.
78. Doenecke, "*Scribner's Commentator*," 278; Jonas, *Isolationism*, 230.
79. "Rugg Defends His Textbooks, Long Attacked," *NYT*, 5 January 1941, D6.
80. "Textbook Writers Reply to Attack; 'Censor' Fight On," *NYT*, 23 February 1941, 1.
81. "Would Debunk Debunkers," *NYT*, 21 March 1941, 20.
82. Cole, *Charles A. Lindbergh*, 105.
83. Lindbergh, *Wartime Journals*, 353, 448.
84. Cole, *Charles A. Lindbergh*, 108.
85. Cole, *Charles A. Lindbergh*, 118; Cole, *Roosevelt and the Isolationists*, 345.
86. Cole, *Charles A. Lindbergh*, 108.
87. Lindbergh, *Wartime Journals*, 353, 365.
88. Cole, *Charles A. Lindbergh*, 108.
89. Lindbergh, *Wartime Journals*, 481.
90. Lindbergh, *Wartime Journals*, 392–93.
91. Cole, *Charles A. Lindbergh*, 111–12.
92. Lindbergh, *Wartime Journals*, 421.
93. Cole, *Charles A. Lindbergh*, 112; Lindbergh, *Wartime Journals*, 430.
94. Anne Morrow Lindbergh, *War Within*, 150–51.
95. Lindbergh, *Wartime Journals*, 430–31, 436, 448.
96. Cole, *Charles A. Lindbergh*, 112–13.
97. Webber, "Orland K. Armstrong," 1 December 1941.
98. Cole, *Charles A. Lindbergh*, 114.
99. Cole, *America First*, 31; Perrett, *Days of Sadness*, 61.
100. Cole, *Charles A. Lindbergh*, 114.
101. Barbara McDonald, America First, to Armstrong, C/O Norman G. Moore, Knoxville Peace Council, Knoxville, TN, 22 May 1941, Armstrong File, Box 43, America First Committee Records, Hoover Institution, Stanford, CA; "Charles I. Dawson [1881–1969], Ex-U.S. Judge, Dies," *NYT*, 26 April 1969, 37.
102. Olson, *Those Angry Days*, 145.
103. Armstrong to McDonald, American First Committee, Chicago, 22 May 1941.
104. Armstrong to McDonald, Speakers Bureau, America First Committee, Board of Trade Building, Chicago, 23 May 1941; McDonald to Armstrong, 23 June [May] 1941; Armstrong to McDonald, 23 May 1941, all from America First Committee Records, Hoover Institution Archives.
105. Armstrong to William J. Baxter, 24 May 1941, Armstrong Papers.
106. Armstrong to Dear Friend Mr. [Mark Revell] Shaw, Melrose, MA, 31 May 1941, Armstrong Papers.
107. Webber, "Orland K. Armstrong," 1 December 1941. Senator Clark, not surprisingly, vehemently objected to conscription. Dunn, *1940*, 176, 181.
108. Perrett, *Days of Sadness*, 162.
109. Mary Ann Philips, *"Fletcher Warren Reporting for Duty, Sir"* (Austin, TX: Nortex, 2006), 58; Olson, *Those Angry Days*, 115–16, 118, 120; Jennet Conant, *The Irregulars: Roald Dahl and the British Spy Ring in Wartime Washington* (New York: Simon & Schuster, 2013), 78–80.
110. "Wheeler Speech in Atlanta Today Postponed When Council Refuses Use of Municipal Hall," *NYT*, 10 July 1941, 1; Cole, *Charles A. Lindbergh*, 114; Berg, *Lindbergh*, 422–23; Dunn, *1940*, 58; Olson, *Those Angry Days*, 325.

111. "Wheeler Speech in Atlanta," 1.

112. Cole, *Charles A. Lindbergh*, 257n15; Webber, "Orland K. Armstrong," 1 December 1941.

113. Armstrong, Washington, DC, to Charles A. Lindbergh, Darien, CT, 10 July 1956, Charles A. Lindbergh Collection, Manuscripts and Archives, Yale University Library, New Haven, CT; Kenneth S. Davis, *The Hero: Charles A. Lindbergh and the American Dream* (Garden City, NY: Doubleday & Company, 1959).

114. Marjorie M. Armstrong, Republic, MO, to Press Relations, Harcourt Brace Jovanovich, New York, 2 February 1971, Lindbergh Collection, Yale University Library.

Chapter Two

Businessmen and Generals

In the summer of 1941, Armstrong was at loose ends. By July, he had drifted out of Lindbergh's orbit, been fired from America First, and resigned from the No Foreign War Committee. America First was not much interested in Japan but rather focused on Europe. As one historian put it, it "did not conduct any concerted campaign to prevent war with Japan."[1] "America Firstism," another scholar declared, "by no means embodied Asia Firstism."[2] As a result, there was a niche among isolationist groups for a new committee devoted to averting war with Japan. It was around this time that the FBI opened an espionage file on the Missourian.[3]

Even while he was still working for America First, his restless mind was contemplating creation of his own organization. In May, he launched plans to create a Committee to Study Pacific Relations (subsequently, the word "study" was dropped) to be composed of prominent Americans dedicated to avoiding war between the United States and Japan. The use of "committee" to describe what today would be called a "political action group" (PAC) was quite prevalent in 1940 and 1941. His group followed on the heels of two other "committees" created to address the question of what the United States should do about the looming threat of war, the interventionist Committee to Defend America by Aiding the Allies and the isolationist America First Committee. Thanks to Armstrong, whose voluminous correspondence has been preserved, it is possible to trace the origins, membership, and history of the Committee on Pacific Relations.

When he began contacting potential recruits, Armstrong hoped to attract thirty to forty members for his committee but in the end had to settle for a dozen or so.[4] It should be noted that in his approaches to prominent Americans, never once did he mention that he was reporting his and his colleagues' anti-interventionist activities to the Japanese embassy nor report that on the eve of war the embassy had pledged to partly finance his committee.

The first candidate Armstrong approached regarding his committee project was William Joseph Baxter, economic consultant and expert on Far Eastern trade as well as managing director of the Baxter International Economic Research Bureau in New York. He apparently got Baxter's name from the Institute of Pacific Relations in New York, which he later recalled gave him the names of people "who might be interested in such a project."[5] Founded in 1925 in Honolulu—subsequently it moved to New York—and terminated in 1960, the institute was the preeminent international organization of scholars, journalists, and other nongovernmental figures interested in discussing problems and relations among nations bordering the Pacific. Two years later, six national councils were created. A secretary general and secretariat were added to manage the daily activities of the institute. The American Council was the best funded and largest. Its first secretary was Edward C. Carter, who served the institute from 1926 until 1949. In 1931, he was appointed the institute's secretary general. The institute also published two journals, *Pacific Affairs*, with the well-known scholar Owen Lattimore as editor from 1933 to 1941, and *Far Eastern Survey*.[6]

Contacting Baxter made sense, for the New York businessman was already active in the America First Committee as head of its New Rochelle chapter.[7] Armstrong also may have been interested in Baxter for two further reasons. First, he was a "money man" who socialized with the rich (as references to him in the *New York Times* revealed). Armstrong may have hoped that Baxter would contribute—as, in fact, he did later—or help raise funds for the Committee on Pacific Relations. When Armstrong called on him, Baxter furnished the names of others who might be interested in the committee.[8] In addition, Baxter was pro-Japanese and anti-Chinese. Author John Roy Carlson described him as the author of "many pro-Japanese tracts."[9] The economic argument for close cooperation between the United States and Japan, observed a historian, was "most ably made" by "investment counselor" Baxter in his 1940 work, *Japan and America Must Work Together!*[10]

In leaning toward Japan, he was representative, at that time, of the attitude of American businessmen. A September 1940 *Fortune Magazine* poll revealed that 40 percent of business leaders favored appeasement of Japan. Fewer than 20 percent came down on the side of an embargo or threat of force aimed at Japan.[11] Moreover, Baxter's pro-Japanese and anti-Chinese beliefs were shared by most of the members of Armstrong's new committee. Finally, like many anti-interventionists, Baxter was anti-British and opposed to Roosevelt.

In February 1941, he published an article titled "War with Japan Coming," which Armstrong probably read (there is a copy in his papers in the archives). The views Baxter expressed in his piece must have drawn Armstrong to him. It made clear that Baxter, like Armstrong, was an isolationist opposed to war with Japan. Like famous pacifist and evangelist E. Stanley Jones, Baxter also was hostile to the British empire. Moreover, like Armstrong, he was conservative, anti-union, and passionately opposed to the New Deal.

Echoing the belief, among those opposed to conflict with Japan, in the existence of a viable Japanese "peace party," Baxter was fervidly against what he termed the "War Party" in the United States. He accused it—in an ironic twist—of educating Americans for "mass hari-kari [hara-kiri or ritual suicide]." He blamed this alleged drive to war on the New Deal, which he pronounced a failure, both domestically and in its foreign policy. In a harbinger of the postwar attacks by right-wing Senator Joseph McCarthy on the State Department, he castigated that institution as "one of the most popular habitats" of New Dealers in recent years. He blamed it and the U.S. Treasury for bringing about the Tripartite Pact concluded by the Axis powers (Germany, Italy, and Japan) in September 1940. The signatories pledged to assist any one of them attacked by a nation not yet a belligerent, which stipulation was obviously aimed at the United States. Ironically, as someone against war with Japan, he believed in forcibly settling international disputes, for which belief he had been accused, he complained, of being an "imperialist." England had already "hopelessly lost" the war, he wrote, but the United States wanted to charge into the European conflict. He claimed that, beginning in February 1941, the U.S. "War Party" had begun to downplay the seriousness of England's situation.

A year ago, he continued, he had come to Florida to pen a book on Japan and the Far Eastern situation. "As a student of the Far Eastern situation for many years," he wrote, he believed Americans were grossly underestimating the role that region would play in this second war. At the beginning of the European conflict in 1939, he continued, he believed Britain would lose. The United States, he argued—no wonder he was accused of being an imperialist—should take over "economic and part military control" of all North and South America (an idea that resembled the head of America First, General Wood's, suggestion that the United States take over the northern portion of South America). He believed it would be "national suicide for us to become involved in the war either in Europe or in Asia." He had always told his clients not to worry about Europe; "the real stage to watch was in the Far East, for that was the area in which American soldiers would most likely be involved." Since Britain had already lost the war, he advised his clients that only one road was still open. Like former U.S. ambassador to Belgium John Cudahy, a major spokesman for isolationism and supporter of America First, and many other anti-interventionists, he saw the possibility of a negotiated peace between England and Germany.[12] Like E. Stanley Jones, though, he feared the possibility of a "salvage operation" in which the United States would protect the British empire's interests in Asia.

If the Japanese knew of Baxter's views, they would have been pleased. "Until recently," he argued in February, "we have read little in the papers about any possible war between the United States and Japan." Since the previous summer (1940), though, he had been convinced the Roosevelt administration was determined to save the British empire's assets. "All denials to the contrary," he wrote, "I have been convinced that this country is getting ready for war in Asia, and not for war in Europe."

In his 1940 book *Japan and America Must Work Together!*, he attempted to demonstrate that it would be "suicide if we permitted our government to create war between the American and Japanese peoples in order to protect the British assets in Asia."[13] In the past year, he had witnessed the State Department and the entire Roosevelt administration "almost go out of their way to aggravate relations with Japan." Writing two weeks following Ambassador Nomura Kichisaburo's arrival in Washington to negotiate a settlement between the two nations, he claimed that "any attempted negotiation for the removal of friction was immediately quashed." Now, he continued, State had told the Japanese that the United States would declare war if Japan tried to take over Dutch or British colonies in Asia. Baxter's Anglophobia led him to rash, emotional, and insupportable assertions. "The history of [Robert] Clive in India," he claimed, "is also a chapter that makes the record of the present dictators in the world look mild by comparison." Clive (1725–1774) was an English East India Company soldier and statesman whose military victories over the French in India in 1751 and 1757 destroyed their power there. Subsequently, he served twice as governor of Bengal and took Calcutta.[14] U.S. "reformers," Baxter argued, claimed to believe in democracy for everyone, "except of course" those ruled by the British in Asia, who had never had any democracy and never would if the British won "the coming showdown in Asia."

Like Armstrong, Baxter approved of the views of Roy W. Howard of the Scripps-Howard press and cited the latter's plea for more American understanding of Pacific problems.[15] Baxter also criticized the U.S. "War Party's" dispatch of Wendell Willkie, the Republican candidate for president in 1940 who was opposed to isolationism, on a mission to China as the president's personal representative. He approvingly noted that General Hugh S. Johnson, former head of the National Recovery Administration (Roosevelt fired him in 1934), opponent of the president's foreign policy, and member of America's First's national committee who had helped launch the committee in September 1940 with a nationwide radio address,[16] had dismissively described Willkie as "P.T. Barnum." "Since we are set on saving the world," wrote Baxter sarcastically, "we had better not leave out Asia."

Americans, he continued, were ignorant of China. In his book, he asserted that "the American public's conception of China and the Chinese government is just about as accurate as the American public's conception of what the 'Wild West' used to be like." He was just as hard on the Chinese as he was on the New Dealers. He echoed some of the contemporary criticism of China by British "China experts," Japanese so-called "liberals" (such as the Japanese ambassador to Britain and future postwar prime minister Yoshida Shigeru), and Baxter's fellow isolationists, such as journalist Ralph Townsend and John Bassett Moore, a historian of American foreign affairs and authority on international law.[17]

Nevertheless, his (and the Japanese) views of China were just as uninformed as those of the vast majority of Americans. He completely overlooked the Chinese revolution and surging nationalism that had been rapidly changing China during the past several decades. Instead, he seemed to settle for "opium" images, writing that the Chinese preferred to dwell in a "dream world, leaving foolish businessmen to concern themselves with world affairs." He believed they had been a failure in the modern industrial age and, in fact, had retrogressed over the past several centuries. In the age of mass production, he continued, the Chinese "have completely failed in every respect," whereas the Japanese had succeeded. Despite the fact that some viewed the Chinese as a "democratic-loving" people making great progress, they had proven themselves an "inferior people, incapable of even maintaining law and order, or anything resembling a democracy." Moreover, he warned, "Little is said about the fact that the great centre of Communism in Asia is in China, and . . . the record of government in China is the blackest of any large country in the world."

Sounding very much like Japan specialist Elizabeth B. Schumpeter, who argued in a 1940 book that Japan was much stronger economically than most people thought,[18] Baxter declared it was the "greatest tragedy of our times" that Americans still thought of the Japanese as a bankrupt nation where the people "make a few toys and other inferior articles." The testimony of most U.S. admirals regarding the Far Eastern situation, he complained, claimed that Japan was so insolvent that she would soon collapse in the event of a war with the United States. He disagreed and predicted that in the event of a Japan–United States conflict, the U.S. bond market would break down before that of the Japanese. Americans underestimated Japan's finances, merchant marine, and naval power, he insisted. In retrospect, he was right when he wrote that those Americans who felt the "coming war with Japan" would be brief were "in for the surprise of their lives." In support of this conclusion, he cited the views of Major General William C. Rivers (see below) and Admiral Yates Stirling Jr.

In April 1941, Stirling made clear that, unlike Baxter, he was no isolationist. Two years earlier, he was opposed to Japanese aggression in China and believed that a Japanese–American war might occur because of "some arrogant and aggressive action" by Japan or a "misstep" by that nation that "drives the United States into a war."[19] At the same time, he supported lend-lease and opposed "defeatist propaganda" that argued the United States should not go to a war it could not win. In addition, he supported U.S. convoying of lend-lease supplies to Britain. His main belief, though, was that lend-lease was immoral, for it meant hiring the British to fight as U.S. mercenaries. The United States, he concluded, should declare war on Great Britain's side. Thus, his argument closely resembled that of journalist and historian Herbert Agar, who wrote later that the Century Group was "not content with giving or selling arms to our friends in order that they might die in our defense."[20]

Meanwhile, Baxter did not ignore the racial dimensions of the Japan–United States crisis. Because the "Yellow Peril" had always been a popular topic in the American press, he argued it would not be nearly as hard to get Americans to fight Japan as it would be to persuade them to fight in Europe again. "All economic common sense," he appealed, "calls for an alliance between the United States and Japan to develop Asia, and not for an alliance between Japan and Germany." Again, he cited press magnate Roy Howard's views. "Japan wants no war with America," the newsman insisted and blamed the crisis on the "bungling" of the Senate Foreign Relations Committee. He called for a little more "tolerance in our psychological approach to Japan, with the recognition of the fact that they are a proud and sensitive people." Meanwhile, Baxter again cited General Hugh Johnson, who in 1940 had denounced, according to Baxter, "the stupidity of our going to war with Japan."

He seemed most worried about Americans' underestimation of a potential foe. His countrymen had "little or no respect for the Japanese military or naval machines, and particularly for Japanese finances"—which made Elizabeth Schumpeter's volume particularly upsetting to some. It was clear why he joined Armstrong and others in the Committee on Pacific Relations. As he had "feared a year ago," the U.S. government was "steadily marching down the road to war with Japan." In his view, "the propaganda machine of the [U.S.] 'War Party' will work at a faster tempo in the weeks ahead to aggravate our already strained relations with Japan." Without an Anglo-German negotiated peace, he insisted, "*I do not see how it is going to be possible to stop the 'War Party' from getting this country involved in a war with Japan that will last for many, many years*" (Baxter's italics and underlining). Numerous people were profiting from the armaments business, he asserted, so the United States seemed anxious to "rush pell-mell to commit national suicide." While the government had been promising not to send troops to Europe, he charged, it had been preparing "behind the scenes" to implement its "pre-destined role as the salvage agent for the British Empire by preparing the ground for a Japanese-American war." He warned his readers to be prepared for a lot of talk about the "Yellow Peril" and "why we must go to war with Japan if the sanctity of the American home is to be protected. The martial music is playing, our opponent has been selected, and all that is needed is a little 'educating' of the American people regarding a nation that even beforehand, they have made up their minds to hate." Getting in one last dig at the New Deal, he warned that once again in history leaders who have failed to produce the "abundant life" at home were turning to foreign adventure.[21]

He proved a hard-boiled Darwinist and apologist for Japan in *Japan and America Must Work Together!*, which ignored the preceding three years of Japanese atrocities in China (most infamously, the "Rape of Nanjing" in 1937–1938). He was clearly disturbed by the increasingly hard-line policy the United States was following in response to Japanese aggression in China as well as America's increasing aid to that country. He was obviously opposed to the anti-Japan and pro-China stance of many in the U.S. government and among the people. He was not afraid, though, to swim against the current. He "fully realized that in opposing the popular viewpoint and saying a 'kind word' for Japan," he would be "called the usual epithets by our many so-called 'liberals.'" For proposing that Japan and the United States work together, he realized he would be called a "'Japanese propagandist', an appeaser, and many other unpleasant names."

Referring to a May 1940 speech he had delivered, he argued that Nature, in the current "Machine Age," had certain "chosen peoples." As a result, "one machine and motor-minded Japanese is worth, to society, a million Chinese." The Japanese were the "'Henry Fords' of Asia" and the "Americans of Asia," while the Chinese "simply do not have what it takes to succeed under the rules contained in the American 'bible.'" He clearly agreed with Armstrong and other members of the future Committee on Pacific Relations that war with Japan should be averted. In both the United States and Japan, he warned, there were "cocky" people who felt they could "fight anybody," and those were the people we must "guard against." If the "chosen American people foolishly elect to fight the chosen Japanese people," he observed, "only one result is inevitable, both will perish in the process." Americans, he argued, had the choice of helping the Japanese to "Americanize" the Asian people or going to war with Japan on the theory that her leaders were wrong in adopting the "'American Bible of Success' and in doing the splendid job she has already done."

He also was a blatant apologist for Japan's expansion (while at the same time criticizing the British empire). The military party, he argued, had solved Japan's overpopulation problem by providing a "safety valve" in the form of a new empire. For that, he enthused, it "so rightly deserves the admiration and loyalty of the Japanese people." He fulsomely praised "Japan's Record as an Empire Builder." He denied the Japanese wanted to "rule the world," an accusation he dismissed as a "childlike charge." On the other hand, his anti-Chinese bias was made even clearer by his chapter titled "'Poor Chinese People'—The Greatest Propagandists in the World," in which he was harshly critical of them. It was incredible that after three years of Japanese invasion and atrocities against the Chinese, he could claim that "only a dreamer" could think that Japanese management in China, which had improved the standard of living, public morality, and public hygiene, "could harm the Chinese people." It was not surprising that he relied heavily for his negative view of China on fellow Committee on Pacific Relations member and pro-Japanese writer Ralph Townsend. The latter, he asserted, had done an "outstanding" job in his "excellent" book *Asia Answers* (1936). In addition, he again referred approvingly to Roy Howard, whom Armstrong also had approached for advice regarding his proposed committee. In conclusion, he wrote, the Japanese were "anything but a 'Yellow Peril.'" Indeed, he argued that trade with them was necessary for American recovery from the Depression.[22] Tellingly, when an FBI agent interviewed Armstrong in March 1942, he handed the agent a copy of Baxter's *Japan and America Must Work Together!* The book, the agent commented, "appears to be Japanese propaganda."[23]

In April 1941, Armstrong wrote to Baxter, although the former's letters make clear the two men had been in touch earlier. He enclosed a copy of the speech he was to deliver the following day to students and townspeople in Columbia, Missouri. The address had been scheduled for the week before, he wrote, but had been postponed. It had expanded into a "much bigger thing than contemplated," he explained, so the Peace Council (in Columbia?) believed it should give it a lot of publicity. He had traveled to Columbia on 14 April, he wrote, and arranged the press releases. The news services had copies of his speech and would publish reports of it the following evening. He had quoted Baxter in his speech, he added, and hoped that reference would be retained in the press release, if Baxter did not object.

As usual, he was pursuing a hectic schedule working for the isolationist cause. He wrote Baxter that he planned to speak in Springfield on 22 April and then at a conference in St. Louis on 23 April. Following that, he would travel to Louisville, Nashville, Atlanta, Raleigh, and end up in Washington on 27 April. He would be in Washington all day on 28 April, he informed Baxter, and attempt to get to New York the following day. He would "report to you," he wrote, before coming. In each city, he would arrange "mass meetings" for "some of our best speakers" in the House and Senate, referring to isolationist senators and representatives. Meanwhile, he explained, there had been a "real reaction" in the Midwest against "convoys and our going to war." He promised to tell Baxter about it when he saw him in New York.[24]

On 29 April, he was still in Washington and wrote Baxter from there to explain the delay in his New York trip and to describe his activities for the isolationist cause. He had had, he wrote, a "most busy and interesting time." He had given two speeches in Missouri, and the crowds were "just as enthusiastic as ever."[25] By the spring of 1941, confirmed one historian, "isolationists were increasingly talking in terms of British defeat."[26] Armstrong echoed this trend. Because Britain was suffering setbacks, he wrote, "there was a "great backwash of reaction against going to war." "'What's the use'—is the talk I now here [sic]." He had visited some southern cities, he reported, and they "really want some meetings down there." In Washington, he had met with a half dozen senators "who will go into that war-minded territory [the South]." Isolationist Senator Robert R. Reynolds (Democrat, North Carolina) would speak in Jacksonville "to take the hide off [Senator Claude] Pepper," who was, in one view, a "die-hard interventionist." Missouri Senator Bennett Champ Clark would travel to Louisville, "gladly, he said, for he wants to take Mr. [Herbert] Agar of the Louisville *Courier-Journal* over the coals."[27]

Agar, one of the most vocal members of the interventionist Century Group, had been appointed editor of the *Courier-Journal* in 1940 and immediately began using it as a platform to agitate for joining Britain in the war. In early 1941, the Century Group closed down. Several of the participants promptly established a new organization dubbed Fight for Freedom, with Agar as one of the founders and a colleague at the Louisville *Courier-Journal*, Ulric Bell, as chairman of its executive committee. Like the Century Group, this new organization supported U.S. entry into the war.[28]

Continuing his 29 April report to Baxter, Armstrong wrote that isolationist senator D. Worth Clark (Idaho) would speak in Raleigh and Senator Gerald P. Nye (North Dakota) in Atlanta. He hoped to be in New York on 1 May, he wrote, and would phone Baxter at his office to arrange a meeting. He had "moved right along on the matter we discussed, and now have it in concrete shape." He enclosed a copy of a press release planned for the following day's afternoon papers, which he believed would "have a wide usage."[29]

Ten days later, he wrote Baxter that he was "disappointed" that "Hell and [Hell'n] Maria Dawes" (a favorite self-description of former U.S. vice president [1925–1929] Charles G. Dawes [1865–1951]), whom he had hoped to see in Chicago, was not there. Seeing him would not have helped his isolationist cause, however, for Dawes was an interventionist. "I am on the trail of several others, though," Armstrong wrote, "and think there will be some good contacts." He then clarified the mysterious reference in his previous letter to "the matter we discussed" and to a press release. The "matter" was evidently the statement that he planned to send to Yale University Professor A. Whitney Griswold at the end of May advocating peace with Japan and the formation of a Committee on Pacific Relations. He enclosed a copy for

Baxter's approval and suggestions. "I think we are on the right track!" he wrote. "If we can get this letter signed by about 100 prominent citizens, favorable to friendly relations in the Pacific, and who really know the situation there, we can strike hard toward the sending of the Committee [members] to Japan, and the working out of further plans." In closing, he expressed gratitude for Baxter's help and encouragement.[30]

In late May, he wrote Baxter that he had been sending "numerous letters on our project." Possessed of a "can-do" attitude as always, he reported the replies had been "uniformly favorable. We must go through with this, and we can." He made clear to the New York businessman that the "letter" he mentioned earlier was the statement calling for a Committee on Pacific Relations that he had sent Griswold and others. The goal was still to obtain a hundred signatures, he wrote, "stating it [is] our purpose to select a Committee on Pacific Relations." He hoped to convene a meeting in early June in Washington or New York of everyone who signed the statement or was interested, and "announce plans for the visiting commission [committee] to go to Japan." In the meantime, he had work to do for America First in Louisville. While there, he promised, he would continue to correspond regarding plans for the committee. He would have "definite plans" prepared when he went to New York again in about a week.[31] Meanwhile, unbeknownst to the potential committee recruits, he kept the Japanese embassy in Washington informed about his progress in organizing the group.

At this time, he also contacted another American businessman, Everett W. Frazar (E. W. Frazar), who had long been involved in business with Japan and had served as president of the American Association in Tokyo for years. For his service, the Japanese government had bestowed on him the Order of the Rising Sun, third class. Given by the emperor himself to Japanese who had made special contributions in their fields, it also was awarded to foreigners who made unique contributions to Japan. Many years before, at an earlier time of tensions between America and Japan (1920), he had traveled to the United States as a representative of the American members of the America-Japan Society in Tokyo to act as a peacemaker. Upon returning to Japan, he proposed that a Japanese "publicity center" be established in the United States. Although much delayed, in 1938 the Japan Center was founded in New York. By the time Armstrong contacted him in 1941, Frazar had business reasons to oppose war with Japan, for such a conflict would result in the freezing of all the assets of companies with which he was involved in Japan, China, and Manchukuo.[32]

On the last day of May, Armstrong wrote to Frazar, once again referring to his mentor Walter Williams, who had been dean of the University of Missouri's School of Journalism when Armstrong was a student there. Both Williams and Frazar were sympathetic to a peaceful rather than a military solution to tensions between the United States and Japan. Armstrong was particularly interested in the fact that Frazar was an "officer in the American Japanese [America-Japan] Society."³³ Founded in 1917 in Tokyo, it included several members who, in the words of an eminent Japan historian, "professed a common interest: perpetuation of harmonious relations between their respective nations." Meetings of the society, the historian continued, were "a forum of significance." In December 1940, it hosted a farewell luncheon for Ambassador Nomura Kichisaburo before he departed for his post in Washington.³⁴

In his letter, Armstrong expressed the wish to see Frazar when he (Armstrong) came to New York but in the meantime hoped he would be a cosigner of his statement. There were "doubtless" many in the America-Japan Society, Armstrong continued, who would be interested in his project. "We contemplate sending a commission to Japan," he explained, to study problems affecting their two countries and to "suggest possible solutions." He invited Frazar to contribute the names of outstanding men and women who might serve on that commission or sign the statement. In closing, he impressed on Frazar that "time is urgent."³⁵

Because he was away from New York when Armstrong's letter arrived, it was early July before Frazar replied. "Naturally, as an American who has lived in Japan for a great many years," he wrote, "I am very sympathetically inclined and ready to do all I can toward the betterment of what seems to be a rapidly widening chasm." Because he was "deeply interested" in business in China as well as in Japan, though, "I would rather not intimately associate myself with any one organization."³⁶

In addition to businessmen, Armstrong was interested in recruiting military men for his committee. Whereas he had some success with civilians, he was spurned by both of the generals he approached. In an August letter to pacifist Mark Shaw, he reported that during his visit to New York a month earlier, he had met with U.S. Army General James G. Harbord. He was "outspoken in his advice to me to go right ahead and let's make a stand against war with Japan." This led the Missourian to confidently assert, "I believe he would act as chairman [of the Committee on Pacific Relations], and that would be all to the good."³⁷ The following day, he wrote Elizabeth Schumpeter that he had spoken "at some length" with Harbord. "He was very anxious for us to go ahead with a conference," he reported, "and intimated he would take a leading part." "I have been thinking he might be willing to be chairman," he wrote, "and if so, that would give it [the committee] considerable impetus."³⁸

There was no question the general would have been an important addition to Armstrong's committee. He had considerable experience in Asia, where beginning in 1902 he served for over a decade as an officer in the Philippine Constabulary. During 1917 and 1918, he was chief of staff of the American Expeditionary Force in France. At the time Armstrong approached him, he was chairman of the board of Radio Corporation of America (RCA). Unfortunately for Armstrong's hopes, however, he was not an isolationist. On the contrary, he supported conscription and, in late May, had spoken in favor of American assistance for Britain.[39]

Moreover, he had mixed feelings about the Japanese. On the one hand, he claimed to understand them and expressed sympathy for what he viewed as the reasons behind their actions. On the other hand, he saw them as a menace to the rest of Asia. In April 1938, he took a lengthy trip through Australia, Southeast Asia, and East Asia. In a series of radio broadcasts following his return, he spoke of the Australians' "faint perception of a shadow arising in the North Pacific," by which they meant Japan. That shadow, he warned, was "further darkened" by Dutch exploitation of the natives in the Dutch East Indies. They did not seem free and were not friendly toward Europeans and Americans. Although Australia and the Dutch East Indies were both afraid of the "growing shadow," he noted, they had nothing else in common. The shadow, he told his listeners, "wears an even deeper hue" in the Philippines. Upon his departure from that American colony, it made him sad to think the "indifference" of the United States might allow the peace and prosperity he had witnessed in the Philippines to change. "The lights on Corregidor were shining bright as we left Manila Bay for the open China Sea," he wrote, "but the rolling echo of the evening gun brought me many thoughts."

He also glimpsed Japan's anticommunist obsession, when his ship docked at Kobe. "The customs authorities were especially efficient," he told his radio audience, "in the matter of Communistic literature of any kind." It was clear, from his broadcast, that he shared that animus (like Armstrong and other members of his committee). He spoke of the Chinese Red Army and the Sian Incident of December 1936, when a warlord general kidnapped the Chinese Nationalist dictator, Chiang Kai-shek. Whatever launched the war in China, he declared, "I cannot resist the conviction that Japan is now fighting the battle of the world against a Communistic Asia."

While in Japan, he reported, he saw little evidence, other than some troop and truck movements, that it had a million men fighting a protracted war in China. Moving on to Hong Kong, he sided with critics of China (such as Ralph Townsend) when he declared the large numbers of people in that port city "threw some doubt on the intense nationalistic spirit of the Chinese, for many of these refugees, if of a nation disposed to fight for its country, would not have been in Hong Kong." It was clear that he contrasted that spirit with the Japanese people's "grim determination" to carry on. In Shanghai, Japanese officers showed Harbord stark evidence of war. He was critical of "white men and women," observing that it was rumored that they had danced and drunk on a hotel roof garden while a "few hundred yards away" thousands of members of an "alien race" had died under a terrible bombardment (as also happened in Peking when the Japanese attacked the previous summer).

His sympathy for Japan probably was the result of his status as military man and businessman; if there was resistance, then one used force to overcome it and to break into markets. He seemed sympathetic to Japan's use of armed force to try to suppress anti-Japanese feelings in China and maintain Japanese trade. His view of the Japanese invasion of China was a confused one, though, based on facile comparisons with the successful U.S. pressure on Japan to open up to the outside world in the 1850s. He compared Japan's pressure on China in the "China Incident" to Commodore Matthew Perry's mission in the 1850s, which used the threat of violence to force Japan to trade with America. "I do not credit the Japanese with the intention of annexation of territory," he averred, "where they are successful in China"—which would have been news to the Chinese, much of whose country the Japanese were then ruling through puppet regimes. As a soldier as well as a businessman focused on the bottom line, he saw the Perry mission as successful, for the Japanese were "our third best customer, and we are theirs." "That was the kind of cooperation," he asserted, "which the Japanese, no doubt, sought in China against absolute boycott of their business." He also expressed his admiration for what he believed to be Japan's lack of corruption in pursuing its war. "I heard no hint," he noted, "that any great family in Japan is enriching itself in this hour of its country's supreme test. Nor is it even suggested that the great business concerns like the Mitsui and Mitsubishi are making unusual profits . . . [nor is Japan] spending her money on propaganda or advertising agencies."

The Chinese resistance to the Japanese occupation of China's northeast region, which the Japanese called Manchukuo, he dubbed "bandits." He claimed that region was an "independent country," although it had the "closest and military understandings with Japan." He justified the Japanese presence there, again comparing it to the United States. It was "as necessary to Japan for protection of her west coast," he declared, "only three hundred miles from Russian territory, as Hawaii is to our west coast." Japan, he added, would fight to preserve the "economic and military understanding . . . she has with the new Empire. She has to if she is to survive." In his final broadcast, he warned that "wise statesmanship" would be needed in the future. He urged Americans to pay more attention to Asia. The struggle between idealism and realism was unending, he argued, and the United States was "a little on the Idealistic side."[40] His sympathetic views of Japan would have made him attractive to Armstrong, if he knew about them. He would have been a good candidate for membership in the Committee on Pacific Relations, for he wanted to avoid war with Japan, so all America's efforts could go toward shoring up a beleaguered Britain.

Elizabeth Schumpeter, for her part, tried to help Armstrong by proposing a possible military recruit for Armstrong's proposed committee. She suggested Armstrong contact isolationist General William C. Rivers, whom Baxter had mentioned approvingly in early 1941. Did Armstrong have on his list, she wondered, a retired army or navy man by the name of Rivers who lived in the New York City area? He had penned several "intelligent" letters to the *New York Times* regarding Japan–United States relations. She offered to check his initials when she returned home.[41]

A man of vast military experience, from fighting Indians at home to serving in the Philippines to World War I commands,[42] William C. Rivers seems to have devoted himself in retirement to writing frequent letters to the *New York Times*. In a 1936 missive, he warned that no one could notice the "unnecessary strain in our relations with Japan without deprecating it and realizing the danger involved." He recommended talks between Japan and the United States as "wise." "Historically," he wrote, "Japan and America should be friends. Strategically and commercially, there are many good reasons why the two principal Pacific powers should be 'Good Neighbors.'"[43] In October 1937, three months after the outbreak of the Sino-Japanese War (1937–1945), he questioned the wisdom of any American cooperation with Britain and France in levying sanctions on Japan. Like some members of Armstrong's committee, he suspected the two European powers needed American assistance to retain the Chinese territories they had forcibly seized in the past. In a startling claim for those times, he argued that Japan was the only country that could help China.[44]

In 1939, he supported the Ludlow Amendment, which would have required a referendum before any war was declared. Rivers, one historian wrote, viewed adoption of Ludlow's proposal as "virtually synonymous with the prevention of war."[45] In December of that year, he became chairman of a National Committee for the War Referendum. The implementation of the amendment, he argued, would "make any administration more hesitant to follow a line of policy likely to result in a war situation."[46] In a letter to the *New York Times* editor in September 1940, he agreed with A. Whitney Griswold regarding Japan policy. "Dr. Griswold believes," he wrote, "there is reason for trying to improve our relations with Japan. Also, that there exists a reasonable basis for such action." He also concurred with Griswold's judgement, in an August 1940 *Harper*'s article, that there was no "region of vital interest to our strategic and domestic welfare" in the Far East.[47] In short, Rivers was the sort of military man the isolationists liked, and they often quoted his opinions.[48] There is no evidence in Armstrong's correspondence, however, that he ever contacted the general.

NOTES

1. Wayne S. Cole, *America First: The Battle against Intervention in World War II* (Madison: University of Wisconsin Press, 1953), 189–93. See also Donald J. Friedman, *The Road from Isolation: The Campaign of the American Committee for Non-participation in Japanese Aggression, 1938–1941* (Cambridge, MA: Harvard University Press, 1968), 90.

2. Justus D. Doenecke, "Explaining the Antiwar Movement, 1939–1941: The Next Assignment," *Journal of Libertarian Studies* 8, no. 1 (1986): 159.

3. Wayne S. Cole, *Charles A. Lindbergh and the Battle against Intervention in World War II* (New York: Harcourt Brace Jovanovich, 1974), 106, 108; Report by W. E. Leishear, FBI, New York, "Japanese [Espionage] Activities in Washington, D.C.," 14 November 1941, report on Terasaki visits to New York, 29 September 1941, and 30–31 October 1941, pp. 27–28, Terasaki Hidenari FBI File No. 65-HQ-37232, FOIA.

4. O. K. Armstrong to Dr. T. T. Brumbaugh, Columbus, OH, 12 September 1941, Orland Kay Armstrong (1893–1987) Papers, 1912–1987 (C4056), State Historical Society of Missouri. The membership list was included in the circular letter he sent out following the 22 September 1941 inaugural meeting of the committee (see below). Armstrong to "Dear Friend," 4 October 1941, Armstrong Papers.

5. O. K. Armstrong to Mr. [W. Forbes] Webber,[Kansas City Division, FBI], 6 March 1942, Armstrong Papers.

6. Paul F. Hooper, "The Institute of Pacific Relations and the Origins of Asian and Pacific Studies," *Pacific Affairs* 61, no. 1 (1988): 98–121; John N. Thomas, *The Institute of Pacific Relations: Asian Scholars and American Politics* (Seattle: University of Washington Press, 1974), 1–8.

7. Armstrong to Webber, 6 March 1942; John Roy Carlson, *Under Cover: My Four Years in the Nazi Underworld of America* (New York: E.P. Dutton & Co., 1943), 256. For biographical sketches of Baxter (1899–1970), see *Marquis Who's Who on the Web* (accessed 18 August 2005); "William J. Baxter, Headed Economic Research Agency," *New York Times* (hereafter *NYT*), 17 April 1970, 30.

8. Armstrong to Webber, 6 March 1942.

9. Carlson, *Under Cover*, 256.

10. Doenecke, "Explaining the Antiwar Movement," 160; William J. Baxter, *Japan and America Must Work Together!* (New York: International Economic Research Bureau, 1940).

11. Warren I. Cohen, *The Chinese Connection: Roger S. Greene, Thomas W. Lamont, George Sokolsky, and American-East Asian Relations* (New York: Columbia University, 1978), 232.

12. Doenecke, "Explaining the Antiwar Movement," 152; Charles A. Lindbergh, *The Wartime Journals of Charles A. Lindbergh* (New York: Harcourt Brace Jovanovich, 1970), 391; Roger B. Jeans, *Terasaki Hidenari, Pearl Harbor, and Occupied Japan* (Lanham, MD: Lexington Books, 2009), 78, 80.

13. Unless otherwise noted, the following discussion is based on Baxter, *Japan and America Must Work Together!*, 5–9, 16, 29, 44, 81–82, 92, 96–97.

14. William Bridgewater, ed., *The Columbia-Viking Desk Encyclopedia*, 2nd ed. (New York: Columbia University Press, 1964), 383; William L. Langer, comp. and ed., *An Encyclopedia of World History* (Boston: Houghton Mifflin, 1952), 534–35.

15. Baxter praised Howard for a series of articles on the Far East. See Baxter, *Japan and America Must Work Together!*

16. Wayne S. Cole, *Roosevelt and the Isolationists* (Lincoln: University of Nebraska Press, 1983), 44–45, 380; Susan Dunn, *1940: F.D.R., Willkie, Lindbergh, and Hitler—the Election amid the Storm* (New Haven, CT: Yale University, 2013), 65–66, 314.

17. Doenecke, "Explaining the Antiwar Movement," 160; Dorothy Borg, "Two Histories of the Far Eastern Policy of the United States: Tyler Dennett and A. Whitney Griswold," in *Pearl Harbor as History: Japanese-American Relations, 1931–1941*, ed. Dorothy Borg and Shumpei Okamoto (New York: Columbia University Press, 1973), 553, 727–28. China, wrote Moore, was not a nation-state but merely a "geographic name." Doenecke, "Explaining the Antiwar Movement," 160. Yoshida was ambassador to Italy and Britain, 1936–1938. The military

looked askance at him for his perceived liberalism and friendship with the United States and Britain. Janet Hunter, comp., *Concise Dictionary of Modern Japanese History* (Berkeley: University of California Press, 1984), 251. China was a different matter for him (as for other Japanese). For criticism of China by Yoshida and the British, see John W. Dower, *Empire and Aftermath: Yoshida Shigeru and the Japanese Experience, 1878–1954* (Cambridge, MA: Harvard University Press, 1988), 133–34, 143.

18. Elizabeth Boody Schumpeter, ed., *The Industrialization of Japan and Manchukuo, 1930–1940: Population, Raw Materials and Industry* (New York: Macmillan, 1940).

19. Yates Stirling, *Sea Duty: The Memoirs of a Fighting Admiral* (New York: G.P. Putnam's Sons, 1939), 308.

20. Rear Admiral Yates Stirling Jr. [1872–1948], "Naval Aid to England: It Would Be More Honorable to Declare War," delivered before the Kiwanis Club of New York, 30 April 1941, *Vital Speeches of the Day*, vol. 7, 485–88; Lynne Olson, *Those Angry Days: Roosevelt, Lindbergh, and America's Fight over World War II, 1939–1941* (New York: Random House, 2013), 145.

21. William J. Baxter, "War with Japan Coming," Baxter International Economic Research Bureau, confidential, 25 February 1941, Armstrong Papers.

22. For Baxter's quotations from Townsend's book, see his *Japan and America Must Work Together!*, 31–32, 35–37, 41. Baxter also cited Rodney Gilbert's *What's Wrong with China* to criticize the Chinese (*Japan and America Must Work Together!*, 31, 33, 35, 39, 42, 84). He recommended both Townsend's and Gilbert's books to readers.

23. Armstrong, Springfield, MO, supplemental report to Webber, Kansas City, FBI, 16 March 1942, Armstrong's FBI File No. 62-45631-18, FOIA.

24. Armstrong to Baxter, New York, 19 April 1941, Armstrong Papers.

25. Armstrong to Baxter, New York, 29 April 1941, Armstrong Papers.

26. Doenecke, "Explaining the Antiwar Movement," 158.

27. Armstrong to Baxter, 29 April 1941.

28. Olson, *Those Angry Days*, 144–45, 213, 323–25.

29. Armstrong to Baxter, 29 April 1941; Cole, *Roosevelt and the Isolationists*, 427.

30. Armstrong to Baxter, New York, 10 May 1941, Armstrong Papers.

31. Armstrong to Baxter, 24 May 1941, Armstrong Papers.

32. "E.W. Frazar [1867–1951] Dies; Trader to the Orient," *NYT*, 15 October 1951, 25; *Marquis Who's Who on the Web* (accessed 18 August 2005); Ogata Sadako, "The Role of Liberal Nongovernmental Organizations in Japan," in *Pearl Harbor as History: Japanese-American Relations, 1931–1941*, ed. Dorothy Borg and Shumpei Okamoto (New York: Columbia University Press, 1973), 462, 710n12; Dorothy Perkins, *Encyclopedia of Japan* (New York: Roundtable Press, 1991), 66.

33. Armstrong to Frazar, New York, 31 May 1941, Armstrong Papers.

34. Robert J. C. Butow, *The John Doe Associates: Backdoor Diplomacy for Peace* (Stanford, CA: Stanford University Press, 1974), 94, 220; Ogata, "The Role of Liberal Nongovernmental Organizations," 462.

35. Armstrong to Frazar, New York, 31 May 1941, Armstrong Papers.

36. Frazar to Armstrong, Springfield, MO, 2 July 1941, Armstrong Papers.

37. Armstrong to Shaw, Melrose, MA, 16 August 1941, Armstrong Papers.

38. Armstrong, Springfield, MO, to Schumpeter, 17 August 1941, Armstrong Papers.

39. Timothy K. Nenninger, "Harbord, James Guthrie (21 Mar. 1866–20 August 1947)," in *American National Biography* (New York: Oxford University Press, 1999), 10:42–43; *Marquis Who's Who on the Web* (accessed 18 August 2005); Joseph E. Persico, *The Eleventh Month, Eleventh Day, and Eleventh Hour: Armistice Day, 1918, World War I and Its Violent Climax* (New York: Random House, 2004), 177; "Gen. Harbord Weds Widow of Col. Brown," *NYT*, 1 January 1939, 29; "Britain Needs Us, Says Gen. Harbord," *NYT*, 25 May 1941, 33; "Gen. Harbord Dies in Home at 81," *NYT*, 21 August 1947, 23; Major General James G. Harbord, Chairman of the Board of the Radio Corporation of America, "Some Observations around the Pacific," a series of three addresses broadcast by the National Broadcasting Company on 30 August, 6 September, and 13 September 1938, 13.

40. Harbord, "Some Observations around the Pacific," 7, 9, 12, 16, 21, 22, 25–28, 30–32.

41. Schumpeter to Armstrong, 23 August 1941, Armstrong Papers; Armstrong to Mrs. Schumpeter, 17 September 1941, R. Elizabeth Boody Schumpeter Papers (A-43), Schlesinger Library, Radcliffe College, Cambridge, MA.

42. "William Cannon Rivers," *Marquis Who's Who on the Web* (accessed 24 July 2006); "Maj. Gen. W.C. Rivers," *NYT*, 11 July 1943, 35.

43. William C. Rivers, "Strain Deplored," *NYT*, 16 February 1936, E9.

44. "Ludlow Urges Use of Neutrality Act to Stop Assistance to Japan," *Washington Post* (hereafter *WP*), 8 October 1937, 6.

45. Manfred Jonas, *Isolationism in America, 1935–1941* (Ithaca, NY: Cornell University Press, 1966), 165–66. See also "Vote on War Abroad Urged by Gen. Rivers," *WP*, 12 May 1939, 13.

46. Cole, *Roosevelt and the Isolationists*, 256–57.

47. William C. Rivers, "Situation in East," *NYT*, 1 September 1940, E7.

48. Doenecke, "Explaining the Antiwar Movement," 160.

Chapter Three

The Professoriat

At the time he contacted the Japanese embassy in May 1941, Armstrong's efforts to recruit American leading lights for his Committee on Pacific Relations went into high gear. In an attempt to recruit Far Eastern "experts" who could lend weight to the committee's undertakings in relations between the United States and Japan, he contacted Professors A. Whitney Griswold, Paul H. Clyde, and Elizabeth B. Schumpeter. Of the three, only Schumpeter responded by wholeheartedly supporting him and his Committee of Pacific Relations.

In May 1941, Armstrong wrote to Griswold, assistant professor of government and international relations at Yale, whom he believed to be an isolationist deeply concerned about the threat of war with Japan. Griswold was a prolific public intellectual in the years leading up to World War II, publishing numerous articles in popular and scholarly journals such as *Annals*, *Asia*, *Events*, *Foreign Affairs*, *Harper's*, and the *Yale Review*.[1] In December 1937, he asserted that U.S. problems in the Far East could be settled only through "direct negotiation with Japan."[2] American pacifists praised his writings. The National Council for the Prevention of War's organ, *Peace Action*, recommended his *The Far Eastern Policy of the United States*, praising it as a "volume of history which may yet play a part in history."[3]

Elizabeth Schumpeter, who became a strong supporter of Armstrong's plans for the committee, also extolled Griswold's volume.[4] Like Schumpeter, Griswold complained that he had suffered some unpopularity in Far Eastern studies circles. In a May 1939 letter to her, he explained that he was interested in her study of Japanese economic development because of "my own appreciation of the great need for objectivity, of which you speak. I, too, have come in for some unpopularity on this score. The emotionalism that blinds not only the public but most of our writers to the true course of events in the Far East is a source of constant worry to me. I feel there is no use arguing with these people and that the only way to attack the problem is through just such honest scholarship as you are attempting to maintain." There was a "tremendous need right now," he continued, for the economic analysis she was working on. "My chief desire," he added, "is to see the task objectively and capably performed." In closing, he offered his assistance with her project.[5] Thus, Schumpeter found a kindred soul in Griswold in those fraught times for Far Eastern studies. Because she was married to one of the leading economists of the time, Harvard University Professor Joseph Schumpeter, and because Griswold had published a classic book on international relations, they were perhaps the only members of the Committee on Pacific Relations with any real name recognition.[6]

At that time, Griswold and Schumpeter saw eye to eye when it came to U.S. policy toward Japan. In September 1939, he wrote her that he had perused her article ("The Problem of Sanctions in the Far East") with the "greatest interest" and asked for reprints. They also were in the same camp when it came to the Far Eastern studies establishment. Griswold wrote he was a "mere kibitzer" when it came to the Institute of Pacific Relations. "I see no use in arguing with such a propaganda group," he declared, "and I intend to address my comments to less emotional and more impartial authorities." He was writing an article, he explained, that would "reflect your views on the embargo." He was afraid, though, that because of the war in Europe—which began the day after his letter to her—the piece would not be printed. In any event, the Nazi–Soviet Nonaggression Pact, signed in August 1939, had "knocked the slats out of [Edward C.] Carter [secretary general of the institute's International Secretariat] and his godsaking [*sic*—godforsaken?] *front populaire*, which is one good thing."[7] Here Griswold was undoubtedly referring to Carter's strenuous efforts to persuade the Soviets to join and participate in the institute, a controversial policy in light of the Russian show trials in the 1930s. Unfortunately for his reputation, Carter accepted the Soviet version of the trials.[8]

The Nazi–Soviet Nonaggression Pact, Griswold continued, had tipped the "balance of power in the Far East in our favor" and rendered the imposition of an embargo on Japan "much less likely." On the other hand, the European war had made a general restriction of exports of "war materials"—that is, "one that will not be a discriminatory sanction on Japan"—much likelier. Although he had been concentrating on German language and history that summer, he assured Schumpeter that he had not let go of his interest in the U.S.'s Far Eastern policy.[9]

Two weeks later, Griswold wrote again to tell her that he planned to use her reprints in his course at Yale. Referring to his article "Facing Facts about a New Japanese-American Treaty," he informed her that he had completed his own piece that was to be published in *Asia* magazine.[10] In November, he wrote Schumpeter that the journal editor was going to publish comments by several scholars, and "[T. A.] Bisson and Co."—Bisson was a well-known Far Eastern scholar associated with the Institute of Pacific Relations—were already "after me hot and heavy." Scheduled to rebut his critics in the February 1940 issue of *Asia*, he asked Schumpeter for help with the economic aspects of his piece.[11] In his article, Griswold argued that a new trade treaty with Japan should be expanded to Manchukuo and Japanese-occupied China and no action should be taken, positive or negative, regarding recognition of Japan's "New Order" in East Asia. Bisson led the opposition to Griswold's proposal, arguing that a treaty that included Japanese-held areas of China would be U.S. "recognition of the 'New Order' with a vengeance." Bisson had credibility on the subject of the Japanese invasion and occupation of large areas of China, having published a book on that subject just two years earlier.[12] Griswold agreed with Schumpeter, however, concerning the dangers of an embargo directed against Japan. "I am still of the opinion," he wrote, "that an embargo would be both extremely dangerous and probably ineffective in bringing about peace in China." On the positive side, he thought the August 1939 Russo-German Mutual Nonaggression Pact and the European war gave the United States a chance to levy more pressure on Japan than otherwise. What did she think? he asked.[13]

In December, Griswold wrote that he was pleased that she generally agreed with the views laid out in his article in *Asia*. In the meantime, he had mailed a rebuttal of his critics to the journal. "It is as strong an argument against an embargo," he told her, "as I could make." Meanwhile, "by all means keep up the good fight against Kurt Bloch and I will endeavor to hold my fort against Bisson." The attack on her by Bloch in the most recent *Pacific Affairs*, he wrote encouragingly, was "very weak indeed." According to Schumpeter, Bloch was a German refugee who had lived in China before he became a research associate at the Institute of Pacific Relations.

The "most glaring fallacy," Griswold asserted, in the embargo argument was that the "more effective it promises to be the more likely Japan will be to resist it by force." In addition, it "made no sense" to simultaneously pressure Russia and Japan. He had faith in the U.S. ambassador to Japan, Joseph Grew, who was "aware of these things, and, if I read the omens correctly, is playing a very shrewd game."[14] Griswold's favorable view of Grew was probably due to the latter's policy of "constructive conciliation" toward Japan and support for Japanese "moderates," such as former ambassador to Britain Yoshida Shigeru. Just as the isolationists' policies were the subject of much dispute in the United States, though, by 1940 Grew's approach to relations between America and Japan was "increasingly controversial." With American public opinion turning against him, by that fall he had ceased siding with the Japanese "moderates" and begun pondering the question of when the United States would have to act against Japan.[15]

In the meantime, Griswold was "immensely" interested in Schumpeter's progress on her book on the Japanese economy. "The more I see of current writings on the Far East," he asserted in December 1939, "the more convinced I am that you are filling the most important remaining gap in our knowledge."[16] After a nine-month silence, in September 1940 he wrote to thank her for sending him a reprint of her Philadelphia talk in April. His silence had not been because he no longer agreed with her. He read the reprint "with great interest and approval," he assured her, and "in fact, I echo your sentiments." In the meantime, he looked forward to seeing her at Yale during the coming year and to meeting her husband,[17] Harvard economics professor Joseph Schumpeter.

Three weeks later, she replied to Griswold that her husband was "shocked" to hear she was "tampering with the integrity of periodicals by suggesting reviewers to them." "He tells me this is never done," she wrote, "and I can see now why there may be something in his point of view." She did not abandon hope, however, that a sympathetic Griswold would review her book, *The Industrialization of Japan and Manchukuo, 1930–1940*. It would be "absolutely natural," she wrote, for him to review a Japan book for the *Yale Review*. "Do you know the editor well enough," she inquired, "that either you or I could suggest it without violating professional etiquette?" She thought Griswold would be especially interested in the introduction and conclusion as well chapters 10, 11, 20, 21, and 22.[18]

The following month (October), Griswold hosted the famous anti-interventionist Charles Lindbergh at a dinner prior to the latter's speech at Yale to nearly three thousand people.[19] In November, Griswold wrote to thank Schumpeter for the copy of her book. He would read "as much of it as I can" for his *Foreign Affairs* piece and do a "serious review" later. "It certainly looks like a wonderful piece of work," he added and wished her luck "for the success of the magnum opus." It was "very pleasant," he added, "to see you and Professor [Joseph] Schumpeter last Saturday."[20]

In the beginning, Griswold favored Japan rather than China, which certainly qualified him for membership in Armstrong's committee. Following the outbreak of the Sino-Japanese War in 1937, he argued the United States should do everything possible to avoid involvement in a war in East Asia. U.S. national interests lay with Japan rather than China, he argued, and therefore it should discard its support for China and instead focus on rapprochement with Japan. In February 1939, he wrote to popular newspaper columnist Walter Lippmann to suggest the terms on which he believed the United States and Japan should iron out their differences. The 1911 U.S.–Japan Commercial Treaty was due to expire in January 1940. In July 1939, the United States notified Japan it would end the treaty after the stipulated six months, following which either country was free to use sanctions at any time and without advance notice.[21] In November, Griswold published an article in *Asia* magazine in which he urged passage of a comprehensive treaty to settle the Japanese–American dispute. This piece became widely known, for Lippmann praised it in his nationally syndicated column (which was perhaps how Armstrong heard of it). Since it was designed to launch public discussion, it was forwarded by *Asia*'s editors to forty prominent people for comment. To counter those who were critical, some of whose responses were published in the December issue of *Asia*, Griswold reiterated his position in the magazine's February 1940 issue.[22] In August, three months after the German conquest of Belgium, the Netherlands, and France, he argued the United States should settle its relations with Japan, so it could focus on the European situation. The United States had failed, he concluded, to find in the Far East an area of "vital interest to our strategic security and domestic welfare." Businessman and isolationist William Baxter concluded after reading the article that Griswold believed there was reason to improve U.S. relations with Japan and a "reasonable basis for such action."[23]

Meanwhile, in May 1941, Armstrong wrote to Griswold to ask for his support. His appeal seemed blind to Japan's aggressive behavior in China and Indochina over the preceding several years. Instead, he cited Walter Williams, who had been dean of the University of Missouri's School of Journalism when Armstrong was a student there. He "used to discuss foreign affairs" with the dean, who was "particularly interested in preserving peace in the Pacific." "There need never be war between the United States and Japan," the dean had declared in 1924–1925, "and there never will be if the intelligent people of both nations seek to understand their mutual problems."[24] By 1941, however, Armstrong was rightly worried that war between the two nations was "almost imminent." It was his "earnest conviction," though, that such a conflict could and should be prevented.

Instead of referring to Griswold's May 1941 article in the *Annals of the American Academy of Political and Social Science*,[25] Armstrong's 31 May letter cited a piece by the Yale historian that had appeared eighteen months earlier—an eternity in view of the rapid development of the world crisis. He knew of Griswold's interest in the problem of how to avoid war with Japan, he wrote, and had read his article in the November 1939 issue of *Asia* "with intense interest and approval."[26] As Lippmann had pointed out, Griswold had argued that negotiations for a new commercial treaty to replace the one that had been allowed to lapse in January could serve as an opportunity to settle American–Japanese differences.[27] According to many sources, Armstrong asserted, Griswold understood American–Japanese questions, and would be "sympathetic to settling those difficulties by some method other than war." Since he was unable to visit him at Yale, he enclosed a statement "some of us" had prepared for possible release. If Griswold was willing to cosign it, Armstrong wrote, "write me at once." If the Yale professor desired to alter the wording "in any way," he added, let him know.[28]

The "security and interests of our nation," the statement began, demanded immediate measures to "strengthen relations . . . between Japan and the United States." Despite the existence of "grave problems" in the Far East affecting U.S. interests, the drafters believed they "need not lead to armed conflict" between the two countries if an "intelligent, vigorous effort is made to understand and adjust them." The first means for the reestablishment of "more friendly relations" between the two countries was to investigate the causes of friction and devise ways of "amicable adjustment." The drafters assured Americans who might object that, although this approach called for cooperation, it "in no sense requires the sacrifice of any American principles, nor the sacrifice of honor on the part of any nation." It was believed, they confidently asserted, that understanding areas of conflict between the two nations would point to solutions "based upon international justice and equity for ourselves, for all peoples of the Orient, and for all nations having interests in the Far East."

The statement expressed concern that conflict in the Far East would hinder U.S. efforts to cope with the European crisis. In rather tortured prose, it emphasized that the European war made it imperative to undertake a "fresh study of our relations in the Pacific with a view to dissolving any adverse forces that would hinder the performing of our responsibilities elsewhere." The drafters reached out to Japan as well, arguing that its maintenance of trade and cultural cooperation with the English-speaking nations had "long proven the wise and sound policy." For the two nations' peoples, they warned, war would "be nothing short of calamitous." In closing, the drafters (Armstrong was the main author) appealed to the American government and people. There was much to be gained in "strengthening our position in the Orient by friendly rather than by antagonistic attitudes." They "respectfully" pointed out to the American people the "opportunity that now presents itself." To act in accordance with the drafters' "opinions and suggestions," they called for immediate creation of a Committee to Study Pacific Relations.[29]

In sending Griswold this statement, Armstrong revealed that he believed the Yale historian could be used to broaden recruitment. He was sending an extra copy of the statement to Griswold, he wrote, so he could forward it to anyone who was interested. He asked the professor to send him a list of such people, so he could send them a copy. He flattered Griswold, writing that he "doubtless knew numbers who are in favor of strengthening relations between our two countries." He then went on to make a request that may have startled the professor. "The plan," he wrote, "contemplates sending a commission to Japan early this summer, to study problems and make a report as to their possible solution by peaceful means." Would Griswold be willing to undertake such a mission? he inquired.[30]

Unfortunately for Armstrong's attempts to recruit Griswold, it was too late. In response to the growing crisis in Asia and Europe, the latter had retreated from his earlier focus on better relations with Japan. In January 1941, he confessed he was "frankly confused . . . as to exactly what course to believe in."[31] In his May article, he declared there would seem "no possibility whatever of a negotiated adjustment in American-Japanese relations," nor did the future "offer very great hope of such." The best that could be hoped for in American–Japanese relations, he concluded, was the current "undeclared peace."[32] By the time he received Armstrong's letter, then, it was clear he had abandoned hope of a negotiated settlement with Japan.

Therefore, in his June reply to Armstrong, Griswold wrote that he was "on the whole, sympathetic with your point of view." "I think it is ominous," he continued, "that so many major military powers have lined up against us, and further that to attempt to fight a war simultaneously on two fronts as far removed as Europe and the Far East would be disastrous." He still believed, he admitted, "it would be advantageous to us if we could arrange some *modus vivendi* with Japan that would permit us to concentrate on the far greater menace of Germany." However, he confessed that he was "perplexed as to the methods to pursue" and was not "inclined to urge any particular policy on anyone." He still retained some confidence in the U.S. government that Armstrong lacked. "I think," he told Armstrong, "that the government is aware of the danger and is taking steps to meet it." He had described his "feelings" on the matter, he told the Missourian, in the May issue of the *Annals of the American Academy of Political and Social Science*. His conclusion could not have been more discouraging to Armstrong. He was "not at the moment sure enough of the right policy to advocate any policy other than the one suggested in this article [that there was no chance of success in American–Japanese negotiations]." He hoped Armstrong would "understand my attitude."[33] Armstrong did not lose hope, though. Five days later, he reported to Schumpeter that Griswold appeared "much disturbed as to the proper move to be made at this time." He hoped, though, that he would "assist us."[34]

Armstrong also wrote to Professor of History Paul H. Clyde at Duke University, who had been mentioned as an outstanding person who understood relations between Japan and America and "might be sympathetic to an attempt to settle those difficulties peaceably rather than by war." Since he could not visit him in North Carolina, he enclosed a copy of the statement he had sent to Griswold and invited him to be a cosigner. He enclosed an extra copy in case Clyde knew anyone else "favorable to strengthening Japanese-American relations." He also asked Clyde for a list of interested parties, so "as large a number as possible may join in the statement." He was obviously anxious to get the ball rolling. "Time is urgent," he declared, and thanked Clyde in advance for a "prompt reply."[35]

In his June response, Clyde, like Griswold, declined to sign the statement. He was in "substantial agreement" with it, he wrote, but "must decline to be one of its co-signers." National unity was more important than confused public opinion, and the time was past for vague proclamations concerning Japanese–American relations. "A national emergency," he explained, "is already in effect by Presidential proclamation. Therefore, public statements of this kind at this time serve only to confuse public opinion and are doubtful aids in promoting any policy." "Any action which is to affect materially Far Eastern policy at this juncture," he continued, "must be presented to the President directly, must be supported by a substantial group representing authoritative opinion, and should be presented privately so as not to embarrass either the President or the Secretary of State." Only the "above procedure," he argued, "would be proper or effective in the present state of the national emergency."[36]

While Griswold and Clyde declined to join Armstrong's campaign to avert war with Japan, Elizabeth Schumpeter proved one of his most enthusiastic supporters during the six months preceding the outbreak of war and stuck with his committee right up until the Pearl Harbor attack ended its brief life. She had received her Ph.D. in economics from Radcliffe in 1934. The following year, she was hired to direct a research project on Japan sponsored by the Bureau of International Research. In 1937, she married the well-known Harvard economist Joseph Alois Julius Schumpeter.[37] By the time Armstrong contacted her in May 1941, she was thoroughly alienated from the Far Eastern studies establishment and ready to join a pro-Japanese group, such as Armstrong proposed, to try to avert war with Japan. Her disaffection was clear in her correspondence with Griswold during 1939 and 1940 and with Stanford history professor Payson J. Treat in 1940.

While ostensibly writing to praise Griswold's *The Far Eastern Policy of the United States* and request permission to quote from it, her sense of frustration with and alienation from the Far Eastern establishment surfaced in her very first letter to him. Writing in January 1939, months before the European war began, she asserted, "I cannot tell you how desirable I think it is to have a volume like yours appear just at present when we stand so much in need of a sense of perspective about our Far Eastern policy and its implications."[38]

Since she mentioned she was working on a book about Japan's economic development, in his reply Griswold asked for a "description of your research project, publications, progress, etc." He had "heard many random accounts of it," he wrote, "but never an authentic one." They seem to have immediately formed a mutual admiration society. "It sounds as if you were performing a great service to American business and diplomacy," he wrote, "not to mention scholarship."[39] In her response, Schumpeter proposed visiting him in New Haven "some time."[40] It was almost four months before he replied. When he did, he invited her to have lunch with Professor Nicholas John

Spykman, director of the Yale Institute of International Studies and "one of the best-known political scientists of his time," and himself to discuss her book.[41]

Subsequently, she forwarded an outline of her first volume as well as copies of an article and two talks she had published since early 1938. She had had "extraordinary difficulty in attempting to appraise the situation since the China Incident," she wrote, "especially since I thought it was necessary to pay some attention to the possibilities of Korea and Manchukuo in the strategic set-up." She again explained her unpopularity in the field of Far Eastern studies:

> I was very much interested in your work because it represented the same kind of effort to be objective in the historical diplomatic sphere that we are making in the economic sphere. . . . There is so much emotion and . . . propaganda at present concerning conditions in the Far East that there is very great need of objective scholarly work. I have made myself very unpopular in Far Eastern circles in the last year and a half because I have persisted in pointing out that there is a tendency to underestimate the economic strength of Japan and to simplify the whole problem in the Far East.[42]

In June, she wrote Griswold that she, like he, had been "worried for a long time about the kind of information which is being published on Far Eastern problems." When they met, she would tell him about her experiences in attempting to "bring about a more scholarly treatment on some phases of these problems."[43] A few days later, she journeyed to New Haven for a luncheon meeting with Griswold and Spykman.[44]

In September, Griswold responded that he hoped she would forward a copy of her article "The Problem of Sanctions in the Far East" to Senator Arthur H. Vandenberg—a conservative Republican from Michigan and one of the leading isolationists. "He follows the subject closely," he wrote, and they had corresponded regarding it. He advised Schumpeter not to tangle with the Institute for Pacific Relations, which would be "utterly futile." She had "the best possible *entree* to that organization," he explained. As an adviser to the institute's Australian Council, she should be able to do a lot. Meanwhile, he still believed the works she was preparing were the "most constructive and badly-needed [*sic*] projects in the field."[45] Tangle with the Institute of Pacific Relations she did, however. An Asian specialist could hardly avoid it in those days, if one wanted to publish the fruits of one's work. It was the only large scholarly organization that focused on Asia. It included most of the Asian specialists in various disciplines. Over its lifetime, a large number of books were brought out with institute assistance, while it also published a pair of the leading journals in the field, *Pacific Affairs* and *Far Eastern Survey*.[46]

In her reply in June to Griswold, she informed him that she had sent Vandenberg a typed version of her article "when the question of a Japanese embargo came up." She had saved a few reprints to send to "suitable" senators "if and when" the issue arose at the beginning of the following year (1940). "We may be so much occupied with Europe," she worried, "that we will forget the Far East entirely." She went on to ponder the situation there. "I wish," she wrote, "we had a real statesman who would attempt to mediate between China and Japan at this time." She thought that "even the Japanese army would be glad to get out of China now so that it would be free to concentrate against Russia." Perhaps thinking of her Japanese friend Ishibashi Tanzan, she wrote, "Certainly the liberal Japanese feel that the Russian-German pact [of 1939] very much alters the situation." In 1911, Ishibashi (1884–1973) had begun work for the *Oriental Economist*, a business magazine with links to Waseda University and a reputation as a stronghold of liberalism. From 1924 until the end of the war, he served as editor in chief. Following the war, he rose to the pinnacle of the Japanese political system, briefly serving as prime minister in the mid-1950s.[47]

As for the internecine struggle in Far Eastern studies, she did not "blame" Griswold "for thinking it pretty futile to do anything about the IPR. I sometimes wonder why I bother myself." The fight must have fulfilled some need, though, for she went on to declare she had had a "very good time baiting [Edward] Carter . . . about Russia and Germany really belonging in the same camp. This was all done very lightly at a polite tennis party." The following year (1940), she was to complain bitterly to Stanford professor Payson Treat about Philip Jaffe, managing editor of *Amerasia*. In the fall of 1939, he was already on her mind. "I have not yet met," she wrote Griswold, "the great Jaffe." In closing, she requested Griswold's assistance with "a few points" in her book's introduction concerning the Far Eastern policy of the Powers and the United States.[48]

Jaffe and *Amerasia* were later to be the subjects of much controversy involving the Institute of Pacific Relations. In 1938, Stanford professor Payson Treat charged that *Amerasia* was a united front and thus a communist-backed journal. In June 1945, the FBI arrested Jaffe, the editor of *Amerasia*, and charged him, along with several others, under the Espionage Act for possession of hundreds of classified documents. Although he had serious contacts with American communists, he got off with a fine of two thousand dollars. It turned out that few of the documents were sensitive, and none had been passed to foreign governments. Jaffe himself denied having engaged in espionage.[49]

Meanwhile, in mid-September 1939, Griswold advised her to send another reprint to Senator Vandenberg "on the pretext that he might have lost the typed copy." He also assured her he would be happy to help with the introduction to her book.[50] Two months later (November), he wrote to inquire if the Russo-German pact had altered the conclusions in her article on sanctions in the Far East.[51]

By this time, it must have been apparent to both scholars that they agreed concerning U.S. policy toward Japan. In December, she informed Griswold that she had read his article in *Asia* magazine and was "very much impressed about [with] the extent to which we agree on this problem." The Russian–German pact, she replied, had not "in any way seriously modified the conclusions set forth in my article in *Pacific Affairs*." She nearly echoed Griswold's words. "I still believe," she insisted, "an embargo would probably be ineffective and might be extremely dangerous. One of the possibilities of an embargo is the possibility of a Russo-Japanese pact." At present, she was writing an article for the journal *Oriental Economist*, whose editor-in-chief was her friend Ishibashi Tanzan, on the "possibility and means of improving Japanese and American relations." Although criticized as pro-Japanese, she was not naïve when it came to the situation in militarist Japan. "I hope," she wrote, "the military will not assassinate the editor."

At the same time, she could not ignore the struggle in Far Eastern studies circles. She was interested to learn that "Bisson & Company" would be "attacking" Griswold in *Asia* magazine and assured him he was not alone. "I was told by Professor [George H.] Blakeslee"—a professor of history and international relations at Clark University and editor of a journal dealing with foreign affairs—"that Kurt Bloch will attack me in the current issue of *Pacific Affairs*." She had not been allowed to read his criticism, she complained, but would have to wait three months for the issue.[52]

Over a year later (January 1941), she wrote to inform Griswold that the editor of *Pacific Affairs* had declined to publish her rebuttal to Kurt Bloch, which she had submitted late because of illness. Since her rebuttal broached "new problems raised by the war in Europe and the termination of the American Trade Treaty with Japan," she would send Griswold several copies to "distribute . . . around New Haven wherever you think they will do the most good." In the meantime, she had participated in a debate sponsored by the Peace Action Council of the Community Church and the Greater Boston Peace Council. "I have the impression," she added, "that I managed to get our point of view across to a fairly substantial number of the audience."

She also expressed a new worry. She wondered why the *New York Times* editor who previously opined on the Japan question had altered his political stance. In June 1939, she noted, he had been "100 per cent" in support of an embargo. He had cited the "same figures and the same kind of language" as the American Committee for Non-participation in Japanese Aggression (led by Harry B. Price). However, in December—several months following the outbreak of war in Europe—he was much more cautious and implied they should take into consideration "Japanese supplies and alternative sources of imports." Even the Committee for Non-participation members were more cautious, she observed. Her opponent in the debate the previous evening, Professor George Nye Steiger, was the organizer of that committee's Boston branch as well as a historian of China.53

In February 1940, Griswold wrote that he looked forward to reading her response to Bloch, whose analysis he considered "confused & rather weak." As for her wondering about the *New York Times* editor, he complimented her. He had "come around," Griswold thought, because of the "strong logic of your facts as opposed to the assumptions of the embargoists [sic]." Up to this point, they had "monopolized attention because they are an organized pressure group." The war in Europe and the world crisis, though, had "called other individuals and groups into action and the facts, though unpopular, are becoming known." In closing, he wondered whether he could review her book when it was published.54 He invited her to choose a journal, granted it was a "reasonably scholarly journal." She almost immediately communicated her assent, for she was certain the Institute of Pacific Relations would "try very hard to discredit the whole study."55

By the time she wrote Griswold again in July 1940, Japan–United States relations had reached a turning point. The United States, in response to the Japanese occupation of the southern portion of French Indochina, froze Japanese assets in the United States.56 The Far Eastern situation made her anxious. "I have a feeling," she lamented, "that we have missed the bus in the last few months, that there was a chance for a reasonable settlement in the Far East which we may not have again for a long time." She had attempted to persuade *Harper's* to publish a "more realistic approach to the whole problem than that put forth by [Professor Nathaniel] Peffer"—a professor of international relations at Columbia University—but the staff informed her that Griswold was writing an article for the magazine.57

With her book finished, she was thinking ahead to the reviews. In her letter to Griswold, she wished both their books would be "required reading for everyone who has anything to do with our foreign policy in the Far East or who writes about it." She especially wanted the *New York Times* and the *Herald-Tribune Book Review* to do a "good review" of her book. Did Griswold have "any idea as to how I could go about accomplishing this?" The volume was not, she insisted, "simply another textbook for economists," and most of it should be interesting to the "intelligent" reader.58

In August, she sent Griswold a reprint of a talk she had delivered in Philadelphia in April.59 Probably alluding to the crisis in United States–Japan relations in July, she explained, "the situation has changed so rapidly that I am not bothering to send many of them out." Changing tack, she asked him to review her book for a historical journal. If he had a preference as to which one, he should let her know. Her husband was going to be at Yale one day a week during the coming year, she added, and she might accompany him "from time to time." She hoped to see Griswold and Professor Spykman then.[60]

Her alienation from the field of Far Eastern studies also was apparent in her correspondence with Stanford University history professor Payson J. Treat, who, like her, participated in Armstrong's Committee on Pacific Relations, a group described as "advocating appeasement of Japan," in the fall of 1941. In 1935, he had been awarded the Order of the Sacred Treasure (third class) by the Japanese government and was viewed as pro-Japanese.[61] He was a specialist on the history of American–Japanese relations and may have been, in 1906, the first professor of Far Eastern history in the United States. The beginning of the Pacific War in December 1941, however, blocked what would have been his fifth trip to Asia.[62]

Treat and Schumpeter corresponded often during 1940.[63] It was clear Treat admired Schumpeter's writings and that they were of like mind when it came to the state of American–Japan relations. In January, he wrote that after he read Schumpeter's article in the September 1939 issue of *Pacific Affairs*, "The Problem of Sanctions in the Far East," he wanted to thank her for "shedding so much light on a badly fogged subject." "I not only valued the article highly," he continued, "I have used it as a reference for serious students who wanted to explore the subject. I think you did a fine job." Moreover, he made clear where his loyalties lay, in the clash between China and Japan, when he inquired about the Chinese Council for Economic Research in Washington, DC, mentioned in her article. Was the council a "propaganda agency?" he inquired. "I am interested in learning all I can about the agencies which are so active in disseminating false or misleading information among our good people."[64]

Two weeks later, she responded that she was "generally so unpopular in Far Eastern circles that I especially appreciate a word of appreciation." She had enclosed, she explained, two or three copies of her reply to Institute of Pacific Relations researcher Kurt Bloch on the subject of sanctions in the Far East. It was supposed to appear in the December issue of *Pacific Affairs*, she explained, but the editor refused to include it, explaining he had already sent the issue to press. She went on to vent her frustration. "I have, of course, great difficulty at present in getting anything published by the Far Eastern organizations." She went on to complain that *Far Eastern Survey*, *Pacific Affairs* (both Institute of Pacific Relations journals), and *Amerasia* had all treated her shabbily. In response to Treat's query about her forthcoming book on Japanese economic developments, she replied that it probably would be published by Macmillan in the spring. Treat and Schumpeter both were very concerned about their mistreatment by editors of Far Eastern studies journals. In his early February reply to Schumpeter, the Stanford professor reported that when he read her account of mistreatment, he forwarded, in the "Strictest Confidence" [Treat's underlining], extracts from her letter as well as from two missives from William Henry Chamberlin—journalist and author, isolationist, and future member of Armstrong's Committee on Pacific Relations—to Dr. C. Martin Wilbur.[65] At that time, Wilbur was assistant curator of Chinese archaeology and ethnology at the Field Museum of Natural History in Chicago. More to the point here, he was writing reviews for *Pacific Affairs*, which, he later recalled, made him "better known in the Sinological fraternity."[66]

As for Treat's inquiry about the Chinese Council for Economic Research, Schumpeter replied that it was often mentioned in *Amerasia*. "I assume," she wrote, "that it is a propaganda agency." Propaganda was clearly a subject she, like Treat, was concerned about. "I wish that some serious person or . . . group," she wrote, "would investigate propaganda activities in the field of Far Eastern Affairs. I have been seriously concerned by what amounts to suppression of ideas and information by a very large group which is both very pro-Chinese and very pro-Russian. The fact that they have the natural sympathies of the American people to work upon gives them a very dangerous advantage."[67]

In response, Treat informed her that one of Stanford's politics instructors had written a dissertation about "propaganda agencies dealing with Far Eastern questions." "He has tried," he explained, "to find out who was *behind* the various *fronts*" (Treat's emphasis). Did she have any information about Kurt Bloch, he inquired, who attempted to "smear your article"? He ended with a blast at the three publications that had, in her view, given her a hard time. "My general impression of the three publications you mentioned," he wrote, "is that *Amerasia* is undiluted Communism, *Pacific Affairs* is party line, and *Far Eastern Survey* is camouflaged party line." In view of his jaundiced view of *Pacific Affairs*, he could not help being "mystified" when the journal published her article. Thus, he was grateful for her explanation.[68] *Pacific Affairs*, she responded, had asked her for an article "only because it [*Pacific Affairs*] had been subjected to a certain amount of criticism by a number of the Canadian and Australian members." Some weeks later, though, she gave him a different explanation. It was "after receiving my letter of March 22, 1939," she wrote, "that Mr. [William L.] Holland asked me to contribute an article to *Pacific Affairs*."[69] Holland served the Institute of Pacific Relations for more than thirty years, beginning as a research assistant in the International Secretariat. At the time Schumpeter wrote him, he was "research secretary." In 1946, he became secretary-general. A New Zealander by birth, he became the institute's most important leader and praised as one able to maintain the confidence of its different elements,[70] a quality in evidence when he invited Schumpeter, who was clearly unhappy with the institute, to submit an article to one of the institute's journals.

In her correspondence with Treat, Schumpeter continued to complain about the "establishment" and detail her attempts to overturn the consensus she believed reigned there. She also explained her falling out with the institute. She explained to Treat that she had been attempting to convince Frederick Field, head of the institute's American Council, that it was a mistake to publish *Amerasia* and "display in general an unwillingness and an inability to comprehend the difficult and complicated situation in the Far East. I have been doing this since the summer of 1938 and gave up only recently when I became convinced it was hopeless."[71]

Secretary of the American Council from 1934 to 1940, Field was the scion of an extremely wealthy family. A study of the institute described him as "personable, hard-working, and a flexible administrator." By the mid-1940s, however, he was openly espousing communist causes, which could not have made him popular in the eyes of Schumpeter, an avowed conservative. In 1937, he helped found *Amerasia* as a vehicle for criticizing Japan's policies in China. He argued institute writers could publish views in this journal that were not appropriate for other institute publications. In 1939, he advocated the American Council take over *Amerasia* as an instrument for airing all sides of political issues in Asia.[72]

Schumpeter also had tried to win over to her side Ada Louise Comstock, a vice president of the American Council, but Comstock "could not believe that such nice people as Mr. Field and Mr. [Edward] Carter could be led astray." In her letter to Treat, Schumpeter enclosed copies of letters exchanged with various institute people and said she had many more she would be happy to share with "anyone like Dr. [C. Martin] Wilbur." She did not plan to pursue the matter, though, because she thought it "useless." Treat could keep the copy of her letter to George Eggleston, editor of the *Scribner's Commentator*, she wrote, but she wanted the rest of them returned.

She also continued to complain about Philip Jaffe, managing editor of *Amerasia*, and did everything but call him a communist. It was a travesty, she argued, that he had been picked as one of a "small, select list of ten Americans" at a recent institute conference in Virginia Beach. He had been "known under three names," she revealed. "He was supposedly a greeting card manufacturer who writes on the Far East with a pronounced Soviet bias and absolutely no regard for the facts. A number of people suspect he is acting for some communist interest." She denied knowledge of that accusation but could "truthly [sic]" write that he was a "most unsuitable person to be working in close collaboration with the I.P.R. [Institute of Pacific Relations]" and to be a delegate at the Virginia Beach conference. "I am now contemplating resigning from the I.P.R.," she wrote, "because this last development has made the situation seem to me to be perfectly hopeless." She did not, however, display the same degree of animus against the *Pacific Affairs* editor, Owen Lattimore. In her letter to Treat, she defended Lattimore as "much more tolerant than any of the other I.P.R. people with whom I have come into contact."[73]

Lattimore was well known for his expertise on China's borders with Central Asia, an area at that time relatively unknown to Western scholars. As editor of *Pacific Affairs* from 1933 to 1941, he accepted no articles on the Soviet show trials in the 1930s. Instead, he argued that the trials, in John Thomas's words, "would aid 'democracy' by giving the average Soviet citizen more ground to protest if victimized in the future by government officials." Meanwhile, what was clear was that when it came to Japan, Lattimore was an interventionist, a position Schumpeter would not have agreed with. After the Sino-Japanese War began, *Pacific Affairs*' coverage generally leaned toward China.[74]

Kurt Bloch was another story, though. Bloch, she informed Treat, was "a second or third rate socialist, economist, journalist." She wrote to both Treat and Griswold that she had just received a "very aggrieved" letter from Bloch accusing her of misrepresenting him and suggesting she distribute a mimeographed statement to that effect. It was "very amusing to her," she wrote, "that these people cannot take a dose of their own medicine."

> They control *Amerasia* and the *Far Eastern Survey* and certainly have great influence in *Pacific Affairs*. They can criticize anyone with little prospect of that person being able to make a reply. If the reply is made, it can only be made months later because they never give an opportunity to do it in the same issue. When finally I went to considerable trouble and expense on this one occasion, he is shocked, surprised and hurt, and makes vague threats.[75]

A few days later, Treat responded that he had read her reply to Bloch with "deep interest and approval." He had given one copy to his Stanford colleague in Japanese history and civilization, Dr. Yamato Ichihashi, and the other to the Hoover Institution Library at Stanford University. The latter, he added, was gathering "propaganda material on the Far East," and her article "shows up the practices of one of the Far Eastern journals."[76] Born in Japan, Ichihashi earned a Ph.D. from Harvard University in 1914. The preceding year, he had accepted the position of professor of Japanese history and government at Stanford University. He was involved in the Institute of Pacific Relations' conferences in 1925 and 1926, according to his papers in the archives. Tragically, he was relocated to the interior after the Japanese attack on Pearl Harbor in December 1941. Following the war, he returned to Stanford to resume teaching.[77]

Meanwhile, Treat reported to Schumpeter that Wilbur had immediately acted on her (and Chamberlin's) complaint. Like Schumpeter and Chamberlin, Treat was alienated from the Far Eastern establishment. He told Wilbur that he had remained a member of the Institute of Pacific Relations' American Council "simply because of his [Wilbur's] relationship with it, but that I did not see how I could continue after the [Philip] Jaffe incident." He referred to Griswold, whom Armstrong tried unsuccessfully to lure into his antiwar movement. "If Professors [Nicholas John] Spykman, Griswold, and others, who are objective and academic students, expressed similar views, perhaps some action might be taken." Treat had joined the American Council when it was launched in 1925 and had attended the first institute conference in Honolulu that year. "I welcomed the Institute as a *fact-finding* body," he wrote Schumpeter, "but no one could use that term in connection with much of its work in the last ten years" (Treat's emphasis). If she went to Japan, he concluded, "please give me the opportunity to talk with you at Stanford."[78] It was eight months, though, before Schumpeter replied. When she did, it was to announce that her book, *The Industrialization of Japan and Manchukuo, 1930–1940*, was going to be published in October. Although she could not send him a copy, she hoped he would inform those on the Pacific coast who might be interested.[79]

In sum, well before Armstrong recruited Schumpeter for his committee in 1941, she was on the outs with America's Far Eastern studies establishment, especially the Institute of Pacific Relations. Regardless, the institute gave her name to Armstrong (addressing her as Mrs. Joseph A. Schumpeter, as was the fashion at the time, rather than Elizabeth Boody Schumpeter),[80] even though the year before she had resigned from the institute because of what she considered its hostile environment.[81] She must have seemed an attractive recruit to Armstrong, for in 1940 she was an author and expert on Far Eastern economics at the Harvard-Radcliffe Bureau of International Research, a contributing editor of the Harvard Economic Service, and an assistant professor of economics at Vassar and Wheaton Colleges, whose friends described her as forthright, honest, staunch, and loyal.[82]

In May 1941, Armstrong wrote to her, once again citing Dean Walter Williams's belief that a Japan–America war need never occur. He also professed his own belief that war with Japan could be prevented. He informed Schumpeter that he had been compiling a list of people, including her, who were interested in Japan–America relations. He enclosed the policy statement he had drafted and invited her to sign it. He asked her to recommend others "sympathetic to the solution of our difficulties in the Far East without resort to war" and promised to send them a copy of his statement as well. In addition, he informed her of the "tentative plan" to send a commission to the Orient to "study problems first-hand this summer, and report possibilities for peaceful settlement" and, although he had never met her, invited her to participate. In closing, he urged her to reply promptly for "time is urgent."[83]

Since Armstrong got her first name wrong in his letter (he addressed her as "Edith" rather than Elizabeth), it was perhaps her feelings of isolation that moved her to overlook the error and swiftly agree to participate. She would happily sign his statement, she wrote, "as I am very sympathetic to your position." She had spent five years at Harvard and Radcliffe's Bureau of International Research, she told him, researching Far Eastern economic problems. The bureau, however, was "now liquidating." Responding to his request for others he might contact, she suggested A. Whitney Griswold, whom Armstrong wrote that same day.[84] Later, Armstrong inflated her list of names—she gave him only two—telling the FBI she had provided the names of people "of distinction in the fields of education, religion, or journalism, who had been in the Far East and knew the problems of Japan and China."[85] She sent him a copy of her controversial book, *The Industrialization of Japan, Korea, and Manchuria, 1930–1940* (which she did not send fellow Far East specialist Payson Treat). It had just been released "a few months ago," she wrote, "and . . . is not popular with our best 'wishful thinkers' because it indicates that Japan is stronger economically than they suppose."[86]

Since they were in touch for the first time, Schumpeter tried to give Armstrong some idea of her beliefs. In April 1940, she explained, she had set forth her general stance in a speech (a copy of which she enclosed) at the Academy of Political and Social Science. Her position, she added, had "only been strengthened by subsequent developments."[87] There was no question but what Armstrong was buoyed by her response. Her letter arrived while he was away on a lecture tour, he wrote a week or so later, and he found her words "encouraging." He made it clear he lacked the time to tackle her enormous book. He had been looking it over, though, and hoped to read it soon. "You must have put enormous time, study, and work into it!" He was hoping to push ahead on his "Japanese project," he continued, and was leaving that evening for Washington, where he anticipated meeting several interested people. Although she had not mentioned diplomat William R. Castle in her letter, he added that he was sorry to learn that the former ambassador to Japan (in 1930) was ill. "He is a dear friend of mine," he declared, "and I was counting on him to assist in the plans."[88] That would have been a coup for Armstrong since the diplomat was close to Charles Lindbergh, the most famous of the isolationists.

A Republican, Castle had served in the State Department from 1919 to 1933 and was undersecretary of state for two years in the Hoover administration during that period. In August 1939, he served as assistant to the chairman of the Republican National Committee. Although a member of America First's national committee, he was sensitive to the struggle of have-not countries against the haves. Before the start of the European war in September, he told the House Foreign Affairs Committee that if war broke out in Europe, it would not be dictatorships versus democracies but have-not nations against the haves. During the summer, Lindbergh proposed to Castle the formation of a small group that could become active in case of a European conflict "with the purpose of keeping this country out of trouble." "I get a great deal from talking to Castle," he wrote, "and he represents an outlook I don't want to lose contact with." Meanwhile, that year the former diplomat expressed opposition to an embargo on Japan. He believed it was inevitable that Japan would control the Asian mainland, which might mean demand for American products.

By October, however, Lindbergh was complaining that Castle was "far too conservative for these times." The following year, the ex-diplomat strongly supported Republican presidential candidate Wendell Willkie against President Roosevelt's bid for a third term. At that time, Armstrong tried to recruit him for the leadership of his No Foreign War Campaign, but Castle declined. In January 1941, Castle, like Armstrong, opposed the lend-lease proposal. In April, he expressed opposition to United States participation in a war designed to stop Japanese expansion. Although, in November, he disapproved of America First playing an active role in the 1942 elections, on 1 December 1941 the organization announced it would participate. Castle, wrote a Japan specialist, argued for "appeasement toward Japan until a very late date." In any event, the Japanese surprise attack on Pearl Harbor derailed any attempt by America First to test its power in an election.[89]

Meanwhile, in his 10 June letter, Armstrong informed Schumpeter that he was going to New York the weekend of 14–15 June and would contact her early the following week. "The plan now contemplates selection of six or eight experts, such as yourself," he continued, "to make an immediate trip to Japan, to study first-hand and report definitely what might be done." Meanwhile, because she had mentioned Griswold's name, he had written to him.[90]

By the time Armstrong met her in the spring of 1941, Schumpeter was known for a "violent hostility" to Roosevelt and for being "very right wing in general" (like Armstrong). Because of her work for the Bureau of International Research, in the late 1930s she began to oppose the U.S. government's Japan policy, which stance was "apparently too much for some people." In 1939, she very much wanted to go to Japan, although the trip never materialized. Perhaps the fact that she never traveled to Japan or its puppet state of Manchukuo helps account for her opinions of them. Anti-interventionist and fellow Committee on Pacific Relations member Ralph Townsend did visit there, however, and yet the experience did not alter his views. She certainly had warm feelings for Japan because of her intensive study of its culture, language, and especially economy. Between 1938 and 1941, she wrote several papers on the Far East, with most of the five she penned in 1941 focused on Japan.

Although the volume Schumpeter edited and contributed to in 1940 was to be criticized for her views of Japan's expansion in Asia and argument that America was partially responsible for it, her interpretation was already clear prior to the book's appearance. Her September 1939 article in *Pacific Affairs*, "The Problem of Sanctions in the Far East," was especially provocative and resulted in the journal opening its pages in a subsequent issue to letters endorsing or opposing Schumpeter's analysis. Her argument was straightforward and must have pleased the Japanese. Economic sanctions would be ineffective, she argued, would not stop the war in China, and, in fact, would lead to a war between the United States and Japan. A recent U.S. poll, she wrote, had demonstrated increasing sympathy for China and support for "some sort of economic pressure on Japan." However, weak economic sanctions on Japan would be ineffective, she believed, while strong ones would result in war. It was doubtful, she argued, that Americans (as well as Britons and Frenchmen) would be willing to aid China in "ways which would lead to becoming involved in a war with Japan." Moreover, stopping such a conflict would not be a short and simple business. The West's denial of raw materials to Japan, she believed, gave "a kind of moral justification to what would otherwise be a [Japanese] campaign of pure aggression." She hastened to add, however, that her argument was not a "justification of the Japanese invasion of China." She recognized the lack of oil was Japan's "greatest strategic weakness." Economic sanctions "could injure Japan very much," she acknowledged, but could not halt the China war without "great danger" of Japanese economic and possibly military retaliation. Cut off from raw materials in the Netherlands East Indies, British Malaya, French Indochina, and the Philippines, she prophetically argued, "who can be sure what the Japanese Army and Navy would do . . . ?" "Partial sanctions will not stop a nation prepared to make every sacrifice for what it looks upon as its national existence," she argued, and "strong sanctions applied after a nation is deeply involved will, in all probability, lead to war."[91]

Three months later, while debating the question of whether to levy sanctions against Japan, *Pacific Affairs* published several responses to Schumpeter's article. A Canadian wrote that, although he viewed the article as a "very able, discriminating and exact statement of one view of this most important question," he was not persuaded her conclusions were "altogether sound" and asked for an article taking the other side of the argument. Another writer agreed with her that Americans had been denied a full and balanced description of the Far Eastern situation but insisted that if they did have the full story, they would have demanded punitive action long ago. By far the most detailed response was from her arch opponent, Kurt Bloch, who favored sanctions. Although they would not immediately stop the war in China, he argued, they would result in an "appreciable weakening" of Japan. Moreover, with the China Incident, the risk of war had grown "appreciably less," and embargoes and boycotts would "clearly not imply the risk of war seriously." Though much of Schumpeter's critique of those supporting an embargo "seemed justified, sound and even insufficient at the time of its publication," he concluded, she had "failed to establish her case for doing nothing."[92]

In 1939, Schumpeter was already complaining she had been "accused of being anything from merely 'pro-Japanese' to a 'Japanese spy.'"[93] Both she and her husband, Joseph, were anti-interventionists and opposed to U.S. economic and diplomatic pressure on Japan. This caused those who read or heard their views to interpret their stance as pro-Japanese. In August, with the German invasion of Poland imminent, Joseph wrote in his diary that he feared Roosevelt was guiding the nation into war.

In March, Schumpeter was convinced, because of her work for the Bureau of International Research, that Japan was much stronger than commonly assumed, and added that the present Sino-Japanese War could not be halted by the United States' economic action within two years. Because of these views, she continued, she was "extremely unpopular in certain Far Eastern circles which are anxious to have the United States take this action whatever the consequences may be." Attempting to clarify her position, she asserted that she liked the Japanese people but had "no sympathy with the Japanese Army and its aspirations in China." She was tough-minded, adding that "even where your sympathies are concerned, you should be somewhat realistic."[94]

Because of her opinions, Schumpeter declared in September 1939, she was "practically ostracized" at the Institute of Pacific Relations. Thus, although she had been a member for six years, she resigned the following year. She also was ostracized by her husband's colleagues at Harvard, where "nearly all" the professors were anti-Japanese. China historian John K. Fairbank later recalled that when, because of her studies, she cited "extenuating or at least causal factors in Japan's expansion," some "Cambridge ladies hissed like geese and asked if I could not somehow squash this viper in their midst." China, he added, "was becoming a moral issue . . . never mind the facts."[95] In short, at the time, U.S. policy in the Far East enjoyed "widespread approval," and the Schumpeters were among the few who opposed U.S. policy across the board.

In July 1940, Schumpeter published yet another provocative piece regarding U.S. policy in the Far East. There was a "distinct possibility," she wrote, "that we might be able to do something in the Far East if we could make up our minds to be at the same time firm, generous, and realistic." She confirmed the view of her colleagues that she was anticommunist when she asserted that a Red menace from the Baltic to the Pacific was a "matter of much more concern than the aspirations of the Japanese military." This fear of communism and Russia was shared by the Japanese military at the time as well as Committee on Pacific Relations members, such as Ralph Townsend and the Reverend John Cole McKim (see chapters 4 and 5). The leaders of America First, like Schumpeter, viewed communism as worse than fascism or National Socialism.[96]

Schumpeter's letters also revealed that anticommunism was a strong force for some in Far Eastern studies. One can glimpse harbingers of the later McCarthy era of the 1950s in the way Schumpeter, in particular, couched her anticommunist remarks. In her July 1940 article, she reiterated that an American embargo would not stop Japan, for that nation had other sources of imports that would make it possible to continue the war. An American embargo on scrap iron would fail to be as effective as its supporters thought, she added, and it was doubtful an oil embargo would have the desired outcome either. It was no longer feasible to pressure nations like Japan, Italy, and Germany with economic sanctions, she argued, "with the ease we once thought possible." "A unilateral embargo on raw materials," she insisted, "is not likely to be effective and would undoubtedly be considered an unfriendly act, which might have unwelcome consequences." Even though the creation of the Japanese puppet state of Manchukuo had been met with the Stimson Doctrine (Nonrecognition Doctrine), "the new state is developing in a most promising way without our blessing, and the chance of its ever being returned to China becomes more and more remote."[97]

Like the famous evangelist E. Stanley Jones, Schumpeter believed the United States bore some of the blame for Japan's aggression in Asia. If the Western powers wanted to stop Japan's territorial expansion, she insisted, they should give it "opportunities for industrial and commercial expansion." She anticipated her American critics as well as a prominent wartime and postwar interpretation of the war's origins in Japan when she continued:

> We do not wish to excuse or justify the Japanese invasion of China and the conduct of the war there, but we do wish to bring this war to an end. Japan has behaved abominably toward China, *but we must share the responsibility* [author's italics], because the situation was becoming an impossible one. Japan could well claim she was being encircled by the political and economic policies of the Western powers. . . . The United States has played a leading part in the "encirclement" of Japan.[98]

In pursuing this argument, Schumpeter anticipated the ABCD (America, Britain, China, and Dutch) encirclement of Japan theory that was popular among right-wing as well as some other Japanese in the postwar period. This belief that the United States and other Western powers were partly responsible for Japanese aggression helps to explain why Schumpeter was unpopular among her colleagues. That dislike only intensified when she took at face value (which accounts for her popularity with the Japanese embassy and Japan's New York consulate general) the assurances of Japanese prewar prime ministers that, as she put it, "Japan wants no Chinese territory and no indemnities." "It would do no harm," she insisted, "to proceed on the assumption that Japan means this." There were "mad extremists in Japan," she admitted, who wanted to conquer all China, the European possessions in the South Pacific, and even North and South America, but "they were in a minority" and outnumbered by those who wanted a more liberal government and a less aggressive foreign policy. Blaming the West again, she asserted that the Japanese liberals' stance had been made more difficult by Western immigration and trade limitations as well as racial discrimination. In closing, she followed the same general line Armstrong and E. Stanley Jones did the following year (1941) by calling on the United States to mediate, to "help the two sides . . . get together and agree on a peace."

These positions were controversial in an American environment overwhelmingly sympathetic to the Chinese. Although peace meant for her the guaranteeing of China's sovereignty and territorial integrity, she also believed it should "provide for Japan's claims to economic and strategic security in North China and Inner Mongolia, and recognize . . . there is a new order [an unfortunate term, since it was used by both the Japanese and Germans to explain their expansionist plans] in Eastern Asia under the leadership of both China and Japan."[99] One thing was certain: words and positions such as these—repeated in her 1940 book *The Industrialization of Japan and Manchukuo, 1930–1940*—were certain to contribute to her unpopularity among her Far Eastern studies colleagues. Ironically, in the same month war broke out with the Japanese surprise attack on Pearl Harbor, she published a paper "How Strong Is Japan?" As one of her biographers quipped, "the world found out quickly."[100]

In contrast to Griswold's uncertainty and confusion and Duke history professor Paul Clyde's refusal to sign Armstrong's statement, Schumpeter, according to Armstrong, demonstrated "intense interest" in the undertaking. In late June 1941, she wrote that she would "very much like" to see him and discuss his project. She asked him to inform her when he came to New York and "give me an opportunity to talk to you." She badly wanted to talk with someone who would understand her views. She could discuss these things with him "very much better" in conversation, she wrote, than by letter. She had been in New York the previous week, she added, and "rather hoped I might run into you." It was only two and one-half hours by train from Taconic, so she could easily get to New York for a few hours. She would be very happy to do "anything possible" to assist him. Referring to his idea of dispatching a commission to Japan, however, she felt "rather doubtful about the usefulness of a mission sent at this moment." It would require "very strong backing and be very carefully planned if it is to be at all influential." She then expanded on what she had told Armstrong earlier about her views, from which it was clear she and Armstrong saw eye to eye:

> For the past four years I have been writing and speaking with a view to giving Americans more information about Japan in the hope of improving American-Japanese relations. It has been a very up-hill fight because there are so many powerful propaganda groups on the other side and because the American people very naturally sympathize with the Chinese. They do not see that the course we are following is not necessarily in the best interests of the Chinese or even in our own best interests. I have discovered that thoughtful Americans are pretty badly informed, and I now know some of the facts which interest them.

Another of the "great difficulties," she wrote, was that "almost no newspapers or periodicals will publish anything on the Far East that is in the least realistic. I have had articles solicited and paid for but not published." Perhaps that was because, like some other members of Armstrong's group, she was not reluctant to blame her own country for Japan's actions. "It has seemed to me that it was a tragic mistake," she asserted, "to push Japan into the Axis pact [Tripartite Pact] because I really believe that the unwise and rather ineffective actions of this country helped bring about this result."

Although reviewers of Schumpeter's 1940 book questioned her reliance on Japanese sources, she told Armstrong she had "fairly useful contacts with liberal intellectual circles in Japan." Ishibashi Tanzan was "a very good friend of mine" and had published articles "extremely critical" of the Japanese militarists. Moreover, her husband was not entirely at sea when it came to Japan. He had "many friends among Japanese economists who studied under him in Austria and Germany." He had taught numerous Japanese students as well as journeyed in Japan.[101]

THE INFLUENCE OF SCHUMPETER'S AND CLYDE'S BOOKS ON JAPAN

In the fall of 1941, Armstrong's contact in Japan's Washington embassy lent him two books by American authors he had striven to recruit for his committee, Schumpeter's *The Industrialization of Japan and Manchukuo, 1930–1940* and Clyde's *Japan's Pacific Mandate*. The first, he commented, was "quite long, but interesting," while Clyde's book "contains very interesting material."[102] Schumpeter was deeply involved in organizing the Committee on Pacific Relations, while Clyde had declined to join the committee. The fact that Terasaki Hidenari selected these books to lend to Americans signified that the Japanese agreed with the books' interpretations. In addition to the Japanese embassy's copy of Schumpeter's massive volume (944 pages), the Japanese consulate in New York bought several copies.[103] Moreover, a translation of her book was published in Japan in 1942.[104]

Unpopular with some of her Harvard colleagues and other Far Eastern scholars, both of which groups overwhelmingly sympathized with China and opposed Japan, Schumpeter threw down the gauntlet in her volume and opened herself to charges of being an apologist for Japan. Much information in the world, she wrote, was "colored by 'wishful thinking' or outright propaganda." Acknowledging the war with China and the resultant "suppression of information" made treatment of recent history "necessarily controversial," she adroitly summarized the argument that attracted the ire of critics:

> It is difficult today for a scholar to be honest about political and economic conditions in the *so-called* [author's italics] totalitarian states. Anyone who

concludes that a country such as Japan had certain legitimate economic grievances, that some of its economic policies and practices have been successful and that it is stronger economically than is commonly supposed, is widely suspected of being a sympathizer with aggression and a member of the "fifth column." This tendency seems rather unfortunate because to overcome aggression, we need to know what helped bring it about and how strongly it is intrenched.[105]

Throughout her book, she hammered away at her argument that Japan was stronger than the skeptics believed and that the West was partly responsible for Japan's drive for empire. "The public," she explained, "is singularly unaware of the extent to which the industrial structure in Japan has been strengthened in recent years." "One reason for this attitude," she continued, "may be the fact that many of the most able students and writers on this subject found the Japanese development so distasteful to them that they could not possibly believe it was sound." That disbelief, she added, was "especially true of several with pronounced leftist sympathies," who had frequently predicted a Japanese economic collapse and revolution during the initial two years of the China Incident (1937–1939).

She disagreed with that interpretation. The Japanese economic recovery from the Great Depression, she emphasized, was "more extensive than in any other leading industrial country." Acknowledging Japan's expansionism, she disclaimed any responsibility to "condemn or justify" it. Her volume was designed to provide information, she explained, which "should make it easier to understand the present situation and possibly to deal with it." Again, she took a shot at her opponents. "Many inaccurate and biased accounts of Japanese conditions," she charged, "are now being circulated, because so many propaganda groups are at work, most of them urging some kind of economic action against Japan." "Where emotions are as much involved as they are in this case," she concluded, "there is bound to be much 'wishful thinking' and some deliberate misrepresentation."

When she went on to aver that Japan, "however much it may have been resented politically," had "improved the economic position" of their colonial subjects, the Koreans and Formosans, she succeeded only in increasing the animus of her critics. It did not diminish her unpopularity when she agreed it was "impossible to approve of the ambitions of the military in Japan," but then went on to argue that Japan was only following in the footsteps of the Western colonial powers and wanted "to do likewise at whatever cost to the peace of the world." She blamed the Western powers' repeated attempts, in recent years, to restrict Japan's access to raw materials in their Far Eastern colonies for Japan's expansion. In doing so, she came across as an apologist for Japan. "If Japan promulgates a 'Monroe Doctrine' for Asia in view of the unexpected developments in the European War during May and June 1940," she wrote, "it cannot be denied that these [Western] policies [of denial of

Japanese access to raw materials in Western colonies in the Far East] furnished some excuse." Japan's "drive toward autarchy and regional economic blocs," she argued, "is *partly* [her italics] the consequence of insecurity and of the illiberal trade practices of the Western democracies in the past." "How far it will go," she added, "will depend on the outcome of the present war [with China] and on political development in the future." Much, she added, would depend on U.S. Far Eastern policy.

Like E. Stanley Jones, Schumpeter saw the United States as partly at fault.[106] She accused her country of "extending the [Monroe] Doctrine" to the Dutch East Indies and French Indochina. Therefore, she was pessimistic about the chances for continued peace between the two countries. "If Japan and the United States both continue to expand their claims in the Far East," she asserted, "it is difficult to see how a war can be avoided." "[It] was so easy to start a war," she concluded, "and so difficult to negotiate a wise and generous peace."[107]

Her book was widely reviewed, mainly in the scholarly journals rather than in the popular press. Considering its massive size and density of fact, that was not surprising. As Schumpeter feared, it turned out to be controversial in the narrow world of economists and Far Eastern specialists. There were nine reviews, with three positive, one neutral, and five critical.

In view of the similarity of views expressed by Schumpeter and Yale's Professor Griswold in their frequent correspondence in 1939 and 1940, it was not surprising that one of the favorable treatments, although not written by Griswold, appeared in the *Yale Review*. The way the reviewer praised her work must have pleased her. In those "tense days" of "heated opinions" and "endless debates," he wrote, it was "refreshing" to discover a book containing a "coolly detached point of view, in which the authors are content to allow facts to speak for themselves." It was the "most comprehensive treatment of the industrialization of Japan for the period covered in any single compilation." His short remarks, he continued, "failed to convey the scope of the work." He used such positive words as "deftly," thoroughly," "well supported," and "careful and painstaking scholarship" to describe the volume. Whereas others criticized Schumpeter and her fellow authors for relying on Japanese journals, government, businesses, and universities for the "basic information"—which the cynic would argue explained, along with its views sympathetic to Japan, why the Japanese embassy and consulate general favored it—the *Yale Review* writer praised this approach. In closing, he termed her study "the most definitive work on recent industrial development in Japan that has yet appeared," and averred, "We are not likely to see its equal for some time."[108]

Other reviewers also were kind. Writing in June 1941—some months following publication of the volume (November 1940) and while Schumpeter was involved in helping Armstrong organize the Committee on Pacific Relations—a reviewer seemed to agree with the analyses presented by Schumpeter and the other contributors to the book. The volume's "elaborate discussion" of statistics, he thought, was necessary because of what Schumpeter described as the "many inaccurate and biased accounts of Japanese conditions which 'wishful thinking' and some deliberate misrepresentation have produced." Japan's recovery from the Depression in the 1930s, he asserted, was a "wonderful achievement misjudged outside Japan." Schumpeter believed, the reviewer continued, that the democracies had much to learn from Japan's recovery. "Chapter by chapter," he continued, "carefully analyzed statistics continue to explode popular fallacies and half-truths about Japan." She did not believe, he explained, that Japan's economy would collapse or become "permanently totalitarian." In conclusion, he acknowledged it had "already become very difficult to write of Japan without being open to the suspicion of selecting material so as to reach whatever conclusion is ideologically most agreeable to the writer."[109] A review in the *Economic Record*, an Australian journal presumably detached from the partisan wars in the United States, agreed with and praised her analyses with nary a critical word.[110] Finally, there was a "neutral" review, in which the author simply repeated Schumpeter's complaints about partisanship without revealing his own position.[111]

The negative reviews were more numerous than the positive and neutral ones. Her critics were quick to respond to her arguments. In a faultfinding review in the Institute of Pacific Relations' *Pacific Affairs* (of which she was frequently critical), a Columbia University business professor criticized her book for its "appalling and unnecessary bulk," adding that it was in her contributions to the volume that "repetition is most evident." He went on to write—in the contemporary climate of strong American sympathy for China and antipathy toward Japan—that a "more serious objection" was her "point of view." In her introduction, he argued, she had presented a "wave-of-the-future defense of totalitarian economic practices." In his view, she seemed to agree that the "record of recovery in the totalitarian or militaristic states as measured by increased production and employment is much better than that in France and the United States" and "in the economic sphere we may be able to learn something from the policies and practices of the more successful non-democratic states." Japan was one of the totalitarian or militarist nations, he continued, and her chapters portrayed a strong Japanese economic structure and "defend Japanese policy of recent years on the mainland of Asia." In addition, she had largely relied on Japanese sources, he claimed, that were "certainly not completely disinterested or objective." In fact, he continued, those sources had been "filled in recent years with claims and paper plans." Taking issue with her argument that Japan was stronger than many believed, he declared there were "many evidences of serious weakness." In his opinion, she saw "a much stronger economy than actually exists." Moreover, he accused her of quoting from a source selectively to prove her case.

Finally, the reviewer turned to the impact of Japan's rule on Formosa (Taiwan), Korea, and Manchuria, insisting that in her work there was no "consideration of the attitude of the native populations of those areas or of their own needs." She failed to note, he continued, that "Japanese exploitation has taken the form of ruthless monopoly to serve Japan's needs." She presented the various programs of control in Manchuria, he complained, as "necessary devices to meet some emergency condition." She failed to acknowledge Japan's economic policies in Manchuria had led to Japanese domination of trade and industry and the exclusion of the Chinese. The greed of Japanese monopolies, he added, had "sometimes threatened to defeat their purpose." In conclusion, he lambasted her for failing to write about the "wholesale seizures and confiscations of Chinese properties in Manchuria and the occupied parts of China." If readers were to learn from what she termed the "policies and practices of the more successful non-democratic countries," he concluded, Japan's ways of ruling its conquered lands also should be explored.[112]

In what was the briefest of the negative responses, an anonymous author in *Foreign Affairs* criticized Schumpeter's and her fellow authors' portrait of Japan's "prosperity and economic invulnerability" as "probably too rosy, due to their excessive respect for not always reliable Japanese statistics."[113] In a more extensive treatment, John B. Condliffe, professor of economics at the University of California, Berkeley, echoed complaints about Schumpeter's reliance on Japanese journals and the publications of the South Manchurian Railway, which "seem so often to have a promotional tinge." Her contributions, he grumbled, were "more diffuse than the rest of the book, less convincing in their arrangement of the argument and more repetitious." That was probably to be expected, he continued, where "hopes rather than achievements, plans rather than facts, potential rather than actual figures are discussed." "Most economists," he continued, "are likely to feel that Mrs. [Professor] Schumpeter has given the benefit of the doubt at almost every difficult point to the somewhat optimistic Japanese estimates now available." In contrast to her more optimistic view, he believed Japan's "enlarged empire" would result in "heavy losses and probably economic disorganization." In discussing the "autarchic yen bloc," he noted her argument that it was an "alternative forced on Japan by the breakdown of international treaties." When he went on to assert, "One would expect her argument to have the same appeal in Japanese circles as Mr. [C. W.] Guillebaud's somewhat similar book had in German circles,"[114] he was right. The support rendered her book by the Japanese embassy in Washington and the consulate general in New York City were proof of that.

The review in the *Annals of the American Academy of Political and Social Science* revealed a mixed mind. It was a "highly important book," the reviewer conceded, but then proceeded to caution that it also was "apt to prove misleading unless used with care." It was "misleading" because it was not up to date. The book's essays were "apparently" written several years earlier, but the volume was not published until late 1940, "largely unrevised and in the present tense." And yet, three years of "total war" had "radically altered Japan's whole economic life and prospects." The viewpoint of 1936 "or even 1938," he wrote, was "outdated today [May 1941]." Despite Schumpeter's attempt to update the story, he complained, "One fails to find here any adequate picture of the dynamic impact of war and the growing difficulties in which Japan has recently been floundering." Japan had been making progress in coping with its population problem until its "military leaders chose the alternative of political aggrandizement." He granted it had been difficult for Schumpeter to assemble her facts because of the "rapidly shifting scene" and decreasing adequacy of statistics. Having made do with slight praise, he returned to the attack, lamenting, "Nowhere, however, does the author lay bare the essential processes of war inflation which are tragically impoverishing the Japanese nation and creating a growing series of bottlenecks in its war effort." "Just as she implies a degree of economic necessity in the policy of continental conquest," he continued, "which is hardly substantiated by the evidence of her own book, so . . . she underestimates the penalties Japan is now paying for that policy."[115]

Finally—in a review published nearly two years after the war had begun and hence open to the same charge levied by the above reviewer against Schumpeter, that of being outdated—she and her fellow authors were taken to task for lacking a "comparative point of view." They dealt with "Japan and nothing but Japan," complained the reviewer (which seemed fine for a book that contained Japan and Manchukuo in its title). Moreover, he complained that Schumpeter was "particularly enthusiastic" in believing Japan's "industrial course is much to her benefit." She "praises repeatedly Japan's economic accomplishments, creating the impression that war-economy increases 'enormously' a country's consumption (p. 482), 'improves' its balance of payments, its industrial structure, and even its finances." She barely notices, he continued, the inflationary strain, decline of living standards, increasing monopolistic pressure, "bureaucratism," and nonproductive distribution of capital and disturbance of "all international relations." She did admit, he conceded, that the growing insufficiency of labor, materials, and equipment threatened to "paralyze the whole economy (pp. 402, 410, 861)." Her recognition of Japan's achievements, he groused, was accompanied by "more or less overt attempts to justify her methods. Illiberal trade policies by the outside world get most of the blame. The appearance is created that the West had brought about an *impasse*, and that Japan acted mainly in self-defense."

He rejected that argument, responding that Japan was ahead of most others and surpassed them "severalfold" in its mercantilist policies. Moreover, it led in devaluation, and as early as the 1920s, its tariff rates were over 100 percent ad valorem. He closed with a strongly worded attack on her (of the book's several contributors, most reviewers' target): "Mrs. Schumpeter even commits the inexcusable error of providing Japan's 'Doctrine' with some semblance of an excuse (pp. 470ff). Such symptoms of a biased partisanship are likely to damage the reputation of an otherwise very valuable book."[116]

The same warm Japanese reception granted to Schumpeter's volume was also extended to Professor Paul Clyde's book. The Japanese embassy distributed copies of it as soon as it was published in 1935.[117] After the Pacific War broke out, the *New York Times* military analyst, Hanson Baldwin, recalled that in 1936 the Japanese naval attaché in Washington had given him a copy of Clyde's book "in an obvious effort to show that Japan had not 'fortified' Micronesia."[118]

What exactly did Clyde write to gain such Japanese approbation? *Japan's Pacific Mandate*, his second book, was a study of Micronesia, the Pacific islands put under Japan's administration as a Class C mandate by the Paris Peace Conference in 1919, an action that was subsequently confirmed by the Council of the League of Nations. Although the 1,400 islands—the Marianas, Marshalls, and Carolines of later Pacific War horror—covered a million square miles of ocean, they comprised only 836 square miles of land populated by fifty thousand natives and 32,000 Japanese.[119] From the 1922 settlement of a Japanese–American dispute over inclusion of the island of Yap in the Japanese mandate until 1932, the islands "rarely commanded so much as a paragraph in the world's news." However, rumors that the Japanese had fortified and were continuing to fortify the main islands arose after Japan seized Manchuria in 1932 and intensified following its 1933 withdrawal from the League of Nations (effective in March 1935). Despite the Japanese navy's denial of any such intentions, those rumors, which the navy blamed on the United States, fueled hostility in the world toward Japan.[120]

In the early 1930s, Japan wanted to alleviate Western suspicions regarding militarization of Micronesia, largely to block an American military buildup in the Pacific.[121] Therefore, in 1934 the Japanese government invited University of Kentucky professor Paul Clyde to visit, which he did during March and April.[122] It was clear he was drawn to the islands by what he called their "notoriety," caused by the Western press rumors that the Japanese had fortified them in violation of the stipulations of their mandate (Article 4). It also was clear how he felt about this. "By the simple process of repetition," he explained, "misinformation acquires the dignity of established facts, and nowhere has this process worked with more telling effect than in the tropical islands of Japan's Pacific mandate." In 1932 and again in 1934, he wrote, the Permanent Mandates Commission of the League of Nations interrogated the Japanese representative concerning his country's pledge not to fortify the islands, and the representative reiterated his nation's promise not to fortify the islands, which satisfied the commission.[123]

The Japanese undoubtedly were pleased with Clyde's book. He praised Japanese administration of the islands under their South Seas Bureau, claiming it worked "easily and effectively" and did not interfere with the natives' "traditional habits and simplicity of life." Relations between the natives and Japanese officials, he added, seemed to be "entirely friendly." Some natives disliked the Japanese, he acknowledged, but the "number is not large."[124] As for education in the islands, Japan's record was "deserving of high praise." It also had been accused, "both in the press and in whispered rumors," he continued, of resorting to forced labor in the islands. During his visit, not surprisingly he saw no evidence of that. He also praised the medical services Japan brought to the islands. Perhaps most important, he concluded from his and earlier Western travelers' observations that as of the spring of 1934 Japan had not violated Article 4 of her mandate, which stipulated that "no military or naval bases shall be established, or fortifications erected in the territory." The rumors of fortifications, he charged, were based on "misinformation or a lack of information."[125]

Perhaps anticipating criticism of his conclusions, Clyde insisted he was "afforded every opportunity by officials of the mandatory government to see and examine Japan's administration, and to gain some acquaintance with the nature of the islands and the character of their native peoples. His actions and itinerary were restricted only by the sailing schedules of the Japanese cargo vessels on which he traveled."[126] Despite his attempt to head off skepticism, though, his conclusions were open to criticism. First, he had visited the mandated islands at the invitation of the Japanese government, and the Japanese embassy distributed copies of his book. Therefore, as soon as the volume was published in March 1935, a reporter criticized it as "open to the objection that it is not as impartial as a study or report made under less interested auspices." Essentially ignoring the evidence in the volume, the reporter concluded, "Impartial opinion will await more 'substantial evidence' than is now available."[127] Meanwhile, the book was widely reviewed. In a vague criticism, one reviewer commented that the "general tone of the volume is one of sympathy for the Japanese administration."[128] Yet another reviewer charged him with "something of a belligerently defensive attitude toward the work which Japan has done in the islands."[129]

Other scholars applauded the book. One reviewer praised his approach to press rumors regarding the islands, observing that "it is all to the good that a cold douche of facts should be administered to the too speculative imaginations of journalists."[130] Another called the book "authoritative" and added that Clyde "refutes beyond doubt the irresponsible charges that the Japanese government has been fortifying these islands in violation of the mandate."[131]

Yet another argued that "warmongers and members of the Yellow Peril school will do well to avoid" the book. Clyde wrote, the reviewer added, "in a manner so mild that it is difficult to detect prejudice." He attributed controversies about the islands "primarily to propaganda conceived in ignorance of actual conditions." No one had ever seen the rumored fortifications, he wrote, and in any event, the islands were unsuitable for forts or naval bases. "The Japanese," he concluded, "certainly are not made to play the role of international villain in this book."[132]

Years later, an American historian criticized Clyde's account of the "cheerful" stevedores and laborers he saw on his 1934 trip to Micronesia. There was "circumstantial evidence," the scholar wrote, that Micronesians were forcibly drafted into the mines for up to four years.[133] Moreover, when Clyde wrote that "Japan's education in the jungle" had "wisely modified the curriculum to meet native intelligence and needs," he exhibited the "patronizing prejudices of the era."[134] The historian agreed with Clyde, however, that in 1934 Japan had not yet militarized the islands.[135]

By the time an official at the Japanese embassy in Washington lent Clyde's book to Armstrong in 1941, however, the situation had drastically changed. According to historian Mark Peattie, militarization proceeded in four stages. From 1934 to 1939, the Japanese navy began to build airfields in the Marianas and Carolines, although as late as 1937 it still had not put any warplanes, troops, or artillery on the islands.[136] A year earlier, though, Japan's secret militarization of the islands was already in full swing.[137] Since this was a military undertaking, the embassy official probably was unaware of it (just as the Japanese embassy staff were ignorant of its military's plans to attack Pearl Harbor).

In any event, even if Clyde's favorable report on the Japanese mandated islands helped Japan's image in 1935, and perhaps even in the fall of 1941, the book, photographs, and film from his 1934 trip proved useful once war came to those islands in the Pacific. As a 1945 press report put it, after Pearl Harbor the book was "read with renewed interest."[138] In April 1942, an officer from the War Department's Military Intelligence Division (G-2) wrote Clyde (on the recommendation of Clyde's colleague at Duke, China scholar Paul M. Linebarger) to request information on the Japanese mandated islands. As subsequent correspondence made clear, Clyde was able to help, although he did reveal some impatience when he reminded the official that he was teaching full time and suggested the Military Intelligence Division consult *Japan's Pacific Mandate* while awaiting his answers to its detailed questionnaire.[139]

Subsequently, the head of the Far Eastern Unit, Bureau of Foreign and Domestic Commerce, Department of Commerce, also asked for his help in its studies of the islands. Clyde replied he had already sent material to the War Department, the Navy Department, and the Far Eastern Division of the

Office of the Coordinator of Information (COI, the predecessor to the wartime Office of Strategic Services or OSS).[140] The U.S. Marine Corps benefited from his photographs of the islands,[141] which must have proved useful in the subsequent American amphibious assaults against some of them. In 1945, Clyde told the press that the seizure of Kwajalein and other Marshall Island atolls was "one of the most decisive achievements of the Pacific war." Without those victories, he added, the current attacks on Truk and Ponape (in the eastern Carolines) would have been impossible.[142]

NOTES

1. Unless otherwise noted, the following discussion of Griswold's views on war, and especially the danger of a conflict with Japan, are based on Dorothy Borg, "Two Histories of the Far Eastern Policy of the United States: Tyler Dennett and A. Whitney Griswold," in *Pearl Harbor as History: Japanese-American Relations, 1931–1941*, ed. Dorothy Borg and Shumpei Okamoto (New York: Columbia University Press, 1973), 561–72; Warren I. Cohen, *The Chinese Connection: Roger S. Greene, Thomas W. Lamont, George Sokolsky, and American-East Asian Relations* (New York: Columbia University, 1978), 297. For brief biographies of Griswold, see Robert L. Gale, "Griswold, Alfred Whitney (27 Oct. 1906–19 Apr. 1963)," *American National Biography*, 9:640–41; *Marquis Who's Who on the Web* (accessed 18 August 2005). In 1950, Griswold was appointed president of Yale.

2. "Neutrality Is Urged," *New York Times* (hereafter *NYT*), 26 November 1937, 8.

3. "Books in a Changing World," *Peace Action* 5, no. 8 (1939): 7.

4. Elizabeth B. Schumpeter to A. Whitney Griswold, 27 January 1939, Elizabeth Boody Schumpeter Papers (A-43), Schlesinger Library, Radcliffe College, Cambridge, MA.

5. Griswold to Schumpeter, 29 May 1939, Schumpeter Papers.

6. Griswold was mentioned in William Bridgewater, ed., *The Columbia-Viking Desk Encyclopedia* (New York: Columbia University Press, 1953; Dell, 1964), 741.

7. Griswold to Schumpeter, 2 September 1939, Schumpeter Papers.

8. John N. Thomas, *The Institute of Pacific Relations: Asian Scholars and American Politics* (Seattle: University of Washington Press, 1974), 11–15.

9. Griswold to Schumpeter, 2 September 1939.

10. Griswold, Department of Government and International Relations, Yale University, New Haven, CT, to Schumpeter, Taconic, CT, 15 September 1939, Schumpeter Papers; Griswold, "Facing Facts about a New Japanese-American Treaty," *Asia*, November 1939, 615–19.

11. Griswold to Schumpeter, Bureau of International Research, Harvard University, Cambridge, MA, 21 November 1939, Schumpeter Papers. Bisson was to be an active participant in the controversies surrounding the Institute of Pacific Studies during the war and in the 1950s. See Thomas, *Institute of Pacific Relations*, 24, 37, 51, 86, 157–58, 164–65.

12. Borg, "Two Histories," 568; T. A. [Thomas Arthur] Bisson, *Japan in China* (New York: Macmillan, 1938).

13. Griswold to Schumpeter, 21 November 1939.

14. Griswold to Schumpeter, 8 December 1939, Schumpeter Papers. For Schumpeter's comments on Bloch's background, see Schumpeter to Treat, 14 February 1940.

15. John W. Dower, *Empire and Aftermath: Yoshida Shigeru and the Japanese Experience, 1878–1954* (Cambridge, MA: Harvard University Press, 1988), 216.

16. Griswold to Schumpeter, 8 December 1939.

17. Griswold, Vineyard Haven, MA, to Schumpeter, Cambridge, MA, 3 September 1940, Schumpeter Papers.

18. Schumpeter to Griswold, 26 September 1940, Schumpeter Papers; Elizabeth B. Schumpeter, ed., *The Industrialization of Japan and Manchukuo, 1930–1940: Population, Raw Materials and Industry* (New York: Macmillan, 1940).

19. Charles A. Lindbergh, *The Wartime Journals of Charles A. Lindbergh* (New York: Harcourt Brace Jovanovich, 1970), 411; A. Scott Berg, *Lindbergh* (New York: G.P. Putnam's Sons, 1998), 412–13.

20. Griswold to Schumpeter, 4 November 1940, Schumpeter Papers. This was the last letter between the two to be found in the Elizabeth Schumpeter Papers.

21. Frederick Moore, *With Japan's Leaders: An Intimate Record of Fourteen Years as Counsellor to the Japanese Government* (New York: Charles Scribner's Sons, 1942), 105–6, 113–14.

22. Borg, "Two Histories," 566–68; Griswold, "Facing Facts," 615–19; Walter Lippman, "Today and Tomorrow," *Washington* Post (hereafter *WP*), 21 October 1939, 9; Griswold, "Should Japan Be Embargoed?," *Asia*, February 1940, 92–96. For several of the responses to Griswold, see *Asia*, December 1939, 682–86.

23. Griswold, "Our Policy in the Far East," *Harper's*, August 1940, 259–67; William J. Baxter, *Japan and America Must Work Together!* (New York: International Economic Research Bureau, 1940), 91.

24. Armstrong, Springfield, MO, to Griswold, New Haven, CT, 31 May 1941, Alfred Whitney Griswold Papers (MS 255), Manuscripts and Archives, Yale University Library, New Haven, CT.

25. A. Whitney Griswold, "An Undeclared Peace," *Annals of the American Academy of Political and Social Science*, May 1941, 179–81.

26. Armstrong to Griswold, 31 May 1941.

27. Lippman, "Today and Tomorrow," 9.

28. Armstrong to Griswold, 31 May 1941.

29. "Statement on Japanese-American Relations," 31 May 1941, encl. Armstrong to Griswold, 31 May 1941.

30. Armstrong to Griswold, 31 May 1941.

31. Griswold to R. Douglas Stuart, 16 January 1941, Griswold Papers; cited in Borg, "Two Histories," 735n73.

32. Griswold, "Undeclared Peace," 179–81.

33. Griswold to Armstrong, 5 June 1941, Orland Kay Armstrong (1893–1987) Papers, 1912–1987 (C4056), State Historical Society of Missouri, Manuscript Collection, Columbia, MO. A draft of this letter, dated 4 June, is in the Griswold Papers.

34. Armstrong to Schumpeter, 10 June 1941, Armstrong Papers.

35. Armstrong to Professor Paul H. Clyde, Duke University, Durham, NC, 31 May 1941, Armstrong Papers.

36. Clyde to Armstrong, 3 June 1941, Armstrong Papers.

37. Unless otherwise noted, the following discussion is based on Mark Thornton, "Schumpeter, Joseph Alois Julius (8 Feb. 1883–8 Jan. 1950)," *American National Biography*, 19:444; Richard Swedberg, *Schumpeter: A Biography* (Princeton, NJ: Princeton University Press, 1991), 121–22, 142–43; Robert Loring Allen, *Opening Doors: The Life and Work of Joseph Schumpeter*, vol. 2, *America* (New Brunswick, NJ: Transaction, 1991), 90–94, 102–3, 112n7, 113n23.

38. Schumpeter to Griswold, 27 January 1939, Schumpeter Papers.

39. Griswold to Schumpeter, 30 January 1939, Schumpeter Papers.

40. Schumpeter to Griswold, 2 February 1939, Schumpeter Papers.

41. Griswold to Schumpeter, 23 May 1939, Schumpeter Papers; Borg, "Two Histories," 561.

42. Schumpeter to Griswold, 26 May 1939, Schumpeter Papers.

43. Schumpeter to Griswold, 2 June 1939, Schumpeter Papers.

44. Griswold to Schumpeter, 6 June 1939; Schumpeter to Griswold, 9 June 1939, Schumpeter Papers.

45. Griswold to Schumpeter, 2 September 1939. Schumpeter's article was published in *Pacific Affairs* 12, no. 3 (September 1939): 245–62. Vandenberg abandoned his isolationist stance following passage of the Lend-Lease Bill in March 1941. Lynne Olson, *Those Angry Days: Roosevelt, Lindbergh, and America's Fight over World War II, 1939–1941* (New York: Random House, 2013), 285–86. By the time of the second Institute of Pacific Relations confer-

ence in 1927, the Australian Council had been established as one of its six original councils. Thomas, *Institute of Pacific Relations*, 3.

46. Thomas, *Institute of Pacific Relations*, passim.
47. Janet E. Hunter, comp., *Concise Dictionary of Modern Japanese History* (Berkeley: University of California Press, 1984), 73.
48. Schumpeter to Griswold, Lamberts Cove, Vineyard Haven, MA, 5 September 1939, Schumpeter Papers; Wm. Theodore de Bary, Carol Gluck, and Arthur Teidemann, comps., *Sources of Japanese Tradition*, vol. 2: *1600–2000*, 2nd ed. (New York: Columbia University Press, 2005), 859, and for a sample of Griswold's liberal views, 859–71.
49. Thomas, *Institute of Pacific Relations*, 23–24, 49–50.
50. Griswold to Schumpeter, 15 September 1939.
51. Griswold to Schumpeter, 21 November 1939.
52. Schumpeter to Griswold, 6 December 1939, Schumpeter Papers.
53. Schumpeter to Griswold, 30 January 1940, Schumpeter Papers. On the committee, see Wayne S. Cole, *Roosevelt and the Isolationists* (Lincoln: University of Nebraska Press, 1983), 348–49, 353; Donald J. Friedman, *The Road from Isolation: The Campaign of the American Committee for Non-participation in Japanese Aggression, 1938–1941* (Cambridge, MA: Harvard University Press, 1968); Cohen, *Chinese Connections*. In 1927, Steiger published a study of the Boxer Rebellion (reprinted in 1966): George Nye Steiger, *China and the Occident: The Origin and Development of the Boxer Movement* (New York: Russell & Russell, 1927).
54. Griswold to Schumpeter, 2 February 1940; Griswold, Vineyard Haven, MA, to Schumpeter, Cambridge, MA, 3 September 1940, Schumpeter Papers.
55. Griswold to Schumpeter, 2 February 1940; Schumpeter to Griswold, 14 February 1940, Schumpeter Papers.
56. Robert J. C. Butow, *Tojo and the Coming of the War* (Princeton, NJ: Princeton University Press, 1969), 223.
57. Schumpeter to Griswold, 19 July 1940, Schumpeter Papers. The Peffer article Schumpeter referred to was probably Nathanel Peffer, "Our Job in the Far East," *Harper's* 180 (April 1940): 489–97.
58. Schumpeter to Griswold, 19 July 1940.
59. Schumpeter to Griswold, 30 August 1940, Schumpeter Papers. This is probably a reference to her article "The Policy of the United States in the Far East," *Annals of the American Academy of Political and Social Science* 210 (July 1940): 98–106.
60. Schumpeter to Griswold, 30 August 1940.
61. Richard W. Leopold, "Historiographical Reflections," in Borg and Okamoto, *Pearl Harbor as History*, 17; *Marquis Who's Who on the Web* (accessed 18 August 2005). The Order of the Sacred Treasure was one of four decorations, dating from 1875, designed to honor those who had made important contributions in their areas. It was awarded by the emperor to both men and women. All four decorations were awarded to foreigners who had made unique contributions to Japan. Dorothy Perkins, *Encyclopedia of Japan* (New York: Roundtable Press, 1991), 66.
62. Cohen, *Chinese Connection*, 302; "Payson J. Treat, Pioneer Historian on Far East," *WP*, 17 June 1972, B6. In 1938, Treat (1879–1972) published *Diplomatic Relations between the United States and Japan, 1895–1905*. He also was the author of a standard textbook, *The Far East: A Political and Diplomatic History*, rev. ed. (New York: Harper & Brothers, 1935).
63. There are no letters between the two scholars in the Schumpeter Papers for 1941.
64. Payson J. Treat, Department of History, Stanford University, Stanford, CA, to Schumpeter, 16 January 1940, Schumpeter Papers.
65. Treat to Schumpeter, 3 February 1940, Schumpeter Papers.
66. C. Martin Wilbur, *China in My Life: A Historian's Own History* (Armonk, NY: M.E. Sharpe, 1996), 47.
67. Schumpeter to Treat, 30 January 1940, Schumpeter Papers.
68. Treat to Schumpeter, 3 February 1940.
69. Schumpeter to Treat, 30 January, 14 February 1940, Schumpeter Papers.
70. Thomas, *Institute of Pacific Relations*, 10.
71. Schumpeter to Treat, 14 February 1940.

72. Thomas, *Institute of Pacific Relations*, 8–9, 23–24.
73. Schumpeter to Treat, 14 February 1940.
74. Thomas, *Institute of Pacific Relations*, 8, 14, 17, 21.
75. Schumpeter to Treat, 14 February 1940; Schumpeter to Griswold, 14 February 1940, Schumpeter Papers.
76. Treat to Schumpeter, 19 February 1940, Schumpeter Papers.
77. Yamato Ichihashi Papers (SC0071), Department of Special Collections and University Archives, Stanford University Libraries, Stanford, CA.
78. Treat to Schumpeter, 19 February 1940.
79. Schumpeter to Treat, 11 October 1940, Schumpeter Papers.
80. O. K. Armstrong to Mr. [W. Forbes] Webber, [Kansas City Division, FBI], 6 March 1942, Armstrong Papers.
81. Swedberg, *Schumpeter*, 142.
82. Schumpeter, "Policy of the United States in the Far East," 106; Swedberg, *Schumpeter*, 122.
83. Armstrong to Dr. Edith [sic—Elizabeth] B. Schumpeter, 31 May 1941, Armstrong Papers.
84. Mrs. Joseph A. Schumpeter, Taconic, CT, to Armstrong, 4 June 1941, Armstrong Papers.
85. Armstrong to Webber, 6 March 1942.
86. Schumpeter to Armstrong, 4 June 1941.
87. Schumpeter to Armstrong, 4 June 1941.
88. Armstrong to Schumpeter, 10 June 1941.
89. Adolf A. Berle Jr., *Navigating the Rapids: From the Papers of Adolf A. Berle*, ed. Beatrice Bishop Berle and Travis Beal Jacobs (New York: Harcourt Brace Jovanovich, 1973), 347; Wayne S. Cole, *America First: The Battle against Intervention in World War II* (Madison: University of Wisconsin Press, 1953), 22, 184; Wayne S. Cole, *Charles A. Lindbergh and the Battle against American Intervention in World War II* (New York: Harcourt Brace Jovanovich, 1974), 111, 116, 209; Cole, *Roosevelt and the Isolationists*, 351, 415; Justus D. Doenecke, "Explaining the Antiwar Movement, 1939–1941: The Next Assignment," *Journal of Libertarian Studies* 8, no. 1 (1986): 160; Lindbergh, *Wartime Journals*, 245n, 272; Berg, *Lindbergh*, 393; Dower, *Empire and Aftermath*, 513n22; Manfred Jonas, *Isolationism in America, 1935–1941* (Ithaca, NY: Cornell University Press, 1966), 224. For Castle's appeasement stance, see his article "A Monroe Doctrine for Japan," *Atlantic Monthly*, October 1940, 445–52. For a brief biographical sketch of him, see Cole, *Charles A. Lindbergh*, 70–71. On his friendship with Lindbergh, see the numerous entries in the colonel's *Wartime Journals*; Cole, *America First*, 178–88.
90. Armstrong to Schumpeter, 10 June 1941.
91. Elizabeth Boody Schumpeter, "The Problem of Sanctions in the Far East," *Pacific Affairs* 12, no. 3 (1939): 245–62.
92. "Comments and Correspondence: Sanctions against Japan?," *Pacific Affairs* 12, no. 4 (1939): 427–38. For Bloch's analysis, see especially 430–38.
93. Swedberg, *Schumpeter*, 142.
94. Swedberg, *Schumpeter*, 142.
95. John K. Fairbank, *Chinabound: A Fifty-Year Memoir* (New York: Harper & Row, 1982), 166.
96. Cole, *America First*, 84.
97. Schumpeter, "Policy of the United States in the Far East," 99, 100, 102–4. The U.S. reaction to Japan's conquest and occupation of the Chinese territory of Manchuria, which it renamed Manchukuo, was the proclamation by Secretary of State Henry Stimson that the United States would not extend official recognition to the Japanese puppet state or to any other demands forced on China. David M. Kennedy, *Freedom from Fear: The American People in Depression and War, 1929–1945* (New York: Oxford University Press, 1999), 501.
98. Schumpeter, "Policy of the United States in the Far East," 103–4, 106.
99. Schumpeter, "Policy of the United States in the Far East," 106.
100. Allen, *Opening Doors*, 2:102.

101. Schumpeter to Armstrong, 26 June 1941, Armstrong Papers; Schumpeter to Griswold, 2 June 1939.

102. Armstrong to "Dear friend Mr. Terasaki," 3 October 1941, Armstrong Papers; Schumpeter, *Industrialization of Japan and Manchukuo*; Paul H. Clyde, *Japan's Pacific Mandate* (New York: Macmillan, 1935).

103. Allen, *Opening Doors*, 2:113n24.

104. E. Shumupeta [Elizabeth Boody Shumpeter], ed., *Nichi-Man sangyo kozoron*, trans. Yukiyama Yoshimasa and Miura Masashi, 2 vols. (Tokyo: Keio Shobo, 1942).

105. Schumpeter, *Industrialization of Japan and Manchukuo*, v–vii.

106. Roger B. Jeans, *Terasaki Hidenari, Pearl Harbor, and Occupied Japan* (Lanham, MD: Lexington Books, 2009), chap. 4 (especially p. 104).

107. Schumpeter, *Industrialization of Japan and Manchukuo*, 6, 26, 45, 59, 62–63, 470–71, 857, 860–61.

108. James H. Shoemaker, review of *The Industrialization of Japan and Manchukuo, 1930–1940*, ed. E. B. Schumpeter, *Yale Review* 30, no. 4 (1941): 845–47.

109. H. F. Angus, review of *The Industrialization of Japan and Manchukuo, 1930–1940: Population, Raw Materials and Industry*, by E. B. Schumpeter, *Canadian Journal of Economics and Political Science* 8, no. 1 (1942): 116–19.

110. G. L. Wood, review of *The Industialization of Japan and Manchukuo, 1930–1940*, ed. E. B. Schumpeter, *Economic Record* 17, no. 33 (1941): 291–97.

111. D. Clark Hyde, review of *The Industrialization of Japan and Manchukuo, 1930–1940*, ed. E. B. Schumpeter, *Southern Economic Journal* 7, no. 4 (1941): 586–87.

112. John E. Orchard, review of *The Industrialization of Japan and Manchukuo, 1930–1940*, by E. B. Schumpeter, *Pacific Affairs* 14, no. 2 (1941): 240–46.

113. *Foreign Affairs* 19, no. 3 (1941): 688.

114. J. B. Condliffe, review of *The Industrialization of Japan and Manchukuo, 1930–1940*, ed. E. B. Schumpeter, *American Economic Review* 31, no. 1 (1941): 126–29; C. W. Guillebaud, *The Economic Recovery of Germany from 1933 to the Incorporation of Austria in March 1938* (London: Macmillan, 1939). From 1927–1930, Condliffe was research secretary of the International Institute of Pacific Affairs. Thomas, *Institute of Pacific Relations*, 7.

115. William L. Lockwood, review of *The Industrialization of Japan and Manchukuo, 1930–1940*, ed. E. B. Schumpeter, *Annals* of the American Academy of Political and Social Science 215 (May 1941): 183–84.

116. Melchior Palyi, review of *The Industrialization of Japan and Manchukuo, 1930–1940*, ed. E. B. Schumpeter, *Review of Politics* 5, no. 3 (1943): 396–99.

117. Elliott Thurston, "Is Japan Fortifying Her Mandate Islands?," *WP*, 26 March 1935, 9.

118. Hanson W. Baldwin, "Japan's Bases in the Mandated Islands," *NYT*, 9 February 1942, 4.

119. Clyde, *Japan's Pacific Mandate*, 13, 36–37, 148–49. His first book was *International Rivalries in Manchuria, 1689–1922* (Columbus: Ohio University Press, 1926).

120. Clyde, *Japan's Pacific Mandate*, 2, 159–60, 168–69, 171; M. Matsuo, review of *Japan's Pacific Mandate*, by Paul H. Clyde, *Pacific Affairs* 8, no. 2 (1935): 228.

121. Mark R. Peattie, *Nan'yo: The Rise and Fall of the Japanese in Micronesia, 1885–1945* (Honolulu: University of Hawaii Press, 1988), 245.

122. Clyde, *Japan's Pacific Mandate*, vi, for a list of the islands he visited. In November 1934, he was still working on the book, which was published in March 1935. *Japan's Pacific Mandate*, 203.

123. Clyde, *Japan's Pacific Mandate*, v, 5, 161–67, 176.

124. Clyde, *Japan's Pacific Mandate*, 77, 81. For criticism of Clyde's work as making the Micronesians "appear as simple-minded puppets . . . rather than as human beings such as the ethnologist knows," see F. M. Keesing, review of *Japan's Pacific Mandate*, by Paul H. Clyde, *International Affairs* 15, no. 1 (1936): 163.

125. Clyde, *Japan's Pacific Mandate*, 37–38, 112, 145–47, 157, 220–24.

126. Clyde, *Japan's Pacific Mandate*, vi.

127. Elliott Thurston, "Is Japan Fortifying Her Mandate Islands?," *WP*, 26 March 1935, 9. For a more positive review, see A. M. Nikolaieff, "Japan's First Line of Defense in the Pacific," *NYT*, 31 March 1935, BR3.

128. Walter Consuelo Langsam, review of *Japan's Pacific Mandate*, by Paul H. Clyde, *Political Science Quarterly* 51, no. 2 (1936): 32.

129. Luther H. Evans, review of *Japan's Pacific Mandate*, by Paul H. Clyde, *Annals of the American Academy of Political and Social Science* 183 (January 1936): 295. For a neutral review, see Harlow J. Heneman, review of *Japan's Pacific Mandate*, by Paul H. Clyde, *American Political Science Review* 29, no. 4 (1935): 706.

130. [Anonymous], review of *Japan's Pacific Mandate*, by Paul H. Clyde, *Contemporary Japan* 4, no. 1 (1935): 95.

131. J. R. Drummond, review of *Japan's Pacific Mandate*, by Paul H. Clyde, *Christian Science Monitor*, 26 June 1935, 11.

132. E. R. K., review of *Japan's Pacific Mandate*, by Paul H. Clyde, *Review of Reviews* 92, no. 1 (1935): 6. For other positive reviews, see John Gilbert Reid, review of *Japan's Pacific Mandate*, by Paul H. Clyde, *Pacific Historical Review* 4, no. 3 (1935): 290–91; M. Matsuo, review of *Japan's Pacific Mandate*, by Paul H. Clyde, *Pacific Affairs* 8, no. 2 (1935): 227–29.

133. Clyde, *Japan's Pacific Mandate*, 147; Peattie, *Nan'yo*, 82–83, 327n4.

134. Clyde, *Japan's Pacific Mandate*, 112; Peattie, *Nan'yo*, 96.

135. Clyde, *Japan's Pacific Mandate*, vi, 222; Peattie, *Nan'yo*, 245–47.

136. Peattie, *Nan'yo*, 247–49. For a description of the importance of these islands in the Pacific War, see Hanson W. Baldwin, "Japan's Bases in the Mandated Islands," *NYT*, 9 February 1942, 4.

137. Peattie, *Nan'yo*, 247–56.

138. "Prof. Paul Clyde, Duke University Historian, Made Long Visit to Jap Mandated Islands," [newspaper not identified], [1945], Box 11, Paul H. Clyde Papers, Special Collections, Perkins Library, Duke University, Durham, NC.

139. Allen L. Edwards, Military Intelligence Division G-2, War Department General Staff, War Department, Washington, DC, to Dr. Paul H. Clyde, Department of History, Duke University, Durham, NC, 22 April 1942; Clyde to Edwards, 24 April 1942; Clyde to Edwards, 2 May 1942, Box 9, Paul Hibbet Clyde and Mary Kestler Clyde Papers, Rare Book, Manuscript, and Special Collections Library, Perkins Library, Duke University, Durham, NC.

140. C. K. Moser, Chief, Far Eastern Unit, Bureau of Foreign and Domestic Commerce, Department of Commerce, Washington, DC, to Dr. Paul H. Clyde, Department of History, Duke University, Durham, NC, 23 May 1942; Clyde to Moser, 28 May 1942, Box 9, Clyde Papers.

141. Paul H. Clyde, Professor of History, to Captain Richard Day, U.S. Marine Corps, 20th Century Fox Studio, Box 900, Beverly Hills, CA, 22 October 1942, Box 9, Clyde Papers.

142. "Prof. Paul Clyde, Duke University Historian, Made Long Visit to Jap Mandated Islands," Clyde Papers.

Chapter Four

Pacifists and Former Missionaries

In addition to a handful of history professors, Armstrong also recruited a few former Christian missionaries to China or Japan for his pro-Japanese Committee on Pacific Relations. Most, if not all, of these figures were pacifists.

One of those ex-missionaries was John Cole McKim, who was born in 1881 in Japan, where his father was a longtime Episcopal bishop. An Episcopal priest like his father, McKim was also a painter. He died in New York City in 1952.[1]

Upon the recommendation of journalist Ralph Townsend, Armstrong invited McKim, who had been involved in religious and educational affairs in Japan for a number of years, to the 22 September 1941 inaugural meeting of the Committee on Pacific Relations.[2] He sent McKim the statement he had prepared in May with a request that he sign and return it if he could not attend the meeting.[3] On 18 September, though, the ex-missionary accepted Armstrong's invitation and wrote that the proposed statement was "admirable." He suggested adding "something to the effect that good relations between the two countries are likely to last if they be placed upon a genuinely equilateral basis." Citing the unequal application of the treaty of February 1911 for Americans in Japan and Japanese in the United States, especially the latter's ineligibility for naturalization, he complained of discrimination against them. Sounding like E. Stanley Jones, he declared that he did not think "good relations with Japan can ever be secure until we withdraw from a position which suggests that they belong to the lowest of races."[4]

McKim, who resided in Peekskill, New York, served as an Episcopal missionary in Japan from 1914 to 1931. This alone made him a potential recruit for Armstrong's committee. Moreover, his views on American–Japanese and American–Chinese relations placed him in a league of his own. He was so pro-Japanese that to call him an apologist for Japanese expansion would be an understatement. In 1920, he published *The Decline of Militarism in Japan*,[5] which was timely, because the victories of the democracies in World War I along with the failure of Japan's Siberian Expedition, which undercut Japanese militarism, contributed to the flourishing of democracy in Japan during the 1920s. In 1939, his brief history of Japan was included in a volume published in New York by a Japanese firm.[6] By this time, he was an isolationist, and served as chairman of the Peekskill chapter of America First as well as a columnist—and, in one view, "Japanese sympathizer" and "propagandist"—for the Japanese organ *Japanese American Review*.[7] When it suspended publication in 1941, this pro-Japanese journal had been in existence for over forty years.[8]

McKim wrote both articles and book reviews for the review. A perusal of his writings reveals him to have been pro-Japanese, anti-Chinese, anticommunist, anti-Soviet, anti-Kuomintang (Guomindang), anti–Chiang Kai-shek, and anti-British. Nearly every piece he contributed defended Japan, whether the accusation was its opium dealing, its taking advantage of the European war to carry out its Far Eastern policies ("Japan's policies have always been of a positive and rather obvious nature"), or its criticism of anti-Japanese authors (Freda Utley was "known . . . for her extreme hatred of Japan and the Japanese").[9] Like other members of Armstrong's committee, he was unhappy that most Americans were sympathetic to China during the Sino-Japanese War (1937–1945), which he attributed to "Chiang [Kai-shek] propaganda in this country." He was particularly irritated by talk of American disloyalty to or betrayal of "China" (his quotation marks).[10] Conversely, he praised books that agreed with his pro-Japanese stance. Reviewing one such work, he observed that its author "no longer has any use for the anti-Japanese propaganda" he had heard before visiting Japan. The book's author approvingly regurgitated the views of future Olympic impresario Avery Brundage, then with the AAU (Amateur Athletic Union), to the effect that the press and some U.S. government officials were biased against Japan. Not surprisingly, McKim concluded, "We heartily commend this book."[11]

His extreme pro-Japanese views blinded him to reality. A week before Pearl Harbor, he argued that the Russo-German conflict meant a Japanese–American war could happen "only if the Roosevelt Administration desires it and intends to force it."[12] It seems never to have crossed his mind that Japan could launch that war with a "sneak attack" on the United States. Such a naïve propagandist brought no sense of realism to Armstrong's committee, already populated with pro-Japanese and anti-Chinese figures, though his views undoubtedly gave comfort to Japanese hoping to avert war between the United States and Japan. Ultimately, though, war was in the hands of neither the American isolationists nor the Japanese diplomats with whom Armstrong was in touch in Washington, but in those of the Japanese military and government establishment or, as it sometimes was called, the "War Party."

It was easy to find McKim's views on the Far East in the mass circulation press as well. From 1932 through 1941, he was an inveterate writer of letters to the editors of the *New York Times*, the *New York Sun*, and the *New York Herald Tribune*. The U.S. government, he wrote in one such missive, has "frequently affronted it [Japan]." Japan "honorably withdrew" from the League of Nations, he argued, and Japanese agencies had probably provided more relief to civilian sufferers in China than those of any other nation. The Kuomintang and its communist allies, he complained, have "offered Japan repeated provocation." Speaking of the Sino-Japanese War—and even adopting the Japanese name for it, the "China Incident"—he claimed Chiang Kai-shek "started the present incident. It is begging the question to speak of Japan's 'aggression' here." Ignoring the evidence for a real obsession with communism, both in China and in Japan, he insisted, despite overwhelming evidence to the contrary, that the latter had "never professed to be primarily concerned with communism, in China." Referring to a letter to the *New York Times* "favoring unfriendly action against Japan," he retorted, "Sure Mr. Stimson has no grounds whatever for speaking of Japan's 'unprovoked aggression against China.'"

Chiang and his allies had "long been preparing the present incident," McKim claimed, and had confronted the Japanese with numerous provocations. A true isolationist, he called for "strict impartiality in dealing with foreign countries and foreign wars." In April 1940, he took issue with a letter writer who thought war with Japan inevitable. "There is not the slightest likelihood of Japan's attacking this country," he scoffed. Perhaps he was thinking of Japan's claim to a "Japanese Monroe Doctrine" in Asia when he wrote there would be no war as long as both countries conceded to the other the right to "'regional' doctrines." In February 1941, he sided with Japan in a dispute with the United States over American fortification of Guam. In April, he agreed with Charles Lindbergh when the latter complained that the minority opposed to peace had "influence" and "a loud voice." Referring to the economic sanctions and freezing of Japanese assets in the United States that followed Japan's move into southern Indochina, in late July McKim called them "economic oppressions" that Washington had inflicted on Japan, but "not because of anything Japan has done—still less done to the United States." The day after he attended the inaugural meeting of Armstrong's Committee on Pacific Relations in September, he defended Japan yet again, writing that it could have easily annexed Manchuria—which it did in all but name, of course—in 1931. He called for recognizing that Japan possessed "in her own vicinity" the same rights the United States claimed to hold in its "neighborhood" (the Monroe Doctrine).[13]

Ironically for someone who was such an extreme apologist for Japan in 1941, his sister, Nellie McKim, also a missionary for the Episcopal Church, spent most of the war in a Japanese internment camp in Manila before being liberated in February 1945.[14] One can only wonder, in the absence of evidence, whether her treatment by the Japanese, the surprise attack on Pearl Harbor, and Japan's wartime atrocities affected his views of that country.

McKim was by no means the only former missionary and pacifist in the Far East whom Armstrong approached on behalf of his committee. On 31 May, he wrote to Mark Shaw, ex-missionary, peace activist, and stalwart member of the National Council for the Prevention of War. Born in 1889, Shaw served as a missionary to Japan from 1922 to 1927. During those years, he spent just three months in China. From 1928 on, he was a member of the Japan Society of Boston. He, along with Frederick Libby and Elizabeth Schumpeter, was among those who most encouraged Armstrong's "Japanese project." The latter was already acquainted with Shaw, having met him earlier in Chicago. Since then, he informed Shaw, "considerable sentiment has grown for this Japanese-U.S. project." He enclosed several copies of the statement he had sent out, adding that all the replies thus far had been "favorable." However, he explained, he needed more signatures. Thus, he asked Shaw for a half dozen or more names of people who "understand Japanese problems and might be willing to back the movement in some way."

Armstrong hoped to travel east early the next week, he continued, unless "I get another assignment from America First" (he had been working for America First in Tennessee and Kentucky), and would contact Shaw. His project, he added, had "nothing to do with my America First activities, of course," but he was "beginning to think it is the most important thing we can do at present." He again called for the dispatch of a commission to Japan, this time seeing it as setting a precedent for settlement of the European war. "If we could make this trip to the Orient," he declared, "and help solve some of the problems there, why not a strong public movement to do the same in Europe?" "It is worth the try!" he enthused. As he had already done with others, he singled out Shaw as special. "I have already suggested," he wrote, "that you be one of the men to make the trip."[15]

During the summer, Armstrong continued his correspondence with Shaw. On 11 August, the latter, who was soon to serve as one of the pillars of the Committee on Pacific Relations, finally responded to Armstrong's earlier letter. He claimed the Missourian's letter had arrived while he was participating in the Round Table on Foreign Policy at the Keep America Out of War Congress in Washington. Because Armstrong had written he would be in the East shortly, Shaw wrote, he kept thinking he would hear from him. Since his receipt of Armstrong's late May letter, Japan had occupied the remainder of Indochina and the United States had frozen all Japanese assets. "The present crisis," wrote Shaw, "only intensifies the need of [for] the plan you had in mind." He had listened to the University of Chicago Round Table and the American Forum Hour discussions of the Far Eastern crisis. He was clearly dismayed by Columbia University Professor Nathaniel Peffer's remark at the

Round Table that it was a "miracle" the three speakers, experts on the Far East, all concurred that the United States should stop Japan with a naval force. "As I listened," Shaw told Armstrong, "I felt that it was not a miracle but a tragedy that such an institution as the University of Chicago Round Table should so completely fail to give the American people an adequate and comprehensive analysis of the Far Eastern problem. Never was the danger from 'blind guides' more real that it is in America today."

Like E. Stanley Jones, Shaw was in touch with the Japanese Christian pacifist Kagawa Toyohiko. "I had an hour's interview with Dr. Kagawa when he was in Boston some weeks ago," he informed Armstrong, "and found him most anxious that everything possible should be done by the Christian people of both Japan and America to prevent the calamity of a war between these two nations." In closing, he asked Armstrong to keep him posted concerning any developments with his "splendid proposal."[16] A Christian, Kagawa became an activist as a member of the Japanese Christian Socialists and garnered a worldwide reputation as a result of his many books and lecture tours.[17]

Armstrong responded almost immediately. "Your letter did me good," he wrote; "It encouraged me, at a time when I need it." He had been contacting friends as well as many persons he had not met but who were "interested in better relations with Japan." But then "the Far Eastern disturbances came along,'" he complained, "and threw things into quietude for a while." Despite this, he continued, some of those he had contacted first "without exception" still wanted to "go ahead with some plan such as I suggested." Meanwhile, he was still traveling a lot. The following day, he wrote Shaw, he was going to Louisville and then south, not to work for America First this time but to finish a magazine article. Afterward, he wanted to go east again. "I have some contacts in Washington, in the senate and in the State Department," he explained, "and I am trying to line them up to support some sort of conference on this Japanese project." He would contact Shaw from Washington or his next stop, New York, and maybe he could "have something definite." In the meantime, what would Shaw think of a conference about 20 September? If "things are not continuously disturbed," he continued, perhaps they could gather a "good representation" before then. He asked Shaw to take a "major part" in the program by presenting a paper laying out some of the data he had that described the resources of the world's empires.[18]

In early September, Shaw responded that Armstrong's letter did him "a great deal of good." He would be "anxious," he continued, to learn the outcome of Armstrong's meetings in Washington. A conference around 20 September, he wrote, would be fine with him. The meeting, he added, should be convened at the earliest date for which arrangements could be completed. He would be glad, he wrote, to "cooperate in any way." Since Armstrong had asked his advice and Shaw was assisting him, he in turn asked for Armstrong's help. He enclosed a revision of his article "Analysis of the Present Situation," along with a "tentative suggestion which either the America First Committee, or a group of other organizations, or all of them together, might make." He asked for Armstrong's "frank reaction," especially how the matter might be "promoted."[19]

A week later, Armstrong replied that Shaw's article could serve as the basis for a paper to be delivered at the major conference on America's Japan relations he and others hoped to convene in October. Meanwhile, he continued, "things are coming rapidly to a head." He had invited about a dozen persons to a dinner meeting on 22 September in New York. The number included Far East "authorities," such as Professor Elizabeth Schumpeter and journalist and author William Henry Chamberlin. He hoped Shaw would attend, but if he could not, at least endorse the statement that they would issue at that time, signed by attendees as well as those who could not be present, such as journalist Ralph Townsend and *Christian Century* editor Paul Hutchinson. It would serve "notice to the country that we plan to prevent war, if possible, with Japan." "I am hoping to raise some finances for this," he continued, "and on the strength of it I can furnish $10 to you if you can be with us." Later, he added, he hoped to "raise considerable [money] for this cause. I have some connections in New York [William Baxter] that have promised me some [funds] to apply on [to] the expense[s] of the later and bigger conference."[20]

On 18 September, Shaw accepted the invitation to attend the dinner meeting. He also readily assented to use of his name in connection with the statement. Did Armstrong know when in October the conference might be held? he wondered. He had been invited to speak in Maine and would like to avoid a conflict, if possible. In closing, he expressed his concern regarding Japanese–American relations. "If the facts regarding the present negotiations with Japan are as stated in this week's issue of *Uncensored*, September 13," he wrote, "then it seems very important that we get all the support we can for those in the state department who would negotiate with Japan. Therefore, more power to you!"[21]

In *Uncensored*, an anonymous author reported that the current negotiations between the United States and Japan had been "stalled" for the previous two weeks. The president, the author claimed, was worried that the rumored terms of a Japanese–American agreement, which the author listed in his article, might open him to charges of "appeasing the aggressors." The author claimed the projected agreement included such U.S. concessions as recognition of the Japanese puppet state of Manchukuo as well as United States and British withdrawal from China. Meanwhile, Japan was "anxious for action," the author argued. Without success in these negotiations, he concluded, Prime Minister Konoye Fumimaro's government might fall—as it did a month later—and be replaced by a "strongly pro-Axis" Matsuoka Yosuke regime.[22] Shaw agreed with the author that lack of progress in the negotiations might lead to the replacement of a moderate government by a strongly pro-Axis one. Both the *Uncensored* author and Shaw were right, for the new regime would be headed by militarist General Tojo Hideki, minister of war from 1940 to 1941, rather than diplomat and politician Matsuoka. This was a very bad sign for the future of U.S.–Japan relations because Tojo regarded war with America inevitable.[23]

Armstrong also approached yet another Christian writer and former missionary, Thorburn T. Brumbaugh. Then residing in Columbus, Ohio, Brumbaugh had served in Japan for seventeen years, where he was director of the Wesley Foundation for students in Tokyo and minister of several churches. The Wesley Foundation was a United Methodist campus ministry that the church sponsored on a nonchurch campus. Brumbaugh also had been a *Christian Century* correspondent for thirteen years in Japan. When Armstrong contacted him, he was on the staff of the student YMCA at Ohio State University in Columbus, where he was finishing his Ph.D.[24]

Brumbaugh received rather late notice of Armstrong's New York City meeting. Only ten days beforehand, Armstrong wrote him that his "good friends," Charles Boss, executive secretary of the Commission on World Peace of the Methodist Church, and Paul Hutchinson, managing editor of *Christian Century*, had asked him to send Brumbaugh a copy of Armstrong's statement on U.S.–Japan relations. "A number of us," he explained, "are greatly interested in trying to prevent open hostilities with Japan." They hoped to meet in New York on 22 September and invited Brumbaugh to join them. "Because of your great knowledge of the problems in the Far East," he wrote, "and your sympathy with our efforts to try to solve them by peaceful means," he hoped Brumbaugh, as well as thirty or forty others, would endorse their statement. He also invited him to the public conference the committee hoped to convene in October.[25]

Brumbaugh immediately granted permission to add his name to the statement, although he thought it was "platitudinous." Nevertheless, Armstrong was right to contact him, for Brumbaugh fitted right in with the committee's pro-Japan slant. In fact, he was perhaps even more radical than Armstrong and the other committee members, for in September he referred to Germany and Italy as "aggrieved." Most people in Japan and the United States, he insisted to Armstrong, wanted peace, and he placed the burden for attaining it on Americans. Could the American people, he wondered, "face up frankly with the facts and make the sacrifices and commitments to the Japanese and other unfortunate and now aroused races and nations of the world which alone can support the structure of world peace and cooperation?" A readjustment of lands, resources, and markets was necessary, and in addition to the interests of the United States and Japan, those of China, Germany, Italy, and other "aggrieved" Europeans and Asians had to be "taken into account." "I fail to find," he continued, "the consciousness of these fundamental readjustments as underlying Japan-American peace in your statement." In fact, he complained, he thought the fourth paragraph of the statement suggested that peace was necessary in the Pacific just so the United States could deal with the European crisis. To help prod the U.S. government "to take cognizance of the real opportunity of mediating the Sino-Japanese conflict," however, he was willing to sign the statement. Nevertheless, he believed Americans needed to "go far deeper into the degree of American responsibility for the present world conditions before assuming that a mere friendly attitude will make for peaceful relations between ourselves and other nations." Although he would not be able to attend the meetings in New York and Washington, he promised to pray that they would result in a "more enlightened and Christian American attitude toward Oriental peoples and the rest of the world in general."[26]

In mid-September 1941, Armstrong contacted Paul Hutchinson, the author of numerous articles on Far Eastern affairs, whom he described as "very helpful."[27] Hutchinson had spent several years in China. In 1916, he went there to serve as editor of the *China Christian Advocate*. From 1916 to 1921, he was responsible for all Methodist publications in China. Following his return to the United States, he wrote and spoke on the Far East. In 1924, he went to work for the *Christian Century*, a nondenominational Protestant journal, as managing editor. In 1932, he published *Storm over Asia*. He also was the author of *What and Why in China*. In the 1930s, he was a leader of the anti-Hitler movement in the United States. In 1947, when he became editor-in-chief of *Christian Century*, it had a circulation of forty thousand.[28] The evangelist and pacifist E. Stanley Jones frequently wrote for *Christian Century*, which was, in the view of one scholar, "undoubtedly the most significant" of the anti-interventionist religious journals.[29]

Despite the fact that Hutchinson advocated peace in the Far East, in March 1941 he was a supporter of Friends of Democracy, which was even more combative than the interventionist organization Fight for Freedom. It hired reporters and investigators to penetrate right-wing extremist groups and antiwar organizations and make public what they were up to. In early 1941, it published a pamphlet about the America First Committee that charged that it was a "Nazi Transmission Belt." The close relationship between Friends of Democracy and Fight for Freedom was made clear when the latter handed out tens of thousands of copies of the widely publicized Friends of Democracy pamphlet. Fight for Freedom members then contributed to the expense of another pamphlet, this one accusing famed isolationist Charles Lindbergh of being a Nazi and "American Hitler." Street battles between supporters of Friends of Democracy and Fight for Freedom supporters and those on the side of America First broke out in New York and other cities.[30]

In June, Hutchinson published an article titled "Peace Aims in Asia" in which he called for the United States to take the initiative in proposing a peace settlement in the Far East that might convince the Japanese militarists there was a way other than war to gain economic and political security. Armstrong apparently read the piece, which might be what led him to contact Hutchinson. As usual with peace advocates at that time, though, they placed the burden for resolving the crisis on American shoulders. There was the barest mention of a required Japanese withdrawal from China (with the proper rewards, of course) as part of the pathway to a peace settlement. The emphasis always seemed to be on persuading the Japanese, through reasoned discourse, not to expand further in Asia.[31]

During a trip in September, Armstrong contacted half a dozen people at the University of Chicago, "most of whom," he declared, "were very favorable." He thought Mr. Price—probably Harry B. Price—who had spent twenty years in Asia, mostly in China, and was head of International House, was "sympathetic, and gave me valuable suggestions."[32] However, Price was a most unlikely candidate for Armstrong's Committee on Pacific Relations, which was sympathetic to the Japanese, for Price was pro-Chinese. Moreover, Price served as executive secretary of the American Committee for Non-participation in Japanese Aggression (the "Price Committee") from 1938 until its demise in February 1941. This group called for an embargo on American war supplies to Japan. It also insisted that Japanese "military aggression" had to be halted before "any just settlement and lasting peace structure" could be established in the Far East.[33] In July 1939, Price claimed forty million Americans were opposed to the sale of war materials to Japan, and 72 percent of Americans in a Gallup poll supported such an embargo.[34] In April 1940, he warned against building up Japan, a potential foe of the United States, in the Pacific.[35] In March 1941, following the demise of the Price Committee, he became a member of the national policy board of the Committee to Defend America by Aiding the Allies and supported its call for increased aid to China and extensions of embargoes on war materials to Japan.[36] In light of Armstrong's and Price's diametrically opposed viewpoints on Japanese–American relations, one wonders what "valuable suggestions" a "sympathetic" Price gave the Missourian.

While attempting to recruit former Far Eastern missionaries for his proposed committee, Armstrong also approached American pacifists, such as Dr. Charles F. Boss Jr., executive secretary of the Commission on World Peace of the Methodist Church from 1936 onward. In 1940 and 1941, he worked closely with Armstrong and E. Stanley Jones. In October 1940, he participated in Armstrong's Emergency Peace Conference and was elected vice chairman of the No Foreign War Campaign.[37] Following the conference, Armstrong informed him that he was "pushing along on plans for the mass meetings, and other things associated with the conference." He was sending out a conference report to "hundreds of our friends," including Boss. The "immediate task" was to "schedule 6 or 8 outstanding mass meetings and prove to the country that we mean business." Thus, he was writing to leaders in a dozen places, in hopes this would produce some outstanding gatherings. Did Boss recommend convening one in Chicago? he inquired. He also hoped to arrange a meeting in St. Louis. He would visit Boss soon, he promised, to discuss plans with him. Although Frederick Libby was out west, Armstrong added that he was in contact with Douglas Stewart—publisher and part owner of *Scribner's Commentator*—and Colonel Charles Lindbergh, which Boss must have found a real coup on Armstrong's part.[38] The following day, he invited Boss to join Libby in speaking on 11 November in Evanston, Illinois. If that was not possible, he added, could he appear on 25 November?[39]

Meanwhile, in December 1940, Chairman Verne Marshall of the No Foreign War Committee mentioned Boss as one of those who had rendered full support to the group.[40] Marshall was shortly to be proven wrong about Boss's support for him, though. The following month, the latter telegraphed Armstrong and demanded a "complete break with [the] Marshall Committee." "We prefer [Senator Burton K.] Wheeler," he wrote, "[as] active or honorary chairman."[41]

Boss was a thoroughgoing pacifist and isolationist. During the years leading up to Pearl Harbor, his name was to be found on any number of peace petitions published in the press. Like many anti-interventionists and pacifists, he opposed war as evil, condemned the draft, and supported conscientious objectors.[42] He also was a member of the national council of the Fellowship of Reconciliation, an antiwar organization founded during World War I and dedicated to the establishment of peace.[43] In January 1938, he supported Congressman Louis L. Ludlow's proposed amendment to the constitution, which would have required ratification of a congressional declaration of war by majority vote of the people for it to take effect. In May 1939, he testified in support of the amendment before a subcommittee of the Senate Judiciary Committee.[44] His antiwar posture seemed to override any distaste for dictatorship. In December, he joined six peace organizations in calling for retention of the U.S. ambassador in Moscow, in spite of the Soviet's attack on Finland, and for resumption of full diplomatic relations with Germany, regardless of the United States' recall of its ambassador following the nationwide German assaults on Jews in November 1938.[45]

He made his pacifist views clear in an appearance before the Democratic Party's Platform Committee in July 1940.[46] In his opposition to conscription, he seemed merely foolish, arguing in August at hearings of the House Military Affairs Committee, following the German conquest of most of western Europe, that the United States "cannot beat Hitler by being like him."[47] With the Germans riding high in Europe, that same month he joined other members of a pacifist Committee to Defend America by Waging Peace—a name perhaps deliberately aimed at the interventionist Committee to Defend America by Defending the Allies—with headquarters in Chicago to urge the United States to unite with Latin American countries and other neutral nations to terminate the war by "joint mediation." The committee's slogan was "keeping this country out of war by ending this war."[48] Similar talk by Senator Burton Wheeler, former president Herbert Hoover, and Charles Lindbergh as well as American "personal friends" encouraged Japanese Ambassador Nomura Kichisaburo to take an interest in mediation of the European war.[49]

Perhaps feeling the pressure of the growing movement for war, in October 1940 Boss joined 277 other clergymen to protest what they claimed was illegal interference with the election rights of "certain minority parties."[50] In December, Boss, as executive secretary of the Methodist Church's Peace Commission, ordered the recruitment of eight million church members in support of an appeal for an "immediate armistice" in Europe and repeal of the draft.[51] It was clear that it was Armstrong's and Boss's isolationism that brought them together. In March 1941, Boss wrote Armstrong that it was good to know that he, "along with some of the rest of us, are keeping up the fight to keep the United States out of war."[52] In May, Boss was one of the sponsors of a three-day National Antiwar Congress in Washington, DC.[53] In October, with U.S. entry into the war less than two months off, he spoke for the Ministers' No War Committee, which was partly funded by America First, in declaring opposition to arming American merchant ships.[54] Following Pearl Harbor, he was a member of the governing committee that replaced the Keep America Out of War Congress with the short-lived Provisional Committee toward a Democratic Peace immediately following the beginning of the war.[55]

NOTES

1. Peter H. Falk, ed., *Who's Who in America Art, 1564–1975* (Madison, CT: Sound View Press, 1999), 2:2137. The entry in this volume spells McKim's name as "Mckin." This may have been the spelling McKim used in the art world (2:2136–37).

2. New York Bureau, FBI, "Rev. John Cole McKim," 15 March 1944, McKim FBI File No. 97-85-9, FOIA.

3. O. K. Armstrong to Dr. [John] Cole McKim, Peekskill, NY, 12 September 1941, Orland Kay Armstrong ("O. K." Armstrong) (1893–1987), Papers, 1912–1987 (C4056), State Historical Society of Missouri, Manuscript Collection, Columbia, MO.

4. John Cole McKim to O. K. Armstrong, Hotel Woodstock, New York, 18 September 1941, Armstrong Papers; William L. Langer, comp. and ed., *An Encyclopedia of World History* (Boston: Houghton Mifflin, 1952), 897.

5. John Cole McKim, *The Decline of Militarism in Japan* (n.p.: n.p., 1920).

6. John Cole McKim, "Nippon, a Brief History," in *Special Japan Day Edition* (New York: Nippon, 1939), issued as *Japanese American Review* 39, no. 2060 (1939).

7. John Roy Carlson, *Under Cover: My Four Years in the Nazi Underworld of America* (New York: E.P. Dutton & Co., 1943), 159, 256.

8. Editorial, *Japanese American Review* 41, no. 2125 (1941): 2. This issue provides a good example of the magazine's pro-Japanese views.

9. John Cole McKim, review of *The Secret Shanghai*, by Jean Fontenoy, *Japanese American Review* 29, no. 2070 (1939): 2; McKim, "Propagandists Have Shed Crocodile Tears to Distort Actual Situation in China," *Japanese American Review* 39, no. 2076 (1939): 1–2; McKim, review of *China at War*, by Freda Utley, *Japanese American Review* 39, no. 2076 (1941): 2, 7.

10. McKim, "Japan Battled Scourge of Cholera in 1879," *Japanese American Review* 40, no. 2091 (1941): 6.

11. McKim, review of *Observations Made on a Trip to Japan*, by J. Russel Wait, *Japanese American Review* 40, no. 2095 (1940): 2, 7.

12. McKim, review of the *Contemporary Review* (August 1941), *Japanese American Review* 41, no. 2125 (1941): 2.

13. McKim, "Ourselves and the Japanese," *New York Times* (hereafter *NYT*), 1 February 1939, 16; McKim, "Comment on Editorial," *NYT*, 19 May 1939, 20; McKim, "In Defense of Japan," *NYT*, 27 May 1939, 8; McKim, "Action Deprecated," *NYT*, 13 January 1940, 7; McKim, "On Minding Our Own Business," *NYT*, 30 April 1940, 18; McKim, "Japan's Position Argued," *NYT*, 26 February 1941, 20; McKim, "An Amendment Offered," *NYT*, 26 April 1941, 14; McKim, "An Elucidation of 'Reprisal,'" *NYT*, 26 July 1941, 14; McKim, "Japan's Position Upheld," *NYT*, 23 September 1941, C22.

14. "New List of Rescued Manila Prisoners," *NYT*, 23 February 1945, 6; New York Bureau, FBI, "Rev. John Cole McKim," 15 March 1944, p. 22, McKim FBI File No. 97-85-9, FOIA; "Last Missionaries Freed in Manila," *Christian Century* 62, no. 12 (1945): 371–72, 381.

15. Armstrong to "Dear friend Mr. [Mark R.] Shaw," Melrose, MA, 31 May 1941, Armstrong Papers. For a biographical sketch of Shaw, see "Mark R. Shaw," National Council for the Prevention of War (NCPW) Collection, reel 41:116 (box 129).

16. Shaw, associate secretary in the Boston area, NCPW, Melrose, MA, to Armstrong, Springfield, MO, 11 August 1941, Armstrong Papers.

17. Janet Hunter, comp., *Concise Dictionary of Modern Japanese History* (Berkeley: University of California Press, 1984), 84.

18. Armstrong, Springfield, MO, to "My dear friend Dr. Shaw," Melrose, MA, 16 August 1941, Armstrong Papers.

19. Shaw to Armstrong, 6 September 1941, Armstrong Papers.

20. Armstrong to Shaw, 13 September 1941, Armstrong Papers.

21. Shaw to Armstrong, New York, 18 September 1941, Armstrong Papers.

22. "Peace in the Orient," *Uncensored*, no. 102 (1941): 1–2. There were 114 issues of this magazine. The first was published in October 1939, while the final issue appeared the day before the Japanese attack on Pearl Harbor.

23. For a biography of Tojo, see Hunter, *Concise Dictionary of Modern Japanese History*, 227–28.

24. "Brumbaugh Takes Student Post," *Christian Century* 58, no. 41 (1941): 1250; "Missionary Task in Asia Stressed," *NYT*, 26 August 1957, 21; "Rev. T.T. Brumbaugh," *NYT*, 17 May 1974, 42. Following World War II, he served as executive secretary of the Board of Missions of the United Methodist Church for Japan, Korea, and the Philippines. In 1946 and 1947, he also was executive director of the Committee for the Establishment of a Christian University in Japan.

25. Armstrong to Brumbaugh, Columbus, OH, 12 September 1941, Armstrong Papers.

26. Brumbaugh, Columbus, OH, to Armstrong, Springfield, MO, 16 September 1941, Armstrong Papers.

27. Armstrong to Terasaki Hidenari, 15 September 1941, Armstrong Papers; Armstrong, Springfield, MO, to Dear Friend [Terasaki Hidenari], 4 October 1941, NCPW, reel 41: 223 (box 280).

28. "Paul Hutchinson, Author, 65, Dead," *NYT*, 16 April 1956, 27. For a biographical sketch of Hutchinson (1890–1956), see *Marquis Who's Who on the Web* (accessed 18 August 2005).

29. Justus D. Doenecke, "Explaining the Antiwar Movement, 1939–1941: The Next Assignment," *Journal of Libertarian Studies* 8, no. 1 (1986): 143.

30. Lynne Olson, *Those Angry Days: Roosevelt, Lindbergh, and America's Fight over World War II, 1939–1941* (New York: Random House, 2013), 324–25; "Nazi Aid Charged to Anti-war Group," *NYT*, 12 March 1941, 15. A recent study argues, based on the failure to register as foreign agents of two of its speakers, that there was some truth to the charge that America First was a "Nazi Transmission Belt." Susan Dunn, *1940: F.D.R., Willkie, Lindbergh, and Hitler—the Election amid the Storm* (New Haven, CT: Yale University, 2013), 237. In the case of one of the speakers she mentions, Ralph Townsend, the story is a bit more complicated (see chapter 7 below).

31. Paul Hutchinson, "Peace Aims for Asia," *Asia* 41, no. 6 (1941): 271–73; Armstrong to Hutchinson, 15 September 1941, Armstrong Papers.

32. Armstrong to Terasaki, 15 September 1941.

33. "Group to Ask Curb on Aid to Japan," *NYT*, 19 January 1939, 3. On the Price Committee, see also Donald J. Friedman, *The Road from Isolation: The Campaign of the American Committee for Non-participation in Japanese Aggression, 1938–1941* (Cambridge, MA: Harvard University Press, 1968); Warren I. Cohen, *The Chinese Connection: Roger S. Greene, Thomas W. Lamont, George Sokolsky, and American-East Asian Relations* (New York: Columbia University Press, 1978); Warren I. Cohen, "The Role of Private Groups in the United States," in *Pearl Harbor as History: Japanese-American Relations, 1931–1941*, ed. Dorothy Borg and Shumpei Okamoto (New York: Columbia University Press, 1973), 435–49, 453–58. For biographies of Price, see Friedman, *Road from Isolation*, 1–2; Cohen, *Chinese Connection*, 300.

34. "40,000,000 Reported for a Japan Embargo," *NYT*, 18 July 1939, 8.

35. "Key to the Far East Held in U.S. Control," *NYT*, 13 April 1940, 7.

36. "British Aid Group Urges U.S. Convoys," *NYT*, 18 March 1941, 10.

37. "Peace-Makers Meet as War Rages Abroad," *Washington Post* (hereafter *WP*), 22 October 1940, 12; "Lindbergh Calls for Avoiding War," *NYT*, 22 October 1940, 12; Wayne S. Cole, *Charles A. Lindbergh and the Battle against Intervention in World War II* (New York: Harcourt Brace Jovanovich, 1974), 110; "'No Foreign War' Campaign," *WP*, 23 October 1940, 6. For a biographical sketch of Boss, see *Marquis Who's Who on the Web* (accessed 12 August 2005).

38. Armstrong to Dear Friend Dr. [Charles] Boss, 29 October 1940, Armstrong Papers.

39. Boss, telegram to Armstrong, Springfield, MO, 30 October 1940, Armstrong Papers.

40. "Anti-war Group Asks Public Aid," *NYT*, 23 December 1940, 9.

41. Boss, Chicago, IL, telegram to Armstrong, C/O Peace Committee Meeting, Bedford Hotel [New York?], 6 January 1941, Armstrong Papers.

42. "War Is Denounced as Futile and Evil," *NYT*, 6 May 1940, 7. His opposition to universal conscription was made clear in "Educators Assail Peacetime Draft," *NYT*, 9 July 1940, 4 (Hutchinson and Libby also signed this anticonscription declaration). On his support for conscientious objectors, see "Conscience and Duty," *WP*, 9 June 1939, 12. For the opposition of many pacifists and isolationists to the draft, see Doenecke, "Explaining the Antiwar Movement," 154–55.

43. "Denies War Poll Slurs Roosevelt," *NYT*, 19 May 1939, 10. Norman Thomas also was active in this organization. It published a magazine, the *New World* (later retitled the *World Tomorrow*), edited by Thomas up to 1921. Manfred Jonas, *Isolationism in America, 1935–1941* (Ithaca, NY: Cornell University Press, 1966), 79.

44. Wayne S. Cole, *Roosevelt and the Isolationists* (Lincoln: University of Nebraska Press, 1983), 257; "Denies War Poll Slurs Roosevelt," 10.

45. "Peace Groups Urge Envoy Stay in Russia," *NYT*, 9 December 1939, 3.

46. "Platform Shaping," *NYT*, 14 July 1940, 1.

47. John B. Oakes, "Draft Essential to U.S. Defense, Says Roosevelt," *WP*, 3 August 1940, 1.

48. "Peace Group Asks Mediation on War," *NYT*, 30 August 1940, 8.

49. Frederick Moore, *With Japan's Leaders: An Intimate Record of Fourteen Years as Counsellor to the Japanese Government* (New York: Charles Scribner's Sons, 1942), 202–3.

50. "Curb on Minorities in 23 States Seen," *NYT*, 20 October 1940, 16.

51. "Methodists to Open Drive for Peace," *WP*, 22 December 1940, 10.

52. [Charles Boss], Commission on World Peace of the Methodist Church, Chicago, IL, to Armstrong, NCPW, Washington, DC, 24 March 1941, Armstrong Papers.

53. "U.S. Leaders Urge President to Take Strong Stand in Speech," *WP*, 26 May 1941, 1; "War Foes to Hold Capital Sessions," *NYT*, 26 May 1941, 12.

54. Robert C. Albright, "Knox, Stimson Join Colleagues in Asking Guns on Ships Quickly," *WP*, 14 October 1941, 1. America First helped the Ministers' No War Committee finance the mailing of isolationist material to 93,000 Protestant ministers. Friedman, *Road from Isolation*, 71.

55. "Anti-war Group Changed," *NYT*, 2 January 1942, 4; Roger Chapman, "Antiwar Movements: World War II," in *Encyclopedia of American Social Movements*, ed. Immanuel Ness (New York: Routledge, 2015), 1079.

O. K. Armstrong election poster, ca. 1930s. Courtesy of Columbia Research Center, State Historical Society of Missouri.

O. K. Armstrong, ca. 1940. Courtesy of Columbia Research Center, State Historical Society of Missouri.

William J. Baxter Sr., 1956. Courtesy of Baxter Investment Management, Riverside, CT.

Frederick J. Libby, ca. 1930s, photograph by Blank-Stoller. Courtesy of Peace Collection, National Council for the Prevention of War, Swarthmore College, Swarthmore, PA.

Payson J. Treat receiving imperial award from Deputy Foreign Minister Shigemitsu Mamoru, 1935. Courtesy of Payson J. Treat Papers, Envelope D, Hoover Institution Archives, Stanford, CA.

Elizabeth Boody Schumpeter, 1941. *Source:* HUGBS 276.90p (45), olvwork369533, Harvard University Archives, Cambridge, MA.

William Henry Chamberlin, n.d. Courtesy of William Henry Chamberlin Special Collection, Archives and Special Collections, Providence College, Providence, RI.

Mark Revell Shaw, n.d. *Source:* Delmar Gibbons Papers, Bentley Historical Library, University of Michigan. Courtesy of the Prohibition National Committee.

Ralph Townsend, 1934. *Source: Overland Monthly and Outwest Magazine* 92 (December 1934): 150.

Chapter Five

Journalists

In order to spread widely his pro-Japan message, especially news of his Committee on Pacific Relations, Armstrong needed to recruit newspapermen. Thus, accepting Elizabeth Schumpeter's advice, in early June 1941 he contacted the foreign correspondent and author, William Henry Chamberlin of the *Christian Science Monitor*.[1] After years (1922–1934) spent covering Russia for that newspaper, from 1935 to 1939 Chamberlin served as its East Asian correspondent. During that time, he published *Japan Over Asia*, which came out the same year the Sino-Japanese War began (1937). In 1941, he joined a number of other figures in participating in the Committee on Pacific Relations that, as one scholar put it, favored "appeasement" of Japan.[2]

By that time, Chamberlin had become a well-known "isolationist." He disliked the term, however, and considered it the "same stupid tyranny of words" as in Russia, Italy, and Germany.[3] In December 1940, he insisted that American liberalism should not pursue another crusade or aggressive war in Asia or Europe out of dislike for totalitarianism and under the illusion that such a conflict could knit together the "broken pieces" of Asia, Europe, and Africa.[4]

Like Elizabeth Schumpeter and Payson Treat, Chamberlin felt alienated from the Far Eastern studies establishment in the United States. In February, Treat wrote Schumpeter that Chamberlin—like Schumpeter, a resident of Cambridge, Massachusetts—had complained to him that the *Pacific Affairs* editor, Owen Lattimore, had mistreated him. Later, he continued, Chamberlin "authorized me to bring it to the attention of Dr. [C. Martin] Wilbur." He had forwarded extracts from Chamberlin's two letters to Wilbur in the "*Strictest Confidence*" (Treat's emphasis).[5] Two weeks later, he reported, Wilbur "at once went to bat on the information which I supplied him" from Chamberlin.[6]

In May 1941, Chamberlin participated in the National Antiwar Congress in Washington, DC, sponsored by seven anti-interventionist organizations, including the Keep America Out of War Congress, the National Council for the Prevention of War, the Fellowship of Reconciliation, and the Women's International League for Peace and Freedom. At a roundtable on foreign policy, he sounded much like E. Stanley Jones when he urged the United States to use diplomacy to make peace between Japan and China and to carry out an "active peace policy." In doing so, he seemed prescient when he warned the United States not to adopt a "total economic boycott of Japan." Seemingly overlooking the September 1940 Tripartite Pact, he warned that halting oil shipments—as happened less than two months after the pact—would "push Japan into the arms of the Axis." "Economic war," he declared, "would be a prelude to naval and military war."[7] It might be possible, he noted, for the United States

> to sponsor a settlement which would provide for the evacuation by Japan of large areas of China which the Japanese have proved unable to occupy effectively and for all-round economic cooperation between the countries in the Far East and American participation in the financial and economic reconstruction which will be necessary both in Japan and China after the deep injuries which the war has inflicted on the economies of both countries.

Disagreeing with Jones, however, he insisted the United States was not an imperialist nation.[8]

As to whether Chamberlin was pro-Japanese, like several other members of the Committee on Pacific Relations, the evidence is scant. In late 1937, he was judged by a reviewer of his book *Japan Over Asia* to give Japan "every possible break." He "finds many good things to say about the people of Japan," the reviewer complained, but "look at what Japan has done to the people of China."[9] It would perhaps be more accurate, though, to argue that Chamberlin favored treating Japan cautiously, lest it react violently.

In his early June 1941 letter to Chamberlin, Armstrong lamented that at present "the possibility of war between our nation and Japan is almost imminent." "Can such a war be prevented?" he asked. It was his "earnest conviction that it can be and should be." He had been putting together a list of those who "understand American-Japanese relations and might be sympathetic to an attempt to settle those difficulties by peaceful means." He enclosed the statement he had drafted and invited Chamberlin to sign it. Since the latter lived in Cambridge, Armstrong mentioned that "Mrs. Joseph Schumpeter" had also signed, perhaps hoping that her husband's name would convince Chamberlin to do likewise. He also asked Chamberlin for the names of anyone else interested in better relations between the United States and Japan. He told Chamberlin that he hoped a "small committee" could be dispatched to Japan to study and research the problems facing the United States.[10]

Because Chamberlin was traveling in the Midwest, it took him two weeks to respond. Armstrong must have been gratified at his reply, for he had found another fervent isolationist. He had his "full permission," wrote Chamberlin, to include his name on the statement. "I am heartily in favor of keeping the United States out of participation in any and all foreign wars," he declared, "and perhaps it would be more feasible to begin a constructive peace effort in the Far East than in Europe, because the Administration, at the moment, seems to be more inclined to be reasonable about Japan than Germany."

Chamberlin then recommended several persons with "Oriental experience" who might be interested in Armstrong's statement. Among them were Treat, whom Armstrong was to contact in September, and Shaw, with whom he was already in touch. He also suggested the former diplomat William Castle as well as Professor Edwin Reischauer of Harvard University. There is no evidence in Armstrong's papers, however, that he contacted either of them, although he referred to Castle as a "dear friend" in a June letter to Schumpeter. "I hope and believe you are one of the people who have not resigned themselves to the 'inevitability' of our involvement in any kind of 'shooting war,'" Chamberlin wrote to Armstrong, "provided there is no attack on this hemisphere."[11]

Armstrong also was very much interested in Roy W. Howard, chairman of the board of Scripps-Howard Newspapers.[12] After visiting Japan and Manchuria in 1933, Howard had returned home to argue for a larger U.S. Navy.[13] During the years 1939 through 1941, however, he became an isolationist and drew close to Charles Lindbergh. As the latter put it in November 1940, Howard was "taking a decided stand with his papers against American intervention." By February 1941, however, Lindbergh had changed his mind and adopted a decidedly unflattering view of Howard. His policy, wrote the famed aviator, "seems to be to stay close enough to center so he will not be caught out, whichever way events turn."[14] Thus, although Howard reluctantly supported lend-lease in February, his newspapers "remained highly suspicious of Roosevelt's interventionism." At the same time, the Scripps-Howard press, according to one study, "gave a national forum to a host of anti-interventionist columnists."[15]

Probably attracted by Howard's positions, Armstrong contacted him. In late May, he reported to businessman William Baxter that Howard had made some suggestions that were "*good*" (emphasis in original). The latter proved cautious, though, perhaps because of his public position as a supposedly objective newsman. Seemingly confirming Lindbergh's judgment, Armstrong wrote that Howard "does not want to stand out in front on this but will give us the behind-the-scenes support needed."[16] Howard also proved sympathetic to Armstrong's Committee on Pacific Relations, although he did not join it. In a cable to Tokyo on 1 November, Ambassador Nomura Kichisaburo reported that Howard was "manifesting great interest in Armstrong's movement." His *New York World-Telegram* was one of the few newspapers that reported on the meeting of the Committee on Pacific Relations in late September. At the same time, he cautioned Tokyo to keep "strictly secret" a Japanese diplomat's meeting with the associate of America First Committee officials (reference to Terasaki's meetings with Armstrong?) since the FBI had the committee under surveillance.[17]

It was clear that Howard, like the members of Armstrong's Committee, wanted to avoid war with Japan. "Japan wants no war with America," he argued in 1940 in a series of articles in the Scripps-Howard newspapers. Because of its material interests in the United States, he continued, it would "like to stabilize her relationship with America on a friendly basis," although he was perceptive enough to add "naturally on a basis of her own choosing." "Her initial terms for such a development would be absurd and impossible," he admitted, "but Japan will trade and negotiate." If the United States was a little more tolerant in its "psychological approach to Japan," recognizing they are a "proud and sensitive people," he insisted that "the present unnecessary antagonism could be dispelled with relative ease." He then fielded a proposal reminiscent of that which both Armstrong and E. Stanley Jones were to broach the following year. A commission composed of Americans with "some understanding of and respect for oriental psychology" should be immediately appointed to study and report to Congress and the president on the "broad and fundamental aspects of the entire oriental situation."[18]

In New York, Armstrong also contacted (Charles) Fulton Oursler,[19] a writer, novelist, and editor of *Liberty Magazine* from 1931 to 1942, regarding his proposal for a committee. He probably knew Oursler because of his (Armstrong's) work as a freelance magazine writer. In August 1936, he had written FBI Director J. Edgar Hoover that *Liberty* wanted an article on "the very subject we discussed—that 'public enemies' should now be considered 'public rats.'"[20] After meeting with Oursler, though, Armstrong was silent regarding the editor's reaction to his idea for a Committee on Pacific Relations, nor did Oursler's name appear on later rosters of the committee. Therefore, one suspects that Oursler was not encouraging when Armstrong went calling. The reason might have been that while he had lectured in Japan, his views differed from the pro-Japanese, anti-Chinese ones of committee members such as Ralph Townsend and others.

At first, Oursler seemed sympathetic toward the views of the isolationists. In April 1940, when the "Phony War" in Europe, which had begun with the German invasion of Poland on 1 September 1939, turned into a real one with the German invasions of Denmark and Norway, he declared, "We are sympathetic toward various countries in their wars but no propaganda has yet made any substantial group of American citizens believe that we should get into the war."[21] Six months later, though, he was warning about fifth columnists and calling, according to a press report, for "denial of free speech and free press to aliens, elimination of 'all the starry-eyed idealists, the fellow-travelers and any actual Communists and Nazis in our Government bureaus and departments', and prohibition of newspapers published in foreign languages," all for the sake of self-defense. Although he cited the danger of Axis fifth columnists, however, he omitted Japan from his list.[22]

If anything, Oursler was pro-Chinese and anti-Japanese. He had some experience of Japanese dictatorship and censorship. In September 1937, Japanese police in Yokohama confiscated a copy of *Liberty* because it contained a piece by Madame Chiang Kai-shek on the Sino-Japanese War that, the Japanese police claimed, was "pure propaganda."[23] The ensuing war seemed to confirm his sympathy for China. Reflecting on a day spent with Madame Chiang two weeks before the Japanese attack on China in 1937, he wrote admiringly about the Chinese, who had "something to die for."[24] Even if he had been inclined to participate in Armstrong's committee, he may have been abroad when it convened its first meeting on 22 September 1941.[25]

Following the September launching of Armstrong's committee, Oursler's *Liberty Magazine* made clear that it—Oursler probably wrote these editorials—had no sympathy for the isolationists. In October, in reaction to Lindbergh's anti-Jewish remarks in his Des Moines speech, the magazine called him "the most dangerous man in the United States of America today." It also slammed America First. In a witty letter to the magazine published the day before the Pearl Harbor attack, Secretary of the Interior Harold Ickes pointed out the inconsistency of the magazine criticizing him in August for saying hard things about Lindbergh and then itself saying even harsher things in October. The magazine editor retorted that before Lindbergh's Des Moines speech, he was "merely an isolationist." After his attack on the Jews, however, he had crossed the line.[26]

The magazine's 11 October issue accused Japanese diplomats in Washington of carrying out propaganda and the following week published an exposé of them. It was hard to stop Japanese propaganda in the country, the author argued, for most of those activities were carried out by embassy or consular personnel protected by diplomatic immunity. The "next dangerous group obviously due for ousting," he promised, "are the Japanese."[27] In fact, Terasaki Hidenari, the chief of propaganda and an intelligence officer as well as Armstrong's main contact in the embassy, was protected by diplomatic immunity. To arrest him, moreover, was to reveal the U.S. government's breaking of the Japanese diplomatic code.[28]

Two weeks before Pearl Harbor, Oursler may have indirectly disclosed his advice to Armstrong during their earlier meeting when he declared in his magazine, "Clearly it is time for all the committees and groups that have sought to bring pressure on public opinion to close up shop and go home."[29]

With the outbreak of war, Oursler assisted the FBI, which had Armstrong under surveillance on the eve of Pearl Harbor. Shortly after the outbreak of the conflict, he resigned as editor of *Liberty Magazine* to take up a post with the FBI.[30]

Armstrong's most controversial journalist recruit for the Committee on Pacific Relations was reporter and former diplomat Ralph Townsend. State Department files revealed that he was appointed to the diplomatic corps in December 1930 and resigned on February 1933.[31] In June 1939, the FBI reported that he had served as vice consul in Shanghai in 1932 and 1933 and in Foochow in 1933.[32] In a subsequent report, the bureau said he had been posted to Shanghai on 10 December 1931.[33]

A committed isolationist, he worked as a publicity agent and public relations counsel for the Japanese Committee on Trade and Information, a propaganda organ backed by the Japanese government. In a 1936 work, *Asia Answers*, he called the Japanese invasion of China an "advance" (the same word used by the Japanese following the war to avoid using the negative word "invasion"). It was a "boon to the majority of [the] Chinese," he claimed, and Japan, as a "staunch opponent of Moscow," was "fighting the white man's battle" in Asia. He also published a series of pro-Japan pamphlets, while urging Americans to maintain neutrality in Asia. He especially targeted those who wanted to make "Americanism mean support for Chiang Kai-shek." "There has been nothing in Japan's relation to us to deserve our hatred of Japan," he wrote, "nor has there been anything in China's relation with us to deserve our support of China."[34]

Less than three months after the Sino-Japanese War broke out in 1937, he wrote a letter to the editor of the *New York Times* in which he contrasted Japan and China to Japan's benefit. Japan was more democratic, he argued, and less militaristic than China.[35] In denouncing China at that time, though, he was in a "small minority." Many of these pro-Japan isolationists concentrated on the advantages to America of siding with Japan rather than focusing on castigating the Chinese. "A good many," concluded one historian, emphasized the United States' "relatively lucrative trade with Japan as compared with China."[36]

In March 1938, he published a pamphlet, "There Is No Halfway Neutrality," in which he argued pro-Red agitators ("a vicious alien movement") and the British were trying, through threats of boycotts, propaganda, and other means, to stir up war between the United States and Japan. Embargoes and boycotts, he argued, would not hurt Japan's war effort nor help China. He dismissed the importance of American oil and metals in Japan's war effort. "Our red minority," he claimed, "[was] eager for [a] U.S. war on anti-red Japan." In short, he saw a vast conspiracy to drag the United States into war with a friendly Japan. His pamphlet carried a blurb by the Reverend John Cole McKim, another of the pro-Japan members of the proposed Committee on Pacific Relations, that praised the publication as the "best statement of [the] case yet." As was usual with pro-Japan figures, Townsend dismissed Chinese "democracy" and labeled Chiang Kai-shek a "dictator." At the same time, he rejected critics' claims regarding "Japanese militarism" and argued instead that China "lead[s] the world in militarism." Japan's expansion had been directed toward Asia, he insisted, and it had never "molested us." He also pooh-poohed claims that Japan was a dictatorship. Moreover, he insisted Japan was more "civilized" than the United States. It was China, he asserted, that was the aggressor in the current war rather than Japan. There was no reason, he concluded, to "single out Japan for hostility."[37]

In calling Chiang Kai-shek a dictator, Townsend agreed with Japanese propaganda. In March 1941, Ambassador Grew had dinner with Vice Foreign Minister Ohashi Chuichi in Tokyo. When President Roosevelt referred to dictatorships in the Far East in a recent speech, Ohashi told Grew, he could not have meant Japan, for "with her many faults, Japan at least was not under a dictatorship." Roosevelt, he went on, must have meant Chiang Kai-shek, "the perfect dictator." He could not, he added, "imagine any country less democratic than Chiang Kai-shek's China."[38]

In November 1940, Townsend criticized the "belligerent pronouncements" of Roosevelt concerning Japan and the "war threat and hate specialists of the present Washington administration." He also took issue with the "internationalist lecturers, commentators, columnists and other spokesmen" calling for "embargoes and boycotts and intensified war threats." He asserted that much of what was carried in the press and on the radio about the Sino-Japanese War was "recognized as totally untrue by any moderately well-informed person." He complained in this fourth year of Japan's invasion of China that the press and radio "all too frequently" tried to convey the impression that the Japanese government had been usurped by a "bloodthirsty, utterly reckless and fanatical gang known as Militarists." There was, he argued, a "relentless anti-Japanese campaign" in the United States and a campaign to "stir war with Japan." And yet, he added, if Japan were defeated, a China dominated by the Soviet Union would be the likely result.

Townsend also appealed to Americans' self-interest as well as the profit motive by arguing that Japan's trade with the United States was far more important than China's. Japan, he asserted, was the "commercial prize of Asia." It would be "prudent," he argued, to preserve U.S. trade with Japan, "our best and largest [market] there [in Asia]." Roosevelt's "Asiatic policy," he claimed, had alienated America's third largest foreign customer. Clearly, he was a Japanese apologist. Only once in his article did he come close to acknowledging that Japan might be to blame for some of the problems in the Far East and between Japan and the United States. The Japanese, he admitted, were not "angels," although, he hastened to add, they had demonstrated as much patience as "could be expected of any people." Japan had never "threatened us, molested us, or attempted to trespass in this hemisphere" and wanted to be "friendly." He failed to mention the December 1937 Japanese sinking of the *U.S.S. Panay*; after all, it did not occur in "this hemisphere." Swimming against the pro-Chinese tide of sentiment in the United States, he insisted the United States was under no "obligation to jeopardize our own peace on behalf of the Chinese." He scoffed at those who argued the United States should help China because it was fighting for democracy, pointing out the absence of Chinese elections and the existence of Chiang Kai-shek's dictatorship. As for supporting China in the Sino-Japanese War, he insisted that if Americans "seek to quarrel with nations because of their quarrels with others, we shall be quarreling most of the time with all countries." In any event, he added, the Japanese were unlikely to change their China policy because of "anything we may do or not do."

Completely ignoring American economic interests throughout Asia as well as Japan's atrocities in China, Townsend repeatedly and flagrantly asserted that for Americans, "there is nothing worth fighting for anywhere in Asia." His was a call to lay off the Japanese. If the United States was not going to fight because "there is nothing for us to fight for in Asia," then "no good purpose is served by threats of fighting, boycotts, or embargoes." He repeatedly blamed Roosevelt and his administration for directing at Japan the "war threats and insults which with no visible good and much visible harm" had characterized their policy. If the United States pursued peace, he insisted, "there are indications that the Japanese will gladly meet us halfway."[39] Halfway across the Pacific at Pearl Harbor, as it turned out.

Townsend continued to air similar arguments throughout 1941. In February, he opposed the Lend-Lease Bill in testimony before the Senate Foreign Relations Committee, declaring that it would make the United States "the unmistakable aggressor against nations which have not sought objectively to molest us."[40] Foremost among those nations, for Townsend, was Japan. He spoke at two local America First meetings on the West Coast. He never delivered a speech, however, under the auspices of America First's headquarters, and the latter seems to have been ignorant of his foreign connections.[41]

In September, Armstrong informed Terasaki Hidenari in Washington that he had visited "at some length" Townsend, whom he described as a staff writer for *Scribner's Commentator*.[42] *Scribner's Commentator* (1939–1942) first appeared in November 1939. It became the voice of the extreme right wing of the isolationist movement. From 1940 to early 1942, George T. Eggleston was its editor, and it had a circulation of thirty thousand. In July 1941, editorial offices moved to Lake Geneva, where E. Stanley Jones and Japanese pacifist Kagawa Toyohiko had met and discussed peace prospects the month before. While most isolationists sympathized with the Chinese in the Sino-Japanese War, *Scribner's Commentator* criticized them. The magazine was linked to Lindbergh, with whom the editors were close. After Pearl Harbor, it disappeared.[43]

In a February 1941 article in the magazine, its publisher had warned that if the United States entered the European War, it would cost four hundred billion dollars, a million dead, and millions of ruined lives.[44] That same month, the magazine opened its pages to one Yakichiro Suma, a spokesman for the Japanese Foreign Ministry. It had "received many suggestions from him," the magazine acknowledged, adding that he had "spent many years in Japan." It should have served as a caution for the pro-Japan group in the United States when subsequently the "portly" Suma was arrested by the military police in Japan.[45] In an article published in the June 1941 issue, "Must We Fight Japan?," Townsend again defended that nation and lambasted China.[46] During the war that ensued, the sensationalistic book *Under Cover* made frequent reference to Townsend's prewar publications—referring to one as a "Nazi best seller"—and frequently labeled him a "Japanese agent" or "Japanese propagandist."[47]

Townsend also wrote for another isolationist publication, the *Herald*. In late October, a magazine called the *Hour* reported on what it termed a fifth column group named the Patriots of the Republic. The Patriots, the magazine claimed, followed the line laid down by the America First Committee. At the latter's meetings, articles from the *Herald* were read to inform attendees of the "latest tactics on the appeasement front."[48]

Meanwhile, in November 1941, while testifying before a federal grand jury investigating *Scribner's Commentator*, its editor, George Eggleston, recalled how the magazine came to hire Townsend. Douglas Stewart, part owner of *Scribner's Commentator*, had heard Townsend speak on a *Town Hall of the Air* radio broadcast. In addition, he had read two of Townsend's books, published by Putnam's and "widely circulated," advocating peace between the United States and Japan. Therefore, he invited Townsend to contribute articles to the magazine. Both Stewart and Eggleston pronounced "first-rate" the two pieces Townsend submitted criticizing the propaganda techniques of prowar authors. Subsequently, Stewart invited Townsend to move to Lake Geneva for the summer and write some more for the magazine. Therefore, in June 1941, Townsend and his wife rented a cottage there.[49] According to a later study of the isolationists, that same year he was made an editor at *Scribner's Commentator*.[50]

NOTES

1. Mrs. Joseph A. Schumpeter, Taconic, CT, to O. K. Armstrong, 4 June 1941; Armstrong to Schumpeter, 10 June 1941, Orland Kay ("O. K.") Armstrong, Papers, 1912–1987 (C4056), State Historical Society of Missouri, Manuscript Collection, Columbia, MO.

2. Ernest R. May, "U.S. Press Coverage of Japan, 1931–1941," in *Pearl Harbor as History: American-Japanese Relations, 1931–1941*, ed. Dorothy Borg and Shumpei Okamoto (New

York: Columbia University Press, 1973), 520; Warren I. Cohen, *The Chinese Connection: Roger S. Greene, Thomas W. Lamont, George Sokolsky, and American-East Asian Relations* (New York: Columbia University Press, 1978), 294. For an abbreviated list of the journals and newspapers for which Chamberlin wrote, see Cohen, *Chinese Connection*. For biographical sketches of Chamberlin (1897–1969), see *Marquis Who's Who on the Web* (accessed 18 August 2005); Cohen, *Chinese Connection*, 294.

3. Ronald Lora and William Henry Longton, eds., *The Conservative Press in Twentieth-Century America* (Westport, CT: Greenwood Press, 1999), 270; John Chamberlain, review of *The World's Iron Age*, by William Henry Chamberlin, *New York Times* (hereafter *NYT*), 30 November 1941, BR1.

4. Manfred Jonas, *Isolationism in America, 1935–1941* (Ithaca, NY: Cornell University Press, 1966), 236.

5. Payson Treat to Elizabeth Schumpeter, 3 February 1940, Elizabeth Boody Schumpeter Papers (A-43), Schlesinger Library, Radcliffe College, Cambridge, MA.

6. Treat to Schumpeter, 19 February 1940, Schumpeter Papers.

7. "Avoidance of War Urged as U.S. Aim," *NYT*, 1 June 1941, 22; "War Foes to Hold Capital Sessions," *NYT*, 26 May 1941, 12. For further press coverage of the congress, see William V. Nessly, "U.S. Leaders Urge President to Take Strong Stand in Speech," *Washington Post* (hereafter *WP*), 26 May 1941, 1, 4.

8. J. Henry Carpenter, "Peace Congress Meets in Capital," *Christian Century* 58, no. 24 (1941): 790–91.

9. Charles Poore, review of *Japan over Asia*, by William Henry Chamberlin, *NYT*, 6 November 1937, 15.

10. Armstrong to Chamberlin, Cambridge, MA, 10 June 1941, Armstrong Papers.

11. Chamberlin to Armstrong, 24 June 1941, Armstrong Papers.

12. Armstrong to Mr. [W. Forbes] Webber, [Kansas City Division, FBI], 6 March 1942, Armstrong Papers.

13. David H. Weaver, "Howard, Roy Wilson (1 Jan. 1883–20 Nov. 1964)," in *American National Biography*, 11:314; *Marquis Who's Who on the Web* (accessed 18 August 2005). During his visit to Japan, Howard was the first American newspaperman to interview the Showa Emperor (Hirohito).

14. Charles A. Lindbergh, *The Wartime Journals of Charles A. Lindbergh* (New York: Harcourt Brace Jovanovich, 1970), 259 and n., 372, 416, 419–20, 432, 452, 518, 522.

15. Justus D. Doenecke, "Explaining the Antiwar Movement, 1939–1941: The Next Assignment," *Journal of Libertarian Studies* 8, no. 1 (1986): 140.

16. Armstrong to William Baxter, 24 May 1941, Armstrong Papers.

17. U.S. Department of Defense, *The "Magic" Background of Pearl Harbor* (Washington, DC: Government Printing Office, 1978), 4:126–27, A-184, A-185; Nomura Kichisaburo, Washington, DC, to Tokyo, 1 November 1941, RG 457, Frank Schuler Papers, FDR Library, Hyde Park, NY; "New Group Seeks U.S.-Japan Amity," *New York World-Telegram*, 25 September 1941, 7.

18. William J. Baxter, *Japan and America Must Work Together!* (New York: International Economic Research Bureau, 1940), 5, 94–96; Roger B. Jeans, *Terasaki Hidenari, Pearl Harbor, and Occupied Japan* (Lanham, MD: Lexington Books, 2009), chap. 4.

19. Armstrong to Webber, 6 March 1942; "(Charles) Fulton Oursler (1893–1952)," *Marquis Who's Who on the Web* (accessed 18 August 2005).

20. Armstrong, Boston, MA, to J. Edgar Hoover, 18 August 1936, FBI File No. 62-45631, FOIA.

21. Lucia Giddens, "Oursler Warns D.A.R. about Propaganda," *WP*, 18 April 1940, 1.

22. "U.S. Ready to Meet Aggressors, Knox Asserts, Warning against Fifth-Column Stabs in the Back," *WP*, 6 October 1940, 5.

23. "Japanese Seize U.S. Magazine," *NYT*, 19 September 1937, 36.

24. Fulton Oursler, *Three Things We Can Believe In* (New York: Fleming H. Revell, 1942), 40.

25. Leonard Lyons, "Bluebird Makes a Bet," *WP*, 19 September 1941, 11. Lyons reported that Oursler was "going to London."

26. "Lindbergh, the Most Dangerous Man in America," *Liberty*, 18 October 1941, 9; "No Apology to Mr. Ickes," *Liberty*, 6 December 1941, 9.

27. Fulton Oursler, "The Last Word," *Liberty*, 11 October 1941, 62; Hallett Abend, "The Japanese Ambassador Plants a Story," *Liberty*, 18 October 1941, 48.

28. Jeans, *Terasaki Hidenari*, 29, 66, 145.

29. [Fulton Oursler], "May She Always Be Right," *Liberty*, 22 November 1941, 9.

30. "Oursler, Liberty Editor, Quits," *NYT*, 4 February 1942, 17. In March 1942, it was revealed during the trial of an alleged German agent that the agent had written several articles for the magazine over the years. Dillard Stokes, "Viereck Lawyer Ousted; Called Judge Biased," *WP*, 4 March 1942, 1. Regardless, during the war the FBI recruited Oursler to work for a newly created secret organization, Special Intelligence Service (SIS), that targeted Latin America. Its task was to destroy the German espionage network in that part of the Western Hemisphere. He worked for the service for three years, and it was said that, thanks to his efforts, thirteen agents infiltrated twelve nations in Central and South America under the cover of being correspondents. Ten years after the war, his participation in SIS was still under wraps. Fulton Oursler, *Behold This Dreamer!*, ed. Fulton Oursler Jr. (Boston: Little, Brown, 1964), 452–54. The SIS saga was first reported in Don Whitehead, *The FBI Story* (New York: Random House, 1956).

31. San Francisco Bureau, FBI, "Ralph W. Townsend; David Warren Ryder—Registration Act, Espionage," 6 December 1939, FBI File No. 65-2193-21, FOIA.

32. M. C. Falkner, San Francisco Bureau, FBI, "Ralph W. Townsend, Registration Act, Espionage," 9 June 1939, FBI File No. 65-2193-4, FOIA.

33. San Francisco, FBI, "'Changed' [*sic*—charged?]: Ralph W. Townsend; David Warren Ryder alias Ray W. Ryder—Registration Act, Espionage," 18 May 1940, Townsend FBI File No. 65-2193-37, FOIA.

34. Jonas, *Isolationism in America*, 36–37. One wonders whether his antiestablishment views were the result of a perceived injustice while he was in the foreign service. In January 1932, his transfer from the Foreign Service School to Shanghai, a desirable post, was canceled, and he was reassigned to Foochow as vice consul. "Seven Promoted in Foreign Service," *NYT*, 17 January 1932, N2.

35. Ralph Townsend, "Clarification Is Sought: Pacifism and Democracy as Applied to China Found Puzzling," *NYT*, 29 September 1937, 22. His pro-Japanese pamphlets included *Does Japan Slam the Door against American Trade in Areas of Japanese Influence in America?* (San Francisco: Japanese Chamber of Commerce, 1938); *America Has No Enemies in Asia* (San Francisco, 1938); *The High Cost of Hate* (San Francisco: Alec Nicoll, 1939); and *Seeking Foreign Trouble* (San Francisco: self-published, 1940). On Townsend's sympathy with Japan in 1941, see James Augustin Brown Scherer, Ralph Townsend, and Charles E. Martin, "Shall We Guarantee Peace in the Pacific?," *Town Meeting* 6, no. 18 (1941): 3–32. For his harsh judgements of the Chinese, see his *Ways That Are Dark: The Truth about China* (New York: G.P. Putnam's Sons, 1933). Two of his books were translated into Japanese before the war. *Asia Answers* (1936) was translated with the title *Beikoku kyokuto seisaku no shinso* (The Truth of America's Far Eastern Policy) (Tokyo: Nihon Kokusai Kyokai, 1937). *Seeking Foreign Trouble* (1940) was translated as *Beika: Amerika gaiko seisaku no kago* (American Dollar: The Errors of America's Diplomatic Policy) (Tokyo: Nihon Keizai Renmeikai Taigai Jimukyoku, 1941). For a list of Townsend's writings, see also Jonas, *Isolationism in America*, 37n6.

36. Doenecke, "Explaining the Antiwar Movement," 160.

37. Ralph Townsend, *There Is No Halfway Neutrality* (San Francisco: self-published, 1938). The consulate bought and distributed some of his writings.

38. Joseph C. Grew, *Ten Years in Japan: A Contemporary Record Drawn from the Diaries and Private and Official Papers of Joseph C. Grew, United States Ambassador to Japan, 1932–1945* (New York: Simon and Schuster, 1944), 375.

39. Ralph Townsend, "Japan—Our Commercial Prize," *Scribner's Commentator* 9, no. 1 (1940): 41–46.

40. "Willkie Due to End Aid Bill Hearing in Senate," *WP*, 11 February 1941, 1.

41. Wayne S. Cole, *Roosevelt and the Isolationists* (Lincoln: University of Nebraska Press, 1983), 553; Wayne S. Cole, *America First: The Battle against Intervention in World War II* (Madison: University of Wisconsin Press, 1953), 121, 124–25.

42. Armstrong to Terasaki Hidenari, 15 September 1941, Armstrong Papers.

43. Justin D. Doenecke, "*Scribner's Commentator* (1939–1942)," in *The Conservative Press in Twentieth-Century America*, ed. Ronald Lora and William Henry Longton (Westport, CT: Greenwood Press, 1999), 273–82. For Eggleston's recollections of the founding of *Scribner's Commentator*, see George T. Egglston, *Roosevelt, Churchill, and the World War II Opposition: A Revisionist Autobiography* (Old Greenwich, CT: Devin-Adair, 1979), 71–73.

44. Robert R. McCormick, "Can America Fight in Europe," *Scribner's Commentator* 9 (February 1941): 90; cited in Jonas, *Isolationism in America*, 270.

45. Armstrong to Terasaki, 15 September 1941, Armstrong Papers; Jonas, *Isolationism in America*, 37; Yakichiro Suma, "A Japanese Speaks," *Scribner's Commentator* 9, no. 4 (1941): 21–23; William Henry Chamberlin, review of *Volcanic Isle*, by Wilfrid Fleisher, *NYT*, 21 September 1941, BR3.

46. *Scribner's Commentator* 10, no. 2 (1941): 96–98.

47. John Roy Carlson, *Under Cover: My Four Years in the Nazi Underworld of America* (New York: E.P. Dutton & Co., 1943), 136, 148, 185, 195, 200, 248, 256, 389, 410.

48. "Precaution against *The Hour*," *Hour*, no. 117, 25 October 1941, 800.20211/605, PS/VH Confidential File, decimal file 1940-44, Record Group 84, National Archives.

49. Eggleston, *Roosevelt*, 141.

50. Jonas, *Isolationism in America*, 37.

Chapter Six

"We Plan to Prevent War, if Possible, with Japan"

The Committee on Pacific Relations

As we have seen in the earlier chapters, Armstrong conducted a "considerable correspondence" with ex-missionaries, editors, professors, journalists, generals, businessmen, pacifists, and others with the goal of forming "some sort of committee" as well as convening a conference at which Far Eastern problems could be discussed. In May 1941, he recalled, he drafted a "tentative form letter"—the statement he sent to Yale University's Professor A. Whitney Griswold—and mailed it to businessman William Baxter in New York, Frederick Libby in Washington, DC, Mark Shaw in Boston, and others. He was busy finishing a book that summer, though, and thus "did little with the project until about the middle of August."[1]

Even while distracted by other matters, though, Armstrong did not lose sight of his idea for a Committee on Pacific Relations. On 23 June, he wrote Terasaki Hidenari, his contact in the Japanese embassy in Washington, that he would get in touch with all those he had contacted earlier regarding "this matter" and ask them to suggest a date for a conference and dinner meeting in the nation's capital in the first days of July. Two or three of those "most active in this matter" would select the date, "with the advice of [Roy] Howard and [Fulton] Oursler." He also promised to start contacting forty or fifty prominent men and women who "should" attend the conference and dinner. "I shall secure their consent," he promised, "to be present." He also would announce a program as well as speakers for the banquet. "The subjects will all be related to the problems of better relations in the Far East." As a journalist, he also knew how important the media would be in his venture.

Therefore, he promised to solicit "strong support for the conference and for the plans to follow" from "favorable" press—Howard's role, judging from the 25 September report in his *New York World-Telegram* on the committee's first meeting—and radio. He would "continue to contact personally senators and congressmen known to be favorable to better Far Eastern Relations." He went on to mention Senator David I. Walsh (Massachusetts), the isolationist chairman of the Senate Naval Affairs Committee; Senator Walter F. George (Georgia), an archconservative (like Armstrong) and internationalist who favored repeal of all neutrality laws, including the arms embargo; and Congressman Hamilton Fish, a Republican isolationist and ranking member of the House Foreign Relations Committee. Many of those, he predicted, would attend the dinner. Finally, he promised that prior to the conference, a "complete plan of further action" would be drafted, to be announced at the meeting. He added his hope that by the end of the week, he would have a "satisfactory response" regarding the conference's time and place.[2] Four days later, he again wrote Terasaki, this time to inform him that "from all over the country have come replies indicating the most intense interest in the plans we have underway [for the committee]." The war in Russia seemed to have "intensified the desire of the American people to strengthen our relations with Japan."[3]

Meanwhile, Armstrong continued to organize his committee. In mid-July, he wrote Terasaki to report that even though he had just arrived home the day before, he was about to leave on a trip to Chicago, New York, Boston, and Washington. Apparently, he was having some success in creating the committee. "Contacts," he enthused, "have been most interesting! . . . Now have a splendid list of those ready to assist us in any efforts we may make." The problem was to recruit "really outstanding men and women." In New York, he reported, he was going to see Elizabeth Schumpeter, and that evening they would meet several more people. "This meeting," he declared, "will be very important, I feel." In addition, he had made plans to meet others in Washington. Only two or three persons he had "counted on" for help were "discouraged and hesitant." Even that did not dent his confidence, for he confidently added that "we can fill their places with many others."[4]

It was perhaps Schumpeter's ostracism from the Far Eastern scholars' community that made her eager to cooperate with Armstrong's efforts to avert war with Japan. Membership on the committee may have given her a renewed sense of belonging to a community of like-minded souls. Several members of the committee, such as Armstrong, Schumpeter, Treat, and Chamberlin, shared a sense of being oppressed by the majority, in Armstrong's case, the interventionists, and in the cases of Schumpeter, Treat, and Chamberlin, the sense of being a beleaguered minority in Far Eastern study circles because of their pro-Japan feelings.

On 12 July, Armstrong wrote Schumpeter that her earlier letter had "warmed my heart!" "It was nice to know," he continued, "that some others, such as yourself, agree that something may be done to halt our drift into war with Japan." During the six months he worked on the "Japanese project," he mentioned his contact with the Japanese embassy only to Frederick Libby, Mark Shaw, and Schumpeter, leaving the rest of the committee members in the dark. He wanted to see Schumpeter, he continued, to "go over all the plans." He hoped to arrive in New York on 16 July and was "quite sure" he would be there most of the following day. He asked that she let him know if they could meet on either of those two days. He also reported on his progress. "Responses to my letters to many outstanding persons," he enthused, "have been most interesting! I think we shall have a line-up of men and women whose word in this matter of U.S.-Japanese relations will mean much." Meanwhile, there was no evidence, during Armstrong's and Schumpeter's months of meetings and correspondence, that her famous husband, Harvard economist Joseph Schumpeter, was involved in Armstrong's "Japanese project." Armstrong seemed interested in meeting her "distinguished husband," though, and asked if "it is possible, allow me to do so."[5]

Four days later, Schumpeter wrote and accepted Armstrong's invitation to meet him in New York and would await a message from him at her club, the Cosmopolitan. If she did not hear from him, she would go to the lobby of the Woodstock Hotel—Armstrong's regular haunt when he visited New York—at 1 p.m. Sounding like a character in a mystery or espionage novel, she informed Armstrong, "I shall be wearing a brown hat."[6] Located at 127 West 43th Street, it was this hotel where former American Communist Party chief Earl Browder spoke in the late 1940s to a group dubbed the "Discussion Circle."[7]

On 17 July, Armstrong reported to Terasaki that his luncheon meeting with Schumpeter, who had "done outstanding work in economic research in the Far East," had been "very successful." They would convene again the following day, he added, to "go over a long list of men and women who have been contacted on behalf of some phase of Japanese relations during the last several years." He also would meet with Roy Howard "to go over the whole matter." "Developments in the foreign situation," he cautioned, "have made the task more difficult, of course, but many of our friends feel we should redouble our efforts."[8] In writing about the "foreign situation," it was possible he was referring to the 22 June 1941 German invasion of the Soviet Union.

That same day, Armstrong jotted down on the back side of an unsent missive the names of some prospective members of his committee, including Schumpeter, William Henry Chamberlin, Mark Shaw, Everett Frazar, and James Harbord.[9] The day after her meeting with Armstrong, Schumpeter mailed Armstrong a list of two dozen more persons to contact for his "Japanese project" and added that she had not included people she knew he had learned about from other sources. "I wish you all possible success," she wrote, "and will be glad to help in any way possible." Referring to his desire to arrange a meeting of those interested in his committee, she feared "it may be difficult to arrange a dinner in the middle of the summer." Her enclosed list included anti-interventionist senators, college presidents, professors, newspaper publishers (such as Robert R. McCormick of the *Chicago Tribune* and Arthur Krock of the *New York Times*), a well-known columnist (Walter Lippmann), and a general. There is no correspondence in Armstrong's papers, however, to indicate he attempted to contact any of these people.[10]

While Armstrong was energetically striving to line up support for his committee, isolationism's heyday was waning. On the eve of war, a best-seller list revealed the leanings of the American reading public; not a single isolationist book reached the top ten. Number one on Pearl Harbor day was William Shirer's *Berlin Diary*, a grim reminder of the Nazi threat.[11] After war broke out, Armstrong explained to the FBI that he had been too busy to pursue organization of his committee during the summer of 1941. During June, July, and August, however, he continued laboring on his "Japanese project," while exchanging letters with Schumpeter, Frazar, and Chamberlin. Progress was slow until late September, though, when he and his recruits met and tentatively established the Committee on Pacific Relations.

Slow progress in planning his New York dinner meeting and subsequent Washington conference obviously got Armstrong down. On 17 August, he wrote Schumpeter that he had been "rather up and down, at times, since we conferred in New York [17 July]. I'll not say I've been discouraged, but things certainly went against us for a while." Commenting on the tensions in American–Japanese relations since late July, he wrote that "things will drift along for some time," but "actual hostilities will not break out." "If such is true," he added, "then let us move along with our plans." On 24 July, the Japanese military had invaded southern Indochina, which was followed two days later by President Roosevelt's order freezing all Japanese assets in the United States.[12]

Referring to an 11 August letter from Shaw, Armstrong told Schumpeter that Shaw had "begged me not to drop the matter [the Japanese project]." Obviously looking ahead to the fall conference on "pacific relations," he explained that Shaw would give a paper and "otherwise be helpful." Did Schumpeter have any more "specific suggestions?" he continued. He would be in the South for a week researching an article before arriving in Washington around 25 August and New York two days later. He asked her to write him at General Delivery, Hoboken, Georgia, adding that this was the "only HOBOKEN [his capitalization] outside of New Jersey!" He would make this place his headquarters in the South. "If for any reason you are coming to Washington," he continued, "and cared to be there in about a week, you might be of help to me there in lining up the speakers, etc., for the conference, and deciding upon a possible date." For the first time, he began to plan the fall conference in late September. "What would you think," he asked, "about September 20th?" He sounded lonely, writing, "Thanks for any word from you."[13]

There was no question that Schumpeter was the most supportive member of Armstrong's group. On 23 August, she replied from Maine to Armstrong's recent letter. "I am glad," she wrote, "that you still believe it to be worth the trouble to attempt to improve our relations with Japan or at least keep them from getting worse. I am very much afraid that if Roosevelt and Churchill decide we must get into the war, they will decide to do it via Japan on the theory that the American people will object less to this approach." (Here she seemed to be flirting with the notion floated by Charles Beard, Charles C. Tansill, and other conservative historians that President Roosevelt used a clash with Japan as a "back door to war.") In response to Armstrong's suggestion that the meeting be held on 20 September, she replied that this day or a date "early in October" would be fine, "if we are still at peace." "Please call upon me," she added, "to help in any way possible." In closing, she invited Armstrong to lunch with her and her husband at their Taconic, Connecticut, home.[14]

After war broke out, Armstrong informed the FBI that he had asked Terasaki whether Japanese embassy representatives should attend "if a conference was held such as I contemplated." The Japanese responded that would be a gesture of friendship, especially if the meeting "attracted wide attention and brought some good speakers and authorities on the Far East." Some of those with whom he was in contact, Armstrong explained to the Japanese, were "of course friends of China as well as of Japan."[15]

After four months of delays caused by the crisis in American–Japanese relations and Armstrong's preoccupation with finishing an article, in September he accelerated cooperation with his American contacts to organize a committee.[16] His efforts can be traced in his correspondence with prospective committee members as well as with the leaders of the National Council for the Prevention of War. On 8 September, he telegraphed Terasaki, "Majority anxious to move quickly as possible but difficult to arrange dinner before Friday nineteenth." He would receive cables that day, he explained, that would determine the date of the dinner.[17] Meanwhile, he later recalled, he informed the Japanese that plans for his and his colleagues' "proposed conference were in abeyance, but that we hoped to make them soon." He and Shaw had discussed how to pay for the conference, he added, and were going to ask William Baxter for his advice.[18]

As planning for the conference progressed, Armstrong seemed mindful of the domestic political peril of working secretly with the Japanese. Thus, he informed William Langdon of the State Department's Division of Far Eastern Affairs that he would be in New York in late September for a meeting with "several interested in preventing war with Japan."[19] Meanwhile, on 11 September, Roosevelt delivered his famous "shoot-on-sight" speech, in which he ordered the U.S. Navy to fire without warning on German and Italian warships if they were spotted in the patrol zone in the Atlantic that the United States had staked out.[20]

While the international crisis deepened, Armstrong continued to report in detail to Terasaki, noting that plans for the committee meeting in New York were "proceeding successfully." He had gotten in touch through travel and mail with many of "our" friends, and it had been decided that 22 September would be the best day to meet, and he had informed everyone concerned. Their "Statement of Purpose" would be announced, and plans for the "larger conference" and "continuing programs of action" would be discussed. Many "who would like to be there cannot be present for various reasons." Therefore, he had mailed copies of the statement to them with a request they endorse it and give permission to use their names. "We shall simply make a start at this meeting Monday," he wrote, "but it will be a very important start." Following the meeting, he added, "the project will be public, with full publicity for such announcements as we feel are helpful." He was optimistic after being "down" during the summer. He had found "tremendous interest" in the committee. He had cast his net widely and been in touch with pacifists, fellow isolationists, at least one big newspaper man, magazine editors (Paul Hutchinson of *Christian Century* and Fulton Oursler of *Liberty Magazine*), university people, religious figures (Methodists, such as E. Stanley Jones and Charles Boss, Baptists, and ex-missionaries such as Harry Price and Mary Brooks), as well as Far East specialists (such as A. Whitney Griswold, Paul Clyde, and Payson Treat). Schumpeter, he was confident, would "take a good lead." He had not been able to meet with newspaper tycoon Roy Howard but hoped to do so later in the week in New York. He would spend "a few hours" in Chicago getting in touch with many of those he had contacted during his visit the week before. Several of them, he reported, were compiling rosters of people they wanted "us" to send the statement to after the Monday dinner meeting. Charles Boss was anxious to help, he wrote, although he could not attend the New York meeting. He would "give us all possible help with his lists of ministers and others," though, and with an article in his journal.[21]

A week before the New York dinner meeting, Armstrong also wrote to *Christian Century* managing editor Paul Hutchinson. After the meeting on 22 September, he promised, he would fill in Hutchinson on those discussions as well as the plans for a Washington conference, at which he hoped Hutchinson would present a paper. In a handwritten note on the carbon copy of his letter, he described Hutchinson as an "outstanding writer and man" who had recommended several others.[22]

On 12 September, Armstrong wrote to journalist Ralph Townsend that it was a pleasure to meet him "the other evening on my hurried visit, and I greatly appreciate the suggestions you gave me." He had received "splendid support" in Chicago for our "Japanese project" from Charles Boss; Paul Hutchinson; William Benton, vice president of the University of Chicago (1937–1945) and adviser to the national director of the America First Committee; and "others of similar caliber."[23] "I think the lineup of talent for the conference,' he continued, "to be held in Washington in a month or so will be impressive." Nearly everyone he had contacted had agreed to endorse his statement, he wrote—in fact, only one (Hutchinson) of the three mentioned above had signed—so their names could be added to the statement issued at the meeting on 22 September. He was "counting on" Townsend endorsing it, too, which Townsend did. He invited him to be one of the three or four speakers at the closing banquet at the upcoming Washington conference. He was aiming high. "A number of senators, Congressmen and Representatives of foreign governments will be there." It was "quite likely," he added, he would be in Chicago again on 17 or 18 September, and "I may get to come up to Lake Geneva again." If not, he would write Townsend.[24] In a brief reply on 15 September, Townsend returned Armstrong's statement with the comment, "I hope your conference does good [sic]." His scribbled comment on the bottom of the statement did not sound like someone subsequently to be accused of being a Japanese agent. "I hope that the beginning relative to Japan in exploring avenues of amity," he urged, "may be extended to *all* nations" (Townsend's emphasis)[25]

While the outbreak of war loomed, Armstrong continued to look for support for his committee from the religious community, especially the Protestants. On 15 September, he informed Terasaki that he was leaving for Louisville that evening for meetings. Many of his Baptist friends, including Mrs. [Mary] Walters [Brooks], he explained, were there for a reunion as well as the dedication of a new structure at the seminary.[26] In Louisville, he "conferred at length" with "various officials" of the Baptist Church, trying to "enlist their leaders to endorse the movement [the committee]." He was in high gear now, writing that he had drawn up a list of publications to which he planned to mail "our" publicity release. Brooks, a church secretary at the First Baptist Church in Gainesville, Florida, and a former Baptist missionary in Japan,[27] gave Armstrong "helpful advice as to enlisting various groups." Since she resided in Florida, she could not attend the September 22 meeting in New York. Nevertheless, he added, she would endorse his statement and attend the October conference in Washington, if possible.[28]

Armstrong had tried earlier to sign her up for the committee. Having misplaced his letter, it was late August before she responded.[29] Like other potential members of the committee, she sympathized with Japan. In one historian's view—disproved by the diversity of the group that supported

Armstrong's pro-Japan campaign—"practically the only group defending the Japanese point of view in America was the missionaries who had returned from Japan," even though "their influence was very limited."[30] Both Brooks and John Cole McKim were examples of this group of missionaries. Brooks, however, seemed more aware of Japan's faults than McKim. She declared that she sympathized with Japan's policy. In view of its small area and large population, she understood that when everyone else was seizing territory, the Japanese needed some also. She was troubled, though, and acknowledged that "perhaps worse of all—they think the time is opportune to plough on." She declared she would "love" to attend the committee meeting. If she knew it would be held in the fall, she would not go on vacation then. She responded to Armstrong's request for the names of "outstanding" and interested men and women who understood the Far East. The problem was that all her nominees were retired. In closing, she appealed to Armstrong, "let's pray hard for Japan—and the fine Christians there."[31]

Armstrong also continued his attempt to recruit specialists on the Far East for his committee. He informed Terasaki that he had sent his statement to "carefully selected authorities on the Far East" throughout the nation. The motive was the same that inspired his approach to A. Whitney Griswold in May. He wanted the persons whose names appeared in the committee's statement to "attract attention because of their knowledge of affairs in the Orient." As a journalist, he was interested in magazine coverage as well. "I am sure," he informed the Japanese agent, "we can get Mr. Townsend to do an article for his magazine [*Scribner's Commentator*]." If *Liberty* would publish one or more pieces on the committee, that would be "splendid." He had other proposals for magazine articles as well.[32]

In early September, Armstrong began to invite people to the first meeting (and the last, as it turned out) of the committee. During the summer, he had not contacted William Baxter. Although he may have been too busy, there also was, as we have noted, some uncharacteristic discouragement on his part. On 8 September, he finally wrote Baxter to apologize for failing to call on him during his last visit to New York. "I grew a little discouraged," he confessed, "over conditions for a little while." Now, however, he was being "urged on every hand to go ahead on our Japanese project." He had recently been in contact with "numerous others" who had encouraged him to "make some definite moves." The "most practical" suggestion, he continued, was that the group meet in New York as soon as feasible to discuss the problem, draw up a plan of action, and prepare a public statement. Although he understood many of their "friends" would not be able to attend, he was sending them the enclosed statement with a request for their views. The meeting would be held at the Woodstock Hotel at 7 p.m., and "it would be my pleasure to have those present as my guests." He would still be in New York the middle of the following week, he wrote, and "shall certainly report to you personally. . . . I value your advice." "I think if we handle this thing right," he enthused, "we can put it over [in] a big way."[33]

Armstrong also telegraphed Schumpeter. She replied that she would attend the meeting, although 19 September would be more convenient.[34] On 17 September, he wrote her that he was leaving Springfield that evening for Chicago before continuing on to New York. He asked her to send a copy of his statement as well as an invitation to attend the dinner to General William C. Rivers. He would be at the Woodstock Hotel all day on 22 September and would be "glad to see him and get his suggestions."

Although Armstrong was "rather tempted" to belatedly accept Schumpeter's August invitation to have lunch in Taconic, since he did not know exactly when he would arrive in New York, he wrote he had better await "more definite planning." He was considering moving on to Boston the day after the meeting, he added, so might spend part of the 23rd with her and her husband. He asked her in closing to invite her husband to join them at the dinner meeting, for he would "enjoy meeting him."[35] Schumpeter replied almost immediately that since classes began at Harvard that day, her husband would be unable to attend. She would be there, though, "as promised."[36]

Armstrong tried once again to enlist the people who had turned him down in the spring or summer. It was apparently encouragement enough for him that Griswold's June letter had expressed sympathy with the Missourian's concerns and supported a practical compromise between the United States and Japan, even though the Yale professor had confessed he was at a loss as to how to proceed. In early September, Armstrong informed Griswold of plans for a "group of us to meet in New York as soon as possible, to talk over the whole problem and to draw up some statement that can be made public. Also, to formulate some continuing course of action." He knew "many of our friends" lived far away and would not be able to attend, so he enclosed his statement of the proposed committee's goals with a request for a response. He also invited Griswold to attend the meeting and requested the names of any other interested parties the professor might know.[37]

There is no record, either in the Armstrong or Griswold papers, of any reply to Armstrong's letter. Nevertheless, the latter did not accept rejection. Despite Griswold's discouraging response in early June and failure to answer his September letter, Armstrong informed the State Department in late September that Griswold had promised to join the Committee on Pacific Relations.[38] Moreover, early the following month, he sent the Yale historian his report on the New York meeting. Despite the tensions between Japan and the United States, he wrote, "we feel that every honorable means should be used to avoid war." His group planned to convene a conference "within the next few weeks," he continued, and he would keep Griswold informed. In the meantime, he invited the professor to forward any advice or suggestions he might have, especially regarding the conference program or other possible committee members.³⁹ There is no record in the archives of any reply by Griswold to this letter either.

He also did not give up trying to woo Paul Clyde. During the summer, he went to Durham to see the Duke professor but had no better luck with him than with Griswold. In September, he wrote the same thing to Clyde that he had conveyed to Baxter a week earlier. He had had "some periods of discouragement," he confessed, "since I saw you in your office some weeks ago." He invited Clyde to the New York meeting. He was aware the professor was not enthusiastic about his endeavor so probably would not attend, so he asked if he could attach his name to his statement. Many were "anxious to see something done to prevent war with Japan," he wrote, "and to lay the basis for mediation in the Chinese conflict." He promised Clyde that the statement made "no commitments, but simply gives notice we hope to do something constructive."⁴⁰

Since Clyde was away from Durham and did not return to Duke until late September, the meeting in New York was over before he replied to Armstrong's appeal. The statement was greatly improved, he wrote, but reminded Armstrong that his own focus was on the United States rather than Japan. "I trust that your efforts," he wrote, "may serve the best interests of the United States." He then declined to permit his name to be used on the statement. It must have been even more discouraging for Armstrong when the professor concluded by writing, "I am not at all sure that your plan for a non-official committee on Pacific relations can accomplish anything at a time such as this."⁴¹ Thus, despite the subsequent claim of a scholar of American–East Asian relations, Clyde did not join Armstrong's committee in 1941.⁴² Armstrong could not take no for an answer, though, and, in a meeting at the State Department five days later, he claimed Clyde had promised to join his committee.⁴³

He also contacted businessman E. W. Frazar again. Even though the New York businessman also had declined to join Armstrong's committee, the latter again refused to take no for an answer. Thus, in September he invited Frazar to attend the New York meeting, which—surprisingly—he did.⁴⁴ On 8 September, Armstrong also followed up his earlier chat with General Harbord with a letter. It was a pleasure to meet the general on the street recently, he wrote, and to speak with him regarding "our plans to strengthen Japanese-American relations." He invited the general to attend the 22 September meeting, adding that his attendance would be "an inspiration to all."⁴⁵

Since Armstrong's July conversation with the general, however, Japan–America relations had been thrown into crisis by Japan's occupation of southern Indochina and the subsequent United States freezing of Japanese assets. As a result, like Griswold and Clyde before him, the general turned him down. "I am sorry," he replied, "that I do not think it will contribute to the situation for me to join in such a discussion." He went on to express sympathy with the group's aims, though, when he wrote, "I most sincerely hope that nothing will happen to provoke hostilities of any kind between Japan and the United States and I am in sympathy with every proper measure that can be taken to strengthen Japanese-American relations." He thought it was a "favorable sign" that the president did not mention Japan in his recent speech on the "war situation."[46]

In the meantime, in late June, journalist William Henry Chamberlin had written Armstrong. He did not reply until early September, however, when he wrote to inform Chamberlin of the upcoming New York meeting, adding that several persons from the Boston area would attend. If too few of them could make it, he would convene a similar gathering in Boston.[47] A week later, he confessed to Chamberlin that he had failed to mail his 8 September letter to the journalist, although in fact he had sent it. He repeated his invitation to the dinner meeting, which Elizabeth Schumpeter would attend. At the meeting, he explained, a statement would be issued calling for establishment of a committee and development of plans for "strengthening relations with Japan." A "major conference" would probably be scheduled for late October in Washington, and he invited Chamberlin to make a presentation. If he was unable to come to the New York meeting, Armstrong promised to call on him in Boston.[48] In a late August letter to Armstrong, Schumpeter had expressed her hope that Chamberlin would be back from Canada in time for the September 22 meeting.[49] On 17 September, however, he informed Armstrong that he would be unable to attend because he was going to be in Canada until the end of September. He hoped they could meet in Boston afterward to "discuss the question of peace in the Far East, in which I am sure our views closely coincide."[50]

In the meantime, Armstrong set about cultivating fresh prospects. Prior to the late September meeting, he continued his attempt to enlist as many prominent Americans as possible. In mid-September, he wrote to Payson Treat. In June, Chamberlin had recommended Treat as one of those "with Oriental experience who would, I think, be interested in your statement."[51] Therefore, Armstrong sent Treat a copy of his statement, claiming that it garnered widespread support. As an obvious inducement for Treat to add his name, he reported that it had the endorsement of Roy Howard. He did not mention, though, that the latter had declined to sign it, preferring to remain in the background. Schumpeter, Chamberlin, Shaw, and "many others who favor strengthening relations with Japan rather than war," Armstrong wrote, also had approved it. Adding his name, he assured Treat, "does not make any commitment except our determination to formulate some plan. That plan and action will come later."[52] Treat promptly replied that he was "happy indeed" to endorse the statement. It was a "well-reasoned statement of the problem" and offered a "constructive program." He asked Armstrong to keep him informed regarding the 22 September meeting.[53]

The same day he contacted Treat, Armstrong also wrote to his friend Charles Boss regarding the "Japanese project" and reported he had had "some splendid response" to it. He had called on Paul Hutchinson and "several others" while in Chicago. In Lake Geneva, he had seen Ralph Townsend, who had been in the Far East "for many years and has written several books and [gathered] much research material on the subject." "All," he wrote, "seem to think we are on the right track in this." He was disappointed, though, that Boss would not attend the New York meeting. He asked his friend to "let me use your name as endorsing the Statement. It makes no commitment except to express our feeling that something should be done to avert war and to use our good offices for mediation in the Japanese-Chinese conflict when possible." He hoped to see Boss when he passed through Chicago on 17 and 18 September. In closing, he cryptically added that he "MUST get the information asked for in the other letter, if at all possible."[54] In the end, however, Boss neither attended the New York meeting nor endorsed the "Japanese project" statement.

Armstrong also approached his old friend Frederick Libby. A pacifist, Libby was a constant presence in Armstrong's life while the latter struggled to organize his committee. In view of his positions regarding Asian affairs over the years, he was a good candidate for membership on Armstrong's committee. The two men had known each other at least since July 1940. At the time, Libby was known as the "dean of American pacifists" but also as an appeaser of Japanese imperialism. In 1940, according to one scholar, he was accused of being willing to "condone Japanese imperialism" to avoid war.[55]

A week before the New York meeting, Armstrong informed his "dear friend Fred" that the "Japanese project is coming rapidly to a head." While he was with America First (May–July 1941), he claimed, "he could do nothing with it." His friends who were knowledgeable about both Japan and China, though, had "urged him not to drop the matter, but to press on with it." He was planning a dinner meeting with a small group, he continued, on 22 September at the Woodstock Hotel in New York. "It would be an informal affair," he informed Libby, "private. If you could possibly be there, I would appreciate it more than I can tell you." He reminded Libby that "some weeks ago" he had shown him the committee statement (the May version). Enclosing a copy, he told Libby it had been revised somewhat in September. They hoped to issue the statement or a similar one at the end of the dinner meeting, he continued, and they also would schedule a conference in Washington, "perhaps around October 24th." They wanted to give "a dozen or more outstanding authorities on Far Eastern questions" time to draft papers. He requested permission to include Libby's name among the statement's signers, if he was unable to attend. As an inducement, he mentioned that Hutchinson and "many others"—ultimately, only a dozen or so were associated with the committee and its statement—unable to attend had granted such permission.

Charles Boss also was "much interested," he informed Libby, and had attempted to unite the antiwar forces. Last week in Chicago, he "gave me some valuable reports on what Dr. [E. Stanley] Jones and others are doing along this line, and advice as to how we might coordinate." In his letter to Libby, Armstrong then touched on the most sensitive question involved in the "Japanese project." "One big problem," he explained, "is to present the whole project in such a matter [sic—manner] that it will not be attacked as a pro-Japanese attempt to let China down. No one connected with this [project] would countenance that, of course. But we must cut straight to the issue[s] of—First, preventing war with Japan; second, mediating in the Chinese[–Japanese] conflict."[56]

Libby promptly responded that he would be unable to attend the "Conference on the Far East" on 22 September. However, he completely endorsed "the Statement that you have asked me to sign and am happy to give you authority to attach my name to it with the names of Paul Hutchinson and others." He asked Armstrong to keep him posted on developments and "let me help you in this highly important task in any way that I can."[57]

Armstrong also attempted to recruit another famous antiwar figure of the time for his campaign to avoid war with Japan. On 16 September, on the eve of his visit to Chicago, he wrote E. Stanley Jones, a Methodist evangelist (Armstrong was a Baptist) active in the peace movement. This was not Armstrong's usual form recruitment letter, but an attempt to win over Jones by convincing him of the Missourian's bona fides in the antiwar movement. Clearly, he hoped Jones's fame as an evangelist could be used to support his (Armstrong's) drive to avert war with Japan and establish his committee.

On his most recent visit to New York, wrote Armstrong, he had stopped by Jones's office, but he was "in the field." Jones may have heard of him, he wrote in mid-September, through some of their mutual friends, such as Charles Boss, Frederick Libby, Kirby Page, or some of the "fine leaders in the peace movement" he had met since he launched his antiwar efforts in the American Legion and other organizations the year before. In 1937, Kirby Page—an author, pacifist, and social evangelist—had published *Must We Go to War?* with fellow evangelist Sherwood Eddy. It was reported that he had made numerous trips to Asia and Europe to study economic and international questions.[58]

"You may recall," Armstrong wrote Jones, that he had organized the No Foreign War Campaign, which "cracked up badly" when Verne Marshall took the reins. Since then, he had been speaking throughout the country. "Our backs are to the wall now, of course," he wrote Jones, "but if every Christian American could read your article in this current *Christian Century*, there would be no further involvement of this country in war!" Paul Hutchinson, he explained, had mentioned Jones's article to him recently in Chicago. "Do accept my hearty thanks" for it, he added.

Armstrong went on to give Jones a history of his interest in "the possibility of preventing war with Japan, and . . . of mediation [of] the Japanese-Chinese conflict." This undoubtedly piqued Jones's interest, for that was exactly what he was working on at that time. He had gotten in touch with many friends, Armstrong wrote, and they were "greatly interested." He was intrigued by Jones's own efforts to mediate in the Sino-Japanese War as well as Japanese–American relations that year. Libby had, he wrote, "told me of your efforts with Dr. Kagawa [Toyohiko] and Dr. [Chester] Miao [Miao Ch'iu-sheng]." Miao was executive secretary of the National Committee for Christian Education in China and a prolific author. Since Jones's meetings with the two gentlemen, Armstrong added, Charles Boss had kept him informed. He then got to the point of his letter and invited Jones to attend the 22 September dinner meeting in New York. He had mailed the enclosed statement all over the nation, he told the evangelist, especially to those who had "lived and worked in Japan and China." If Jones could not attend, Armstrong asked, would he allow his name to be used in support of the statement?[59]

Jones may not have wanted to play second fiddle to Armstrong, for he did not reply to his letter until the day after the meeting and then with platitudes. He had read Armstrong's letter with "great . . . interest," he wrote, and thanked him for what he said and his "splendid work."[60] A week later (30 September), however, he answered Armstrong's letter again (as if he had made no note of his previous reply). "I am grateful beyond words," he wrote, "that you are helping [not leading] in this campaign to keep America out of the war." He did not endorse Armstrong's statement but merely apologized for not having time to "send you word about endorsing your meeting." He was sure, though, that "it got on without it."[61] Following the meeting, Armstrong recalled that, although Jones could not attend, Shaw, Schumpeter, Baxter, McKim, and "a few others" were present. Jones had an excuse, for at that time he was leading a retreat for ministers and speaking to an evening rally in Detroit.[62] In any event, judging from the lack of well-known figures among the attendees, Armstrong's endeavor was fated to be a Quixotic effort.

INAUGURAL MEETING OF THE COMMITTEE ON PACIFIC RELATIONS

Armstrong later described the prospective committee's first meeting. "We had dinner at the Woodstock [Hotel]," he recalled, "then adjourned to a private alcove where we discussed the possibility of our committee and a conference. The result was set forth in a letter," he continued, "which I mimeographed when I got home some days later."[63] Perhaps as a result of his earlier contact with Roy Howard, the meeting was reported in the latter's *New York World-Telegram* (as well as in the anti-interventionist Hearst papers).[64] Three days after the gathering, Armstrong and Mark Shaw (now secretary and chairman of the committee, respectively) announced in the *World-Telegram* that the committee had been founded to "strengthen relations between the United States and Japan and to urge mediation of the Sino-Japanese conflict." Armstrong declared that people nationwide who understood the problems in the Far East and were "sympathetic to efforts to prevent war with Japan" were being invited to join the committee. Sometime in October, he added, the group would convene a conference in Washington on Pacific relations. According to the committee's statement, "We are of the opinion that the security and interests of our nation demand that immediate steps be taken to halt the feelings of tension between Japan and the United States and to look toward solution of difficulties between the two nations by peaceful means." In closing, the article identified the committee organizers as Ralph Townsend of *Scribner's Commentator*; Paul Hutchinson, associate editor of *Christian Century*; Frederick Libby, chairman of the National Council for the Prevention of War; William Henry Chamberlin, author and former newspaper correspondent in Tokyo; and Payson Treat, professor of history at Stanford University.[65] The article did not say how many of these organizers attended the 22 September meeting (Libby, as we know, was not present).

In a cable to Tokyo dispatched several weeks later (1 November), the Japanese embassy reported the meeting of the committee and mentioned the names of some of those who attended. In addition to Armstrong, Ambassador Nomura Kichisaburo reported, Mark Shaw was present as "temporary chairman" and William Henry Chamberlin as a "special member." Payson Treat also attended, he noted. The Japanese were pleased that the meeting was covered in the *New York World-Telegram* and believed the reason was that Roy Howard, the paper's publisher, was "manifesting great interest in Armstrong's movement." The gathering, the ambassador added, was also reported in the Hearst newspapers.[66] A few days later, he added that, except for the Hearst papers and the *New York Daily News*—whose publisher was an isolationist—a Japanese–American war seemed "far more popular" than a German–American one in other American papers and magazines.[67]

The fact that newspapers reported this meeting of Armstrong's group was not surprising, for some, like the Scripps-Howard press, routinely gave a platform to isolationists. The Hearst press, for its part, gave Boake Carter, an isolationist radio commentator, a daily column. In addition, owner William Randolph Hearst penned a daily column in which he commented on foreign policy.[68] He agreed with the anti-interventionists in not believing that Japan was aggressive and believing it was possible to reach an accommodation with it. He did not invariably concur with the anti-interventionists, though; he sided with a minority of isolationists when he insisted on retaining the Philippines.[69]

AFTERMATH OF THE COMMITTEE'S MEETING

Once his committee was launched, Armstrong faced the problem of funding the organization as well as the major conference it hoped to convene later. That would not be easy in those latter days of the Great Depression. The day after the Woodstock Hotel meeting, he wrote Shaw, he had a lengthy conversation with William Baxter. "He feels," Armstrong wrote, "that this thing is big enough to go into properly, and thinks we should have a finance committee, raise enough money to hire the help needed, and thus put the committee generally on a firm foundation." "I wonder if it can be done," he mused. "I realize how hard it is to get money these days, but we shall have to have some if we do anything at all."[70] Shaw replied two weeks later that they needed funds if they were to accomplish "anything at all worth-while."[71]

In addition to money problems, trouble with the committee's name followed almost immediately. On 1 October, Robert W. Barnett, who was with the American Council of the Institute of Pacific Relations, wrote to Acting Committee Chairman Shaw. Mentioning several members of the group, Barnett declared that the group was to be congratulated on the "distinguished participation" in your project. His own institute, wrote Barnett, was nonpolitical, and the American Council and other member councils of the institute had not proposed a "positive political program of action." The Committee on Pacific Relations' program, however, consisted of "explicit advocacy of a removal of feelings of tension between Japan and the United States and a solution of difficulties between the two nations by peaceful means. This aim is, of course, political." Fearing confusion with his own organization, he suggested the committee change its name. "The Committee for Peaceful Change in the Pacific" or "The Committee for Improving Japanese-American Relations," he argued, "might satisfactorily describe your group without leading to confusion of the character and purpose of our two organizations." In response, Shaw scribbled on Barnett's letter, "I think this point is well-taken."[72]

A few days later, Shaw sent a copy of the letter to Armstrong. He thought it broached "a point which I think deserves careful consideration." "Personally," he asserted, "I think it would be much better to have a name that would not be so easily confused with the Institute. Both for *our* sake and theirs. The average layman would not keep the distinction clearly in mind" (Shaw's emphasis). He sounded like Elizabeth Schumpeter when he argued it would be particularly good to have a different name from the institute because "we do *not* favor a 'positive' (war) policy whereas many individuals in the Institute do seem to favor such a policy whether the Institute ... does or not." As for what name the committee should adopt instead, he suggested that, in addition to Barnett's two proposals, the committee consider "Committee on American–Far East Relations," if they did not want to limit the group to American–Japanese relations.[73]

Subsequently, Institute of Pacific Relations officials wrote to all the members of the new committee to protest the name of the group. On 20 October, Armstrong reported the dispute to Terasaki. The letter he received was "polite enough," he conceded, and the writer apparently spoke for the whole institute. "I shall show you his letter," he promised, "when I come [to Washington]." The official, he continued, wrote that they "'welcomed' any such move as ours, but hoped there would be no conflict of names." He might have echoed Schumpeter when he asserted, "Of course, it is well known that they now speak for the pro-Chinese group."[74] In any event, the fact that there was a group, the Committee on Pacific Relations, dedicated to opposing such widespread pro-Chinese views must have cheered his Japanese contacts.

According to a later study, the committee planned a one-day conference, to which several outstanding personages would be invited, in Washington, DC, in October. Although pleased with the interest and publicity the committee had aroused, Armstrong agreed with the group's decision to postpone that conference so that it could be carefully planned and thus successful.[75] Here, Libby's advice might have been influential. Unaware, naturally, of Japan's plans for an attack on Pearl Harbor in early December, he argued that the committee could accomplish little before Christmas. Instead, the grand old pacifist suggested that Armstrong attend a conference of Quakers, who planned to meet at the Old Quaker Church in Washington in November. Probably more decisive, though, was Armstrong's plan to work on a book in October with a collaborator, Mr. [Leonidas] Westervelt, of Douglaston, Long Island.[76]

ARMSTRONG'S MEETING AT THE STATE DEPARTMENT, 30 SEPTEMBER 1941

In late September, Charles Boss wrote Armstrong that he was "glad to hear of your success ... with the meeting on Japan. Please send me the details in a confidential letter."[77] Following the dinner in New York, Armstrong plunged into a whirlwind schedule to drum up support for his committee. All the while, he was careful to keep the U.S. government informed about his attempts to ward off war with Japan. On the last day of September, he reported to the State Department on the establishment of the committee. He met with William Langdon, who ten days later was to pen a stiff memorandum to

Secretary of State Cordell Hull concerning Japanese espionage in the United States. Armstrong handed him copies of the committee's prospectus, which included a list of its members as well as its statement and explained the purposes of the group. He informed Langdon that the committee planned to invite several interested and outstanding figures to attend a one-day conference in Washington in October to discuss Pacific relations. He hoped that a State Department representative would attend the banquet following the conference.

It was clear Langdon did not have a high opinion of Armstrong's views. During their conversation, he reported, Armstrong "indicated a strong non-interventionist [isolationist] viewpoint."[78] Many isolationists did not believe the United States had material stakes in the Far East "worth a war,"[79] and Armstrong clearly was one of them. He believed, according to Langdon, that "we have no stake in the Far East worth the candle and, consequently, that we ought to make a deal of some kind with Japan rather than follow the present road to war." When Armstrong asked him, "What specifically are the causes of our quarrel with Japan?" Langdon no doubt took pleasure in obliging him. The "deterioration in our relations with Japan," he lectured Armstrong, "was due chiefly to the infringement of our commercial and other rights in China and other Japanese-occupied regions in the Far East, and to violations of general principles which we are upholding in various ways in all parts of the world." When Armstrong asked for advice as to how the committee might help improve relations with Japan, Langdon tartly replied that "some study might be made of the particulars of the causes of American complaint." When Armstrong inquired how that might be accomplished, Langdon suggested reading the department's press releases or expanding the committee's membership to incorporate representatives of those whose losses at Japanese hands had triggered American complaints, such as mission boards carrying out philanthropic and cultural activities in the Far East and business corporations with major interests in Asia. Armstrong, Langdon complained, knew about the mission boards but "ruled out American business concerns on the ground that they would be biased in the committee's proceedings."[80]

In their meeting, Armstrong informed Langdon that, in addition to those listed in the committee's prospectus, the following had "promised" to join the committee: E. Stanley Jones, signifying the isolationist and pacifist currents had merged; Robert L. Flowers, president of Duke from 1941 to 1948;[81] Duke professor Paul H. Clyde; Professor A. Whitney Griswold of Yale University; General James G. Harbord; and E. W. (Everett Welles) Frazar, whom Armstrong described as an "old-time trader in Japan."[82] In fact, only one of the men on this list (Frazar) supported Armstrong and his committee.

It was certainly an eclectic group. While Jones was dead set against war with Japan, Griswold had lost all hope for a peaceful settlement between the United States and Japan. Nor was it clear why Flowers and Clyde would have "promised" to support the committee (even though the latter had published a book six years earlier that some readers viewed as favorable to the Japanese).[83] In view of Lindbergh's and Griswold's experiences with Armstrong including them in his committee despite their refusals to participate, it is clear he misled the State Department about the roster of his supporters.

In any event, he explained to Langdon why he had launched the committee. For a long while, he told the diplomat, he had studied and written about international affairs and had believed in using peaceful means to solve international disputes. He had first become interested in the Far Eastern crisis, he continued, when he presented a plaque at a memorial service for *Christian Science Monitor* correspondent Frank H. Hedges, who had died in Japan eighteen months earlier, at the University of Missouri's School of Journalism. He continued to be forthcoming about his contacts with foreign officials, informing Langdon that two diplomats at the Japanese embassy in Washington had (in the diplomats' words) "earlier endorsed the formation of the Committee on Pacific Relations."[84]

ARMSTRONG RESUMES EFFORTS TO EXPAND THE COMMITTEE

Shortly after this meeting, Armstrong returned home, from whence he announced the results of the 22 September meeting in a circular letter on 4 October.[85] In this missive, he reported that at his invitation a small group had met in New York to "discuss the problems of strengthening our relations with Japan" and reached six decisions. First, they issued the enclosed statement "as being substantially the sentiment of American people informed on Far Eastern problems and anxious to take steps to prevent war with Japan." It received "good coverage" in some newspapers, he wrote, especially the *Journal-American* and the *World-Telegram*. The news services also published the statement, with "varying results." Second, the committee decided to distribute the statement to those interested in "cooperating in our endeavor." This was being done, he assured his readers, as names were forwarded to him in "increasing numbers." Third, they had decided to ask for the help of peace organizations in obtaining "public information and cooperation." He had mailed the committee statement to officers of such groups throughout the country and requested their cooperation and suggestions. Fourth, the committee agreed to convene a Conference on Pacific Relations in Washington. "Recognized authorities on Far Eastern problems and particularly on Japanese-American relations," he explained, would be invited to participate. The "acting officers," which meant Shaw and Armstrong, were responsible for the arrangements, but the full committee would select the date. Fifth, they needed to raise funds for the conference and for "some continuing program." Finally, the New York meeting had agreed to establish the Committee on Pacific Relations with membership composed of everyone who had endorsed its statement. Three members would serve as acting officers until the conference, when a more permanent organization "may be perfected." He then listed the dozen members of the committee as Shaw, Armstrong, Schumpeter (chairman of the Washington conference program committee), Libby, Baxter, Chamberlin, McKim, Hutchinson, Townsend, Brooks, Brumbaugh, and Treat.[86]

Three days later, Armstrong wrote to Shaw, McKim, and Schumpeter to report on the planned Washington conference. His letters to Shaw and Schumpeter (and to his friend Libby) were always lengthier than those he sent other committee members. Moreover, while he informed Shaw, McKim, and Schumpeter that he was in touch with the Japanese, he did not let the other committee members in on the secret. He informed Shaw that he had taken "several short trips" following their 22 September meeting. Previously, he had telegraphed Shaw but now had time to mail him a full report. He described his meeting with Baxter the day after the New York dinner. The next step, he wrote, was to hold a conference in Washington with forty or fifty of the nation's "best authorities on the Far East" in attendance. Because both Griswold and Clyde had turned him down and Schumpeter was a bit of an outcast at Harvard, this seemed an impossible dream. He suggested to Shaw that the meeting not be held until late October, lest it be "unprepared and unsupported." Or should they wait six more weeks? he asked. He promised not to write any of the other members except Schumpeter—who, along with Shaw, was the most committed to his "Japanese project"—to whom he would send a letter resembling the one he sent to Shaw.[87] Two days later, he forwarded a brief report on the committee to Shaw. He was sending it to "everyone on my list of correspondents," he wrote, and to "peace societies, publications and other media of publicity, over the country." "It has been a terrific job," he explained, adding he hoped it would "produce some good."[88]

That same day, he wrote McKim that he expected to hear soon from Shaw and Schumpeter regarding conference plans. Some members had advised him not to hurry but to prepare a "real successful meeting, well attended and attracting considerable attention." "I feel," he commented approvingly, "that is good advice." In late October, they might be able to meet again at "our Washington conference," but if not then, then maybe "shortly before Thanksgiving." He would keep him informed. In closing, he flattered McKim, who by all accounts was an odd bird, writing that he had heard "so many favorable things about you" and would rely on his advice and assistance.[89] Two days later (9 October), he sent McKim a short note enclosing the "mimeographed report of our [New York] meeting, which I am sending widely all over the country. I am hoping that it will increase the interest in our project."⁹⁰

Finally, he wrote Schumpeter that he had been "rather busy" since returning home. He had had "some interesting reactions to our little meeting and its attendant publicity. The N.Y. papers did it up well, I thought. The news services carried it to some extent. Most of the letters were entirely favorable." Foremost in his mind was the question of the committee's fall conference. He had written to ask Shaw how long they should "allow before the next move." He wanted to pose the same question to her, he added. He was in favor of convening the conference in Washington. Within the next "week or ten days," he explained, he would have more names for the committee and "assurance of fine support." He realized, however, that a conference could not be arranged "on short notice." He would prefer to hold it in two months, if necessary, during the Christmas holiday rather than just convene another committee meeting or dinner. If Schumpeter agreed, should they drop the notion of calling a conference in October? He could shore up interest by holding a dinner in Chicago to which they could invite Hutchinson, Townsend, Boss, and others. They could follow up with a Boston meeting with those in that area attending. They also could hold another meeting in New York as well as the one in Washington. Maybe, he added, "there might be one somewhere in the southwest." All these meetings, he concluded, would lead up to a conference, "perhaps in December." As always, he solicited her suggestions and worried about money. "We shall have to face the matter of money," he wrote, "and Mr. Baxter, who has given me some help, said he would assist in organizing a committee for that important task." He asked for her views as "soon as possible." In the meantime, he would contact Shaw and others.⁹¹ Without waiting for her reply, on 9 October he sent her a copy of his report on the New York dinner meeting.⁹²

The same day that Armstrong sent Shaw the meeting report (9 October), the latter wrote Armstrong to complain that the Missourian had left him in the dark. He did not have a copy of the news release Armstrong had given the press nor had he seen anything in the Boston papers or the *New York Times*. As a result, he was a "little embarrassed how to answer people who mentioned it to me." He did not see all the New York papers regularly, he added, so he did not know which paper or date to consult after he heard the news release had been published. As for Armstrong's request for advice concerning the timing of the conference, he thought it should be convened "as soon as it can be done well." He did not know the extent of Armstrong's preparations, he added, but the end of October "seems a little soon." However, it should be held before Thanksgiving, if possible, for *Uncensored* magazine and other sources had revealed that negotiations between the United States and Japan were "more or less at a standstill, and 'are deteriorating.'" He believed the crisis would come when the German–Russian war was decided.

If Russia lost, "as now seems likely," Japan would be "less inclined to make major concessions."

For someone present at the dinner hosted by Armstrong on 22 September, Shaw seemed uninformed about the Missourian's thinking. Did he want a temporary organization to "make an immediate public protest against war with Japan," he asked, or a "permanent committee with office and staff to promote better Japanese-American relations and with a more constructive and conciliatory policy than the Institute [of Pacific Relations] seems now to take?" Or was Armstrong going to leave it to the Washington conference to decide what the next move should be?

The date of the conference, he wrote, would depend on "how soon you could get some real funds, and how soon the group of the caliber we need could be enlisted." He was planning to attend the National Council for the Prevention of War conference in Washington on 14 and 15 November, he wrote, so "just before or just after" that would be convenient for him, but possibly not for others. Replying to Armstrong's earlier query, he asserted that if they waited six weeks, that would mean the week following Thanksgiving. Since many of the university men might be on holiday the weekend after Thanksgiving, he wondered whether that would be a desirable date. "How many of your people are there," he asked Armstrong, "who would effected [sic] by such a factor?"

Had Armstrong seen Robert Maynard Hutchins? Shaw continued. Hutchins was an ardent isolationist, a prominent member of America First, and a friend of Lindbergh's. He also was president of the University of Chicago (1929–1951). Had Armstrong had any other responses, Shaw inquired, to the "new movement of which you spoke?" Whether Shaw meant the Committee on Pacific Relations—in which case it would be an odd way for the committee's acting chairman to refer to it—or some other "movement," perhaps broached at dinner on 22 September, was not clear. In any event, Shaw acknowledged, "America First seems to be the most active agency in the field at present." The America First Committee in Boston, Shaw reported, had asked him to go to Chicago the following week to "press the adoption of the larger financial program which I have been urging."[93] This assignment must have made plain to Armstrong that Shaw's primary loyalty was to America First.

On 9 October, Armstrong also sent a brief report on the September meeting to Libby. He apologized for the delay, but he had been "so much on the go" since he left New York. He did not mention that the week following the New York meeting, he had visited the State Department in Washington. Moreover, he delayed writing Libby until five days after he sent out his circular letter to "friends" reporting on the meeting. They had a "most interesting discussion," he wrote. There had been an "excellent reaction . . . from the publicity," so he hoped they could move swiftly to "some worthwhile program." A note of realism crept into his report. "I realize the odds are against us, but I am leaving no stone unturned to make our Statement and project as effective as possible."

Following up on his promise in the 4 October circular letter, Armstrong informed Libby he was sending his report and statement to all the peace groups on his lists and included an extra copy for Libby's files. Always on the lookout for publicity for the committee, he told Libby the two documents would be worth "at least some mention" in *Peace Action*,[94] for they marked a beginning of "what could develop into a vigorous program." He was coming to Washington soon, he continued, and would "of course" like to chat with Libby "on this and other plans." He was in touch with "some of our friends" to try to raise funds, which "as you know is a major problem." A worthwhile conference in Washington would require "financing," he wrote, and several of his friends in New York had suggested ways to raise money.[95]

In a second letter that same day, this one marked "Confidential," Armstrong felt compelled to explain to Libby why Shaw had been invited to serve as acting chairman of the committee. It "seemed best," he wrote, to ask Shaw to serve until they could "perfect some more permanent organization." He had been "very helpful and interested," he went on, "and seemed anxious to fill some place of leadership in this project." Shaw, Schumpeter, and he concurred that if the committee was to "render a permanent service," they should find a "very outstanding man" as chairman. Therefore, he asked for Libby's suggestions.[96] In a letter written four days later, Libby replied that he would be glad to discuss the committee when Armstrong arrived in Washington.[97]

October 9 was clearly Armstrong's day for reporting to committee members or other interested parties, for he also wrote to Brooks, Brumbaugh, Treat, Hutchinson, Townsend, E. Stanley Jones, Chamberlin, and Clyde. In each letter, he enclosed a brief report of the 22 September meeting and added that he was sending it "widely to publications all over the country, to stimulate public interest in our project." They had their "little meeting" in New York, he wrote Brooks, "and made a start at least with our project to strengthen relations with Japan." He had told everyone about her, and they were anxious to meet her. The conference would not be held until December, he explained, because it would take a long time to prepare. He assured her that he would keep in touch and hoped she would be able to attend the conference.[98] He told Brumbaugh that everyone at the 22 September meeting had been grateful for his "helpful advice and stimulating suggestions." No slouch at flattery, he asserted that Brumbaugh was "certainly . . . blessed with the esteem and regard of our best leaders all over the nation." He invited Brumbaugh to present a paper "on any angle of this question which you think best" at the Washington conference. In closing, he promised to keep Brumbaugh informed.[99]

That same day, he thanked Treat for allowing his name to be used on the statement. They planned to convene a conference in December in Washington, he informed the professor, and promised he would be "inclined to advise setting the date to convenience you," in case Treat had plans to be in the East. In closing, he asked if Treat had any suggestions concerning publicity.[100] Everyone, he informed Hutchinson that same day, "spoke of you in terms of highest regard, and it was a pleasure to tell them I had visited you and discussed our project briefly with you." He invited Hutchinson to read a paper on some aspect of the Far East problem at the December conference. He clearly wanted to keep up with him. He wrote that it was probable he would be in Chicago again in a week or ten days and promised to visit him again. "I do feel that we have started something worthwhile, and I am anxious to see it continue on a sound basis."[101] Finally, his letter to Townsend also offered flattery. "Everyone spoke in highest terms of yourself," he wrote, "and it was a pleasure to tell them that I had seen you recently." He had been busy mailing the report of the meeting and other material, he continued, to "peace societies, publications and other media of publicity." The next step would be the Washington conference, which he had originally hoped could be convened in October. He hoped to go to Chicago soon and "possibly on to Lake Geneva" to solicit further advice from Townsend.[102]

He also sent a copy of the meeting report to E. Stanley Jones. He was still "tremendously interested" in Jones's conversations with Kagawa Toyohiko and "representatives of the Chinese people" (Chester Miao) concerning mediation. Therefore, he invited him to be one of the key speakers at the Washington conference and "give us a summary of what you think can be done in this regard," and promised to stay in touch with the evangelist.[103]

In his letter to Chamberlin, he repeated his invitation to the author and journalist to present a paper at the December conference. All of us are volunteers, he wrote, and had no funds yet "although Mr. Frazar, who attended our meeting, made several valuable suggestions."[104] That same day, Shaw wrote Armstrong from the Boston area that he had seen Chamberlin that day when the latter spoke on Russia to the Women's International League for Peace and Freedom. He was interested in the Washington conference, wrote Shaw, but was "not sure" he could make it.[105] Finally, despite Clyde's refusal to allow his name to be used on the statement and his negative assessment regarding the committee's chances, Armstrong sent him a copy of his report on the founding of the group.[106]

On 11 October, Armstrong wrote to Baxter, too. He had been busy mailing out a brief report to people nationwide, he reported, and to publications that "might give us some publicity." All the replies had been "favorable," he continued, with "most urging me and our group to move at once into something tangible." The next move, he argued, should be a "fairly large conference, to attract national attention." He sounded a note of pessimism, though.

Perhaps thinking of the difficulties of Prime Minister Konoye Fumimaro's government in Japan, he observed that "developments in the Far East are not so good." Since Hitler was "smashing into Russia," "it handicaps our efforts greatly." No doubt Armstrong meant that it was difficult to argue for peace with Japan, a member of the Axis powers, when those nations seemed a greater threat to the United States with every passing day. Armstrong was nothing if not feisty, though, writing that he "was not inclined to give up the fight." As soon as he finished mailing the publicity materials by the middle of the following week, he would write Baxter to propose a "new course of action."[107]

That same day, he wrote again to Frazar, enclosing his report on the 22 September meeting. Most of their publicity, he informed him, had been "very good." The next step would be a conference in Washington. As "you suggested when you met with us in New York," he continued, that would involve a lot of preparation and time. Moreover, "I expect our relations in the Far East to become rather acute again in the next few weeks and that may delay things." Perhaps it was a hint to businessman Frazar when Armstrong went on to raise the question of financial support for the committee's efforts. He felt that "we should raise at least finances enough to carry on the office work for the next few months, in an earnest attempt to avert war if possible."[108] Unlike Baxter, though, there is no evidence Frazar took the hint.

That same day, Armstrong also sent his report on the 22 September meeting to General Harbord. "Tensions between our nation and Japan continue," he wrote, "but we feel that every honorable means should be used to avoid war." He informed the general of plans for a Washington conference "sometime within the next few weeks."[109] In late October, Harbord replied that he was "very much interested in the maintenance of peaceful relations with Japan." He took a tack like Clyde's, however, in declining to participate in the work of Armstrong's committee. "Things are in such a status with regard to our public relations in various directions," he declaimed, "that I, as a Retired Army Officer, do not think it prudent for me to engage in any conferences in which I might find myself, as a soldier, at variance with the policies of the Commander-in-Chief."[110]

Meanwhile, on 11 October, Armstrong received a letter from the trusty Schumpeter. Referring to his 9 October committee report, she exclaimed, "I admire your energy and good will!" As usual, she had a suggestion for him. "I wonder," she wrote, "if we couldn't interest Hugh Byas in this venture (and perhaps get him to speak at the meeting when it is held)." Two or three weeks ago, she explained, Byas, who until 1941 had served as a correspondent for the *New York Times*, had published a lengthy letter in that newspaper advocating "patience in our attitude and actions toward Japan."[111] As was the case with Schumpeter's recommendation that Armstrong contact General Rivers, there is no evidence the Missourian ever contacted Byas.

Having finally received Armstrong's 7 October letter, a week later Schumpeter penned a lengthy and worried reply. She agreed with him that more time was necessary to organize a "really effective conference." She also thought the series of dinner meetings in various cities might well arouse "preliminary interest." She would be happy to work with Shaw to schedule one in Boston. She asked for extra copies of Armstrong's report on the committee meeting and volunteered to write to people who might join the committee. "I know you want me to be extremely frank with you," she continued, "about everything." Two points worried her. The first was the committee chairmanship. She "liked Mr. Shaw personally," she hastened to add, "but I am afraid some people would consider him simply a professional peace-worker." In his place, she hoped "someone of undoubted prominence and ability, truly interested in our project, will turn up, who will be willing to serve as chairman." Like Armstrong, she also was concerned about money. She hoped funds would be found but warned, "I trust the sources will be carefully investigated." She was worried about Baxter. "My own reason for some slight anxiety about Mr. Baxter," she wrote, "is the advice given me by a friendly Japanese." "You know," she warned, "the interventionists are quite capable of taking drastic advantage of any small slip."[112] Sure enough, at the National Council for the Prevention of War conference in Washington in mid-November, Armstrong was warned about a person who sounded very much like Baxter (see chapter 7).

Meanwhile, in late October, Armstrong reported to Terasaki on his efforts to expand the committee. "The reactions to our project" he assured him, "have been interesting indeed." After the Hearst Sunday papers reported on it, committee members received letters, mostly favorable, from far and wide. He had continued to mail out reports on the meeting and the committee statement, he reported, and had requested they be given "wide publicity." He then moved on to the question of the proposed conference in Washington. Committee members, especially Shaw and Schumpeter as well as "a number who have become interested since the publicity," he wrote, all argued that the Washington conference "MUST [his capitals] be planned long in advance." He was "anxious to move at once" but would not have their support if he did not consult with them in fixing the conference date and speakers. Baxter had "very kindly furnished some finance" but more would have to be found among "our friends." He had written ten key committee members and friends, including Townsend, Schumpeter, and Chamberlin, to solicit their views regarding a series of smaller conferences or dinner meetings, and all replies thus far had been positive.

The "Chicago group," Armstrong informed Terasaki, had invited him to lunch on 23 October. He would call on Boss and Hutchinson beforehand to "see what we may plan." He would also prepare publicity material for Boss, editor of the *World Peace Newsletter*, which went to "many thousands all over the country." He also had sent publicity material to Hutchinson for *Christian Century*, of which he was associate editor. In addition, he had scheduled a meeting with the editor of *Rotarian* magazine and another with the editor of *Kiwanian Magazine*. That same day, he would travel up to Lake Geneva to meet with Townsend and the editors of *Scribner's Commentator* to discuss some articles and cartoons for that magazine.[113] He also had been invited by "some on the West coast" (Payson Treat?) to travel out there, he wrote, and the "Boston crowd (Shaw, Schumpeter, Chamberlin, etc.)" wanted him to attend a dinner there. He obviously was itching for action. "It would be no task, with Dr. Libby's help," he told Terasaki, "to work up a small dinner at Washington, a sort of preliminary conference, to lay plans for the bigger."

In the meantime, though, there were three problems to resolve. The first was whether to visit William Randolph Hearst, a prominent anti-interventionist. In the summer of 1941, Charles Lindbergh had spent three days at Hearst's home in California.[114] Armstrong wanted to visit Hearst and "planned to go," he informed Terasaki, but had been bogged down with correspondence. He also had "felt [it] best to await developments since the international scene was changing so rapidly." In addition, he seemed to be awaiting instructions from the Japanese. He could go this week, "if desired," and thought it would be "worth the try." He seemed to be asking for money. "I find that the fare is some more than I thought, but $250 would cover it." His second pressing problem, he wrote, was whether to go ahead with small meetings, like the one he was going to attend in Chicago, which would lead up to the large meeting "sometime in November." He promised he would report on that when he returned from Chicago. Finally, he broached the money question once again, wondering whether they should immediately act to get their project well funded by "friends," especially those in New York. There was the expense of his half-time stenographer to whom he had contributed "a huge amount of my time." He needed a Washington office, a full-time secretary to work under committee members' direction with "myself remaining as secretary," and the need for well-established publicity contacts. "We could then," he promised, "hit this thing very hard." If they did not operate in this way, he warned, they would fail. He had faith, though, that the funds could be found. Baxter, Frazar, and "numerous others interested in Japanese trade would help." If they could find $3,000, the job could be done." "Reports from Washington," he concluded, "are very bad, as you know." "If we can make this movement large enough," however, "it will succeed in preventing war." "If not," underestimating how close the outbreak of war was, he predicted war would come "within two or three months."[115]

On 21 October, Shaw informed Armstrong that he was staying in Chicago for several days, probably until 23 October. If the Missourian came, he continued, he would like to see him. In the meantime, he could be contacted at the America First office there. He then inquired about the date and plans for the Washington conference. Like other members of the Committee on Pacific Relations as well as some America First anti-interventionists, Shaw blamed his own country rather than Japanese aggression for the crisis in Japanese–American relations. Writing just after the resignation of Prime Minister Konoe Fumimaro's government on 16 October and the ascension of General Tojo Hideki as prime minister two days later, Shaw complained: "Too bad our government did not show enough interest in negotiations with Japan to keep Konoye [Konoe] in power."[116] Even though Shaw was in Chicago and wanted to see him if he passed through, Armstrong later reported he "missed him."[117]

On 27 October, Shaw was still in Chicago. He seemed increasingly anxious about the state of Japanese–American relations as well as the status of the committee's proposed Washington conference. "With Secretary [of the Navy Frank] Knox saying that hostilities may break our [out] any time within twenty-four hours between Japan and the United States," he wrote, "the times are indeed becoming urgent in the Pacific as well as in the Atlantic." He probably would be in Chicago the remainder of the week, he noted, and invited Armstrong to write. If the latter was going to be "up this way, of course I would want to see you."[118]

Meanwhile, the establishment of the Committee on Pacific Relations did not go unremarked by critics. In late October, in an issue that found its way by mid-November to the State Department's Division of Foreign Activity Correlation as well as its Division of Far Eastern Affairs, the *Hour* magazine disparaged the founders of the committee as "well-known Propagandists and Appeasers." On 25 September, it reported, the press had divulged the establishment of the committee, whose goal was "strengthening relations between the United States and Japan and urging mediation in the Japanese-Chinese conflict." Organizers Shaw and Armstrong—the same man, the magazine pointed out, who had been acting chairman of Verne Marshall's No Foreign War Committee—issued a statement signed by several "prominent citizens" (the *Hour*'s quotation marks). "We who have joined in this pronouncement," it declared, "are of the opinion that the security and interests of our nation demand that immediate steps be taken to halt the feelings of tension between Japan and the United States." It had investigated, the magazine reported, the statement's signatories. One of them, Ralph Townsend, had written "a number of rabidly anti-Chinese works." The Japanese Chamber of Commerce was reported to have given him "regular orders for quantity lots" of his pamphlets. His publications, it charged, were "used as propaganda material by key U.S. Fifth Columnists." James True, right-wing "dean of American 'anti-Semites,'" had praised him, asserting that he fulfilled "one of the nation's greatest needs." Moreover, the magazine added, Townsend was an employee of the America First organ *Scribner's Commentator*.

The magazine also criticized several other committee members, including Baxter, McKim, and Treat. Baxter was a New York resident and president of the Silk Research Bureau of America, the magazine explained, who has been "active for some time in spreading favorable publicity for Japan." His book, *Japan and America MUST Get Together* (sic—*Japan and America Must Work Together!*), was full of photographs produced by Japanese propaganda bureaus. "McKimm" [sic] regularly wrote for the *Japanese American Review*, which was published by a Japanese propaganda agency registered with the State Department (actually, the publisher of the journal was registered with State). Treat also had contributed to the *Japanese American Review*. A typical comment in one of his articles, the *Hour* complained, was, "I happen to be more concerned about the righteousness of our own conduct than about the shortcomings of Japan." These persons who "so eagerly" backed the committee's programs made clear the group's "true nature," the magazine concluded.[119]

Despite such criticism, Armstrong continued to work on the committee. On 18 October, he informed Libby that he would visit Washington soon and talk with him "privately." "Many letters of advice and proffered assistance have come in on the matter of Japanese-American Relations," he wrote, "but those most interested urge no hasty action." They feel that the conference should be "worked out with great care and with sufficient time to ensure its success." Undoubtedly referring to the crisis in Tokyo that culminated in the resignation of the Konoe cabinet on 16 October—something that might have convinced less tenacious people to abandon plans for an organization dedicated to averting war with Japan—Armstrong admitted that events of the past several days "present a very dark picture." Rather than give up, however, he insisted they "go forward." He closed by flattering Libby. "I wish all peace leaders could think as clearly and express themselves as forcefully as you have in the recent releases which have reached me!"[120]

In late October, Armstrong traveled to Boston and then New York. In Boston, he met with a former resident of Japan, Dr. G. Sidney Phelps, who promised to speak at the committee's conference.[121] Committee member Chamberlin had suggested him as one of those with "Oriental experience" who might be interested in Armstrong's statement. Phelps, Chamberlin continued, had served in the YMCA in Japan but was then retired.[122] While in Boston, Armstrong also met with Chamberlin as well as "others." He did not see Shaw, who was in Chicago.[123]

On 30 October, Armstrong attended a rally in New York where he heard speeches by Lindbergh, America First supporter and former diplomat John Cudahy, and isolationist Senator Burton K. Wheeler.[124] The following day, he suggested to Terasaki that a second meeting of the committee be held, this time in Washington, to discuss American–Japanese relations.[125] This proposal revealed that, according to one historian, he was an "energetic, impulsive, courageous, patriotic, aggressive, emotional, 'banty rooster' type."[126] Terasaki, for his part, pressured him to meet with Secretary of State Hull to "state as strongly as possible" the committee's goals. The result of such a meeting, Terasaki added, would determine whether the committee would survive or be terminated. Meanwhile, according to Ambassador Nomura, arrangements had been made for Armstrong to come to Washington soon to "carry out this program."[127]

Thus, the Japanese were fully cognizant of Armstrong's maneuvers. Nomura reported to Tokyo that the Missourian would keep in touch with the embassy and plan the organization of the Committee on Pacific Relations, whose objective would be promotion of friendly relations between Japan and the United States. "It will be promoted by Americans," Nomura wrote, "and will have . . . the appearance of being financed by American money (although a portion of the actual expense will be born [sic] by this office)." This revelation of Japanese funding for the committee was very dangerous for Armstrong and his fellow committee members, for it opened them to the charge of being unregistered foreign agents. The first meeting, the ambassador continued, had been held in New York, where Shaw, the former secretary of the YMCA in Japan, was named temporary chairman.[128]

Nomura did not mislead Tokyo on the strength of the proposed committee. At present, he wrote in his 1 November dispatch, it had no influential members. It was sponsored by Americans, though, and, with its establishment and expansion, "it is hoped that American public opinion can be made more friendly toward Japan." The embassy, he added, had instructed Armstrong to report to the State Department on the committee's activities.[129] By this time, Armstrong was no stranger around the department, having already visited once in June and twice in September. Following trips to Boston and New York, in November he paid two further calls to State. When he inquired at the department prior to his November visits, he discovered "things were more critical than supposed."[130] While in Washington, he also planned to attend a dinner at the Raleigh Hotel, an America First event at which former ambassador John Cudahy was to speak.

Although the Committee on Pacific Relations subsequently disappeared from Japanese diplomatic cables, Armstrong did not. On the eve of the war, there were two vulnerable points about him and his committee. One was the Japanese willingness to partly fund the committee, even though Armstrong was not registered as a foreign agent. The second was the presence on the committee of a man (Townsend) who was to end up in prison in 1942 because of his pro-Japanese activities and, in particular, official Japanese subsidy of the publication and circulation of his writings.

Meanwhile, despite the blow to his committee resulting from the prosecution of Townsend (see chapter 7), in the fall of 1941 Armstrong maintained a frenetic pace. In October, he traveled to Canada to collect data for an article on that country's aviation. In early November, he went to Canada again. It was a quick trip, for in a couple of days he was back in Springfield, where he delivered a pacifist speech titled "The Great Task for Intelligent People in the Years Ahead to Drive War from the World" to junior high school students.[131] That same day, he was scheduled to deliver a speech for America First in St. Louis.[132] On 14 and 15 November, he was back in Washington for the National Council for the Prevention of War meeting at the Quaker Meeting House.[133]

All that time, he was reporting to the Japanese embassy, which promptly forwarded the information he provided to Tokyo. He barely hinted to the acting chairman of his committee, however, that he was in touch with the Japanese. In an understatement, on 7 November he wrote Shaw that he had had "a most busy time." Hearing from both the State Department and the Japanese embassy how critical relations between the two countries were, he wrote, he "decided it was time to act, and *suggested at both places* [author's emphasis] that a small group of us meet with Sec. Hull as soon as possible, to lay before him the necessity for continuing the far eastern talks." Referring to Japanese special envoy Kurusu Saburo's imminent arrival in Washington, he wrote that now "there might be a chance to keep things open; otherwise, my guess is that the new cabinet [with Army General Tojo Hideki as prime minister] will explode into war."

He tried to line up support for a meeting with Hull. G. Sidney Phelps thought it a "good idea," Armstrong wrote, and would be in Washington on 14 November.[134] In a letter to Schumpeter on 8 November, he praised Phelps as being "very well informed on all the questions relating to the far east. He has been there most of the time since 1905. I put it up to him as to what we might do to have some influence upon the immediate crisis." Phelps "agreed it might do some good to see Mr. Hull." Since E. Stanley Jones, whom Armstrong described as an "outstanding religious leader" "very much interested in peace in the Orient," also was going to speak in Washington on 14 November, Phelps suggested to Armstrong that in the afternoon he, Armstrong, Shaw, Jones, and Schumpeter call on Hull. He also recommended Galen M. Fisher (1873–1955) be included.

As a result of Phelps's suggestion, Armstrong informed Shaw that he had gone to New Haven to see Fisher, "whom we had tried to find, you remember, and he also thought much of the idea, and gave me a number of names, whom he thought should be there [at the meeting with Hull]."[135] Fisher was visiting in New Haven, Armstrong wrote Schumpeter. "He said he knew the situation was critical. Said he would be glad to be present at the conference with Hull, unless something comes up in the next few days to prevent [it]." Meanwhile, Armstrong reported he was going to Cambridge (Massachusetts) to meet with Phelps.[136]

He had striven to identify and recruit for his committee people with deep knowledge of the Far East, which Fisher certainly possessed. He had served as a YMCA secretary in Japan for over twenty years (1897–1919). From 1921 until 1934 or 1935, he had been executive secretary of the Rockefeller Institute of Social and Religious Research in New York. As such, he had supported social service research projects in Asia and the United States.[137] In 1939, he was counselor on education and research of the American Council of the Institute of Pacific Relations. He took a personal interest in the Sino-Japanese War. That same year, he served as editor of a collection of articles titled *The Effects of the Sino-Japanese Conflict on American Educational and Philanthropic Enterprises in China*. Japanese mistreatment of those enterprises was a never-ending source of conflict between the State Department and the Japanese between 1937 and 1941.[138] In May 1941, he was editor of a short work titled *How the Oriental Press in San Francisco Has Treated Sino-Japanese War News*.[139]

In early November, Armstrong wrote Shaw that he had tried to visit some of the people Fisher had recommended, especially Raymond Leslie Buell, who had served as president of the Foreign Policy Association from 1933 to 1939. However, he was then out of town. A *Fortune* magazine editor and vehement interventionist, he had been Wendell Willkie's foreign policy advisor. He was a prolific international relations specialist, although he lacked any background on Japan or China. In 1940, he published a work titled *Isolated America*. Despite the title, his book made clear he was not an isolationist.[140] Meanwhile, Armstrong opined to Shaw that they did not need many people for the visit to Hull; Shaw, Schumpeter, Phelps, Libby, Fisher, and "one or two others" would be enough. In the meantime, he looked forward to seeing Shaw in Washington. "Let us do this thing [meet with Hull], and then make plans for a continuing piece of work," probably the committee's Washington conference.[141]

In early November, Armstrong wrote Schumpeter, who, along with Libby and Shaw, was his most faithful committee member and correspondent. This was his first letter to her since he had sent his report on the committee to her a month earlier. Clearly, he was disturbed at the state of Japanese–American relations. He had a "most interesting trip east recently," he reported, and was sorry he had not been able to visit her. In a first reference to his Japanese contacts in his correspondence with her, he divulged that he had "called on some of my friends at the Japanese Embassy and found that the situation is very critical." He unburdened himself, repeating much of what he had written the day before to Shaw. "I was so troubled about it all," he confessed, "that I went to Boston to see Mr. Phelps, and, if possible, see Mr. Shaw and Mr. Chamberlin." He had succeeded in calling on Phelps, Chamberlin, and Galen Fisher, he reported, but Shaw was in Chicago and did not plan to return east until after the National Council for the Prevention of War meeting in Washington in mid-November. Therefore, he had wired Shaw to solicit his views regarding what a delegation to Hull should say to "impress him with our desire for the government to keep the talks going with Japan, particularly since the new envoy [Kurusu] is coming soon."

He then got to the real point of his letter. "I do want you to be with us!" He had been in New York but had been unable to see her because he had to leave for "an engagement here in Missouri." Hoping to get her to join them in the visit to Hull, he told her he had the "promise of another $100, which I wanted to divide with those who can come, to help pay the expenses. I think $15 of it could be spared for you, if you desire some help." He also wrote he might be able to get someone in Washington to pay for their hotel. "We badly need some money," lamented Armstrong, "and shall have to have some." "I have been out considerable money myself," he added, "as I know we all have, but perhaps we can get some budget underwritten soon."

Armstrong went on to explain that they would visit Hull "as individuals" and not as "an official action by our committee, as there would not be time for that by Friday." However, their committee might then join in and implement "some permanent sort of project, if we can avoid war for the next several weeks." He then invited Schumpeter to come to Washington on 14 November. If she arrived on 13 November, he added, "Some of us will be there for that night and do some planning." He was "quite sure" Shaw and Phelps and perhaps Fisher would be present. In addition, he had invited Dr. William C. Johnstone of George Washington University to join them. He would leave for Washington—probably from Springfield—on 11 November, Armstrong concluded, and stay at the YMCA in Washington.[142]

On the evening of 13 November, Armstrong planned to meet "our friends who are here" (quoted in an FBI wiretap transcript), who were perusing a lot of material. The following morning (14 November), he was going to attend a "series of conferences," probably a reference to the National Council for the Prevention of War meetings.[143] On 14 November, Armstrong and Shaw prepared a letter that they would deliver the next day to Secretary Hull, "on behalf of numerous of our friends who have contributed to its ideas and who are especially interested in problems in the far east," to express "opinions and suggestions relative to our relations with Japan." They wished "only to be of any assistance possible." Their letter reflected the approach of Armstrong's earlier mentor, the late Dean Walter Williams, to the possibility of a Japanese–American war. They realized that relations in the Far East were "extremely difficult," they wrote, but they felt that "our [Japan's and the United States'] problems need not lead to armed conflict between our country and Japan, providing an intelligent effort is made on the part of our citizens to understand them." They then proposed five measures for Hull's consideration. Perhaps owing to the recent charges accusing committee member

Townsend of being a Japanese agent, they took a fairly hard line with Japan and eschewed the pro-Japan, anti-China stance of some Japanese apologists.

Writing three weeks before Pearl Harbor, they recognized that Japan's aggressive expansion in Asia—the July move into southern Indochina that brought on the U.S. embargo and freeze—was part of the problem. Their first proposal was that negotiations with Japan should continue, "providing that Japan agree to refrain from any further military or other action that might aggravate the situation during the period of the discussion." Second, because U.S. "restrictive measures" had created the danger of a war that would be "calamitous" to both countries, they urged negotiations for the resumption of trade "on a normal basis" begin. This "should be contingent," however, "upon Japan's willingness to cooperate in reasonable measures to restore peace in China and recognition of Chinese territorial sovereignty." "An indication of this," they added, "would be a token withdrawal of troops."

Having made demands of Japan, they then described its rewards for refraining from further aggression and softening its China policy. "As a gesture of our willingness to recognize certain fundamental need on the part of Japan," they wrote, "the export of a reasonable amount of materials essential to normal Japanese industrial activity should be allowed." Acknowledging the Japanese fear of communism,[144] they called on the U.S. government to "promise the use of its good offices to encourage" the Soviet Union's observance of its April 1941 "non-aggression pact" (Neutrality Pact) with Japan. Their argument could be criticized as "pro-Japan," for after flirting with the idea of violating the Neutrality Pact and attacking the Soviet Union following Germany's invasion of that country in June, by early September the Japanese had postponed any military action against the Soviets until at least the spring of 1942. The reason was that Japan had decided to move south instead of north in Asia, which led to the seizure of southern Indochina in July.[145] Finally, Armstrong and Shaw called for a meeting of all countries with interests in the Pacific to take up the military, economic, and political problems of the region.[146]

Thus prepared, the next day (15 November), Armstrong and Shaw called on State's William Langdon, whom Armstrong already knew from their meeting six weeks earlier. Langdon summoned Cecil W. Gray—Hull's assistant and "gatekeeper," whom Hull described as a "marvel of vigilance, efficiency, loyalty and all equipment for loyal service"—whom Armstrong claimed he had "known for some years." Gray explained that the secretary, according to Armstrong, "would be glad" if Shaw and Armstrong met with Raymond Mackay, assistant chief, Far Eastern Division, instead of him.[147]

When Shaw and Armstrong met with Mackay, Phelps, Fisher, Johnstone, and Schumpeter were absent from their delegation. The day before, Schumpeter had wired that she had just received his 8 November letter with the invitation and was "so sorry not to be with you."[148] Four days later, she wrote

Armstrong that she was working on an article for the *Austro-Asiatic Bulletin* in Melbourne titled "Is Japan's Industry Strong Enough for a Pacific War?" The following evening, she was scheduled to speak on Hartford radio (WTIC) on the topic "Will the United States and Japan Remain at Peace?" Like Armstrong, she was worried about an imminent war with Japan.

> I suppose the next few days will decide whether . . . there is any use in our going on with our effort to improve American-Japanese relations. I am afraid that the issue of peace or war in the Pacific depends almost entirely on how much the Administration wants to get into war at this time. It is so much easier to get the country into a war with Japan in the beginning. I sincerely hope that it can be avoided but I really think that the chances are at least 50-50 in favor of war.[149]

While Schumpeter worried about war, in the 15 November meeting with Mackay, Armstrong stated that he and Shaw, "on behalf of numerous friends," had written Hull the previous day proposing, in Mackay's summary, "certain views and suggestions looking toward a peaceful solution of Pacific problems." During the meeting, Shaw embarked on a twenty-minute, "rambling, repetitious" statement on the Far Eastern situation. He argued that, thanks to Western influence, Japan wanted a high standard of living, but because it lacked the means to achieve it was, in Mackay's summary, "now greatly discontented." Since it had learned "modern ways" primarily from the United States, Shaw continued, "the American people are in some sense responsible for the existing situation." Finally, he asserted that it would be "preferable" to attain a peaceful solution, rather than resort to war, to resolve Japanese–American problems.

Mackay gave the two men a "diplomatic" response. He assured Shaw that the U.S. government "had given and would continue to give constant and searching consideration to the question of our relations with Japan and that it would, as in the past, make every appropriate effort to attain by peaceful means a just and enduring solution of Pacific problems." The two men, he concluded, "seemed entirely satisfied" with his "general statement" and thanked him for the opportunity to communicate their views before they took their leave.[150]

Armstrong immediately disclosed the meeting to Terasaki at the Japanese embassy. His delegation, he reported, was received "most cordially" that morning at the office of Mackay, Maxwell Hamilton's associate in the Division of Far Eastern Affairs. They spent almost an hour discussing their suggestions with him and planning "future contacts and cooperation." They then went to Hull's office and handed a copy of their suggestions to Gray, his secretary, as Hull had requested, and discussed "matters briefly with him." Three weeks before Pearl Harbor dashed all hopes for peace in the Pacific, Armstrong cheerfully informed the Japanese that he was "happy to report that there was the best of reaction from Mr. Mackay, from Mr. Gray, and from Mr. Langdon as well, whom Mr. Shaw and I went to see briefly."

On the back of a copy of his letter to the embassy, he jotted two lists, which probably had been typed and given to State as the delegation's suggestions. To say Mackay was in "full agreement" with them was Armstrong's hearing what he wanted to hear. The first list, titled "Summary of Immediate Suggestions," called for "unfreezing" money and credits, restoration of trade relations "at least upon some temporary or working basis," and restoring the flow of oil to Japan. The second list, titled "For Long-Time Program," called for Japan to have access to raw materials or "the 'open door' policy" for Japan, recognition of Manchuria (Manchukuo), permanent trade relations, the guarantee of Japan's rights to trade in China, and a guarantee "against *communism* [Armstrong's emphasis] from Russia or China." All Japan had to do in return was to recognize the territorial integrity of China, which Japan, as a signatory of the 1922 Nine-Power Pact, had already acknowledged but violated with its attacks first on Manchuria and then on China proper (although it did not publicly repudiate the pact). Mackay, Armstrong added, "seemed in full agreement" with these "proposals."[151]

Perhaps the key word was "seemed." It must have been painful for Mackay to sit and listen to these amateurs' "suggestions." They would have given the Japanese everything they wanted, at a cost of promising something they had already agreed to in the 1922 Nine-Power Pact, only to violate repeatedly in their attacks on China. In short, Armstrong and the Committee on Pacific Relations supported Japanese demands in the negotiations taking place between the two governments. The Japanese could point to Armstrong and his colleagues and argue that prominent Americans wanted the same things Japan was demanding, and hence those demands must be reasonable. As usual, no one consulted the Chinese, who would have been outraged—as Chinese Ambassador Hu Shi was with E. Stanley Jones[152]—if they had known what the Committee on Pacific Relations was proposing for their country. In any event, in Armstrong's telling, Mackay simply pointed out that "certain things would be demanded of Japan, in return for which a program would be offered." With Japanese special envoy Kurusu Saburo due to arrive in Washington the same day (15 November) for what ended up being last-ditch efforts for peace between the two countries, Mackay, according to Armstrong, believed "some of it [the "program"] depended upon what the new Japanese envoy might convey from his government."

Armstrong and Shaw also informed Mackay of the current and future plans of the Committee on Pacific Relations.[153] Although the State official did not mention the committee in his relatively terse memorandum on the meeting, Shaw and Armstrong handed over what Mackay vaguely referred to as "certain relevant papers." In addition to a copy of Shaw's and Armstrong's 14 November letter to Hull, they gave Mackay a copy of Armstrong's 4

October report on the intention to formally establish a Committee on Pacific Relations, a copy of his group's 22 September statement laying out their reasons for creating the committee, and a copy of the program of the National Council for the Prevention of War conference being held on 14 and 15 November.[154] Although Armstrong had written Libby in October that he might miss the conference, he attended after all.[155]

Armstrong and Shaw also informed Mackay that "other friends," "Dr. [E. Raymond?] Wilson" and "Mr. [G. Sidney] Phelps" especially,[156] would accompany them in more "personal" visits to the State Department "soon" and that "a wider program was being prepared." In addition, the delegation left with Mackay a roster of the committee as well as the names of those who had participated in the "deliberations of the last few days." They invited Mackay or Hull to contact any of them "for further talks at any time." Armstrong was, as ever, optimistic. "On the whole," he wrote, "I am personally encouraged that considerable good might be done within the immediate future."[157]

The day after the National Council for the Prevention of War conference ended, Armstrong reported that he had engaged several persons to participate in a radio debate on Japan. That same day (16 November), he and Shaw worked all evening on material for the broadcast.[158] The following day, Armstrong scheduled the broadcast, to be carried on 107 stations, for 23 November, and invited two speakers, Shaw and Congressman Frederick C. Smith of Ohio.[159]

Meanwhile, on 17 November, two days after Armstrong met with Mackay, Coordinator of Information (the predecessor to OSS) William J. Donovan wrote the State Department to request lists of American or European propaganda agents working for the Japanese. Fletcher Warren of the Division of Foreign Activity Correlation at State asked George Atcheson Jr. of the Division of Far Eastern Affairs whether his branch could supply any of the information Donovan sought. Among the Americans and Canadians Atcheson named was Ralph Townsend. Atcheson described him as a former Foreign Service officer who was "understood to write for *Scribner's Commentator*." He was one of those, Atcheson wrote, who had engaged in or been suspected of engaging in "propaganda or publicity work favorable to the Japanese Government." On 1 December, the acting chief of State's Division of Foreign Activity Correlation sent Donovan two lists, which included both Townsend and Armstrong.[160]

The day of the radio broadcast, Armstrong traveled to New York "to work." The next day, Shaw stayed at the same New York hotel as Armstrong. On 25 November, the latter returned to Washington.[161] The following day (26 November), Shaw resigned from the Committee on Pacific Relations. He forwarded his letter of resignation, he wrote Armstrong, "in harmony with our phone conversation of last evening." The National Council for the Prevention of War office would send a news release to the two newspapers that published the original story about the committee that mentioned his name. "They may not bother to use it," he added wryly. He could not depart without offering Armstrong some final words of advice regarding the committee. It had "never been really organized," he wrote, but was simply composed of those who signed the statement. Armstrong should start all over again, he advised, and select those he wanted and those who would permit their names to be cited as members. He also urged Armstrong to change the committee's name. That would avoid it being confused with the Institute of Pacific Relations, which was "of a different nature."

He also was concerned about their 15 November meeting at the State Department. As they had given Mackay a copy of the committee statement identifying Shaw as acting chairman, he explained to Armstrong, he was sending the State official a copy of his resignation letter "just for his information." He had seen Mackay that week and made clear to him that in their earlier letter to Hull, they had written as "interested individuals." He had explained to Mackay there had been no time to circulate the letter to other members of the committee. Moreover, he told the State official that the committee had not progressed sufficiently to have "any Executive committee that might be authorized to speak for the group."

He made clear to Armstrong that dropping out of the committee did not mean he was abandoning his efforts for peace in the Far East. The day before, he had a "very worthwhile" meeting with Senator Elbert D. Thomas (D-Utah) on the Far Eastern situation. Thomas had served as a Mormon missionary to Japan from 1907 to 1912 and published a book in Japanese. He also was a member of the Chinese Political and Social Science Association and had published a work titled *Chinese Political Thought* (1927). From 1933 until 1951, he served in the U.S. Senate.[162]

Shaw also informed Armstrong that he had a "very good talk" with former diplomat William Castle. That evening, Shaw was going to speak at the club of Congressman Frederick Smith, who also was opposed to war with Japan. Finally, he was going to call on E. Stanley Jones when the evangelist returned to Washington the following day. In closing, he told Armstrong that since he had been traveling for almost a month, it was time to return to work in Melrose.[163]

"As you know," Shaw wrote in his formal letter of resignation, "it was with much reluctance that I consented to let my name be used as 'acting chairman' of the group seeking to organize a Committee on Pacific Relations, both because I felt that there were others much better qualified than I for this position, and because I feared that owing to other duties I could not give it the time and effort needed to complete the organization of a representative committee." He had delayed submitting his resignation to Armstrong and the "other members of the group interested" in hopes someone "better qualified" might be "enlisted." However, "in justice to you and the others, as well as to myself, I should not try to continue in the capacity of 'acting chairman' and so I send you my resignation to be effective as of today."

He assured Armstrong he was in "hearty sympathy" with the group's purpose, "the promotion of better understanding between America and Japan and the avoidance, if possible, of any outbreak of hostilities between these two countries which have been friends and allies for nearly ninety years." Over that period, he added, the United States had achieved great influence on Japanese life and thought. "It would be a real calamity for all concerned," he warned, "if in the strain of the present complex and critical situation we should allow ourselves to take hasty steps which could cause us to lose that influence." They could "render much greater service to the constructive solution of the problems of the far east by an understanding, sympathetic, albeit a sometimes firm, friendship with all the peoples in that troubled area than we could by allowing ourselves to be maneuvered into the position of an actual or threatened participant in that tragic conflict [the Sino-Japanese War]."[164] Shaw's resignation letter was followed by a National Council for the Prevention of War news release in Washington that closely followed the text of the letter.[165]

Armstrong later told the FBI that he was in Washington on Saturday, 29 November. He was obviously mistaken, though, when he claimed he "attended" a radio broadcast on the "Japanese question" that featured Shaw, Congressmen Smith of Ohio and Bertrand W. Gearhart of California, and Robert Aura Smith of the *New York Times*.[166] The broadcast, titled "What Should Be Our Policy toward Japan," took place on 23 November, with Shaw—still described as acting chairman of the Committee on Pacific Relations—one of the four debaters. Shaw's statements must have persuaded some that the committee was a pro-Japan organization. If the Japanese listened, they would have been pleased with his defense of the Japanese side of the dispute between the two countries. At such a tense time in American history, with the fate of peace between Japan and America hanging in the balance, Shaw calmly declared "we should be factual, not emotional." He praised the Japanese for their ninety years of progress, calling them "capable, industrious, dynamic, progressive and patriotic." They were "justly proud of their own Oriental culture and long-honored history," he noted, and had "moved faster than any other eastern people in adopting western ways." It was unfair to tie them to an "unjust status quo" in the Pacific that was the result of British, French, and American aggression. Japan, he declared, had not "committed anywhere near the aggressions that Great Britain has." In addition, he concluded, "when Japan sought to meet her growing but legitimate needs through the regular channels of trade and commerce, she found herself repressed and obstructed by the previous aggressors, now the great possessors, Britain, France, Russia and America."[167]

Following the 7 December Japanese attack on Pearl Harbor, Armstrong's Committee on Pacific Relations vanished, destroyed by events in the world of action. He immediately canceled a meeting scheduled for Boston as well as the committee's proposed conference in Washington.[168] A week later, he wrote to Schumpeter that he had not had a chance to acknowledge her 18 November letter, and "since that time much has happened! Or am I telling you?" He went on to console her as well as himself. "Of course, we did all we could, and have that satisfaction. I put a tremendous lot of time and effort and expense into it and am only sorry that I failed." He stubbornly refused to give up, though. "As soon as I think the country is ready for it, I am going to try to interest a number of my friends in the formation of a national committee for a just and lasting peace. That will give us a chance to go ahead with our research at least."[169] In the meantime, he penned a note of appreciation to the State Department. "Seems incredible," he wrote, "that affairs could move so swiftly and tragically after all the efforts of your department and of so many of us interested in peace in the Pacific. Thanks for your kindnesses to us. Best regards to Mr. Hull and others of your associates in this difficult time."[170]

His old friend Charles Boss had not given up either. In a letter to Armstrong on Ministers' No War Committee stationery five days after Pearl Harbor, he reported that groups were planning to convene over the following four or five days in New York, Chicago, and perhaps other places to "discuss what churchmen should do in the light of the present situation." He tried to encourage Armstrong. "The fellowship of all who have worked in the cause of peace," he wrote, "will grow stronger under the tests through which we must go."[171]

NOTES

1. Orland Kay Armstrong to [W. Forbes] Webber, [Kansas City Division, FBI], 6 March 1942, Orland Kay Armstrong (1893–1987) Papers, 1912–1987 (C4056), State Historical Society of Missouri, Manuscript Collection, Columbia, MO; Armstrong, Springfield, MO, to Dear Friend, 4 October 1941, National Council for the Prevention of War (hereafter NCPW), reel 41: 223 (box 280).

2. Armstrong, Atlanta, GA, to Mr. Terasaki, Japanese Embassy, Washington, DC, 23 June 1941, Armstrong Papers; David M. Kennedy, *Freedom from Fear: The American People in Depression and War, 1929–1945* (New York: Oxford University Press, 1999), 346.

3. Armstrong to the Honorable Mr. Terasaki, Japanese Embassy, Washington, DC, 27 June 1941, Armstrong Papers.

4. Armstrong to the Honorable Hidenari Terasaki, 12 July 1941, Armstrong Papers.

5. Armstrong to Elizabeth Boody Schumpeter, 12 July 1941, Armstrong Papers.

6. Schumpeter, Taconic, CT, to Armstrong, 16 July 1941, Armstrong Papers.

7. Earl Browder, *The Decline of the Left Wing* (Yonkers, NY: self-published, 1948); Earl Browder, *Chinese Lessons for American Marxists* (Yonkers, NY: self-published, 1949).

8. [Armstrong] to Mr. Terasaki, [17 July 1941], Armstrong Papers.

9. "a." [Armstrong] to Mr. Terasaki, 17 July 1941, Armstrong Papers; Armstrong to Dear Friend, 4 October 1941.

10. Schumpeter to Armstrong, 18 July 1941, Armstrong Papers.
11. Richard R. Lingeman, *Don't You Know There's a War On? The American Home Front, 1941–1945* (New York: G.P. Putnam's Sons, 1970; Perigee Books, 1980), 273.
12. Armstrong to Schumpeter, 17 August 1941, Armstrong Papers; Kennedy, *Freedom from Fear*, 505, 510.
13. Armstrong to Schumpeter, 17 August 1941.
14. Schumpeter, Seal Harbor, ME, to Armstrong, 23 August 1941, Armstrong Papers.
15. Armstrong to Webber, 6 March 1942.
16. Warren I. Cohen, "The Role of Private Groups in the United States," in *Pearl Harbor as History: American-Japanese Relations, 1931–1941,* ed. Dorothy Borg and Shumpei Okamoto (New York: Columbia University Press, 1973), 452–53.
17. Western Union telegram to H. Terasaki, 8 September 1941, Terasaki Hidenari FBI File No. 65-HQ-37232, FOIA.
18. Armstrong to Webber, 6 March 1942.
19. Armstrong to Webber, 6 March 1942.
20. Wayne S. Cole, *America First: The Battle against Intervention in World War II* (Madison: University of Wisconsin Press, 1953), 159.
21. Armstrong to Terasaki, 15 September 1941, Armstrong Papers; Armstrong to Dear Friend, 4 October 1941.
22. Armstrong to Paul Hutchinson, *Christian Century*, Chicago, IL, 15 September 1941, Armstrong Papers. There is no evidence in Armstrong's papers that Hutchinson replied to his letter.
23. Armstrong to Ralph Townsend, C/O *Scribner's Commentator*, Lake Geneva, WI, 12 September 1941, Armstrong Papers; Lynne Olson, *Those Angry Days: Roosevelt, Lindbergh, and America's Fight over World War II, 1939–1941* (New York: Random House, 2013), 233–34.
24. Armstrong to Ralph Townsend, C/O *Scribner's Commentator*, Lake Geneva, WI, 12 September 1941; Charles A. Lindbergh, *The Wartime Journals of Charles A. Lindbergh* (New York: Harcourt Brace Jovanovich, 1970), 484n246; Wayne S. Cole, *Roosevelt and the Isolationists* (Lincoln: University of Nebraska Press, 1983), 380. Following the war, Benton served in the State Department (1945–1947) before becoming a Democratic senator from Connecticut (1949–1953). Lindbergh, *Wartime Journals*, 484n246.
25. Townsend to Armstrong, 15 September 1941, Armstrong Papers.
26. Armstrong, Chicago, to Mr. Terasaki, 11 September 1941; Armstrong to Mr. Terasaki, 15 September 1941, Armstrong Papers.
27. Armstrong to Dear Friend, 4 October 1941; Mary Walters Brooks (Mrs. Carlyle), Gainesville, FL, to Armstrong, Springfield, MO, 26 August 1941, Armstrong Papers. Her husband was an assistant at the same church.
28. Armstrong to Terasaki, 15 September 1941.
29. Brooks to Armstrong, 26 August 1941.
30. Donald J. Friedman, *The Road from Isolation: The Campaign of the American Committee for Non-participation in Japanese Aggression, 1938–1941* (Cambridge, MA: Harvard University Press, 1968), 90.
31. Brooks to Armstrong, 26 August 1941.
32. Armstrong to Terasaki, 15 September 1941.
33. Armstrong, Springfield, MO, to William Baxter, New York, 8 September 1941, Armstrong Papers.
34. Armstrong to Schumpeter, 17 September 1941, Armstrong Papers; Schumpeter, telegram to Armstrong, 8 September 1941, Armstrong Papers.
35. Armstrong to Schumpeter, 17 September 1941.
36. Schumpeter to Armstrong, 19 September 1941, Armstrong Papers.
37. Armstrong to Griswold, New Haven, CT, 8 September 1941, Armstrong Papers.
38. Memo of conversation between William R. Langdon, Division of Far Eastern Affairs, and Armstrong, 30 September 1941, Department of State, 740.0011 Pacific War/553, National Archives.

39. Armstrong to Griswold, 11 October 1941, Alfred Whitney Griswold Papers (MS 255), Manuscripts and Archives, Yale University Library, New Haven, CT.

40. Armstrong to Dr. [Paul H.] Clyde, 12 September 1941, Armstrong Papers.

41. Clyde, Duke University, Durham, NC, to Armstrong, Woodstock Hotel, New York, 25 September 1941, Armstrong Papers.

42. Warren I. Cohen, *The Chinese Connection: Roger S. Greene, Thomas W. Lamont, George Sokolsky, and American-East Asian Relations* (New York: Columbia University Press, 1978), 294.

43. Memo of conversation between Langdon and Armstrong, 30 September 1941.

44. Armstrong to Everett W. Frazar, New York, 8 September 1941; Armstrong to Frazar, 11 October 1941, Armstrong Papers.

45. Armstrong to General James G. Harbord, Chairman, National Broadcasting Co., RCA Building, New York, 8 September 1941, Armstrong Papers.

46. Harbord to Armstrong, 15 September 1941, Armstrong Papers. Harbord may have referred to Roosevelt's fireside chat on 11 September regarding the German sinking in the Atlantic of the U.S. destroyer *Greer*.

47. Armstrong to William Henry Chamberlin, Cambridge, MA, 8 September 1941, Armstrong Papers.

48. Armstrong to "My dear friend Mr. Chamberlin," 15 September 1941, Armstrong Papers.

49. Schumpeter to Armstrong, 23 August 1941.

50. Chamberlin, Halifax, Nova Scotia, Canada, to Armstrong, 17 September 1941, Armstrong Papers.

51. Chamberlin to Armstrong, Springfield, MO, 24 June 1941, Armstrong Papers.

52. Armstrong to Dr. Payson Treat, Department of Oriental History, Leland Stanford University, Palo Alto, CA, 13 September 1941, Armstrong Papers.

53. Treat to Armstrong, 16 September 1941, Armstrong Papers.

54. Armstrong to "Dear friend Charles [F. Boss Jr.]," 13 September 1941, Armstrong Papers.

55. Cohen, "Role of Private Groups in the United States," 425, 430, 445; Cole, *America First*, 90.

56. Armstrong to Frederick J. Libby, NCPW, Washington, DC, 15 September 1941, Armstrong Papers. A copy of this letter may also be found in the NCPW archives: Armstrong to Libby, 15 September 1941, NCPW, reel 41: 223 (box 280).

57. Libby to Armstrong, Woodstock Hotel, New York, 19 September 1941, NCPW, reel 41: 223 (box 280). A copy may also be found in the Armstrong Papers.

58. Armstrong to Dr. E. Stanley Jones, Clifton Springs, NY, 16 September 1941, Armstrong Papers; "Kirby Page," *Marquis Who's Who on the Web* (accessed 14 July 2006).

59. Armstrong to Dr. E. Stanley Jones, 16 September 1941; Charles Bright and Joseph W. Ho, eds., *War and Occupation in China: The Letters of an American Missionary from Hangzhou, 1937–1938* (Lanham, MD: Rowman & Littlefield, 2017), 121n220. Armstrong was referring to Jones's article "America United—on What Level?," *Christian Century* 58, no. 38 (1941): 1139–41.

60. Jones, Rochester, NY, to "My dear Doctor [*sic*] Armstrong," 23 September 1941, Armstrong Papers.

61. Jones to Armstrong, 30 September 1941, Armstrong Papers.

62. Armstrong to Webber, 6 March 1942; Armstrong to Dear Friend, 4 October 1941; "And So Forth," *Christian Century* 58, no. 32 (1941): 988.

63. Armstrong to Webber, 6 March 1942. In this report to the FBI, Armstrong included a copy of that letter along with "other material." Armstrong probably was referring to the 4 October circular letter he sent after he returned to Springfield (see below).

64. Nomura Kichisaburo, Washington, DC, to Tokyo, dispatch no. 1029, 1 November 1941, RG 457, Frank Schuler Papers, FDR Library, Hyde Park, NY; A. Scott Berg, *Lindbergh* (New York: G.P. Putnam's Sons, 1998), 422.

65. "New Group Seeks U.S.-Japan Amity," *New York World-Telegram*, 25 September 1941, 7.

66. Nomura to Tokyo, 1 November 1941.

67. Nomura Kichisaburo, "Diary of Kichisaburo Nomura, June–December 1941," in *The Pacific War Papers: Japanese Documents of World War II*, ed. Donald M. Goldstein and Katherine V. Dillon (Washington, DC: Potomac Books, 2004), 199; Susan Dunn, *1940: F.D.R., Willkie, Lindbergh, and Hitler—the Election amid the Storm* (New Haven, CT: Yale University Press, 2013), 60.

68. Justus D. Doenecke, "Explaining the Antiwar Movement, 1939–1941: The Next Assignment," *Journal of Libertarian Studies* 8, no. 1 (1986): 141. Carter coauthored an isolationist diatribe, which, by 1938, was in its third printing. Boake Carter and Thomas H. Healey, *Why Meddle in the Orient: Facts, Figures, Fictions, and Follies* (New York: Dodge, 1938).

69. Doenecke, "Explaining the Antiwar Movement," 160.

70. Armstrong to Mark R. Shaw, 7 October 1941, Armstrong Papers.

71. Mark Shaw to Armstrong, 9 October 1941, Armstrong Papers. "Possibilities in this line . . . ," Shaw added, but the remainder of the text is missing in the archives copy.

72. Robert W. Barnett, American Council, Institute of Pacific Relations (hereafter IPR), to Mark R. Shaw, Melrose, MA, 1 October 1941, NCPW, reel 41: 116 (box 129). The committee members listed by Barnett included Armstrong, Townsend, Hutchinson, Libby, Chamberlin, and Treat.

73. Shaw to Armstrong, 9 October 1941.

74. Armstrong to "My dear friend Terry [Terasaki Hidenari]," 20 October 1941, Armstrong Papers.

75. Cohen, "Role of Private Groups in the United States, " 453; memo of conversation between Langdon and Armstrong, 30 September 1941.

76. Armstrong to Webber, 6 March 1942.

77. Charles [F. Boss Jr.], executive secretary, Commission of World Peace of the Methodist Church, to Armstrong, 30 September 1941, Armstrong Papers.

78. Memo of conversation between Langdon and Armstrong, 30 September 1941.

79. Doenecke, "Explaining the Antiwar Movement," 160.

80. Memo of conversation between Langdon and Armstrong, 30 September 1941.

81. "Robert L. Flowers, Duke Ex-President," *NYT*, 25 August 1951, 9. For a biographical sketch of Flowers (1870–1951), see *Marquis Who's Who on the Web* (accessed 18 August 2005).

82. Memo of conversation between Langdon and Armstrong, 30 September 1941. Probably drawing on the above State Department memo, a historian described Griswold as a member in 1941 of the Committee on Pacific Relations. Cohen, *Chinese Connection*, 297.

83. A noted U.S. historian described Clyde as a member of the Committee on Pacific Relations, which supported appeasement of Japan, in 1941. Cohen, *Chinese Connection*, 296. He probably reached that conclusion, though, on the basis of Langdon's memo, which he cited. A search of the Paul Hibbet Clyde and Mary (Kestler) Clyde Papers in Duke University's Rare Book, Manuscript, and Special Collections Library yielded no evidence of Clyde's membership in the committee. Investigation of the Robert L. Flowers Papers (boxes 15 and 16) at Duke University's Archives, Perkins Library, also failed to unearth any evidence of his participation in the committee. Therefore, it is certain Armstrong did not have the two men's permission to identify them as members of his Committee on Pacific Relation.

84. Memo of conversation between Langdon and Armstrong, 30 September 1941. On Hedges, see Ernest R. May, "U.S. Press Coverage of Japan, 1931–1941," in *Pearl Harbor as History : American-Japanese Relations, 1931–1941*, ed. Dorothy Borg and Shumpei Okamoto (New York: Columbia University Press, 1973), 514–17, 519–20, 525, 530.

85. Armstrong to Dear Friend, 4 October 1941.

86. Armstrong to Dear Friend, 4 October 1941.

87. Armstrong to Shaw, 7 October 1941.

88. Armstrong to Shaw, 9 October 1941, Armstrong Papers.

89. Armstrong to My Dear Friend Dr. [John Cole] McKim, 7 October 1941, Armstrong Papers.

90. Armstrong to Reverend John Cole McKim, Peekskill, NY, 9 October 1941, Armstrong Papers.

91. Armstrong to Schumpeter, 7 October 1941, Armstrong Papers.

92. Armstrong to Schumpeter, 9 October 1941, Armstrong Papers.
93. Shaw to Armstrong, 9 October 1941; Berg, *Lindbergh*, 411, 473; Lindbergh, *Wartime Journals*, 475n241, 556.
94. Following the war—coincidentally, on the fourth anniversary of the Pearl Harbor attack—Armstrong wrote Libby to subscribe to this magazine. Armstrong, Springfield, MO, to Libby, Washington, DC, 7 December 1945, NCPW, reel 41: 223 (box 280). In his reply, Libby asked Armstrong to "be sure to give me a ring always when [you're] in Washington." Libby to Armstrong, 4 January 1946, NCPW, reel 41: 223 (box 280).
95. Armstrong to Libby, 9 October 1941, NCPW, reel 41: 223 (box 280). There is a copy of this letter in the Armstrong Papers.
96. Armstrong to Libby, 9 October 1941.
97. Libby to Armstrong, 13 October 1941, Armstrong Papers.
98. Armstrong to Mary [Walters Brooks], 9 October 1941, Armstrong Papers.
99. Armstrong to Dr. T. T. Brumbaugh, Columbus, OH, 9 October 1941, Armstrong Papers.
100. Armstrong to Treat, 9 October 1941, Armstrong Papers.
101. Armstrong to Paul Hutchinson, Associate Editor, *Christian Century*, Chicago, IL, 9 October 1941, Armstrong Papers.
102. Armstrong to Townsend, 9 October 1941, Armstrong Papers.
103. Armstrong to E. Stanley Jones, 13 October 1941, Armstrong Papers.
104. Armstrong to Chamberlin, 9 October 1941, Armstrong Papers.
105. Shaw to Armstrong, 9 October 1941.
106. Armstrong to Clyde, 9 October 1941, Armstrong Papers.
107. Armstrong to Baxter, 11 October 1941, Armstrong Papers.
108. Armstrong to Frazar, 11 October 1941.
109. Armstrong to Harbord, 11 October 1941, Armstrong Papers.
110. Harbord to Armstrong, 22 October 1941, Armstrong Papers.
111. Schumpeter to Armstrong, 11 October 1941, Armstrong Papers; May, "U.S. Press Coverage of Japan," 525. On Byas, see May, "U.S. Press Coverage of Japan," 514–17, 519–20, 524–26.
112. Schumpeter to Armstrong, 14 October 1941, Armstrong Papers.
113. Armstrong to Terasaki, 20 October 1941.
114. Berg, *Lindbergh*, 422.
115. Armstrong to Terasaki, 20 October 1941. Several lines and perhaps even a third page are missing from the original letter in the Armstrong Papers. John C. Konzal, Manuscript Specialist, State Historical Society of Missouri, Manuscript Collection, Columbia, MO, to author, 13 October 2005.
116. Shaw to Armstrong, 21 October 1941, Armstrong Papers.
117. Armstrong to Webber, 6 March 1942.
118. Shaw to Armstrong, 27 October 1941, Armstrong Papers.
119. "Pro-Japanese Agency Established," *Hour*, no. 117, 25 October 1941, 800.20211/605, PS/VH Confidential File, decimal file 1940-44, RG 84, National Archives.
120. Armstrong to Libby, 18 October 1941, NCPW, reel 41: 223 (box 280).
121. Armstrong, New York, to Shaw, 7 [November 1941], Armstrong Papers; Armstrong to Webber, 6 March 1942.
122. Chamberlin to Armstrong, 24 June 1941.
123. Armstrong to Shaw, 7 [November 1941]; Armstrong to Webber, 6 March 1942.
124. Armstrong to Shaw, 7 [November 1941]. For a brief summary of Lindbergh's speech, see Cole, *Charles A. Lindbergh*, 191–92.
125. Nomura to Tokyo, 1 November 1941. The version of this message published in U.S. Department of Defense, *The "Magic" Background of Pearl Harbor* (Washington, DC: Government Printing Office, 1978), 4:126–27, A-185, omitted Armstrong's and Shaw's names.
126. Cole, *Charles A. Lindbergh*, 112.
127. Nomura to Tokyo, 1 November 1941.
128. Nomura to Tokyo, 1 November 1941; U.S. Department of Defense, *"Magic" Background of Pearl Harbor*, 4:126–27, A-185. The version in the Schuler Papers omits the sen-

tence: "It will be promoted by Americans and will have . . . the appearance of being financed by American money (although a portion of the actual expense will be born [sic] by this office)."

129. Nomura to Tokyo, 1 November 1941.
130. Armstrong to Shaw, 7 [November 1941].
131. W. Forbes Webber, Kansas City, FBI, "Orland K. Armstrong alias O.K. Armstrong, Espionage—G[erman]," 1 December 1941, Armstrong FBI File No. 62-45631-12, FOIA.
132. Armstrong to Shaw, 7 [November 1941].
133. Armstrong to Webber, 6 March 1942; Armstrong to Libby, 18 October 1941.
134. Armstrong to Shaw, 7 [November 1941].
135. Armstrong to Shaw, 7 [November 1941].
136. Armstrong to Schumpeter, 8 November 1941, Armstrong Papers.
137. "Galen M. Fisher, 81, Social Worker, Dies," *NYT*, 3 January 1955, 27. For a biographical sketch of Fisher, see *Marquis Who's Who on the Web* (accessed 10 October 2005).
138. Galen M. Fisher, ed., *The Effects of the Sino-Japanese Conflict on American Educational and Philanthropic Enterprises in China* (San Francisco, CA: American Council, IPR, 1939).
139. Galen Merriam Fisher, ed., *How the Oriental Press in San Francisco Has Treated Sino-Japanese War News* (San Francisco, CA: San Francisco Bay Region Division, American Council, IPR, 1941).
140. Armstrong to Shaw, 7 [November 1941]; Raymond Leslie Buell, *Isolated America* (New York: Alfred A. Knopf, 1940); Dunn, *1940*, 90. For a biographical sketch of Buell (1896–1946), see *Marquis Who's Who on the Web* (accessed 19 July 2006).
141. Armstrong to Shaw, 7 [November 1941].
142. Armstrong to Schumpeter, 8 November 1941. In January 1945, Johnstone was dean of the School of Government at George Washington University as well as a member of the American Council, IPR.
143. C. A. Kahrhoff, "Japanese [Espionage] Activities in Washington, D.C.," 18 December 1941, pp. 12–14, Terasaki Hidenari FBI File No. 65-HQ-37232, FOIA.
144. Gwen Terasaki, *Bridge to the Sun* (Chapel Hill: University of North Carolina University Press, 1957; Newport, TN: Wakestone Books, 2000), 35–36; William J. Sebald, *With MacArthur in Japan: A Personal History of the Occupation* (New York: W. W. Norton, 1965), 96.
145. Robert J. C. Butow, *Tojo and the Coming of the War* (Princeton, NJ: Princeton University Press, 1969), 207, 209, 212, 216–17, 219n, 220–21n, 342.
146. Shaw and Armstrong to the Hon. Cordell Hull, Secretary of State, Washington, DC, 14 November 1941, NCPW, reel 41: 116 (box 129).
147. Armstrong to Webber, 6 March 1942.
148. Schumpeter wire to Armstrong, 14 November 1941, Armstrong Papers.
149. Schumpeter to Armstrong, 18 November 1941, Armstrong Papers.
150. Raymond Mackay, Division of Far Eastern Affairs, memo of conversation, "Relations with Japan," 15 November 1941, 711.94/2526, National Archives and Records Administration.
151. Armstrong to Terasaki, 15 November 1941, Armstrong Papers; Butow, *Tojo*, 78, 106–7, 194n18, passim.
152. Roger B. Jeans, *Terasaki Hidenari, Pearl Harbor, and Occupied Japan: A Bridge to Reality* (Lanham, MD: Lexington Books, 2009), 121.
153. Armstrong to Terasaki, 15 November 1941.
154. Shaw and Armstrong to Hull, 14 November 1941 (with the notation, "Copy for Mr. Mackay"); Armstrong, Acting Secretary, to Dear Friend, 4 October 1941; "Proposed Statement on Japanese-American Relations," 22 September 1941 (with the notation it was made public on 23 September 1941); "Our Share in Building the Kind of World We Want to Live In," Workers' Conference, 14 and 15 November 1941, Friends' Meeting House, Washington, DC, sponsored by the NCPW; attached to Mackay, memo of conversation with Shaw and Armstrong, 15 November 1941.
155. Armstrong to Libby, 18 October 1941.
156. Armstrong to Terasaki, 15 November 1941. By "Dr. Wilson," Armstrong may have meant E. Raymond Wilson, a lifelong peace activist. Although Armstrong asserted Phelps had resided in Japan (see above), he may have meant Wilson, who studied in Japan in 1926 and 1927. From 1931 to 1943, Wilson worked as educational secretary for the peace section of the

American Friends Service Committee. During 1936 and 1937, he participated in the Emergency Peace Campaign. Beginning in July 1940, he concentrated on opposition to the draft and support for conscientious objectors. In January 1941, he called for a "negotiated peace" with the United States as mediator. "Wilson, E. Raymond (20 Sept. 1896–27 June 1987)," *American National Biography*, 23:570–71; "Hitler Praised at Peace Session," *Washington Post* (hereafter *WP*), 12 January 1941, 2; "E. Raymond Wilson Dies; Spokesman for Quakers," *WP*, 29 June 1987, B4.

157. Armstrong to Terasaki, 15 November 1941.

158. Kahrhoff, "Japanese [Espionage] Activities in Washington, D.C.," 18 December 1941, 16; FBI wiretap, 16 November 1941, FBI file on Terasaki.

159. Kahrhoff, "Japanese [Espionage] Activities in Washington, D.C.," 18 December 1941, 18–19.

160. [Colonel William J. Donovan, Coordinator of Information], 17 November 1941; Fletcher Warren, Division of Foreign Activity Correlation, Department of State, to Mr. [George] Atcheson [Jr.], Division of Far Eastern Affairs, 21 November 1941; [George] Atcheson [Jr.], Division of Far Eastern Affairs, to [Fletcher] Warren, Division of Foreign Activity Correlation, 24 November 1941; George A. Gordon, Acting Chief, Division of Foreign Activity Correlation, to Colonel William [J.] Donovan, Coordinator of Information, 1 December 1941, with encl. lists dated 27 and 28 November 1941, 894.20210/126, decimal file 1940-1944, Record Group 59, National Archives.

161. Armstrong to Mr. Webber, 6 March 1942; Kahrhoff, "Japanese [Espionage] Activities in Washington, D.C.," 18 December 1941, 25–26.

162. *Marquis Who's Who on the Web* (accessed 20 July 2006).

163. Shaw to Armstrong, 26 November 1941, Armstrong Papers.

164. Shaw to Armstrong, acting secretary for the Committee on Pacific Relations, 26 November 1941, NCPW, reel 41: 223 (box 280). A copy of Shaw's letter is also in the Armstrong Papers.

165. NCPW news release, Washington, DC, n.d., no title, NCPW, reel 41: 223 (box 280).

166. Armstrong to Webber, 6 March 1942; James B. Reston, "U.S.-Japan Talks at Critical Point in Bids for Truce," *NYT*, 24 November 1941, 1.

167. Reston, "U.S.-Japan Talks," 1; "Forum Debaters See 2-Ocean War Possible," *WP*, 24 November 1941, 16.

168. Armstrong to Terasaki, Japanese Embassy, Washington, DC, n.d., Armstrong Papers.

169. Armstrong to Schumpeter, Cambridge, MA, 14 December 1941, Armstrong Papers.

170. Armstrong to Far Eastern Division, State Department, Attention: Mr. [Raymond] Mackay, n.d., Armstrong Papers.

171. Boss to Armstrong, 12 December 1941, Armstrong Papers.

Chapter Seven

The FBI and Pro-Japan Isolationists

"[Armstrong's Japanese project] will be promoted by Americans and will have . . . the appearance of being financed by American money (although a portion of the actual expense will be born [sic] by this office)."—Ambassador Nomura Kichisaburo[1]

"It does not appear that he [Armstrong] ever received any financial remuneration from the Japanese Government."—Assistant Attorney General Wendell Berge[2]

The Committee on Pacific Relations' goal was to find a way to prevent war with Japan. In attempting to do so, one of its major problems was to avoid being attacked as a pro-Japanese effort to betray China. O. K. Armstrong had assured Frederick Libby that "no one connected with this [organization] would countenance that, of course." Nevertheless, because of its activities as well as its membership—especially Armstrong, Ralph Townsend, William Baxter, and John Cole McKim—the committee was open to charges of, at least, appeasing Japan and, at worst, serving as unregistered Japanese agents.[3] During the fall of 1941, while the members of the committee were lobbying the administration against war with Japan, several members of the group, including Elizabeth Schumpeter, were being investigated by the FBI.[4]

The origin of such investigations was clear. In May 1940, as the German armies overran the Low Countries (Belgium, the Netherlands, and Luxembourg) and France, President Franklin Roosevelt suggested that FBI Director J. Edgar Hoover check up on critics of the president's national defense policies. In doing so, he approved the use of "listening devices" to gather information on "persons suspected of subversive activities . . . including suspected spies" and suspected "fifth columnists." By the end of the month, Hoover had carried out background checks on 131 critics, including isolationist

Charles Lindbergh, on whom the director had maintained a dossier since the 1930s, and other leaders of the America First Committee. As a critic emphasized, Hoover was not acting on his own but "harassing isolationists under orders from the White House."[5]

In order to show that it had nothing to hide, one of his targets cooperated. At the invitation of America First, in June 1941 the bureau investigated the files of its national headquarters as well as its Chicago chapter. The following month, it was rumored that the FBI had begun tapping Lindbergh's and America First's phones. Many years later, Lindbergh's wife, Anne, insisted that the bureau had tapped her husband's telephone.[6] A Lindbergh biographer, however, could find no evidence in bureau files, declassified as the result of a Freedom of Information Act (FOIA) request, of wiretapping.[7] In November, Roosevelt also asked the U.S. attorney general whether a grand jury could look into America First's funds.[8]

That same month, the House Committee on Un-American Activities (known as the Dies Committee after Congressman Martin Dies) also investigated America First. Its head, the chairman of Sears, Roebuck's board of directors, General Robert E. Wood, granted it full access to the organization's files without a subpoena.[9] In the meantime, Tokyo ordered its Washington embassy to investigate the American isolationists, too. Since it could not get access to Lindbergh, the undisputed star of the movement, it approached an anti-interventionist of lesser standing, Orland Kay (O. K.) Armstrong.

FBI INTEREST IN WRITER AND ACTIVIST O. K. ARMSTRONG

The intelligence community had been interested in Armstrong even before Pearl Harbor. In early October 1941, personnel from the Office of Naval Intelligence, army intelligence, and the FBI held their weekly conference at the office of the commandant of the Third Naval District in New York City. The district's Naval Counter-Intelligence Section sent a memorandum, subsequently forwarded to the FBI director, to the district intelligence officer reporting (obviously from New York press accounts) on the formation and membership of the Committee on Pacific Relations. It also quoted from the statement issued by Armstrong following the meeting.[10] Hoover forwarded the memorandum to the FBI's special agent in charge (SAC) in Washington, DC.[11] The following day, he instructed the agent to investigate whether Armstrong's activities might be "in violation of the Espionage Statutes or otherwise inimical to the internal security of our country."[12] In doing so, he added Armstrong to the list of committee members (Schumpeter, Townsend, and McKim) under investigation as possible Japanese agents.

In late October, Armstrong began to suspect that his mail was being read.[13] It was clear the FBI had him under surveillance, and an agent noted the bureau files contained "numerous references" to him. Agents reported that he had visited New York for a few days at a time and "on many occasions" had traveled to Washington.[14] On 31 October, they reported his contacts with the Japanese embassy. He was, the agent added, "a member and would-be leader of anti-war groups," before which he had delivered numerous speeches. The agent reported he "possibly is interested in preventing war between Japan and this country." Revealing its dated nature, the report stated that he was one of three members of the American Legion's Foreign Relations Committee.

Interestingly, he and Hoover had met before when he interviewed the FBI chief in 1936. He had planned to publish the interview under the director's name in an article titled "Influence of Politics in Crime."[15] When he sent the manuscript to Hoover to vet, he was not above flattering him. "Your public speeches," he wrote, "have been so tremendously able and thought-provoking, there is no reason, it seems to me, why your influence as head of the FBI should not be thus augmented by a few well-chosen articles. I stand ready to help!"[16] Despite the flattery, Hoover denied his request and instructed him not to mention his name either as author of the article or in connection with its preparation.[17]

Following Pearl Harbor, it was extremely risky, as might be expected, to be identified as pro-Axis. Although the FBI's Kansas City Division had concluded on 1 December, a few days before the Japanese surprise attack on Hawaii, and reaffirmed three days following the attack, that there was no evidence of illegal activity by Armstrong and thus it was closing his case, his post–Pearl Harbor public views—brought to the bureau's attention by a resident of Armstrong's hometown—drew renewed FBI scrutiny. A few days after Pearl Harbor, an indignant Springfield citizen sent the bureau a copy of an article Armstrong had published in the *Springfield Leader and Press* only three days after the attack. The title of his piece, "We Brought War on Ourselves, Peace-Maker Armstrong Says," was, to say the least, provocative in those tense and dark days following the disaster at Pearl Harbor.[18]

The newspaper's editor obviously knew Armstrong. "Most Springfieldians," he wrote, knew Armstrong as a Drury College (Springfield) alumnus, American Legionnaire, past state legislator, magazine author, and antiwar advocate. He was an "ardent and active opponent of the war," the editor continued, and "one of the chief organizers of the Committee on Pacific Relations, created for the sole purpose of avoiding a Japanese-American war by peaceful negotiation and understanding." Having returned to Springfield on 5 December, four days later Armstrong had intended to return to Boston (where Lindbergh was scheduled to speak the following day) and then to

Washington to resume his "Japanese-American peace efforts." "Now," the editor explained, "he doesn't know what he'll do."[19]

Hoover himself took an interest in Armstrong's article. The outcome of his case, though, was quite different from Townsend's. In April 1942, the Department of Justice's Assistant Attorney General Wendell Berge wrote in a memorandum to Hoover that "it does not appear that he ever received any financial remuneration from the Japanese Government." This was a critical point if Armstrong, unlike Townsend, was to escape prosecution as a Japanese agent. Berge wanted to be sure, though, so he asked Hoover to check Armstrong's bank account to see whether he had received funds from the Japanese or German governments, a request the director passed on, three weeks later, to the FBI's Kansas City office.[20] By 9 May, Armstrong was safe from prosecution. On that day, the FBI's Kansas City office responded that Armstrong had not received any money from foreign sources.[21]

Because Hoover seems to have failed to inform the Criminal Division of the Department of Justice of the resolution of the Armstrong case, in October Assistant Attorney General Berge again asked him for information on the Missourian. This time Hoover replied promptly. He informed Berge that the 9 May report of the Kansas City office had been sent to the Division of Records. The division, Hoover added, now had all the reports on Armstrong, and "no further investigation is contemplated in the absence of a further request from your office."[22] The fact that prior to Pearl Harbor Japanese Ambassador Nomura apparently did not get around to honoring his promise to Armstrong to partly fund the Committee on Pacific Relations probably saved Armstrong from being charged as an unregistered Japanese agent and possibly, like Townsend, ending up in prison.

The fact that he bent over backward to appear helpful and cooperative probably also helped ensure his fate would be different from that suffered by Townsend. In concluding the 6 March 1942 memorandum that he drafted at the FBI's request, he wrote, "I hope you and your office will call upon me for any further information or help I may be." In the end, the investigation did not go beyond the FBI and the Criminal Division of the Department of Justice, and he was not called before a grand jury. The lack of a money trail coupled with his detailed explanation of his motives and actions obviously satisfied the bureau and marked the end of official government interest in his prewar contacts with the Japanese.[23]

Nevertheless, he was cautious in the years that followed. Charges that he had been "pro-Japan" before the war haunted his future political career. As the 1942 election for the Missouri legislature revealed, Armstrong's prewar isolationist activities created problems for him. As an isolationist and author, he knew George Eggleston, the editor of *Scribner's Commentator* and the *Herald*, the two isolationist publications with which Townsend was associated.[24] Moreover, in November 1941, *Scribner's Commentator* had been investigated by a Washington grand jury gathering information on German agents as well.[25] During Townsend's trial, however, Armstrong escaped being tarred with the broad brush wielded against these publications. During the war, he may have avoided Eggleston because of the latter's association with the trial. Therefore, he did not visit the editor until the war was over and the trial was safely in the past. In October 1945, Armstrong wrote Lindbergh that he had visited "our mutual friend" Eggleston in New York for the first time since the war began, adding he had "simply failed to see him since he got out of the service." "Of course," he concluded, "both he and I mentioned you with pleasant recollection."[26]

Although the FBI officially closed his case, there were sporadic additions to his FBI dossier in subsequent years (1947–1964).[27] Remarkably, considering his close call, in the postwar years he had nothing but praise for the FBI ("one of the best run organizations in the government").[28] He claimed that he and the FBI head were "good friends," congratulated Hoover on his "long and splendid leadership" of the bureau, and praised his "tremendous and public-spirited activities on behalf of the people of this nation."[29] In short, he flattered Hoover just as he did Lindbergh.

FBI INVESTIGATION OF JAPAN SPECIALIST AND PROFESSOR ELIZABETH B. SCHUMPETER

Just as in the cases of several of her fellow members of the Committee on Pacific Relations, Schumpeter's views on Japan attracted the attention of the FBI. After the beginning of the war in Europe in 1939, the bureau placed both her and her famous husband, Harvard economics professor Joseph Schumpeter, under surveillance as security risks. Elizabeth especially attracted FBI attention with her publication in 1940 of a volume on Japan's economy. The bureau was convinced she was a propagandist for Japan. Therefore, much of her dossier focused on the question of whether her book was propaganda. The bureau was also interested in her contacts with the Japanese consulate while she was preparing the book. It did not go unnoticed that the Japan Institute in New York, a branch of Japan's propaganda organization, purchased 250 copies of her massive book, some of which it sold to the Japanese Chamber of Commerce.[30]

Thus, by the time Armstrong contacted her in May 1941, she had a reputation, deserved or not, of being "pro-Japan." It did not help matters that she, like Townsend, was considered a right-winger. In November, she reported to Armstrong that she was having trouble with mail delivery of her Japanese newspapers and periodicals. "I have been carrying on correspondence with the Solicitor for the Post Office," she wrote, "which I think may interest you." She enclosed copies of the correspondence, adding she had not received a reply to her most recent letter. "As soon as I have all the facts," she wrote, "I hope to give this problem a little publicity."[31]

Meanwhile, as contributor of four of the seven chapters (357 of 933 pages) in her book on the Japanese economy, she gained a reputation as an expert on current Asian economic and political affairs. As a result, in November, while the Committee on Pacific Relations was attempting to expand and exert some influence, she was contacted by the Office of Production Management in Washington about a possible job. When she was turned down a few weeks later, she was sure it was because she possessed the "wrong" views of Japan. She was probably right, for the FBI suspected her book was propaganda for the Japanese. After "propaganda analysis," the bureau concluded rather tentatively, "*perhaps* 10 percent of it could be construed as propaganda, *maybe* [author's italics]." The bureau was particularly interested in the fact that she had gotten in touch with the Japanese consulate in New York while she was working on the volume. No doubt the bureau thought it damning that the consulate bought several copies of her book (Japan's Washington embassy also had a copy on hand).[32]

Meanwhile, because of journalist William Henry Chamberlin's views on Japan, in May 1941 the FBI launched an investigation of him also. It uncovered nothing, however, except the ordinary activities of a journalist and author. Therefore, at the end of its investigation, it shifted its attention from Chamberlin as an independent target to using him to "ascertain whether Elizabeth B. Schumpeter is engaged in Japanese espionage activities."[33]

Surveillance of the Schumpeters, husband and wife, continued throughout the war. Because of her contacts with the Japanese, the FBI was more interested in her than in her husband. FBI Director Hoover pressured the bureau's Boston office to come up with evidence on which to charge her with being a propaganda agent. In February 1942, however, the best the division could do was to accuse her of writing books "praising Japan and previous to Pearl Harbor [she was] in favor of Japanese over Chinese." Following two interviews with her in 1944 as well as study of her publications, it terminated its investigation. When the Schumpters' file was forwarded to the Criminal Division of the Department of Justice, Attorney General Tom Clark concluded there was insufficient evidence to charge them. In a December 1944 memorandum to Hoover, he wrote that prosecution of them was "not contemplated by the Criminal Division."[34]

During the war, she continued to study Japan and the Japanese language. In 1944, though, her proposal to a press for a book on Japan's economy was rejected. Although she continued her research on the country, she never again tried to publish a book about it.[35] Several years following the war (July 1951), her name once again appeared in an FBI report, this time in response to a query from Senator Pat McCarran's Senate Judiciary Committee.[36] Operating through its offshoot, the Internal Security Subcommittee, it was especially interested in the Institute of Pacific Affairs, Schumpeter's old bête noire, and any signs of communist influence in the United States.[37]

FBI INVESTIGATION OF JOHN COLE McKIM

In light of his numerous pro-Japanese utterances, it may have been McKim that Frederick Libby had in mind when he informed Mark Shaw in November 1941 that, in addition to the charge against Ralph Townsend of being a foreign agent, "we hear that there is another member of the Committee [of Pacific Relations] liable to the same charge."[38]

It should have been no surprise that the FBI investigated McKim on suspicion of being an unregistered Japanese agent or, at the very least, "an apologist for Japan." As in the case of Townsend, people complained that McKim was "anti-American" and a "paid agent of the Japanese Government."[39] It did not help that the day before the Pearl Harbor attack, he mailed a letter to the Japanese consulate general in New York that asserted, "It fills me with pride to be called a 'loyal and diligent' defender of Japan."[40]

The bureau's investigation of McKim began in March 1940 and was not closed until December 1944, when Assistant Attorney General Tom Clark ruled that the FBI's evidence was insufficient to prosecute McKim for violation of the Foreign Agents Registration Acts (the letter was dated the same day Clark terminated the investigation of Elizabeth Schumpeter).[41] The bureau's objective, as in the cases of Schumpeter and Townsend, was to prove that McKim had been paid by the Japanese to publish pro-Japan views. Although he was indeed paid for the articles and book reviews he wrote for the *Japanese American Review*,[42] which was published by the Nippon Publishing Company, the FBI failed to prove that McKim was a Japanese stooge. In fact, it concluded that McKim was, in the words of the FBI's New York City Bureau, an "eccentric but harmless individual." One informant even referred to him as a "crackpot." He was "addicted," an informant reported, to writing letters to the *New York Times*. When interviewed, he insisted his sole wish was for the United States to remain neutral. He also was naïve, for he told an FBI agent that the Japanese were incapable of carrying out propaganda in the United States.[43] In April 1940, the FBI described him as a character about town in Peekskill, wearing black knee britches and, since he was "stone deaf," carrying around his neck a long rubber tube with a trumpet on one end and an ear piece at the other.[44]

In January 1940, someone (name blacked out) representing the Nippon Publishing Company registered with the State Department.[45] From 1939 to 1941, whilst McKim was writing for it, the *Japanese American Review*, with a circulation of ten to fifteen thousand copies, was funded by the Japanese consulate, which received the monies from Japanese firms.[46] In February

1942, a Japanese clerk in the former Japanese consulate in New York confirmed that the journal was funded by the Japanese. Each month, he recalled, Kondo Shinichi from the consulate general gave the magazine a check for two thousand dollars. It was a bimonthly journal distributed free throughout the country, the informant explained for, in the FBI's words, "the purpose of propaganda for the Japanese Government."[47]

The bureau also knew about McKim's involvement with Armstrong's Committee on Pacific Relations.[48] In November 1943, an FBI informant—undoubtedly the person affiliated with the Overseas Department of the National Council of the Episcopal Church mentioned later in this FBI report—related how he had seen McKim's name in a press article in September 1941 announcing the formation of the committee. Not wanting to see war break out between Japan and the United States, he asked McKim to place his name on the committee's mailing list. McKim referred him to "some man in a small town near Cleveland" whom he said was the sponsor of the committee (Armstrong was in Missouri, and Townsend, Wisconsin). That person informed him that the committee was being organized, anticipated having a headquarters in Washington, DC, and would put his name on its mailing list as soon as the committee was established. He had heard nothing further regarding the group, however, the informant noted.

On 22 September, four persons besides himself attended the committee's founding dinner, McKim told an FBI agent in 1943. He did not have to rely on memory, for he kept a diary that contained an entry for 22 September. One of the attendees was Japan businessman and trader Everett W. Frazar (the other names are blacked out in the FBI report). One member's—probably Mark R. Shaw, who was associated with the prohibition movement in the United States—chief aim seemed to be the establishment of Prohibition in Japan. McKim had been interested in the committee, he told the agent, because he wanted to stop the United States from fighting Japan or any other nation. The committee's aim, he added, was the creation of mutual understanding and friendly relations with Japan. He himself was interested in everything having to do with the Far East, since he was born and had spent much of his life there. The committee members had scant time between late September and the early December attack on Pearl Harbor, he added, to organize. He was unaware of any results of its planning to open a committee office in Washington.

Although the founding of the committee drew some criticism when it was announced in the newspapers, it also attracted another supporter. A few days after the meeting, McKim informed Armstrong that he had just received a letter from one F. M. Nishio of the Cementex Company, apparently a tool manufacturing firm. Nishio wrote that he had just read in the previous evening's newspaper about the creation of the Committee on Pacific Relations. Noting that McKim was one of the "sponsors," he asked that his name be added to the mailing list, to which McKim replied he would forward his name to Armstrong.⁴⁹

On 4 October 1941, McKim continued, a statement had been published and dispatched to officers of peace organizations across the country with a request that they cooperate with the committee. However, McKim explained, the war broke out before the committee reached the point of active operations. Since Pearl Harbor, he had heard no more about the group. After its inaugural meeting, he had not taken part in its activities other than corresponding with Armstrong (name blacked out in the FBI report, but there is correspondence between the two men in the Armstrong Papers) between 22 September and 7 December 1941. Those communications, advised an FBI agent, were available in the files of the New York Field Division.

Its interest obviously piqued, FBI agents met with McKim in December to inquire about the committee. McKim recalled that a certain person (name blacked out in the FBI report), at a third party's urging, had written to him on 12 September to invite him to the 22 September meeting. The Armstrong Papers at the University of Missouri filled in the blanks. It was Townsend, himself under investigation by the FBI at the time of the committee's founding, who recommended that Armstrong invite McKim to the committee dinner. Armstrong then sent McKim a copy of the committee statement and asked for his endorsement, if he was unable to attend.⁵⁰

FBI INVESTIGATION OF RALPH TOWNSEND

Ralph Townsend was the only member of the Committee on Pacific Relations to be imprisoned as a result of his prewar pro-Japan isolationist activities. He was convicted for failure to register as a Japanese agent. He had spoken before at least two local America First meetings on the West Coast, although never under the auspices of its national headquarters. The committee leaders, concluded one historian, "appear to have had no knowledge of the foreign connections of Townsend."⁵¹

Of the committee members listed in the Committee on Pacific Relations prospectus, State Department official William Langdon took special note of Townsend, on whom, he noted, the FBI had a "sizeable dossier."⁵² It was the State Department, Townsend's former employer, that launched the investigation of him. In February and again in April 1939, State, and even President Roosevelt, received letters complaining about Townsend's allegedly pro-Axis views expressed in his booklet *The High Cost of Hate* (1939), a copy of which the department forwarded to the FBI. This booklet and an earlier one, wrote one complainant, were sent to him free and out of the blue and were clearly pro-Japanese propaganda. The publications, he added, obviously were being mailed in large numbers. A few days later, another offended citizen sent the booklet to State with the comment that Townsend was "in the employ of Japan." He also had been told, the writer continued, that Townsend had delivered pro-Japan speeches at private parties. If he was not registered with State as a Japanese employee, "I think his activities would warrant investigation." He ended with the hope that something could be done to halt the circulation of such "rank propaganda" in California. Finally, another irate citizen wrote to denounce *The High Cost of Hate*, which he termed "propaganda of the Berlin-Rome-Tokio [Tokyo] Axis." If Townsend was not registered as a "hired agent" of Germany, Italy, or Japan, he concluded, "perhaps you will deem it appropriate to have an investigation made as to his activities."[53]

State obviously took these demands for investigation of Townsend seriously. In May 1939, Assistant Secretary of State George S. Messersmith sent FBI Director Hoover a copy of *The High Cost of Hate*. He thought someone might have subsidized its publication and asked Hoover to initiate a "discreet inquiry." The director requested the SAC in San Francisco—Townsend lived in Oakland, California—to investigate the writer's sources of income, his "affiliations with any subversive activities," his bank account, and his state income tax returns. The bureau, he added, had requested Townsend's U.S. income tax returns for 1935 through 1938. Hoover also enclosed a copy of *The High Cost of Hate*. Obviously, Messersmith and Hoover suspected the Japanese government was financing Townsend's publications, which would make him an unregistered Japanese agent. Perhaps feeling the pressure from State, Hoover made clear the matter was urgent, writing it was "imperative" the SAC give it "immediate investigative attention" and report "at the earliest possible date."[54] Ironically, some months later it was reported that Townsend did not file federal income tax returns for 1935 and 1938 because his income was insufficient.[55]

An American adviser to Ambassador Nomura later revealed that "two or three fairly good [American] writers" had accepted Japanese payments. He had not met them but had seen their pamphlets. Some came from California—where Townsend lived—he recalled. Curious to see how Japan's record in China could be defended, he had read some of the pamphlets. All were "spoiled" by the biases of the writers, with one "strongly anti-British and anti-New Deal." A Boston newspaper published a critical front-page article on the pamphleteers, he added. Nomura's adviser used these pamphlets to criticize Japan's propaganda activities in the United States as doing more harm than good.[56]

The first report from the FBI's San Francisco bureau followed barely a month later (June 1939), with copies, as was to be the case throughout the investigation, going to the State Department, Naval Intelligence, and G-2 (Intelligence) at the War Department. Townsend, the bureau reported, was the author of several pro-Japanese books, such as *Ways That Are Dark* and

Asia Answers. Moreover, in 1937, he had visited Japan. He also had been heard on the radio defending the Japanese invasion of China. Despite this pro-Japan record, the report added, he was not registered as a foreign agent. The bureau claimed that he was receiving payment in cash, "probably" from "some Japanese agency" in San Francisco.[57]

In October 1939, the bureau submitted another report on him to headquarters, this one noting that his mail was being read. The most interesting thing about the report was its mention of a letter to him from the N.Y.K. Line (Nippon Yusen Kaisha Steamship Company), which entity the FBI had mentioned earlier as a possible source of Japanese government payments to him.[58] Less than a month later, the bureau reported that informants had asserted he was a "paid propagandist" of the Japanese government who received $250 to $350 a month, "presumably" from the Japanese consul. The government-controlled Japanese Committee on Trade and Information, an informant noted, knew him well. The Japanese consulate had distributed copies of at least one of his books, *Ways That Are Dark*, through the mail.[59] In February 1940, the FBI began reporting to Assistant Secretary of State Adolf A. Berle Jr.[60]

In April, another mail cover, this one for thirty days, was placed on Townsend.[61] In May, the San Francisco bureau reported that a confidential informant had informed it that Townsend had received ten thousand dollars from the Japanese and eight thousand from the German government over the past year. The bureau reported that the Japanese Chamber of Commerce, in its pamphlet *Does Japan Slam the Door against American Trade in Areas of Japanese Influence in Asia* had quoted portions of Townsend's June 1938 radio broadcast "Is Japan a Threat," with his permission (the first page of the pamphlet contains his letter of permission). The FBI's mail cover revealed that he also had received a letter from the German consulate general in San Francisco.[62]

Meanwhile, complaints by citizens alleging he was a Japanese or German agent continued to arrive in Washington, with one such letter leading Senator Claude Pepper of Florida to add his voice to the chorus calling for an investigation of him.[63] During 1941, Townsend continued to stir up complaints with his booklets, such as *Seeking Foreign Trouble* (1940) and *The High Cost of Hate*, which seemed to pop up all over the country and even in hotels in Harbin in Japanese-controlled Manchuria as well as at a university in the Philippines. Assistant Attorney General Berge reported that it was unknown whether Japanese or Germans had distributed the booklets.[64] Commenting on an FBI report on one recipient of *Seeking Foreign Trouble*, Hoover noted that this person may have received the booklet "as part of a general plan to circularize pro-Japanese propaganda in the United States."[65]

A report from the FBI's Seattle bureau also noted publication of this newest booklet as well as his earlier *America Has No Enemies* (1938), which "discounts the prevalent opinion that Japan is inimical to the United States." It was a "brief," the bureau added, that tried to demonstrate that the United States "would not be justified in making war on Japan." A confidential informant who knew Townsend, who had been pro-Chinese until the last two or three years, helped resolve some of the mystery as to why he had become pro-Japan. Two years earlier, the informant claimed, Townsend told him he wrote propaganda for the Japanese government because he needed money. The bureau added that its report was being sent in case Townsend had not "complied with the provisions of the Alien Registration Act." When the bureau again interviewed the informant two months later, however, he was not sure he had ever met Townsend after all. The FBI's sources, it turned out, were the Chinese consuls in Seattle and San Francisco—not exactly disinterested parties.[66] The FBI's San Francisco office promptly reported that Townsend was "not a registered agent of the Japanese," so he was being investigated to see if he was violating the Registration Act.[67] This was the charge on which he was later convicted.

As the investigation dragged on, Hoover became increasingly exasperated and critical of the San Francisco bureau. In January 1941, he wrote to complain that a promised report had not been received. He added that the Townsend investigation was "one of the Registration Act cases the Bureau believes should receive thorough, continuous, and expeditious attention, in order to determine whether a violation of the Act has occurred."[68] At Hoover's request, in February FBI headquarters compiled a report based on information gathered to date on Townsend. In his books, the report noted, he "debunked" Japanese economic movement into South America and "quotes statistics to justify Japanese aggression in Manchuria." From March 1938 to May 1939, he made numerous and substantial deposits to his bank account. The FBI thought "various Japanese agencies" had guaranteed good sales of his booklets by purchasing a certain number of copies. The War Department believed he had served in the consular service long enough to make good connections and then had resigned to write pro-Japanese materials.[69]

In early February 1941, Townsend testified in Washington against the Lend-Lease Bill. It was three months before FBI headquarters in Washington sent a copy of that testimony to the San Francisco bureau investigating him.[70] Under pressure from Hoover, in late February the bureau filed a lengthy report. Townsend's books, it wrote, had been widely distributed in the United States, and as a result the bureau had received numerous complaints. There were frequent reports that he was being financed by the Japanese government. Townsend argued that Japan was a barrier to communism in Asia, the bureau wrote, and opposition to Japan's policies in Asia was leading to a communist revolution in the United States. Twenty-one thousand copies of *Seeking Foreign Trouble* had been sent out, and he was still taking orders. The 14 February issue of the magazine *Friday* charged that the Japanese Chamber of Commerce in San Francisco had purchased his booklets "in great quantities" and mailed them for him.[71] It was interesting that neither the antiwar National Council for the Prevention of War nor the Women's International League for Peace and Freedom had recommended distribution of *Seeking Foreign Trouble*.[72]

Three months later, Hoover had become obsessed with the Townsend case. In May 1941, he complained that the last report had been submitted in February. "Since this is a case in which I am vitally interested," he wrote, reports should be sent in more frequently than in the past. When would one be submitted? he demanded.[73] The response was swift. On 4 June, the San Francisco bureau dispatched a ten-page report. It included an informant's claim that Townsend was doing propaganda work for Japan. Moreover, in a speech in January, he had defended Japan. There was nothing in the report, however, to conclusively prove that he was a paid agent of the Japanese government.[74]

By June, Hoover was clearly annoyed by the lack of evidence linking Townsend to the Japanese government. It was clear that he wanted to charge him with violation of the Foreign Agents Registration Act, but he needed solid evidence to do so. There was no question but what Townsend's writings and radio speeches were pro-Japan. The issue was whether the Japanese government paid him for them. If not, they were simply an expression of his freedom of speech, however offensive they were in light of the growing threat from Japan.

In late June, Hoover again lost patience. "Advise immediately," he cabled the San Francisco office, when a report on Townsend would be submitted.[75] Obviously, the government was getting ready to charge him, for on 5 July, Hoover instructed San Francisco that the investigation "must be confirmed within thirty days."[76] Meanwhile, Assistant Attorney General Berge mulled over the evidence already collected. "The allegation is made," he wrote Hoover, that the Japanese Chamber of Commerce had bought "large quantities" of Townsend's publications. Reports demonstrate that Townsend "may be" working for the chamber. "Allegation" and "may be," however, were as far as he was willing to go.[77]

Nevertheless, his memorandum gave Hoover another club with which to belabor his hapless San Francisco SAC. In August, he forwarded a copy of Berge's memorandum to the latter, adding rather threateningly that he would "expect that you will comply with this request."[78] Less than a month later, he demanded the SAC "immediately wire explanation for failure to submit report by August fifth as directed and date report will be submitted."[79] Two days later, the San Francisco bureau sent a sixteen-page report on Townsend. The Japanese Chamber of Commerce was a registered agent of a foreign principal, the bureau reported. An informant had "always taken it for granted" that Townsend worked for the Japanese in San Francisco. Large numbers of his booklets were delivered to Japanese companies. Another source reported that Townsend had complained to him that the post office had blocked mailing of some of his booklets. The FBI report also included synopses of his radio speeches, which were generally pro-Japanese and anti-Chinese.[80]

In September 1941, a Federal District grand jury in Washington, DC, began to investigate foreign propaganda in the United States. The hearings seemed mostly to focus on German propaganda. In a close parallel to Japanese consulates' purchase of Townsend's pamphlets, a German agent had purchased and distributed reprints of isolationist congressmen's speeches from the *Congressional Record*. Unfortunately for America First, it was entangled in the ensuing scandal.[81]

Meanwhile, one of the committee members on whom Armstrong counted was in deep trouble. In a memorandum prepared by Internal Revenue agents and forwarded by Hoover to the SAC in San Francisco in September, Townsend was accused of serving as a "Japanese propagandist" and was on a list of "Japanese suspects." It summarized Townsend's arguments in *Ways That Are Dark: The Truth about China* and *Seeking Foreign Trouble*. The former booklet, it pointed out, was a "fierce denunciation" of China, which was contrasted unfavorably with Japan. The latter booklet was an argument against involvement in war with Japan.[82] As a historian later put it, Townsend castigated the Chinese people as "epitomizing *Ways That Are Dark*."[83]

That same month, Hoover again chastised the SAC in San Francisco, demanding that he "comply with my wishes."[84] Searching for the source of what he believed to be Japanese payments to Townsend, Hoover asked the State Department for any information regarding registration as a foreign agent of the Committee on Trade and Information in San Francisco. He correctly believed that it was no longer registered with the secretary of state.[85]

In early October, Hoover blew up at the SAC in San Francisco. "I am not at all pleased with the manner in which this investigation [of Townsend] is progressing and with the manner in which the information obtained has been developed." He believed Townsend was in violation of the Registration Act as an agent of the Japanese government or some other foreign principal. He then tore apart the SAC's report of 12 September. "Inaccurate reporting . . . predominates in this report." He was frustrated that the agents could not prove Townsend was a Japanese agent liable for prosecution for violation of "Section 233, Title 22, U.S. Code." In criticizing the agent, he let slip references to a "prosecutor" and "a successful prosecution." This case, he concluded, "I consider of vital interest and importance." The Criminal Division of the Department of Justice was also interested and looked for evidence against Townsend in the SAC's reports. Meanwhile, it seemed Hoover's mind was already made up. The agent should keep in mind "what he is attempting to prove," wrote the director, and organize the material "in such a manner as to so indicate. . . . I must insist upon detailed, accurate reporting."[86]

By mid-October, it was obvious that Townsend was about to be summoned before the grand jury. "It has now become imperative," Hoover insisted, that "investigation of this case be completed at the earliest possible moment." He ordered the SAC to assign three agents to the case and submit the first report no later than 22 October. The vital point, he added, was the identity of the foreign principal and Townsend's relationship with it. To charge him, the bureau had to prove that the foreign principal was associated with the Japanese government. When the bureau had enough evidence, he directed, it should interview Townsend.[87]

It was at this point, in late October, that the FBI examined Townsend's passport, probably when he turned it in along with his application for a new one. It revealed that from June to August 1937, just when the Sino-Japanese War broke out, he had traveled to Japan and Manchukuo, "visiting cities not open to tourists." Moreover, his articles were published in the English editions of two Japanese newspapers.[88] The last document in his FBI file was dated 31 October.

On 6 November, a grand jury labeled Townsend a person of interest. Although still not charged with any crime, he was summoned to testify before the grand jury eighteen days later.[89] In early November, according to a later account, "lightning struck" the Committee on Pacific Relations as well as Armstrong personally when it was reported that committee member Townsend had been charged with accepting money to serve as a Japanese agent. On 8 November, Frederick Libby wrote Mark Shaw that Armstrong had been in Washington for a couple of days. "We had already heard," he continued, "that Mr. Ralph Townsend, one of the members of your Committee on the Far East [sic], was to be charged with being a foreign agent and receiving foreign money, and we hear that there is another member of the Committee liable to the same charge" (McKim? Baxter?). Libby thought that Armstrong had been "doing his best to clear the Committee with the State Department of responsibility for the conduct of these two men." This matter, he concluded, "would wait until you [Shaw] come."[90] There was no doubt that Townsend was a vehement Japanese sympathizer and isolationist. By the time of the inaugural meeting of the proposed Committee on Pacific Relations, the FBI already had accumulated a "sizeable dossier" on him.[91]

To be fair, Armstrong had doubts about Townsend all along. In a September 1941 letter to Charles Boss, he reported that he recently had visited Townsend in Lake Geneva, Wisconsin. The latter, he wrote, "may be a trifle on the too-vigorous pro-Japanese side."[92] Did he know Townsend was under intense surveillance by the FBI? It began, after all, while the Missourian was attempting to recruit Townsend for his Committee on Pacific Relations between May and September.⁹³ In March 1942, three months after war broke out, he told the FBI that at a conference he attended in mid-November 1941—the National Council for the Prevention of War meeting in Washington on 14 and 15 November—someone (name censored by FBI; Libby or Shaw?) "regretted" the inclusion of three persons (names censored) on the list of members of the Committee on Pacific Relations. At that time, the FBI was investigating Townsend, McKim, and Schumpeter. Decades later, the bureau responded to an FOIA request that it had no file on Baxter.

In 1942, Armstrong divulged to the FBI that he had been told by an informant "in confidence" that one of the objectionable members of his committee—clearly, Baxter—had done work for the "Japanese railroad, or some other agencies of a semi-public nature, in connection with his International Economic Council or agency in New York." This member "never made any reference," Armstrong explained to the bureau, "to any connections with the Japanese government." His informant told Armstrong that because committee members were, in the words of Armstrong's memorandum to the FBI, "entirely unselfish in their interest, they should not be mixed up with any who had done commercial work for the Japanese government or private interests." Armstrong agreed. He had spoken to the person who had worked for the Japanese railway, he recalled, and he had "promised to contribute to the expense of the committee and the proposed conference." Following 7 December, however, "nothing came of that . . . of course."⁹⁴

Here, Armstrong was being disingenuous with the FBI, for in October 1941 he had informed Terasaki Hidenari at the Japanese embassy that Baxter had contributed to the expenses of the committee.⁹⁵ Moreover, if Baxter did not tell Armstrong about his connections with the Japanese government, nor did it appear Armstrong told the New York businessman about his own relationship with officials (especially diplomat, propaganda chief, and intelligence official Terasaki Hidenari) at the Japanese embassy in Washington. In its commentary on Armstrong's March 1942 "supplemental report," the FBI suggested that committee member E. W. Frazar could be the person with Japanese connections since he had spent decades working in Japan and, as a representative there for Baldwin Locomotive Works, had a railroad connection. However, when the bureau went on to connect the mystery man with the International Economic Research Board (*sic*—Bureau), and Armstrong revealed this person had promised to contribute to the committee and its conference expenses, it became plain that the mystery man could only have been Baxter. This person, the FBI reported, was said to have done work for the Japanese railways or "some other agencies of a semi-public nature." Another member of the committee (name censored in the FBI report) concluded that "his [Baxter's] motives for peace with the Japanese may have been encouraged by remunerative gain." In handing in his "supplemental report" to the FBI in March 1942, Armstrong promised that if further information "concerning the above Subject [Baxter] was desired it would be readily forthcoming upon request."[96]

While the FBI investigated Committee on Pacific Relations members Armstrong, Schumpeter, and McKim, Townsend was the only committee participant who was imprisoned. The State Department believed he was a foreign agent. In September 1938, it sent him a copy of the "Rules and Regulations Governing the Registration of Agents of Foreign Principals under the Act of Congress Approved June 8, 1938 (Public No. 583—75th Congress)" as well as the registration form. In a response the following month, he flatly denied he was a foreign agent, claiming that "no activities of mine come within the purview of the regulations cited." None of his talks or publications on foreign affairs, he insisted, had been financed by foreigners. His books and booklets had been sold on a purely commercial basis. He concluded with a vehement defense:

> I do not believe any utterance of mine in any public address or published work could reasonably be interpreted as soliciting partisan sympathy for any nation other than America. On the contrary, the aim in all has been to stress the impropriety of such partisanism [sic] in America, and the desirability of maintaining toward all nations and foreign factions with which our government is at peace a supporting public opinion of uniform neutrality, with good will, rather than discriminations of hate toward some and maudlin sentimentality for others, the basic principle.[97]

In an intriguing handwritten note on Frederick Libby's 8 November 1941 letter to Mark Shaw, one of the two men (the signature is illegible) noted that the "Institute for Propaganda Analysis listed him [Townsend] as a Japanese agent back in 1939."[98] In January 1939, an investigator at the institute cabled the State Department to inquire whether Townsend was "listed with State Department as Japanese Propagandist?" He added he would welcome an "immediate" reply. State replied that very day that Townsend had not registered under the Registration Act of June 1938.[99]

In fact, what the institute wrote was considerably subtler. Townsend, it reported, self-published his writings and insisted that Japan did not pay for them. His motive was patriotism, he claimed, and noted his name was not on the State Department's official list of foreign propagandists. The institute's journal, *Propaganda Analysis*, which took as its mission the destruction of myths fabricated by belligerents in the war, then concluded: "This is true. Actually, the Japanese aren't paying Mr. Townsend to write the pamphlets, and they aren't giving him money to publish them. However, the Japanese Chamber of Commerce in San Francisco buys the pamphlets and sends out thousands of them."[100] According to George Eggleston, editor of *Scribner's Commentator*, the grand jury prosecutor learned of this and summoned Townsend to testify.[101]

It was probably an earlier Department of Justice investigation in San Francisco that led to Libby's early November 1941 alarm about Townsend. According to Eggleston, in October 1941, he, magazine part-owner Douglas Stewart, and several magazine staffers were subpoenaed to appear before the federal grand jury that had begun work in July in Washington.[102] In early November, the *Washington Post*, reporting the proceedings of the grand jury investigating German agents and the isolationist publication *Scribner's Commentator*, noted that two weeks earlier the sales and promotion manager of that magazine had given Townsend a "mammoth," "closely guarded, secretly compiled master" mailing list of anti-interventionists compiled by the isolationists. On 6 November, two days prior to Libby's letter to Shaw, Townsend became a person of interest to the grand jury but still had not been charged with anything. Scheduled to testify before the grand jury on 24 November, he temporarily disappeared, which set in motion a nationwide search for him. The "anti-interventionist writer," however, still was being sought merely as a "key witness" in the special grand jury's investigation of German agents.[103]

It was not until a week later that the press ominously described Townsend as a "spokesman . . . for the appeasement of Japan."[104] After the special grand jury was convened in Washington, the *Washington Post* sent a reporter to Lake Geneva to investigate *Scribner's Commentator* and the *Herald*. He spun a tale of the "anti-British *Herald*" receiving funds in an unbelievable and mysterious way. The *Herald*, he reported, was not a "crude Nazi propaganda sheet or blatantly unreasoning anti-interventionist handbill" but as sophisticated a paper as its sister publication, *Scribner's Commentator*. He detailed the business arrangements of both publications. Its editorials and advertisements (for example, for the America First Committee) made clear it was an isolationist publication. He pointed out that the *Herald* had stopped publication because it had run out of money. "One of those who appeared in the *Herald* venture "ostensibly as a staff writer," the reporter added, "was Ralph Townsend, now the object of a nation-wide search by federal agents."[105] Meanwhile, in 1941, the FBI began tapping the phones at *Scribner's Commentator* (just as it was said to be tapping the phones of Lindbergh and America First).[106]

In addition to being pro-Japanese, both *Scribner's Commentator* and the *Herald* were anti-Semitic. Therefore, the America First Committee's national officers were "cautious in their relations" with them, even though, according to one writer, "many supporters of America First held antisemitic views." Nevertheless, it cooperated with the publications. Their staffs helped America First's headquarters and some local chapters to mail isolationist materials. America First leaders allowed the publications to publish their speeches, and some chapters distributed issues of the publications.[107]

Although at first sought only as a witness before the special grand jury investigating German agents as well as *Scribner's Commentator* and the

Herald, following Pearl Harbor things became darker for Townsend. Four days after the attack, a Washington columnist advised his readers to "be on the lookout for" Townsend, whom he described as the author of a book advocating "appeasement of Japan." The Washington grand jury, he continued, "hears that Townsend has a pro-Japanese mailing list."[108] On 16 December, he finally appeared before the grand jury, which was now no longer limited to the investigation of German agents but expanded to encompass "Axis" agents. For the first time, press coverage of Townsend's tribulations used the word "Jap." Townsend, the press reported, had recently advocated that the United States "pursue a policy of neutrality and peace with the Axis powers." The report added, though, that he now believed in assisting the war effort in every possible way.[109] In its report on his grand jury appearance, the press asserted that Townsend had "written sympathetically of Japan's ambitions in Asia" and had "numerous connections in Japanese commercial and government circles there."[110]

After nearly three months of investigations, the axe descended. In January 1942, nearly two months after the beginning of the war, Townsend was arrested in Lake Geneva, where evangelist E. Stanley Jones had talked peace with Kagawa Toyohiko in June 1941 and where *Scribner's Commentator* and the *Herald* had been published up until Pearl Harbor. In January 1942, *Scribner's Commentator* closed down with a "WIN THE WAR" issue. According to its editor, it received "hundreds of letter lamenting our demise."[111]

Townsend and five others, according to the press, were accused of "conspiring to conceal that they were Japanese agents" by failing to register under the Foreign Agents Registration Act.[112] In February 1942, the press reported that complaints about Townsend's writings, especially *America Has No Enemies in Asia*, had "provoked a Department of Justice investigation *last autumn* [author's italics]," and two special prosecutors had spent weeks before a federal grand jury in San Francisco collecting the evidence that resulted in Townsend's indictment in late January.[113]

The Washington, DC, grand jury that had begun to investigate foreign propaganda in mid-1941 indicted Townsend and several others for criminal conspiracy for failing to register as Japanese agents and thus violating the Foreign Agents Registration Act. The indictment accused Townsend of writing, editing, and distributing pamphlets, such as *America Has No Enemies in Asia*, financed by the Japanese consul general in San Francisco. The Japanese, it was reported, paid Townsend and five others more than $175,000 for propaganda work. The indictments, it was reported, were the result of an investigation launched in November 1941 by two special assistants to the attorney general.[114]

In March 1942, Townsend, identified as a former editor of the *Herald*, a "flagrantly pro-Axis enterprise," and a contributor to *Scribner's Commentator*, pled guilty to accepting money to write articles and make speeches on behalf of the Japanese without registering as a foreign agent, although a charge of criminal conspiracy was dropped. As public relations counsel and publicity agent for the Japanese Committee on Trade and Information, it was charged, he received "substantial compensation."[115] Several of his publications, including *The High Cost of Hate*, *There Is No Halfway Neutrality*, and *America Has No Enemies in Asia*, it was asserted, were "designed in Tokyo" and paid for by the Japanese consulate general in San Francisco. He was allowed to remain free on $5,000 bond, however, and remanded to a probation officer.[116]

Now routinely labeled in the press a "Japanese (or Jap) agent," even though his editor at *Scribner's Commentator* scoffed that Townsend was "no more an enemy agent than Bob Hope,"[117] in June he was sentenced to eight months to two years in prison. In doing so, the judge referred to him as a "Hirohito hireling" who had committed a crime that was "repulsive, obscene and macabre." The government accused him of serving as a "front man" for the San Francisco Japanese Committee on Trade and Information, a propaganda agency financed by the Japanese government by way of its consulate general in San Francisco.[118] In July, his appeal for a reduction of his sentence on the grounds he did not mean to violate the law when he failed to report his connection with the Japanese committee was denied.[119]

He also was indicted for sedition—for conspiring to undermine the morale of the military—along with *Scribner's Commentator*, America First, and many other individuals and organizations. In October, the press reported the case might be tried in a month.[120] From his cell in the District (of Columbia) Jail, he argued that the sedition charge was inspired by "extremists" who wanted to "punish me for my perfectly honorable and legitimate pre-war stand for United States neutrality." Even though he had pled guilty, he insisted, "Nothing I ever had to say was ever directed by any foreigner. I was never anybody's foreign agent. All I published was independently written and 100 percent American."[121] In the fall of 1942, he also was accused of accepting $2,250 from a pro-German sympathizer to pay for distribution of fifteen thousand propaganda pamphlets titled *The Truth about England*.[122]

After several months in jail, he was released, "thanks to the heroic efforts" of isolationist Senators Robert Taft, Burton Wheeler, and Gerald Nye, according to *Scribner's Commentator* editor George Eggleston.[123] Subsequently, he apparently resumed his career as a freelance writer. As time passed, his 1942 conviction and jail term were rarely mentioned. In 1943, the sensationalistic book *Under Cover* by John Carlson did cite his conviction and the thousands of copies of his pamphlets that he printed.[124] Between 1968 and 1972, he corresponded with a retired naval officer who had been a cryptographer at Pearl Harbor when the Japanese attacked and, in retirement, was working on a revisionist work on World War II and its origins. Thus, he seemed associated with the right-wing, anti-Roosevelt, revisionist writers on the war. In January 1968, he wrote that he would be "right proud" to meet George Wallace, the Georgia right-wing segregationist. In February, he became involved in what he referred to as a "tax wrangle." In 1971, one of his correspondents wrote Townsend to assure him that he did not tell an acquaintance about Townsend's past "troubles."[125]

More than six decades later, the Japanese right wing effusively praised a new translation of Townsend's 1933 book *Ways That Are Dark: The Truth about China*. The book, explained a reporter, "contrasts an allegedly dirty, devious nation with the trustworthy, hardworking Japanese, and bitterly criticizes the then-U.S. government for opposing Japan's attacks on China. . . . For the right wing here [in Japan], he is a hero."[126]

Meanwhile, two days after Pearl Harbor, with the "prevention of war" objective of his organization dashed by the Japanese action, at least for the time being, Frederick Libby announced that his organization, the National Council for the Prevention of War, would dedicate itself to achievement of a negotiated peace at the earliest possible moment in the war.[127] This by no means went unnoticed by the public. In a note to Libby a week after Pearl Harbor, one Aleck Hamilton wrote that he had noticed Libby was executive director of the National Council for the Prevention of War and "agitating for a negotiated peace." "Unfortunately for your argument," he continued, "too many people remember that you participated in forming the Committee of [sic] Pacific Relations not long ago." While it had appealed for better relations between the United States and Japan, he observed, at the same time it included "too many persons suspected of acting as Japanese propagandists."[128]

NOTES

1. U.S. Department of Defense, *The "Magic" Background of Pearl Harbor* (Washington, DC: Government Printing Office, 1978), 4:126–27, A-185.

2. Wendell Berge, Assistant Attorney General, Department of Justice, memo for Mr. J. Edgar Hoover, Director, FBI, 10 April 1942, FBI File on Orland Kay Armstrong, FOIA.

3. Warren I. Cohen, "The Role of Private Groups in the United States," in *Pearl Harbor as History: American-Japanese Relations, 1931–1941*, ed. Dorothy Borg and Shumpei Okamoto (New York: Columbia University Press, 1973), 302, 452.

4. Although author John Roy Carlson labelled Baxter, Townsend, and McKim "pro-Japanese" in his 1943 polemic *Under Cover*, he did not mention Schumpeter. John Roy Carlson, *Under Cover: My Four Years in the Nazi Underworld of America* (New York: E.P. Dutton & Co., 1943).

5. Curt Gentry, *J. Edgar Hoover: The Man and the Secrets* (New York: W. W. Norton, 1991), 225–27; Wayne S. Cole, *Charles A. Lindbergh and the Battle against Intervention in World War II* (New York: Harcourt Brace Jovanovich, 1974), 129; Charles A. Lindbergh, *The Wartime Journals of Charles A. Lindbergh* (New York: Harcourt Brace Jovanovich, 1970), 515; Joyce Milton, *Loss of Eden: A Biography of Charles and Anne Lindbergh* (New York: HarperCollins, 1993), 397–98.

6. Cole, *Charles A. Lindbergh*, 117–18, 129; Anne Morrow Lindbergh, *War Within and Without: Diaries and Letters of Anne Morrow Lindbergh, 1939–1944* (New York: Harcourt Brace Jovanovich, 1980), xxii.

7. Milton, *Loss of Eden*, 398.

8. Cole, *Charles A. Lindbergh*, 129.

9. Wayne S. Cole, *America First: The Battle against Intervention in World War II* (Madison: University of Wisconsin Press, 1953), 118.

10. P. N. Foxworth, Assistant Director, FBI, to Director, FBI, 10 October 1941, FBI File on Armstrong, FOIA.

11. John Edgar Hoover, Director, FBI, to Special Agent in Charge (hereafter SAC), Washington, DC, 23 October 1941, FBI File on Armstrong, FOIA.

12. Hoover to SAC, Washington, DC, RE: Orland K. Armstrong, aliases: O. K. Armstrong, Mr. "A"; Espionage (J[apan]), 4 October 1941, FBI File on Armstrong, FOIA.

13. Armstrong to "My dear friend Terry [Terasaki Hidenari]," 20 October 1941, Orland Kay Armstrong (1893–1987) Papers, 1912–1987 (C4056), State Historical Society of Missouri, Manuscript Collection, Columbia, MO.

14. William E. Leishear, "Japanese [Espionage] Activities in Washington, DC," n.d., 32; FBI wiretap, 31 October 1941, FBI File on Terasaki Hidenari, FOIA.

15. Memo from Harry M. Kimball to D. M. Ladd, FBI, U.S. Department of Justice, Washington, DC, 31 October 1941, FBI File on Terasaki Hidenari, FOIA.

16. Armstrong to J. Edgar Hoover, "Chief," FBI, Washington, DC, 18 August 1936, FBI File No. 62-45631-4, FOIA. Although in signing the letter Armstorng identified himself as a member of the Missouri legislature, he used American Legion, Department of Missouri, Child Welfare Commission, letterhead.

17. Hoover to Armstrong, 1 September 1936, Armstrong, FBI File No. 62-45631-4, FOIA. When Armstrong appealed, Hoover's assistant, Clyde Tolson, reaffirmed Hoover's decision. Clyde Tolson, memo for the director, FBI, U.S. Department of Justice, 17 November 1936, FBI File on Armstrong, FOIA.

18. [Name blacked out], Springfield, MO, to FBI, Washington, DC, with copies of newspaper articles, n.d. [received by FBI on 18 December 1941], FBI File on Armstrong, FOIA.

19. Armstrong, "We Brought War on Ourselves, Peace-Maker Armstrong Says," *Springfield Leader and Press*, 10 December 1941, FBI File on Armstrong, FOIA.

20. Berge memo for Hoover, 10 April 1942; Hoover to SAC, Kansas City, MO, 1 May 1942, FBI File on Armstrong, FOIA.

21. R. E. Sherk, Kansas City, MO, FBI, "Orland K. Armstrong, alias O. K. Armstrong; Internal Security—J[apan] and G[ermany]; Sedition Act," 9 May 1942, FBI File on Armstrong, FOIA.

22. Hoover memo for Assistant Attorney General Berge, 22 October 1942, FBI File on Armstrong, FOIA.

23. O. K. Armstrong to [W. Forbes] Webber, [Kansas City Division, FBI], 6 March 1942, Armstrong Papers.

24. For Armstrong's connection with George Eggleston between September and December 1940, see Lindbergh, *Wartime Journals*, 393, 408–9, 417, 422, 428, 430–31.

25. Dillard Stokes, "2 Magazine Officials Accused of Obstructing Nazi Probe Jury," *Washington Post* (hereafter *WP*), 6 November 1941, 1

26. Armstrong to Lindbergh, 25 October 1945, Charles A. Lindbergh, Manuscripts and Archives, Yale University Library, New Haven, CT.

27. "Orland K. Armstrong," 6 August 1947, FBI File on Armstrong, FOIA.

28. SAC, WFO [Washington Field Office], to Director, FBI, 21 February 1951, FBI File on Armstrong, FOIA.

29. SAC, WFO, to Director, FBI, 26 February 1951; Armstrong to Hoover, 18 July 1964; Armstrong to Hoover, 28 November 1964, FBI File on Armstrong, FOIA.

30. New York City bureau, FBI, report of Elizabeth B. Schumpeter, 12 April and 15 May 1943, FBI File on Schumpeter, FOIA; Roger B. Jeans, *Terasaki Hidenari, Pearl Harbor, and Occupied Japan* (Lanham, MD: Lexington Books, 2009), 44.

31. Schumpeter to Armstrong, 18 November 1941, Armstrong Papers.

32. Robert Loring Allen, *Opening Doors: The Life and Work of Joseph Schumpeter*, vol. 2, *America* (New Brunswick, NJ: Transaction, 1991), 102, 113nn23–24.
33. Boston office, FBI, reports on William Henry Chamberlin and Elizabeth B. Schumpeter, 1 and 22 July 1941, FBI File on Schumpeter, FOIA.
34. Allen, *Opening* Doors, 2:93–94. The first document in Elizabeth Schumpeter's FBI file is dated July 1941. Tom C. Clark, Assistant Attorney General, to Director, FBI, 1 December 1944, FBI File on Schumpeter, FOIA (released to me on 14 March 2006).
35. Allen, *Opening Doors*, 2:151.
36. A. H. Belmont to D. M. Ladd, FBI, 14 July 1951, FBI File on Schumpeter, FOIA.
37. John N. Thomas, *The Institute of Pacific Relations: Asian Scholars and American Politics* (Seattle: University of Washington Press, 1974), chap. 4.
38. Cohen, "Role of Private Groups in the United States," 453.
39. Loyal American to Mr. [Walter] Winchell, 19 December 1941, FBI File on John Cole McKim, FOIA; New York Bureau, FBI, "Rev. John Cole McKim," 15 March 1944, FBI File on McKim, FOIA.
40. McKim, Peekskill, NY, to H.I.J.M. [His Imperial Japanese Majesty?], Consulate General, New York, 6 December 1941, encl. with Hoover to SAC, New York, 4 May 1942, FBI File on McKim, FOIA. McKim enclosed clippings of his and others' letters published in the *New York Sun* as well as a piece he had submitted to the *Peekskill Star*.
41. Tom C. Clark, assistant attorney general, to Director, FBI, 1 December 1944, FBI File on McKim, FOIA.
42. Several articles and book reviews McKim contributed to the magazine between February 1939 and October 1941 are reproduced in New York Bureau, FBI, "Rev. John Cole McKim," 15 March 1944, 34–80.
43. New York City Bureau, FBI, "Reverend John Cole McKim," 22 April 1940 and 10 July 1944, 5, FBI File on McKim, FOIA.
44. New York City Bureau, FBI, "Reverend John Cole McKim," 22 April 1940.
45. Special War Policies Unit, War Division, Washington, DC, to Reverend John Cole McKim, D.D., P.O. Box 242, Peekskill, NY, 24 November 1942, encl. Special War Policies Unit, War Division, memo for Mr. J. Edgar Hoover, Director, FBI, 25 November 1942, FBI File on McKim, FOIA.
46. Loyal American to Mr. [Walter] Winchell, 19 December 1941, FBI File on McKim, FOIA; New York Bureau, FBI, "Rev. John Cole McKim," 15 March 1944, 4–12, 16–17, 27.
47. R. L. Morgan, special agent, memo for the [FBI] Director, Attention: Mr. Ladd, "Japanese Diplomatic Corps, Internal Security," 19 February 1942, box 10, folder: 1942, Homestead Hotel, Internal Security Reports, Memoranda, Roy Leonard Morgan Papers (MSS 93-4), Special Collections, University of Virginia Law School, Charlottesville, VA. On Kondo Shinichi, see Jeans, *Terasaki Hidenari*, 36–38, 46, 75, 89.
48. Unless otherwise noted, the following recollections of McKim regarding the committee are based on New York Bureau, FBI, "Rev. John Cole McKim," 15 March 1944, 19–21.
49. McKim to Armstrong, 27 September 1941, Armstrong Papers.
50. Armstrong to McKim, 12 September 1941, Armstrong Papers.
51. Cole, *America First*, 79, 121, 124–25. A frequent America First speaker, the female flier Laura Ingalls, also was convicted, in her case for failing to register as a German agent, and sentenced to two years in prison. Geoffrey Perrett, *Days of Sadness, Years of Triumph: The American People, 1939–1945* (New York: Coward, McCann & Geoghegan, 1973; Penguin Books, 1974), 218. Perrett argued that she was simply an "ultraisolationist and a political innocent."
52. Memo of conversation between William R. Langdon, Division of Far Eastern Affairs, and Armstrong, 30 September 1941, Department of State, 740.0011 Pacific War/553, National Archives.
53. Tom J. Terral, Little Rock, AR, to President Franklin D. Roosevelt, White House, Washington, DC, 18 April 1939, encl. a copy of his letter to Ralph Townsend as well as a copy of *The High Cost of Hate*, 800.01B11 Registration—Townsend, Ralph/22, encl. with Secretary of State to Attorney General, 13 July 1939, FBI File on Ralph W. Townsend, FOIA; [name blacked out], San Francisco, CA, to Cordell Hull, Secretary of State, Department of State,

Washington, DC, 14 February 1939; [name blacked out] to State Department, Washington, DC, 26 February 1939; Maurice Leon, New York, to Department of State, Washington, DC, 17 April 1939; 800.01B11 Registration—Townsend, Ralph/2, 3, 517; all three encl. with Secretary of State to Attorney General, 13 July 1939. During the investigation of Townsend, his 1939 pamphlet *There Is No Halfway Neutrality* was not mentioned. Manfred Jonas, *Isolationism in America, 1935–1941* (Ithaca, NY: Cornell University Press, 1966), 300.

54. Hoover to SAC, FBI, San Francisco, CA, "Re: Ralph Townsend, Registration Act," 5 May 1939, FBI File on Townsend, FOIA. Messersmith, a former minister to Austria (1934–1937), served as assistant secretary of state from 1937 to 1940. Breckinridge Long, *The War Diary of Breckinridge Long: Selections from the Years 1939–1944*, ed. Fred L. Israel (Lincoln: University of Nebraska Press, 1966), 1n1.

55. Hoover to SAC, San Francisco, CA, 19 December 1939, FBI File on Townsend, FOIA.

56. Frederick Moore, *With Japan's Leaders: An Intimate Record of Fourteen Years as Counsellor to the Japanese Government* (New York: Charles Scribner's Sons, 1942), 64–65.

57. Hoover to Assistant Secretary of State George S. Messersmith, 1 July 1939, File No. 65-2193-4, FBI File on Townsend, encl. M. C. Falkner, San Francisco FBI Bureau, "Ralph W. Townsend, Registration Act; Espionage," 9 June 1939, FBI File on Townsend, FOIA.

58. San Francisco Bureau, FBI, "'Changed' [Charged?]: Ralph W. Townsend; David Warren Ryder—Registration Act; Espionage," SF File No. 65-89, 10 October 1939, FBI File on Townsend, FOIA; Falkner, "Ralph W. Townsend—Registration Act; Espionage," 9 June 1939, encl. with Hoover to Messersmith, 1 July 1939, with copies to Rear Admiral Walter S. Anderson, Director, Naval Intelligence, Navy Department, Washington, DC, and Col. E. R. Warner Mccabe, Assistant Chief of Staff, G-2, War Department, Washington, DC.

59. San Francisco Bureau, FBI, "Ralph W. Townsend; David Warren Ryder—Registration Act, Espionage," 6 November 1939, FBI File on Townsend, FOIA.

60. FBI to Assistant Secretary of State Adolf A. Berle Jr., 15 Feburary 1940, FBI File on Townsend, FOIA.

61. N. J. L. Pieper, SAC, San Francisco, CA, to Director, FBI, Washington, DC, 1 May 1940, FBI File on Townsend, FOIA.

62. San Francisco, FBI, "'Changed' [Charged?]: Ralph W. Townsend," 18 May 1940.

63. Senator Claude Pepper to J. Edgar Hoover, Director, FBI, 26 June 1940, FBI File on Townsend, FOIA.

64. B. E. Sackett, FBI, SAC, New York, to Director, FBI, Washington, DC, 28 August 1940; A. E. Demaray, Acting Director, National Park Service, U.S. Department of the Interior, Washington, DC, to Hoover, Washington, DC, 22 October 1940; A. G. Berens, SAC, St. Paul, MN, to Director, FBI, 30 October 1940; M. L. Richmond, SAC, Houston, TX, to SAC, San Francisco, CA, 31 October 1940; Jessie Bernard, Assistant Professor of Sociology, Lindenwood College, St. Charles, MO, to J. Edgar Hoover, FBI, Washington, DC, 1 November 1940; Florence W. Schaper, Director, Student Guidance and Personnel, Lindenwood College, St. Charles, MO, to J. Edgar Hoover, FBI, Washington, DC; E. J. Gebern, SAC, Denver, CO, to SAC, San Francisco, CA, 7 November 1940; W. L. Listerman, SAC, Cleveland, OH, to Director, FBI, Washington, DC, 7 November 1940; V. W. Peterson, SAC, to Director, FBI, Washington, DC, 16 December 1940; "Ralph W. Townsend; David Warren Rydr, alias Ray W. Ryder," 21 January 1941; J. D. Swenson, SAC, Portland, OR, to Director, FBI, 8 January 1941; G. B. Norris, SAC, Saint Louis, MO, to SAC, San Francisco, CA, 27 January 1941; L. H. Gourley, American Consul, American Consulate General, Harbin, Manchuria, to Secretary of State, "Distribution of Ralph Townsend Propaganda Booklet, 'Seeking Foreign Trouble,'" Despatch No. 22, 25 November 1940, encl. with memo for J. Edgar Hoover, Director, FBI, by Wendell Berge, Acting Assistant Attorney General, Department of Justice, Washington, DC, 1 February 1941; Arthur L. Carson, Silliman University, Dumaguete, Negros Oriental, Philippines, to Director, FBI, 7 February 1941; John Edgar Hoover, Director, FBI, to [name blacked out], New York, 18 June 1941, FBI File on Townsend, FOIA.

65. Hoover to SAC, Portland, OR, 23 January 1941, FBI File on Townsend, FOIA.

66. S. J. Drayton, SAC, Seattle, WA, to SAC, San Francisco, 17 October 1940; San Francisco, FBI, "Ralph W. Townsend; David Warren Ryder, alias Ray W. Ryder," 31 January 1941, FBI File on Townsend, FOIA.

67. N. J. L. Pieper, SAC, San Francisco, to SAC, Seattle, WA, 31 October 1940, FBI File on Townsend, FOIA.
68. Hoover to SAC, San Francisco, 14 January 1941, FBI File on Townsend, FOIA.
69. E. A. Tamm, FBI, memo for the Director, 6 February 1941, FBI File on Townsend, FOIA.
70. John Barry Hubbard, FBI, San Francisco Bureau, report on Ralph Townsend and David Warren Ryder, with aliases, 21 February 1941, p. 11; FBI, Washington, DC, "Ralph W. Townsend," 17 May 1941, FBI File on Townsend, FOIA.
71. Hubbard report on Ralph W. Townsend and David Warren Ryder, 21 February 1941.
72. San Francisco, FBI, report on Ralph W. Townsend and David Warren Ryder, with alias, 26 March 1941, FBI File on Townsend, FOIA.
73. Hoover to SAC, San Francisco, 28 May 1941, FBI File on Townsend, FOIA.
74. Hubbard report on Ralph Townsend and David Warren Ryder, with aliases, 4 June 1941, FBI File on Townsend, FOIA.
75. Hoover to SAC, San Francisco, 26 June 1941, FBI File on Townsend, FOIA.
76. Hoover to SAC, San Francisco, 5 July 1941, FBI File on Townsend, FOIA.
77. Wendell Berge, Assistant Attorney General, Department of Justice, memo for Mr. Hoover, Director, FBI, 13 August 1941, FBI File on Townsend, FOIA.
78. Hoover to SAC, San Francisco, 19 August 1941, FBI File on Townsend, FOIA.
79. Hoover to SAC, San Francisco, 10 September 1941, FBI File on Townsend, FOIA.
80. FBI bureau, San Francisco, report on Ralph W. Townsend and David Warren Ryder, with aliases, 12 September 1941, FBI File on Townsend, FOIA.
81. Cole, *America First*, 122–23.
82. Memo for the files, "Ralph Townsend," encl. with Hoover to SAC, San Francisco, 24 September 1941, FBI File on Townsend, FOIA.
83. Justus D. Doenecke, "Explaining the Antiwar Movement, 1939–1941: The Next Assignment," *Journal of Libertarian Studies* 8, no. 1 (1986): 160.
84. Hoover to SAC, San Francisco, 29 September 1941, FBI File on Townsend, FOIA.
85. [Hoover] to Assistant Secretary of State Adolf A. Berle Jr., 30 September 1941; Hoover to N. J. L. Pieper, SAC, San Francisco, 31 October 1941, FBI File on Townsend, FOIA.
86. Hoover to SAC, San Francisco, 2 October 1941, FBI File on Townsend, FOIA.
87. Hoover to SAC, San Francisco, 13 October 1941, FBI File on Townsend, FOIA.
88. FBI report on Ralph W. Townsend, Washington, DC, 20 October 1941, FBI File on Townsend, FOIA.
89. Dillard Stokes, "2 Magazine Officials Accused of Obstructing Nazi Probe Jury," *WP*, 6 November 1941, 1; Dillard Stokes, "U.S. Hunting Key Nazi Probe Witness," *WP*, 25 November 1941, 1.
90. Frederick Libby, Executive Secretary, National Council for the Prevention of War (hereafter NCPW), Washington, DC, to Shaw, C/O America First Committee, Chicago, IL, 8 November 1941, NCPW, reel 41: 116 (box 129); Cohen, "Role of Private Groups in the United States," 453.
91. Memo of conversation between Langdon and Armstrong, 30 September 1941.
92. Armstrong to Dear Friend Charles [F. Boss Jr.], 13 September 1941, Armstrong Papers.
93. C. A. Kahrhoff, "Japanese [Espionage] Activities at Washington, DC," 18 December 1941, p. 4, FBI File on Terasaki; "Ex-Envoy [John Cudahy] Warns of Nazis' Strength; Tells of Bombings," *WP*, 5 November 1941, 21.
94. Armstrong, supplemental report to [W. Forbes] Webber, FBI, Kansas City, MO, 11 March 1942, FBI File on Armstrong, FOIA.
95. Armstrong to Terasaki, 20 October 1941.
96. "Everett Welles Frazar," *Marquis Who's Who on the Web* (accessed 18 August 2005); Armstrong, supplemental report to Webber, 11 March 1942.
97. Joseph C. Green, Chief, Office of Arms and Munitions Control, to Ralph Townsend, Brooklyn, New York, 15 September 1938; Ralph Townsend, Box 347, San Francisco, CA, to Joseph C. Green, Chief, Office of Arms and Munitions Control, Department of State, Washington, DC, 19 October 1939; 800.01B11 Registration—Townsend, Ralph/1-2, encl. with Secretary of State to Attorney General, 13 July 1939, FBI File on Townsend, FOIA.

98. Libby to Shaw, 8 November 1941.
99. Harold Lavine, Institute for Propaganda Analysis, New York, to Joseph C. Green, Chief of Arms and Munitions Control, Department of State, 30 January 1939, 800.01B11 Registration—Townsend, Ralph/11; Cordell Hull, Secretary of State, to Harold Lavine, Institute for Propaganda Analysis, New York, 30 January 1939, encl. in Secretary of State to Attorney General, 13 July 1939.
100. "War in China," *Propaganda Analysis* 2, no. 5 (1939): 30–31; Doenecke, "Explaining the Antiwar Movement," 142.
101. George T. Eggleston, *Roosevelt, Churchill, and the World War II Opposition* (Old Greenwich, CT: Devin-Adair, 1979), 150.
102. Eggleston, *Roosevelt*, 136; for Eggleston's recollections of his appearances before the grand jury, see chap. 14.
103. Stokes, "2 Magazine Officials Accused," 1; Stokes, "U.S. Hunting Key Nazi," 1.
104. Dillard Stokes, "Lake Geneva's 'Boom' Fizzles as Pro-Nazis Disappear," *WP*, 30 November 1941, 1.
105. Dillard Stokes, "Mysterious $30,000 Is Given to Pro-Nazi Paper Printed at Lake Geneva," *Capital Times*, 30 November 1941; Cole, *America First*, 122.
106. Eggleston, *Roosevelt*, 109.
107. Cole, *America First*, 133, 136, 140.
108. Leonard Lyons, "Phone's Ringing for . . . ," *WP*, 11 December 1941, 16.
109. Dillard Stokes, "Probe Jury Will Question Writer Today," *WP*, 16 December 1941, 14.
110. Dillard Stokes, "Jury to Probe Jap Activities up to Attack," *WP*, 17 December 1941, 38.
111. Eggleston, *Roosevelt*, 156.
112. Dillard Stokes, "Scribner's Writer Seized as Japan Agent," *WP*, 29 January 1942, 1.
113. Dillard Stokes, "Propaganda Helped Lull U.S. Outposts," *WP*, 8 February 1942, 1.
114. "Six Are Indicted as Japan's Agents," *NYT*, 29 January 1942, 15; Stokes, "Scribner's Writer," 1; Stokes, "Propaganda," 1
115. "Admits Work for Japan," *NYT*, 28 March 1942, 3; "Writer Guilty as Jap Agent," *WP*, 28 March 1942, 13.
116. "Viereck Setup," *WP*, 19 May 1942, 1. George Sylvester Viereck was a German agent who was convicted in 1941 for failure to register with the State Department. Susan Dunn, *1940: F.D.R., Willkie, Lindbergh, and Hitler—the Election amid the Storm* (New Haven, CT: Yale University Press, 2013), 237–38.
117. Eggleston, *Roosevelt*, 150.
118. "Tokyo Agent Sentenced," *NYT*, 13 June 1942, 5; Dillard Stokes, "Griffin Denies Memory of Viereck Pay," *WP*, 13 June 1942, 19.
119. "Townsend, Jap Agent, Asking Shorter Term," *WP*, 16 July 1942, 7; "Lesser Term Is Denied to Townsend," *WP*, 18 July 1942, 3.
120. "Named in Sedition Indictment," *NYT*, 24 July 1942, 8; Dillard Stokes, "28 Indicted in Wide Conspiracy to Corrupt Army and Navy," *WP*, 23 July 1942, 1; "3 Cases Involving Subversity May Go to Trial in Month," *WP*, 11 October 1942, 10.
121. "Townsend Enters Denial," *NYT*, 4 August 1942, 20; "Draft Board Asked to Find Suspects," *WP*, 4 August 1942, 14.
122. Drew Pearson, "Merry-Go-Around," *WP*, 26 October 1942, 14.
123. Eggleston, *Roosevelt*, 150.
124. Carlson, *Under Cover*, 413–14.
125. Ralph Townsend and Charles C. Hiles correspondence, 1968–1972, Charles C. Hiles Collection, accession no. 1448, American Heritage Center, University of Wyoming, Laramie, WY.
126. Gregory Clark, "New Mindset Is the Only Salve," *Japan Times*, 11 October 2004, 1–5, http://www.gregoryclark.net/jtoct11.html.
127. "Pacifist Group Shifts to Negotiated Peace," *NYT*, 9 December 1941, 11.
128. Aleck Hamilton Jr. to Frederick Libby, 15 December 1941, with accompanying 10 December 1941 clipping from the *New York Post* (not in file), NCPW, reel 41: 223 (box 280).

Conclusion

Why another book on the American isolationists? Their story has been told often ever since historian Wayne S. Cole's first book on them was published more than six decades ago (he wrote two more on the topic over the subsequent two decades). My purpose in writing this book is to call attention to an overlooked chapter in the story of isolationism. While most historians have focused on the anti-interventionists who concentrated on blocking their country from joining the European Allies following the outbreak of war in 1939, a small but interesting group in the isolationist movement during its heyday in 1940 and 1941, the Committee on Pacific Relations, has been neglected. During that brief period, a conservative politician from Missouri, O. K. Armstrong, along with a handful of determined but little-known Americans from nearly every walk of life except the military worked hard to convince their countrymen they should not go to war with Japan. By the late 1930s and early 1940s, however, it was naïve of them to believe that an agreement could be reached between America and Japan to avoid armed conflict.

HISTORICAL SETTING

The "Great Debate" between interventionists and anti-interventionists was driven as much by ominous events in the outside world as by speeches and publications by the two sides during these years. One has only to describe the situation that drove Americans to take sides in the struggle over whether to intervene or not: the steady encroachments of Germany and Italy in western Europe culminating in the subjugation of every democracy except Britain, which by May 1940 stood alone.

There were clashes on at least four major issues between isolationists and interventionists from the beginning of the war in Europe up to the Japanese attack on Pearl Harbor in December 1941. In each case, the isolationists opposed attempts by President Franklin Roosevelt and the interventionists (or internationalists) to prepare the country for what they believed to be eventual war with Germany. The isolationists, such as Armstrong and pacifist Frederick Libby, opposed the revision of the neutrality acts of the 1930s, which barred the dispatch of arms to any and all belligerents, to permit the export of war supplies to beleaguered Great Britain and China, which was suffering under the onslaught of militarist Japan.

The anti-interventionists also opposed sending lend-lease supplies to Britain and China. Both Armstrong and isolationist journalist Ralph Townsend vehemently attacked the Lend-Lease Bill in testimony in the Senate in early 1941, calling it an attempt to take America into war. Following passage of the bill, huge amounts of lend-lease supplies were being sunk by German submarines. Despite this, the isolationists opposed the use of American destroyers to escort the ships carrying those desperately needed supplies to Britain. Thus, in the spring of 1941, Armstrong wrote that there was a big reaction in the Midwest against convoys. The isolationists' argument against approval of lend-lease and convoys was that they would inevitably embroil the United States in war.

Finally, the anti-interventionists opposed conscription as also making war more likely. Armstrong was careful to note that his eldest son was too young for the draft though, the intended message being that he was not opposed to conscription for personal reasons. As lifelong pacifists, both Libby and Charles Boss, who figure in our story, vehemently opposed conscription.

FIRST MEETING OF THE COMMITTEE ON PACIFIC RELATIONS

The high point of the committee's short life (September–December 1941) was probably its meeting in New York in late September to plan its organization, platform, and publicity. That evening, they affirmed their dual goals of preventing war with Japan and mediating in the Sino-Japanese War. In a statement following the meeting, Armstrong summarized six decisions the committee had made (see chapter 6). Unfortunately, war broke out before they could convene their planned Washington conference on Pacific relations, which was to create a more permanent organization.

DESCRIPTION OF THE COMMITTEE

The Committee on Pacific Relations was a tiny group compared to the isolationist America First Committee, founded in the fall of 1940. The Japanese ambassador in Washington bluntly reported to Tokyo that the committee had no influential members. The "sparkplug" was Armstrong, who journeyed throughout the East, South, and Midwest striving to recruit prominent people for the committee. In addition, he wrote numerous letters to potential members, flattering them and entreating them to join. The committee members' attitudes toward Japan ranged from vehemently pro-Japan to those who simply wanted to avert war between Japan and the United States.

There was some overlap in personnel between America First and the Committee on Pacific Relations. Thus, from May to July, Armstrong worked for the former in attempting to organization the antiwar movement in the South and also helped found an America First chapter in his hometown. Pacifist Mark Shaw also worked for America First even while serving as acting chairman of Armstrong's committee.

The committee comprised an informal grouping of a dozen or so members who had endorsed Armstrong's May 1941 policy statement (as revised in September). Those participants included professors with broad knowledge of the Far East, pacifists committed to averting war, ex-missionaries who had served in the Far East, businessmen (the committee badly needed money), newspaper men (publicity was critical), and other professionals. Armstrong simply ignored those who turned him down and continued to list them as members (as he did when he met with a State Department official in November). He was a very tenacious individual, the sort who when you told him no became even more determined to plow on through every obstacle. He had terrific energy and, although sometimes "low," persevered.

BELIEFS OF COMMITTEE MEMBERS

The members of the committee shared several beliefs. Most of them (for instance, Libby, E. Stanley Jones, and William Baxter) opposed the British Empire and did not see any difference between the growing Japanese empire and centuries-old British imperialism. Although not a member of Armstrong's committee, pacifist and evangelist Jones believed that a war with Japan would end up protecting the British Empire in Asia. Shaw thought the British Empire had outdone Japan in aggressive actions. They also shared with many other isolationists the feeling that America's participation in World War I had been a disaster for America, with vast expenditure of blood and treasure and little gained.

This deep disillusionment with America's experience in the previous war fed a current of pacifism in the ranks of the committee, too, as could be seen in the participation of Libby, the "dean of pacifists," as well as Shaw. Even though pacifist Boss was not a member of the committee, he supported Armstrong in his demands for peace. Members of the committee also were active in the numerous peace councils found throughout America in those days.

While committee members were criticized for siding with the Japanese oppressors of China, they justified their beliefs and actions by arguing that communism would be worse than fascism and the Japanese militarists. They (for example, Armstrong, Townsend, Professor Elizabeth Schumpeter, and former missionary John Cole McKim) saw their pro-Japan sentiments as the lesser enemy in the face of the threat of worldwide communism. Libby bluntly declared the ultimate winners in a Japan–America war would be communism and Stalin.

Several of the members of the Committee on Pacific Relations were also opposed to Roosevelt and the New Deal, including Baxter, Armstrong, and Schumpeter. Far from being liberal, they were even more conservative (right wing) than the members of the Republican-dominated America First Committee. Armstrong further burnished his reputation as a right-winger when he attacked school texts and their authors.

Several of the committee members also were angry with the major association of Asian scholars, the Institute of Pacific Relations. Schumpeter believed she was ill treated by the institute, which dominated her field of Far Eastern studies, and bitterly criticized several of its staffers and writers. Her articles were rejected for publication by institute journals. She was not given an opportunity to rebut criticism of her writings published in one of those periodicals, *Pacific Affairs*. In addition, she complained of being ostracized by the institute. As a result, in 1940, she resigned from it.

Ironically, the institute continued to haunt her even after she resigned. When it learned that the new organization that Schumpeter and others belonged to was named the Committee on Pacific Relations, an institute representative protested the name was too similar to the Institute of Pacific Relations and demanded the committee change its name. The committee leadership seemed willing to do so because the political stances of members of the two organizations were often quite different. Armstrong passed on this information on the controversy over the name to his contact, Terasaki Hidenari, at the Japanese embassy, with the comment that the institute was pro-Chinese.

Schumpeter often complained of unpopularity, and even being called a Japanese spy, in Far East study circles because she criticized a general tendency to underestimate the economic strength of Japan. She also worried about propaganda in the Far East studies field by pro-China groups. She found kindred souls in anti-interventionists Professor Payson Treat of Stanford University and correspondent and author William Henry Chamberlin, both of whom also were alienated from the Far Eastern studies establishment.

In addition, Schumpeter discovered that in 1939 Yale University professor A. Whitney Griswold also was unpopular in Far East studies circles because of his anti-intervention tendencies. He joined Schumpeter in battling against the Institute of Pacific Relations. He hosted Lindbergh for dinner at Yale in October 1940, worried along with Schumpeter about the dangers of placing an embargo on Japan, and at that time was sympathetic to Japan. By the time Armstrong tried to recruit him for his committee in May 1941, Griswold had drifted away from isolationism. Professor Paul Clyde of Duke University also rejected Armstrong's invitation to join his committee at a time when Clyde believed national unity was imperative. Like Griswold, he also declined to sign Armstrong's May 1941 statement.

FINANCING THE COMMITTEE

Meanwhile, the committee needed funds to pay for publicity materials and Armstrong's travel and to set up an office and staff in Washington. One of the members, financier William Baxter, contributed funds for the committee's work. Armstrong hoped businessman E. W. Frazar would chip in, but there is no evidence he ever did. Schumpeter had "slight anxieties" about Baxter, thanks to a tip from a "friendly Japanese," and urged that the sources of donations to the committee be carefully vetted. Baxter may have been the unknown committee member Armstrong was warned about in mid-November. The Japanese embassy also promised partial financial support, but there is no evidence the committee ever received the monies, which saved Armstrong from Townsend's fate of being charged as an unregistered Japanese agent.

THE WASHINGTON CONFERENCE

A central goal in the planning by Armstrong and his colleagues after the New York meeting was to convene a conference on Pacific affairs in Washington as soon as possible. Thus, Armstrong invited committee members to deliver papers at the meeting. He hoped to make a big splash with the Washington conference by inviting congressmen and senators as well as officials from the Japanese embassy to attend. The tragedy for the committee was that its leaders kept postponing it. They first spoke of holding it in October, then around Thanksgiving, and finally in late December, by which time their plans were overtaken by the reality of war. Armstrong, the eternal optimist, continued to have faith as late as October that if his movement could be made large enough, they could prevent war with Japan.

THE SINO-JAPANESE WAR (1937–1945)

The committee's formation and activities took place in the shadow of the Sino-Japanese War. While many Americans sympathized with the invaded Chinese, the members of the committee leaned toward the Japanese in hopes of preventing war between the United States and Japan and mediating in the

Sino-Japanese conflict. In the summer of 1941, Armstrong wanted to send committee members (such as Schumpeter and Shaw) to Japan to study the problems between the two countries and suggest possible solutions. This was not always easy in the atmosphere of widespread sympathy among the U.S. population for the underdog China. In fact, some members of the committee were anti-China, especially Baxter, Townsend, and McKim. McKim and Townsend went furthest in criticism of China and opposed China's leader, Chiang Kai-shek, and the Nationalist Party (Kuomintang) as well. For McKim, Japan could do no wrong, and he refused to believe that it would ever attack the United States.

As isolationists and pro-Japan figures in a time of growing danger from that nation's aggression, members of the committee were alienated from the national conversation, which was slowly tending toward an interventionist consensus when the Japanese surprise attack on Pearl Harbor eliminated the isolationist opposition. Committee members were unable to meet with either President Roosevelt or Secretary of State Cordell Hull, whom Japanese agent Terasaki Hidenari urged Armstrong to visit. A few of them did visit the State Department but were shuttled off to lower-ranking diplomats for interviews.

As a result of their views, committee members were the targets of the slings and arrows of outraged fellow citizens or what Harvard professor John K. Fairbank referred to as the "hisses" of "Cambridge ladies" who disagreed with isolationists such as Schumpeter. In late October, an article in a magazine criticized the committee, paying special attention to Townsend. It also lambasted Baxter, McKim, and Treat, all of whom it criticized for generating pro-Japan propaganda. Curiously enough, Armstrong, the leader of the pro-Japan isolationists, spent scant time and energy on discussion of Japan's record in East Asia. In fact, like many Americans in those days, he may have been ignorant of the real situation in the Far East.

WORSENING SITUATION IN THE FAR EAST

While Armstrong and his colleagues were working against war during the summer and fall of 1941, tensions between the United States and Japan increased as Japan's invasion of southern Indochina in July and General Tojo Hideki's assumption of the office of prime minister in mid-October drove the two countries closer to conflict. In November, Armstrong and Shaw were forced by events to admit that Japan's aggression in Asia was part of the problem and, in a letter to Secretary of State Hull, put more of the burden for maintaining peace on Japan. At that time, committee member Schumpeter estimated the chances of war with Japan as 50–50.

KEEPING THE JAPANESE INFORMED

While working for peace, Armstrong, the de facto leader of the committee, kept Japanese propaganda chief and intelligence agent Terasaki Hidenari in Washington informed about its activities, while telling very few members of his committee of this contact. Immediately after Armstrong and Acting Committee Chairman Shaw met with officials at the State Department in mid-November, the Missourian informed the Japanese embassy of their discussions, which the embassy then just as promptly reported to Tokyo. Ambassador Nomura Kichisaburo did not realize that the Americans were intercepting, decoding, translating, and reading his reports to Tokyo conveying what Armstrong told him regarding the committee. Armstrong also kept Terasaki and the embassy apprised of the committee's plans for a conference in Washington in the fall or early winter of 1941.

FBI INVESTIGATIONS OF COMMITTEE MEMBERS

Although comprising a mere handful of activists, the committee (along with the America First Committee) attracted the attention of the FBI and its bulldog director, J. Edgar Hoover. Several of its members, such as Armstrong, Schumpeter, Townsend, McKim, and Chamberlin, were placed under surveillance, including in some cases mail covers, wiretapping (approved by President Roosevelt for subversives, spies, and fifth columnists), and the compilation of dossiers that included their writings, speeches, and isolationist activities. In addition, the State Department's intelligence arm accused Armstrong and Townsend of serving as propagandists for the Japanese.

These FBI investigations yielded few results, and in the end only one committee member was convicted of a crime. In January 1942, Townsend was charged with failure to register under the Foreign Agents Registration Act. The evidence was thin, for payment was indirect. The Japanese authorities purchased thousands of his pamphlets rather than paying him directly. In the end, he was the only committee member convicted of being an unregistered Japanese agent and served several months in jail before being released following the appeal of several isolationist senators.

The Townsend story may help explain why Armstrong was careful to inform the State Department in late September and mid-November of the committee's activities and membership, even telling State that two officials at the Japanese embassy had "endorsed" the creation of the committee. He fared better than Townsend, for in May 1942 the FBI closed its investigation of him, rendering him safe from prosecution. Nevertheless, the suspicion that he had been "pro-Japan" hung over him during his wartime and postwar political career.

Schumpeter and her Harvard economist husband, Joseph, were placed under surveillance as security risks throughout the war. The Criminal Division of the Justice Department terminated the investigation of her when it was unable to prove she was an unregistered Japanese agent or propagandist. Chamberlin was investigated but swiftly cleared. McKim was suspected of serving as a paid agent of the Japanese government, and not until late in the war (December 1944) was his case closed for lack of evidence.

In late November, the committee began to come apart, even before Pearl Harbor destroyed it once and for all, when Acting Chairman Shaw resigned. In doing so, he rightly pointed out that the committee had never been really organized. Two weeks before the attack on Pearl Harbor, he fulsomely praised the Japanese in a radio broadcast titled "What Should Be Our Policy toward Japan," which must have persuaded any doubters that his committee was pro-Japan.

One cannot help concluding, after reading the personal correspondence and FBI dossiers of members of the Committee on Pacific Relations, that most of them were terribly naïve. Although Schumpeter believed that Japan had behaved "abominably" toward China, she also wrongly thought the "mad extremists" in Japan were in the minority. Japan was only copying the Western colonial powers, she insisted. In the face of the Nazi threat and the brutality of the Japanese Imperial Army (the "Rape of Nanjing" is just one example), committee members persisted in considering the preservation of peace in the late 1930s and early 1940s a matter of speeches, writing, and committee work. In doing so, some of them, such as Baxter and Armstrong, came across as apologists for Japan's expansion.

They won no friends by laying part of the blame for the deteriorating Far East situation on their own country. Schumpeter, Jones (though not a member of Armstrong's committee), Shaw, Thorburn Brumbaugh, and Paul Hutchinson all believed the United States bore some of the blame for Japan's aggression in Asia. Committee member Chamberlin, on the other hand, denied America was an imperialist country.

Pity President Roosevelt, who saw clearly what must be done in the face of the two-front threat from Europe and Asia but was hampered in acting by the opposition of the one-third of the American population who sympathized with the isolationists. Unfortunately for the Committee on Pacific Relations, during the months when Armstrong was trying to enlarge it and use it to lobby for a peaceful settlement with Japan, isolation's heyday was nearly over. He was anything but a quitter, though, and only a week following Pearl Harbor, he was back at work, this time calling for creation of a national committee for a "just and lasting peace."

HISTORICAL SIGNIFICANCE FOR THE PRESENT

The very terms "isolationism" and "America First" still live, proof that once again, as William Faulkner's character said, "The past is never dead. It's not even past."[1] After decades in abeyance, at present "America First" views have replaced the postwar idea that the United States had a duty and responsibility to be a leader in world affairs and that not all international affairs hinge on the question of whether America is being cheated on the bill. Moreover, once again the FBI has been called on to investigate foreign influence, this time on America's election process. Instead of Japan, though, today it is Russia (and possibly China).

NOTE

1. William Faulkner, *Requiem for a Nun* (New York: Library of America, 1994), 535.

Epilogue

The Afterlife of an Isolationist

With the coming of war, America First "swiftly entered the annals of public discourse tainted."[1] In the 1942 elections, several well-known isolationists were defeated, including four prominent senators and a leading congressman. Those who failed at reelection included Senators Gerald P. Nye, Burton K. Wheeler, Robert M. La Follette Jr., and C. Wayland Brooks as well as Congressman Hamilton Fish.[2] In the 1944 elections, there was further opposition to prewar isolationists, and senators, such as Nye, and representatives, like Fish, were again defeated.[3]

However, "noninterventionist efforts did not," wrote one historian, "prove fatal for some."[4] In 1942, Armstrong was one of those who survived the taint of prewar isolationism. In August, he wrote Charles Lindbergh that he had just won the primary election for the Missouri legislature in his district "against an opponent who was put up by the old 'war' crowd who fought me in my peace efforts." Instead of lying low in the aftermath of Pearl Harbor, he was defiant. He had been foolish to run, he admitted, but "I plan now to go ahead and make 'em like it" and run for governor in 1944. He had "rough going after Pearl Harbor," he confessed. "Some of American Legion Commander Milo J. Warner's henchmen in Indianapolis," he charged, had barred him from the legion on a "technicality." When Pearl Harbor occurred, he had forgotten to renew his membership, and on those grounds, "the local post refused to accept his dues."[5] Meanwhile, in addition to his work for the war effort and his political campaigning, he informed Lindbergh, he continued to write for *Readers' Digest* (from 1944 until his death), *Nation's Business*, *Country Gentlemen*, and "many more" magazines.[6]

He ended his letter to Lindbergh on a cheerful note. "There can be no doubt," he asserted, "that efforts to smear those who honestly pointed where we were heading are failing, as they should." Perhaps in a bid to demonstrate his patriotism, he informed the colonel that he was "doing considerable writing in the War Department offices, on material which the 'morale' boys feel will help the war effort, and I hope so. I shall continue to help win this thing." He then added, in a possible allusion to his future political ambitions, "But I have plans that go beyond that."[7]

Despite his stubborn attempts to justify his stance before the war—he never lost his upbeat approach to difficulties and setbacks—isolationism was extremely unpopular, as might have been expected, after Pearl Harbor. In February 1942, far away in Tokyo, Ambassador Joseph Grew jotted in his diary that "national isolationism" was an "anachronism," and the "practical logic of 'splendid isolationism', or bloc isolationism, has gone forever."[8] Closer to home, even Broadway exhibited signs of disillusionment with isolationism. Although it was a failure, Lillian Hellman's play *The Searching Wind* was described by one historian as an attempt to "damn isolationists for all time."[9] In 1942, a leading religious journal seems to have been correct in labeling isolationism a "dead political issue."[10] On 21 April, the Republican National Committee passed a resolution that repudiated isolationism as a party belief.[11]

The electorate had not forgotten either. In November 1942, Armstrong informed Lindbergh that he had won election to the Missouri legislature "handily," but it had been a "real fight." Shortly before the election, he reported, the "Legionnaire and super-patriot crowd" distributed a handbill "attacking my patriotism and making me all but a Nazi and Jap spy. It was really pretty bad." The day before the election, he continued, there was an hourly radio announcement calling for his defeat, because "I had . . . mixed with questionable characters in my peace activities."[12]

There was another factor in Armstrong's political fortunes, though, and that was his opposition to President Roosevelt's New Deal. The evening before the election, he wrote, he was attacked by a "mean, contemptible and vicious fellow who hates all who have not kissed the President's program from the start."[13] Following the war (May 1946), he again criticized the New Deal. He had just returned from Washington, he wrote, and was "struck with the confusion, bickering and downright inertia of the place. The New Deal crowd are fearful, and well they might be. It's a mess."[14]

After his victory in the 1942 election, he lashed out in a press interview at the attacks on him. His election to the Missouri legislature demonstrated, he told an interviewer, that the people "do not hold it against anyone who worked honestly to try to keep this country out of war." Nevertheless, he strongly objected to being called an "isolationist." He obfuscated the issue when he declared he had "always been in favor of cooperation between nations." "And the minute this country got into the war," he added, "every American worth shooting [sic] was in favor of winning it, of course. The election showed that people resent casting reflections [aspersions] on a man's patriotism because he hoped we could keep out of it."[15]

In 1944, he ran for the post of Missouri lieutenant governor but was defeated.[16] He was not the only prewar isolationist to be rebuffed at the polls that year. Missouri Democratic Senator Bennet Champ Clark also went down in defeat.[17] Armstrong's loss was despite his use of a campaign biography bare of references to his activities during 1940 and 1941,[18] the peak years of his career as an isolationist. That same year, he resumed his letter writing to Secretary of State Cordell Hull. In a January 1944 missive, he told Hull he "remembered my former interviews with you, with great pleasure"—even though there is no evidence Armstrong ever met Hull himself. He addressed Hull as though he was an elected representative of the people instead of a diplomat on whose shoulders rested the heavy burdens of planning for the postwar world. "Surely you are free to tell me, and any of my friends who are interested," he wrote, "the answers to three simple questions." Those questions clearly were motivated by Armstrong's fears regarding the Soviet Union's postwar intentions vis-a-vis the Baltic states, Eastern Europe, and even Western Europe. In closing, he told Hull he planned to "follow this letter to your office soon, and perhaps you can give me the answers in person." Six days later, he once again failed to get a meeting with Hull but did manage to meet with Charles E. Bohlen, chief, and Elbridge Durbrow of the Division of Eastern European Affairs. During the meeting, the diplomats maintained that only the secretary could answer Armstrong's first two questions and declared they did not understand his third query. Consequently, Armstrong pressed them to forward his letter to Hull. "Throughout the conversation," they added, "Mr. Armstrong was entirely agreeable." A month later, Bohlen wrote Armstrong to elaborate on the latter's questions.[19]

At the end of the war, there was no embrace of isolationism, as had occurred following World War I. Instead, there was overwhelming support for U.S. membership in the United Nations. For this, Americans had to thank, in part, President Roosevelt's constant references to the damaging mistakes of the isolationists' ideas.[20] Armstrong served one term in the U.S. House of Representatives from 1951 through 1952 (both the *New York Times* and *Washington Post* obituaries erred in claiming he had two terms). Neither obituary mentioned his career as an isolationist before World War II—let alone his covert relationship with propaganda chief and intelligence agent Terasaki Hidenari and others in the Japanese embassy.[21]

As for Armstrong's hero, during the war Lindbergh stayed in touch with isolationist colleagues from the prewar period.[22] Following the war, however, it was Armstrong who initiated contact with him. In 1956, he informed the colonel that he had named his son Charles Lindbergh Armstrong.[23] In letters to Lindbergh, whom he fervently admired—for years, the first letter he wrote in a new year was to Lindbergh—he again described the strain of running for office after Pearl Harbor with an isolationist background. At the beginning of 1944, he wrote, "Naturally, I remember with some joy and more sorrow the days of our association in a cause we felt—we knew—was right." He tried to cheer up Lindbergh, although he could just as well have been referring to himself. "Time brings changes—but will bring to you a greater measure of vindication, and of opportunity to serve, than most people realize."[24] Although he frequently wrote to Lindbergh, he did not see him often. In late 1944 and again in late 1945 or early 1946, the two did meet in Washington, DC.[25]

In May 1952, while Armstrong was still serving in the U.S. House of Representatives, he wrote Lindbergh from London: "What you did twenty-five years ago [referring to Lindbergh's transatlantic flight] was historic; what you have done since then may prove to be of even greater significance. Although many have not understood your motives nor agreed with all your actions, I am sure in my own mind that the future will vindicate all that you tried to do in the interests of peace on earth and goodwill toward men. So long as I live, I shall not forget the work we did together."[26]

Armstrong continued to write Lindbergh until 1956 (there are no further letters from Armstrong to Lindbergh in the Yale University archives after that year). In July of that year, he wrote the colonel about the donation of electronic chimes to the people of Hiroshima and the ceremony at which Armstrong would make the presentation speech on behalf of the Hiroshima Peace Center. Friends who contributed to the project would have their names inscribed on a scroll to be displayed permanently in the Peace Center Building. He told Lindbergh he would "like so much" to include his (Lindbergh's) name. In fact, it seems to have been a pitch for a contribution from Lindbergh, who was perhaps put off.[27] His last letter to Lindbergh asked him to autograph a photograph for a friend (which also may not have pleased the reclusive aviator).[28]

By 1971 (Lindbergh died in 1974), Marjorie Armstrong was writing in place of her elderly husband, and they were no longer writing directly to the Lindberghs. Instead, they wrote to the colonel care of his publisher to let the Lindberghs know that they had enjoyed his book, *Wartime Journals*, and believed to be a "highly significant record of some of this country's most painful experiences." By chance, she added, they had met Lindbergh's son and congratulated him on his father's "superb book." She reminded Lindbergh that their youngest son, Charles Lindbergh Armstrong, was his namesake.[29]

Epilogue

NOTES

1. A. Scott Berg, *Lindbergh* (New York: G.P. Putnam's Sons, 1998), 433.
2. Wayne S. Cole, *Charles A. Lindbergh and the Battle against Intervention in World War II* (New York: Harcourt Brace Jovanovich, 1974), 229.
3. Richard R. Lingeman, *Don't You Know There's a War On? The American Home Front, 1941–1945* (New York: G.P. Putnam's Sons, 1970; Perigee Books, 1980), 349.
4. Wayne S. Cole, *America First: The Battle against Intervention in World War II* (Madison: University of Wisconsin Press, 1953), 188.
5. O. K. Armstrong to Colonel [Charles A. Lindbergh], 22 August 1942, Charles A. Lindbergh Collection, Yale University Library, New Haven, CT. Two years earlier, Warner had been elected the legion's national commander at the same meeting in which the neutrality resolution sponsored by Armstrong and others had been violently rejected. "Legion Yells Down a Neutrality Call," *New York Times* (hereafter *NYT*), 27 June 1940, 12.
6. Armstrong to [Lindbergh], 24 August 1942, Lindbergh Collection; "O.K. Armstrong, 93, Journalist and Teacher," *NYT*, 17 April 1987, B6; "Orland Kay Armstrong," *Washington Post*, 17 April 1987, C4.
7. Armstrong to [Lindbergh], 22 August 1942.
8. Joseph C. Grew, *Ten Years in Japan: A Contemporary Record Drawn from the Diaries and Private and Official Papers of Joseph C. Grew, United States Ambassador to Japan, 1932–1945* (New York: Simon and Schuster, 1944), 516–17.
9. Lingeman, *Don't You Know There's a War On?*, 289.
10. "Primaries Show 'Isolationism' a Dead Political Issue," *Christian Century* 59, no. 34 (1942): 1021.
11. Breckinridge Long, *The War Diary of Breckinridge Long: Selections from the Years 1939–1944*, ed. Fred L. Israel (Lincoln: University of Nebraska Press, 1966), 259.
12. Armstrong to [Lindbergh], 12 November 1942, Lindbergh Collection.
13. Armstrong to [Lindbergh], 12 November 1942.
14. Armstrong to Lindbergh, 11 May 1946, Lindbergh Collection.
15. "Armstrong Has Definite Plans for Program in Legislature," unknown newspaper [Springfield paper?], n.d., Lindbergh Collection.
16. Armstrong to Lindbergh, 4 February 1945, Lindbergh Collection.
17. Lynne Olson, *Those Angry Days: Roosevelt, Lindbergh, and America's Fight over World War II, 1939–1941* (New York: Random House, 2013), 451.
18. M. J. Golden, Republican Committeeman, 21st Ward, Springfield, MO; Chairman, Third Greene County District, "A Letter from O.K. Armstrong's [Campaign] Chairman," 14 December 1943, encl. in Armstrong, Missouri House of Representatives, to "My dear friend Charles [A. Lindbergh]," 1 January 1944, Lindbergh Collection.
19. Armstrong, Missouri House of Representatives, to Secretary of State Cordell Hull, Department of State, Washington, DC, 22 January 1944; Charles E. Bohlen, Chief, Division of Eastern European Affairs, memo of conversation with Armstrong, 28 January 1944; Bohlen to Armstrong, Springfield, MO, 25 February 1944, 740.0011 European War 1939/32828, decimal file 1940-44, RG 59, NARA.
20. Lingeman, *Don't You Know There's a War On?*, 351.
21. "O.K. Armstrong, 93, Journalist and Teacher," B6; "Orland Kay Armstrong," *Washington Post*, 17 April 1987, C4.
22. Cole, *Charles A. Lindbergh*, 230.
23. Armstrong to Lindbergh, 10 July 1956, Lindbergh Collection.
24. Armstrong to Lindbergh, 1 January 1944, Lindbergh Collection.
25. Armstrong to Lindbergh, 1 January 1945 and 11 May 1946, Lindbergh Collection.
26. Armstrong, London, to Lindbergh, 21 May 1952, Lindbergh Collection.
27. Armstrong to Lindbergh, 1 January 1945 and 11 May 1946.
28. Armstrong to Lindbergh, 10 July 1956.
29. Marjorie M. Armstrong, Republic, MO, to Press Relations, Harcourt Brace Jovanovich, New York, 2 February 1971, Lindbergh Collection.

Bibliography

I. MANUSCRIPTS

America First Committee Records. Hoover Institution, Stanford, CA.
Armstrong, Orland Kay (1893–1987), Papers, 1912–1987 (C4056). State Historical Society of Missouri, Manuscript Collection, Columbia, MO.
Clyde, Paul H. Special Collections, Perkins Library, Duke University, Durham, NC.
Clyde, Paul Hibbet, and Mary Kestler Clyde Papers. Rare Book, Manuscript, and Special Collections Library, Perkins Library, Duke University, Durham, NC.
Griswold, Alfred Whitney Papers (MS 255). Manuscripts and Archives, Yale University Library, New Haven, CT.
Hiles, Charles C., Collection. Accession no. 1448. American Heritage Center, University of Wyoming, Laramie, WY.
Lindbergh, Charles A. Manuscripts and Archives, Yale University Library, New Haven, CT.
Morgan, Roy Leonard Papers (MSS 93-4). Special Collections, University of Virginia Law School, Charlottesville, VA.
National Council for the Prevention of War, 1921–1975 (DG 023). Swarthmore College Peace Collection, Swarthmore, PA.
Schuler, Frank, Papers. Franklin Delano Roosevelt Library, Hyde Park, NY.
Schumpeter, Elizabeth Boody Papers (A-43). Schlesinger Library, Radcliffe College, Cambridge, MA.

II. FBI DOSSIERS

Armstrong, Orland Kay. FBI File No. 62-45631, FOIA.
Chamberlin, William Henry. FBI File No. 100-32226, FOIA (same file as Schumpeter).
McKim, John Cole. FBI File No. 97-85, FOIA.
Schumpeter, Elizabeth Boody. FBI File No. 100-32226, FOIA.
Terasaki Hidenari. FBI File No. 65-HQ-37232, FOIA.
Townsend, Ralph W. FBI File No. 65-2193.

III. MEMOIRS AND SECONDARY WORKS

Abend, Hallett. "The Japanese Ambassador Plants a Story." *Liberty*, 18 October 1941, 14–15, 48.
Allen, Robert Loring. *Opening Doors: The Life and Work of Joseph Schumpeter.* Vol. 2, *America*. New Brunswick, NJ: Transaction, 1991.
Angus, H. F. Review of *The Industrialization of Japan and Manchukuo, 1930–1940: Population, Raw Materials and Industry*, by E. B. Schumpeter. *Canadian Journal of Economics and Political Science* 8, no. 1 (1942): 116–19.
[Anonymous]. Review of *Japan's Pacific Mandate*, by Paul H. Clyde. *Contemporary Japan* 4, no. 1 (1935): 95–98.
Baxter, William J. *Japan and America Must Work Together!* New York: International Economic Research Bureau, 1940.
Berg, A. Scott. *Lindbergh*. New York: G.P. Putnam's Sons, 1998.
Berle, Adolf A., Jr. *Navigating the Rapids: From the Papers of Adolf A. Berle*. Edited by Beatrice Bishop Berle and Travis Beal Jacobs. New York: Harcourt Brace Jovanovich, 1973.
Borg, Dorothy. "Two Histories of the Far Eastern Policy of the United States: Tyler Dennett and A. Whitney Griswold." In *Pearl Harbor as History: Japanese-American Relations, 1931–1941*, edited by Dorothy Borg and Shumpei Okamoto, 561–72. New York: Columbia University Press, 1973.
Borg, Dorothy, and Shumpei Okamoto, eds. *Pearl Harbor as History: Japanese-American Relations, 1931–1941*. New York: Columbia University Press, 1973.
Bridgewater, William, ed. *The Columbia-Viking Desk Encyclopedia*. 2nd ed. New York: Columbia University Press, 1964.
Bright, Charles Bright, and Joseph W. Ho, eds. *War and Occupation in China: The Letters of an American Missionary from Hangzhou, 1937–1938*. Lanham, MD: Rowman & Littlefield, 2017.
Brinkley, David. *Washington Goes to War*. New York: Alfred A. Knopf, 1988.
Browder, Earl. *Chinese Lessons for American Marxists*. Yonkers, NY: self-published, 1949.
———. *The Decline of the Left Wing*. Yonkers, NY: self-published, 1948.
"Brumbaugh Takes Student Post." *Christian Century* 58, no. 41 (1941): 1250.
"Buell, Raymond Leslie." *Marquis Who's Who on the Web* (accessed 19 July 2006).
Butow, Robert J. C. *The John Doe Associates: Backdoor Diplomacy for Peace*. Stanford, CA: Stanford University Press, 1974.
———. *Tojo and the Coming of the War*. Princeton, NJ: Princeton University Press, 1969.
Carlson, John Roy [Arthur Derounian]. *Under Cover: My Four Years in the Nazi Underworld of America*. New York: E.P. Dutton & Co., 1943.
Carpenter, J. Henry. "Peace Congress Meets in Capital." *Christian Century* 58, no. 24 (1941): 790–91.
Carter, Boake, and Thomas H. Healey. *Why Meddle in the Orient? Facts, Figures, Fictions, and Follies*. New York: Dodge, 1938.
Castle, William R. "A Monroe Doctrine for Japan." *Atlantic*, October 1940, 445–52.
Chapman, Roger. "Antiwar Movements: World War II." In *Encyclopedia of American Social Movements*, edited by Immanuel Ness, 1077–79. New York: Routledge, 2015.
Clyde, Paul H. *International Rivalries in Manchuria, 1689–1922*. Columbus: Ohio University Press, 1926.
———. *Japan's Pacific Mandate*. New York: Macmillan, 1935.
Cohen, Warren I. *The Chinese Connection: Roger S. Greene, Thomas W. Lamont, George Sokolsky, and American-East Asian Relations*. New York: Columbia University Press, 1978.
———. "The Role of Private Groups in the United States." In *Pearl Harbor as History: Japanese-American Relations, 1931–1941*, edited by Dorothy Borg and Shumpei Okamoto, 421–58. New York: Columbia University Press, 1973.
Cole, Wayne S. *America First: The Battle against Intervention in World War II, 1940–1941*. Madison: University of Wisconsin Press, 1953.

———. *Charles A. Lindbergh and the Battle against American Intervention in World War II.* New York: Harcourt Brace Jovanovich, 1974.
———. *Roosevelt and the Isolationists, 1932–45.* Lincoln: University of Nebraska Press, 1983.
"Comments and Correspondence: Sanctions against Japan?" *Pacific Affairs* 12, no. 4 (1939): 427–38.
Conant, Jennet. *The Irregulars: Roald Dahl and the British Spy Ring in Wartime Washington.* New York: Simon & Schuster, 2008.
Condliffe, J. B. Review of *The Industrialization of Japan and Manchukuo, 1930–1940*, ed. E. B. Schumpeter. *American Economic Review* 31, no. 1 (1941): 126–29.
Curcio, Vincent. *Henry Ford.* New York: Oxford University Press, 2013.
Davis, Kenneth S. *The Hero: Charles A. Lindbergh and the American Dream.* Garden City, NY: Doubleday, 1959.
De Bary, William Theodore, Carol Gluck, and Arthur Teidemann, comps. *Sources of Japanese Tradition.* Vol. 2, *1600–2000*. 2nd ed. New York: Columbia University Press, 2005.
Doenecke, Justus D. "Explaining the Antiwar Movement, 1939–1941: The Next Assignment." *Journal of Libertarian Studies* 8, no. 1 (1986): 139–62.
———. "*Scribner's Commentator* (1939–1942)." In *The Conservative Press in Twentieth-Century America*, edited by Ronald Lora and William Henry Longton, 273–82. Westport, CT: Greenwood Press, 1999.
Dower, John W. *Empire and Aftermath: Yoshida Shigeru and the Japanese Experience, 1878–1954.* Cambridge, MA: Harvard University Press, 1988.
Dunn, Susan. *1940: FDR, Willkie, Lindbergh, Hitler—the Election amid the Storm.* New Haven, CT: Yale University Press, 2013.
Eggleston, George T. *Roosevelt, Churchill, and the World War II Opposition.* Old Greenwich, CT: Devin-Adair, 1979.
E. R. K. Review of *Japan's Pacific Mandate*, by Paul H. Clyde. *Review of Reviews* 92, no. 1 (1935): 6.
Evans, Luther H. Review of *Japan's Pacific Mandate*, by Paul H. Clyde. *Annals of the American Academy of Political and Social Science* 183 (January 1936): 295.
Fairbank, John K. *Chinabound: A Fifty-Year Memoir.* New York: Harper & Row, 1982.
Falk, Peter H., ed. *Who's Who in America Art, 1564–1975.* Vol. 2. Madison, CT: Sound View Press, 1999.
"Fisher, Galen M." *Marquis Who's Who on the Web* (accessed 10 October 2005).
"Flowers, Robert L." *Marquis Who's Who on the Web* (accessed 18 August 2005).
"Frazar, Everett Welles." *Marquis Who's Who on the Web* (accessed 18 August 2005).
Friedman, Donald J. *The Road from Isolation: The Campaign of the American Committee for Non-participation in Japanese Aggression, 1938–1941.* Cambridge, MA: Harvard University Press, 1968.
Gale, Robert L. "Griswold, Alfred Whitney (27 Oct. 1906–19 Apr. 1963)." *American National Biography*, 9:640–41. New York: Oxford University Press, 1999.
Gentry, Curt. *J. Edgar Hoover: The Man and the Secrets.* New York: W. W. Norton, 1991.
Grew, Joseph C. *Ten Years in Japan: A Contemporary Record Drawn from the Diaries and Private and Official Papers of Joseph C. Grew, United States Ambassador to Japan, 1932–1945.* New York: Simon and Schuster, 1944.
Griswold, A. Whitney. "Facing Facts about a New Japanese-American Treaty." *Asia*, November 1939, 615–19.
———. "Should Japan Be Embargoed?" *Asia*, February 1940, 92–96.
———. "An Undeclared Peace." *Annals of the American Academy of Political and Social Science*, May 1941, 179–81.
Guillebaud, C. W. *The Economic Recovery of Germany from 1933 to the Incorporation of Austria in March 1938.* London: Macmillan, 1939.
Heneman, Harlow J. Review of *Japan's Pacific Mandate*, by Paul H. Clyde. *American Political Science Review* 29, no. 4 (1935): 706.
"Historical Introduction." National Council for the Prevention of War, electronic finding aid. Swarthmore College Peace Collection, Swarthmore, PA.
Hutchinson, Paul. "Peace Aims for Asia." *Asia* 41, no. 6 (1941): 271–73.

Hyde, D. Clark. Review of *The Industrialization of Japan and Manchukuo, 1930–1940*, ed. E. B. Schumpeter. *Southern Economic Journal* 7, no. 4 (1941): 586–87.

Jeans, Roger B. *Terasaki Hidenari, Pearl Harbor, and Occupied Japan*. Lanham, MD: Lexington Books, 2009.

Jonas, Manfred. *Isolationism in America, 1935–1941*. Ithaca, NY: Cornell University Press, 1966.

Jones, E. Stanley. "America United—on What Level?" *Christian Century* 58, no. 38 (1941): 1139–41.

———. "And So Forth." *Christian Century* 58, no. 32 (1941): 988.

Keesing, F. M. Review of *Japan's Pacific Mandate*, by Paul H. Clyde. *International Affairs* 15, no. 1 (1936): 163.

Kennedy, David M. *Freedom from Fear: The American People in Depression and War, 1929–1945*. New York: Oxford University Press, 1999.

Krebs, Gerhard. "The Spy Activities of Diplomat Terasaki Hidenari in the USA and His Role in Japanese-American Relations." In *Leaders and Leadership in Japan*, edited by Ian Neary, 190–205. Richmond, UK: Curzon Press, 1996.

Langer, William L., comp. and ed. *An Encyclopedia of World History*. Boston: Houghton Mifflin, 1952.

Langsam, Walter Consuelo. Review of *Japan's Pacific Mandate*, by Paul H. Clyde. *Political Science Quarterly* 51, no. 2 (1936): 32.

"Last Missionaries Freed in Manila." *Christian Century* 62, no. 12 (1945): 371–72, 381.

Leopold, Richard W. "Historiographical Reflections." In *Pearl Harbor as History: Japanese-American Relations, 1931–1941*, edited by Dorothy Borg and Shumpei Okamoto, 1–23. New York: Columbia University Press, 1973.

Libby, Frederick Joseph. "Time Approaches for Mediation in Far East." *Peace Action* 6, no. 6 (1940): 2.

———. "We Cannot Win a War with Japan." *Peace Action* 7, no. 2 (1940): 2.

———. "You Won't Forget Japan." *Peace Action* 6, no. 4 (1939): 1–2.

"Libby, Frederick Joseph." *Marquis Who's Who on the Web* (accessed 12 August 2005).

Lindbergh, Anne Morrow. *War Within and Without: Diaries and Letters of Anne Morrow Lindbergh, 1939–1944*. New York: Harcourt Brace Jovanovich, 1980.

Lindbergh, Charles A. *The Wartime Journals of Charles A. Lindbergh*. New York: Harcourt Brace Jovanovich, 1970.

"Lindbergh, the Most Dangerous Man in America." *Liberty*, 18 October 1941, 9.

Lingeman, Richard R. *Don't You Know There's a War On? The American Home Front, 1941–1945*. New York: G.P. Putnam's Sons, 1970; Perigee Books, 1980.

Lockwood, William L. Review of *The Industrialization of Japan and Manchukuo, 1930–1940*, ed. E. B. Schumpeter. *Annals of the American Academy of Political and Social Science* 215 (May 1941): 183–84.

Long, Breckinridge. *The War Diary of Breckinridge Long: Selections from the Years 1939–1944*. Edited by Fred L. Israel. Lincoln: University of Nebraska Press, 1966.

Lora, Ronald, and William Henry Longton, eds. *The Conservative Press in Twentieth-Century America*. Westport, CT: Greenwood Press, 1999.

Loureiro, Pedro. "Japanese Espionage and American Countermeasures in Pre-Pearl Harbor California." *Journal of American-East Asian Relations* 3, no. 3 (1994): 197–210.

"MacNider, Hanford (2 Oct. 1889–17 February 1968)." *American National Biography*, 14:280–81. New York: Oxford University Press, 1999.

Marquis Who's Who on the Web. https://marquiswhoswho.com/.

Matsuo, M. Review of *Japan's Pacific Mandate*, by Paul H. Clyde. *Pacific Affairs* 8, no. 2 (1935): 227–29.

May, Ernest R. "U.S. Press Coverage of Japan, 1931–1941." In *Pearl Harbor as History: Japanese-American Relations, 1931–1941*, edited by Dorothy Borg and Sumpei Okamoto, 511–32. New York: Columbia University Press, 1973.

McKim, John Cole. *The Decline of Militarism in Japan*. N.p.: n.p., 1920.

———. "Japan Battled Scourge of Cholera in 1879." *Japanese American Review* 40, no. 2091 (1941): 3, 6.

———. "Nippon, a Brief History." In *Special Japan Day Edition*. New York: Nippon Publishing Company, 1939; issued as *Japanese American Review* 39, no. 2060 (1939).
———. "Propagandists Have Shed Crocodile Tears to Distort Actual Situation in China." *Japanese American Review* 39, no. 2076 (1939): 1–2.
———. Review of *China at War*, by Freda Utley. *Japanese American Review* 39, no. 2076 (1941): 2, 7.
———. Review of *Contemporary Japan* (August 1941). *Japanese American Review* 41, no. 2125 (1941): 2.
———. Review of *Observations Made on a Trip to Japan*, by J. Russel Wait. *Japanese American Review* 40, no. 2095 (1940): 2, 7.
———. Review of *The Secret Shanghai*, by Jean Fontenoy. *Japanese American Review* 29, no. 2070 (1939): 2.
Milton, Joyce. *Loss of Eden: A Biography of Charles and Anne Lindbergh*. New York: HarperCollins, 1993.
Moore, Frederick. *With Japan's Leaders: An Intimate Record of Fourteen Years as Counsellor to the Japanese Government*. New York: Charles Scribner's Sons, 1942.
Nenninger, Timothy K. "Harbord, James Guthrie (21 Mar. 1866–20 August 1947)." In *American National Biography*, 10:42–43. New York: Oxford University Press, 1999.
"No Apology to Mr. Ickes." *Liberty*, 6 December 1941, 9.
Nomura Kichisaburo. "Diary of Kichisaburo Nomura, June–December 1941." In *The Pacific War Papers: Japanese Documents of World War II*, edited by Donald M. Goldstein and Katherine V. Dillon, 136–221. Washington, DC: Potomac Books, 2004.
Ogata Sadako. "The Role of Liberal Nongovernmental Organizations in Japan." In *Pearl Harbor as History: Japanese-American Relations, 1931–1941*, edited by Dorothy Borg and Shumpei Okamoto, 459–86. New York: Columbia University Press, 1973.
Olson, Lynne. *Those Angry Days: Roosevelt, Lindbergh, and America's Fight over World War II, 1939–1941*. New York: Random House, 2013.
Orchard, John E. Review of *The Industrialization of Japan and Manchukuo, 1930–1940: Population, Raw Materials and Industry*, by E. B. Schumpeter. *Pacific Affairs* 14, no. 2 (1941): 240–46.
Oursler, Fulton. *Behold This Dreamer!* Edited by Fulton Oursler Jr. Boston: Little, Brown, 1964.
———. "The Last Word." *Liberty*, 11 October 1941, 62.
———. "May She Always Be Right." *Liberty*, 22 November 1941, 9.
———. *Three Things We Can Believe In.* New York: Fleming H. Revell, 1942.
"Oursler, (Charles) Fulton." *Marquis Who's Who on the Web* (accessed 18 August 2005).
"Page, Kirby." *Marquis Who's Who on the Web* (accessed 14 July 2006).
Palyi, Melchior. Review of *The Industrialization of Japan and Manchukuo, 1930–1940*, ed. E. B. Schumpeter. *Review of Politics* 5, no. 3 (1943): 396–99.
"Peace in the Orient." *Uncensored*, no. 102 (1941): 1–2.
Peattie, Mark R. *Nan'yo: The Rise and Fall of the Japanese in Micronesia, 1885–1945*. Honolulu: University of Hawaii Press, 1988.
Perkins, Dorothy. *Encyclopedia of Japan.* New York: Roundtable Press, 1991.
Perrett, Geoffrey. *Days of Sadness, Years of Triumph: The American People, 1939–1945*. New York: Coward, McCann & Geoghegan Perrett, 1973; Penguin Books, 1974.
Persico, Joseph E. *The Eleventh Month, Eleventh Day, and Eleventh Hour: Armistice Day, 1918, World War I and Its Violent Climax*. New York: Random House, 2004.
Philips, Mary Ann. *"Fletcher Warren Reporting for Duty, Sir."* Austin, TX: Nortex, 2006.
"Primaries Show 'Isolationism' a Dead Political Issue." *Christian Century* 59, no. 34 (1942): 1021.
Reid, John Gilbert. Review of *Japan's Pacific Mandate*, by Paul H. Clyde. *Pacific Historical Review* 4, no. 3 (1935): 290–91.
"Rivers, William Cannon." *Marquis Who's Who on the Web*.
Scherer, James Augustin Brown, Ralph Townsend, and Charles E. Martin. "Shall We Guarantee Peace in the Pacific?" *Town Meeting* 6, no. 18 (1941): 3–32.

Schumpeter, Elizabeth Boody, ed. *The Industrialization of Japan and Manchukuo, 1930–1940: Population, Raw Materials and Industry*. New York: Macmillan, 1940.
———. "The Policy of the United States in the Far East." *Annals of the American Academy of Political and Social Science* 210 (July 1940): 98–106.
———. "The Problem of Sanctions in the Far East." *Pacific Affairs* 12, no. 3 (1939): 245–62.
Sebald, William J. *With MacArthur in Japan: A Personal History of the Occupation*. New York: W. W. Norton, 1965.
Sherwood, Robert E. *Roosevelt and Hopkins: An Intimate History*. Rev. ed. New York: Universal Library, Grosset and Dunlap, 1950.
Shoemaker, James H. Review of *The Industrialization of Japan and Manchukuo, 1930–1940*, ed. E. B. Schumpeter. *Yale Review* 30, no. 4 (1941): 845–47.
Steiger, George Nye. *China and the Occident: The Origin and Development of the Boxer Movement*. New York: Russell & Russell, 1927.
Stirling, Yates. *Sea Duty: The Memoirs of a Fighting Admiral*. New York: G.P. Putnam, 1939.
Suma, Yakichiro. "A Japanese Speaks." *Scribner's Commentator* 9, no. 4 (1941): 21–23.
Swedberg, Richard. *Schumpeter: A Biography*. Princeton, NJ: Princeton University Press, 1991.
Terasaki, Gwen. *Bridge to the Sun*. Chapel Hill: University of North Carolina Press, 1957; Newport, TN: Wakestone Books, 2000.
Thomas, John N. *The Institute of Pacific Relations: Asian Scholars and American Politics*. Seattle: University of Washington Press, 1974.
Thornton, Mark. "Schumpeter, Joseph Alois Julius (8 Feb. 1883–8 Jan. 1950)." *American National Biography*, 19:443-45. New York: Oxford University Press, 1999.
Townsend, Ralph W. *America Has No Enemies in Asia*. San Francisco: self-published, 1938.
———. *Does Japan Slam the Door against American Trade in Areas of Japanese Influence in America?* San Francisco: Japanese Chamber of Commerce, 1938.
———. *The High Cost of Hate*. San Francisco: Alec Nicoll, 1939.
———. "Japan—Our Commercial Prize." *Scribner's Commentator* 9, no. 1 (1940): 41–46.
———. *Seeking Foreign Trouble*. San Francisco: self-published, 1940.
———. *There Is No Halfway Neutrality*. San Francisco: self-published, 1938.
———. *Ways That Are Dark: The Truth about China*. New York: G.P. Putnam's Sons, 1933.
Treat, Payson. *Diplomatic Relations between the United States and Japan, 1895–1905*. 3 vols. Gloucester, MA: P. Smith, 1963.
———. *The Far East: A Political and Diplomatic History*. Rev. ed. New York: Harper & Brothers, 1935.
U.S. Department of Defense. *The "Magic" Background of Pearl Harbor*. 5 vols. Washington, DC: Government Printing Office, 1978.
U.S. Department of State. *Foreign Relations of the United States, Japan: 1931–1941*. 2 vols. Washington, DC: U.S. Government Printing Office, 1943.
"War in China." *Propaganda Analysis* 2, no. 5 (1939): 30–31.
Weaver, David H. "Howard, Roy Wilson (1 Jan. 1883–20 Nov. 1964)." In *American National Biography*, 11:314. New York: Oxford University Press, 1999.
Whitehead, Don. *The FBI Story*. New York: Random House, 1956.
Wilbur, C. Martin. *China in My Life: A Historian's Own History*. Armonk, NY: M.E. Sharpe, 1996.
"Wilson, E. Raymond (20 Sept. 1896–27 June 1987)." *American National Biography*, 23:570–71. New York: Oxford University Press, 1999.
Wood, G. L. Review of *The Industrialization of Japan and Manchukuo, 1930–1940*, ed. E. B. Schumpeter. *Economic Record* 17, no. 33 (1941): 291–97.

IV. INTERVIEWS

Kato Masuo. Interviews by Roy L. Morgan, Worth McKinney, and Harold Nathan, 6, 7, and 8 February 1946. Box 1, folder: [IMTFE] (IPS), February–July 1946, Interrogations of Japanese Officials. Roy L. Morgan Papers, University of Virginia Law School, Charlottesville, VA.

V. JOURNALS AND NEWSPAPERS

Christian Science Monitor
Japanese American Review
New York Times
New York World-Telegram
Peace Action
Washington Post

Index

ABCD (America, Britain, China, Dutch) encirclement of Japan theory, 74
Academy of Political and Social Science, 70
Addams, Jane, 18
Agar, Herbert, 40, 43
Amerasia, 62, 65–66, 67, 68
America First Committee, 1–2, 5, 25; and anti-communist views of, 15, 73; attacked as "Nazi Transmission Belt" by Friends of Democracy, 98, 103n30; criticized by *Liberty Magazine*, 109; discredited by war, 199; and Emergency Peace Conference, 18; and Europe orientation, 8; and fascists and communists, 5, 20; and FBI, 27, 108, 164; and Fight for Freedom, 98; and Friends of Democracy, 98; and German agent, 176; and *The Herald*, 180; and Hitler, 8; House Committee on Un-American Activities investigation of, 164; and Ingalls, Laura convicted as German agent, 185n51; and Japan, 8, 9–10, 35, 70, 108; membership of, 5, 19, 25, 27, 38, 70–71, 92, 123, 138, 145; and Ministers' No War Committee, 16, 101, 104n54; National Speakers Bureau of, 27–28; and 1942 elections, 71; and No Foreign War Campaign, 19, 20; and No Foreign War Committee, 20, 21, 22; opposition to aid to Great Britain, 5; opposition to Lend-Lease Act, 4; and pacifists, 16, 17; and Patriots of the Republic, 113; and Pearl Harbor attack, 71; and recruitment efforts in the South, 27–28, 29; revival of "America First" concept today, 197; and *Scribner's Commentator*, 21, 144, 180; and Thomas, Norman, 17; and Women's International League for Peace and Freedom, 16. *See also* Lindbergh, Charles A.
America-Japan Society (Tokyo), 44–45
American Association in Tokyo, 44
American Committee for Non-Participation in Japanese Aggression, 63, 99
American Communist Party, 62
American Forum Hour, 94
American Friends Service Committee, 18
American Legion, 16, 18, 24–25, 26
American Legion Magazine, 14, 24
American Socialist Party, 17
Annals of the American Academy of Political and Social Science, 57, 59, 81
Anti-interventionists. *See* isolationists
Armstrong, Charles Lindbergh, 30, 201, 202
Armstrong, Marjorie, 30, 202
Armstrong, Orland Kay ("O.K."): and America First, 19, 20, 25, 27–28, 28,

29–30, 35, 44, 94, 128, 147; and American Legion, 13, 14, 16, 16–17, 18, 24–25, 26, 129, 165, 184n16, 199, 200; and *American Legion Magazine*, 14, 24; and anti-British speeches of, 29; anticommunism of, 24, 201; and army intelligence, 164; and Assistant Attorney General Wendell Berge investigation of, 166; and Baptist Church, 13, 123; and Baxter, William, 28, 36, 43, 107, 117, 121, 124, 130, 136, 140, 142, 143; and Benton, William, 123; and Boss, Charles, 97, 99, 101, 122, 123, 128, 129, 130, 133, 142, 156, 177; and Brooks, Mary, 122, 123, 139; and Brumbaugh, 97, 139; and Byrd, Admiral Richard E., 13; and campaigns against vice in Kansas, 13; and Canada, 146; and Castle, 70, 71; and Chamberlin, 96, 106–107, 119–120, 127, 139, 142, 148; and Clyde, 53, 59–60, 76, 84, 122, 126, 134–135, 139, 140, 159n83; and commission to Japan, 44, 45, 58, 69, 71, 75, 94; and Committee on Pacific Relations, 1, 3, 9, 23, 27, 28, 35, 43–44, 53, 58, 70, 91, 105, 117, 120, 135, 156, 164, 165; conservatism of, 24, 25; and Coordinator of Information, 153; and Criminal Division, Department of Justice, 166; criticized by *The Hour* magazine, 144; and Cudahy, John, 145, 146; and Department of Justice investigation of, 166; and Division of Records, FBI, 166; and Donovan, William J., 153; and education of, 13, 44, 57, 165; and Emergency Peace Conference, 18, 19, 99; and FBI investigation and reports on, 14, 17, 18, 27, 29, 35, 42, 110, 120, 121, 155, 163, 164–165, 166, 167, 178; and Federal Iterali des Ancient Combatants, 13; Fisher, Galen M., 147, 148, 149; and Flowers, 134–135, 159n83; and Ford, Henry, 17; and Frazar, Everett, 119–120, 126, 134, 140, 141, 143, 178; and Griswold, 43–44, 53, 57–59, 70, 71, 117, 122, 124, 125, 134–135, 159n82; and Harbord, James, 119, 126, 134, 141; and Hiroshima Peace Center, 202; and Hoover, J. Edgar, 108, 164, 165, 166, 167; and House of Representatives, 201, 202; and Howard, Roy, 107–108, 117, 119, 122, 127, 131; and Hull, Cordell, 146, 147, 148–149, 149–150, 151, 151–152, 154, 201; and Hutchinson, Paul, 96, 97, 98, 99, 122–123, 128, 130, 139–140, 142; as isolationist, 14, 35, 200–201; and Japanese Embassy contacts and support, 14, 25, 27, 35, 44, 53, 76, 135, 136, 146, 147, 148, 152, 164, 165; and Johnstone, William C., 149, 161n142; and Jones, E. Stanley, 23, 122, 129, 129–130, 134–135, 139, 140, 147; Kansas City Division, FBI, 165, 166; and Lend-Lease Act, 23; and Libby, Frederick J., 19–20, 94, 100, 117, 119, 128–129, 129, 130, 133, 136, 138–139, 143, 145, 160n94, 163; and Lindbergh, Anne, 26; and Lindbergh, Charles, 13, 23, 25, 28, 30, 35, 100, 135, 145, 165, 167, 199–200, 200, 201–202; and Mackay, Raymond, 150, 151–153, 154; and MacNider, Hanford, 19; and magazine articles by, 199; and Marshall, Verne, 22, 23, 26, 129; May 1941 policy statement of, 3, 43, 57–58, 117, 128; and McKim, 91, 130, 136; and military men, 45; and Missouri Legislature, 13, 166, 199, 200; and Missouri Writers Guild, 13; and New Deal, 200; and New York inaugural meeting of Committee on Pacific Relations, 95, 96, 97, 117, 121, 122, 124, 128, 128–129, 130–131, 170; and No Foreign War Campaign, 18, 21, 25, 71, 129; and No Foreign War Committee, 20, 21–22, 23, 35; and Office of Naval Intelligence, 164; opposition to Roosevelt of, 24, 29, 200; and Oursler, Charles, 108, 109, 117, 122; and pacifists, 17; and "People's Campaign against War", 23; and Phelps, G. Sidney, 145, 147, 148, 153, 161n156; and post-Pearl Harbor article in the *Springfield Leader and Press*, 165; and Price, Harry B., 99, 122; and recruitment drive in the South, 27, 27–28, 29, 42–43, 43, 44, 94; and reports to the U.S. State Department, 121, 125, 126, 134–135, 146; in Republican Party, 13; and school textbooks debate, 24; and Schumpeter, Elizabeth, 45, 53, 59, 69, 71, 76, 94, 96, 105, 106, 107, 118, 119, 119–121, 122, 125, 127, 130, 136, 137, 139, 141, 142, 147, 148–149, 150–151, 156, 167; and Shaw, Mark, 28, 45, 94, 95, 107, 117, 119, 120, 121, 127, 130, 132, 136, 139, 142, 144, 145, 147, 148–149, 153, 155; Smith, Frederick C., 153; and Terasaki Hidenari, 109, 112, 117–118, 119, 121, 122, 123, 124, 133, 142–143, 145, 151, 178, 201; and Townsend, 96, 110, 112, 123, 124, 128, 139–140, 142, 143, 146, 177; and Treat, Payson, 65, 107, 122, 127, 139–140; and U.S. Department of State, 156, 177; and U.S. Department of State, Division of Foreign Activity Correlation, 144, 153; and U.S. generals, 2; and War Department office of, 200; and Warner, Milo J., 199, 203n4; and *Wartime Journals*, 202; and Washington conference, 96, 97, 117, 121, 123, 127, 133, 134, 135–137, 139, 139–140, 142, 156; and Westervelt, Leonidas, 133; Williams, Walter, 44, 57, 69, 149. *See also* Baxter, William J; Chamberlin, William Henry; Committee on Pacific Relations; isolationism; Japan; Libby, Frederick J.; Lindbergh, Charles A.; McKim, John Cole; Schumpeter, Elizabeth Boody; Shaw, Mark R.; Townsend, Ralph W.

Asia Answers, 42, 110
Asia magazine, 54–55, 57, 63
Atcheson, George Jr., 153
Atlanta, 29
Atlantic Conference, 15
Australia, 46
Austro-Asiatic Bulletin, 150

Baldwin, Hanson, 82
Baldwin Locomotive works, 178
Barnett, Robert W., 132, 133

Baxter, William J., 36–44; and absence of FBI file, 178; anti-British empire views, 38, 41; anti-China bias of, 39, 41, 42, 50n22; anti-communism of, 39; as apologist for Japan, 38, 39, 41; author of *Japan and America Must Work Together!*, 36, 38, 41, 42, 145; Baxter International Economic Research Bureau, 36, 178; and Committee on Pacific Relations, 132, 137; criticized by *The Hour*, 145; and FBI investigation of, 178; and financial support for Committee on Pacific Relations and its proposed Washington conference, 96, 178; and Griswold, 57; imperialist views of, 37; and Japanese business ties of, 178; and negotiated peace between Germany and Britain, 37, 40; opposition to New Deal of, 37, 41; opposition to Roosevelt, 36; opposition to war with Japan, 37, 40–41; and Silk Research Bureau of America, 145; *Under Cover* labels as pro-Japanese, 183n4; and "Yellow Peril", 40, 41, 42. *See also* Armstrong, Orland Kay
Beard, Charles, 121
Bell, Ulric, 43
Benton, William, 123, 157n24
Berge, Wendell, 166, 173
Berle, Adolf A. Jr., 173
Bisson, T.A., 55, 63, 85n11
Blakeslee, George H., 63
Bohlen, Charles E., 201
Boss, Charles, 97, 99–101, 122
British Malaya, 72
British Security Coordination, 29
Brooks, C. Wayland, 199
Brooks, Mary Walters, 122, 123
Browder, Earl, 119
Brumbaugh, Thorburn, 97, 102n24
Buell, Raymond Leslie, 148
Burke-Wadsworth Selective Service Act. *See* Selective Service Act
Byas, Hugh, 141
Byrd, Richard E., 13

Carlson, John Roy, 36
Caroline Islands, 82

Carter, Boake, 131, 159n68
Carter, Edward C., 36, 54, 62, 67
Castle, William R., 70–71, 107, 154
Cementex Company, 170
Century Group, 5, 43
Chamberlin, William Henry, 66; and alienation from Far Eastern Studies circles, 3, 68, 105; and Armstrong, 105, 145; and Committee on Pacific Relations, 106; and FBI investigation of, 168; and Japanese report on, 131; and National Antiwar Congress, 106; and rejection of term "isolationism", 105
Chiang Kai-shek, 46
Chiang, Madame, 109
Chicago Tribune, 120
China Christian Advocate, 98
"China Incident.". *See* Sino-Japanese War
Chinese Council for Economic Research, 65, 66
Chinese Red Army, 46
Christian Century, 96, 97, 98, 122, 130, 131, 143
Christian Science Monitor, 105, 135
Churchill, Winston, 15, 121
Clark, Bennet Champ, 24, 29, 43, 201
Clark, D. Worth, 43
Clark, Tom, Assistant Attorney General, 168, 169
Clive, Robert, 38
Clyde, Paul H., 75, 87n62, 89n122; accused of pro-Japan views, 83; and book and research materials useful to U.S. military in Pacific War, 84; and conclusion that Japan had not fortified Micronesia as of 1934, 83, 84; and criticism of *Japan's Pacific Mandate*, 89n124; and Micronesia trip in 1934, 84; and reviews of *Japan's Pacific Mandate*, 82–84
Cole, Wayne S., 2, 189
Columbia, Missouri, Peace Council, 42
Columbia University, 79
Commission on World Peace of the Methodist Church, 97, 99
Committee to Defend America by Aiding the Allies, 4, 21, 35, 99, 101

Committee to Defend America by Waging Peace, 101
Committee on Pacific Relations, 1, 23, 45, 108; and abortive Washington conference, 193; and anti-China views of, 194; and anti-communist views of, 73, 192; and apologist for Japan, 196; and Baxter's financial support of, 96; blamed their own country for Far East crisis, 196; and conservatism of, 192; criticism of, 194; disparaged by *The Hour*, 144; and Far Eastern crisis, 9; and FBI investigations of, 163, 164, 179, 195–196; and Howard, 107; and Institute of Pacific Relations demands committee change name, 132, 192; and Japan policy, 35, 108; and Japanese inside information on committee, 195; and Japanese report to Tokyo, 131; and Japanese support of, 23, 27, 36; and May 1941 call for formation of the committee, 58; members alienated from Far Eastern studies circles, 192; membership of, 3, 28, 35, 36, 40, 42, 47, 53, 65, 71, 75, 91, 92, 93, 94, 105, 123, 136, 170, 178, 183; naivete of members, 196; and New York dinner meeting of, 95–96, 97, 108, 130–131, 135; and opposition to Institute of Pacific Relations, 192; and opposition to New Deal, 192; opposition to pro-China line, 192; and opposition to domestic propaganda, 14; and opposition to Roosevelt, 192; organization of, 35, 120; ostracized as pro-Japan, 3; overlap in membership with America First, 191; and peace councils, 191; and prevention of war with Japan, 10; and pro-Japan stand, 106, 110; and shared beliefs of members, 191; and Sino-Japanese War, 193; unorganized nature of, 2; and U.S. State Department, 134, 152; and Washington conference of, 96, 97, 98. *See also* Armstrong, Orland Kay
Committee to Study Pacific Relations. *See* Committee on Pacific Relations
Comstock, Ada Louise, 67
Condliffe, John B., 80, 89n114

Congressional Record, 176
Conscription. *See* Selective Service Act
convoy policy debate, 4, 25, 40, 42, 190
Coordinator of Information, 84
Cosmopolitan Club, 119
Cudahy, John, 37, 146

Davis, Kenneth, 30
Dawes, Charles G., 43
Dawson, Charles, 27
Democratic Party Platform Committee, 100
Department of Commerce, 84
Department of Justice, 166
Detzer, Dorothy, 17, 18
Dies Committee. *See* House Committee on Un-American Activities
Dies, Martin, 164
Does Japan Slam the Door against American Trade in Areas of Japanese Influence, 173
Drury College, 13, 165
Dunn, Susan, 2
Durbrow, Elbridge, 201
Dutch East Indies, 9, 46, 72, 78

Economic Record, 79
Eddy, Sherwood, 129
The Effects of the Sino-Japanese Conflict on American Educational and Philanthropic Enterprises in China, 148
Eggleston, George T., 20, 21, 24, 67, 112, 113, 166, 180
Emergency Peace Conference, 18, 19
Espionage Act, 62, 164
Episcopal Church, 93, 170

Fairbank, John K., 73
The Far Eastern Policy of the United States, 53, 60
Far Eastern Survey, 36, 61, 65, 66, 68
Faulkner, William, 197
Federal Bureau of Investigation (FBI), 1, 2, 62, 197
Fellowship of Reconciliation, 100, 106
Field, Frederick, 67
Fight for Freedom Committee, 5, 43, 98
Fish, Hamilton, 118, 199

Fisher, Galen M. *See* Armstrong, Orland Kay
Flowers, Robert L., 134
Foreign Affairs, 56, 80
Foreign Policy Association, 148
Formosa. *See* Taiwan
Fortune Magazine, 36, 148
Frazar, Everett W. ("E.W."), 44, 119, 126, 170, 178
Freedom of Information Act, 164
French Indochina. *See* Indochina
Friends of Democracy, 98

Gearhart, Bertrand W., 155
George, Walter F., 118
German-Soviet Treaty of Friendship and Alliance, August 1939, 54, 55, 62, 63
Germany, 7
Gilbert, Rodney, *What's Wrong with China*, 50n22
Gray, Cecil W., 150, 151
Great Britain, 6; and American support for, 7, 46; debate in United States over aid to, 4; isolationists criticism of, 29, 36
"Great Debate," 1939-1941, 2, 3, 27, 189
Great Depression, 77, 132
Greater Boston Peace Council, 63
Grew, Joseph C., 55, 111, 200
Griswold, A. Whitney, 53–59, 75; and Institute of Pacific Relations, 54, 61, 63; and Japan policy, 54–55, 56; and Lindbergh, 56; and Schumpeter, 3, 53–55, 56, 60–62, 62–64, 68, 78; and Sino-Japanese War, 56; and Treat, 68; and unpopularity in Far Eastern studies circles, 53–54; and Vandenberg, 61, 62. *See also* Schumpeter, Elizabeth Boody
Guam, 93
Guillebaud, C.W., 80

Hamilton, Maxwell, 151
Harbin, 173
Harbord, James G., 45, 119, 126
Harper's Magazine, 48, 64
Hart, Merwin K., 20
Harvard University, 73, 76, 107
Hearst newspapers, 131, 142
Hearst, William Randolph, 131, 143
Hedges, Frank H., 135

Hellman, Lillian, 200
The Herald, 113, 166, 180, 181
Herald-Tribune, 64, 93
Hitler, Adolf, 8, 22
Holland, William L., 66
Hong Kong, 9
Hoover, Herbert, 101
Hoover Institution, 68
Hoover, J. Edgar, 108, 163, 164
The Hour, 113, 144
House Committee on Un-American Activities, 164
How the Oriental Press in San Francisco Has Treated Sino-Japanese War News, 148
Howard, Roy W., 38, 40, 42, 107–108, 122, 127; and Japanese report on, 131
Hu Shi, 152
Hull, Cordell, 7, 134
Hutchins, Robert Maynard, 138
Hutchinson, Paul, 98–99, 122, 129, 131

Ichihashi Yamato, 68
Ickes, Harold, 109
India, 9
Indochina, 9, 57, 72, 78
Inner Mongolia, 75
Institute of Pacific Relations, 36, 54, 62, 68, 86n45, 138, 148; protests name of Armstrong's committee, 132–133. *See also* Schumpeter, Elizabeth Boody
Ishibashi Tanzan, 62, 63, 76
Isolationism, 1, 197; and anti-British views of, 7, 43; British opposition to, 29; and defeats of, 3–4; and influence of World War I on, 3; and Japan, 8, 9; and rejection of by Republican National Committee following war, 200; as traditional policy of the United States, 3; and unpopularity after Pearl Harbor, 200; and waning of, 120
Isolated America, 148
Italy, 7, 18

Jaffe, Philip, 62, 67, 68
Japan : and American businessmen, 36; and American isolationists, 6, 164; and American pacifists, 6, 7; anti-communism of, 46, 150; atrocities in China by, 41, 112; and Chiang Kai-shek, 111; and "China Incident", 8, 46; diplomatic code broken by the U.S., 109; expansion of, 6, 8; Foreign Ministry of, 6, 113; and Indochina, 64, 94, 120, 150; and League of Nations, 82; and Lindbergh, 6, 164; and Micronesia, 82; and "New Order" in Asia, 55, 75; and Nine-Power Pact, 152; and non-aggression pact with the Soviet Union, 150; Order of the Rising Sun, third class (awarded by emperor), 44; Order of the Sacred Treasure, third class, 65, 87n61; and "peace party" in, 37; and President Roosevelt, 6; and Siberian Expedition, 92; and South Seas Bureau, 83; and menace of, 46; U.S. freezes assets of, 94, 120; and "War Party" in, 92
Japan Center (New York), 44
Japan Institute, 167
Japan Over Asia, 105, 106
Japanese American Review, 92, 145, 169
Japanese Chamber of Commerce, 167
Japanese Christian Socialists, 95
"Japanese Project.". *See* Committee on Pacific Relations
Johnson, Hugh S., 38, 40
Jones, E. Stanley, 10, 37, 74, 75, 78, 91, 95, 98, 99, 106, 108, 112, 152, 181
Journal-American, 135

Kagawa Toyohiko, 95, 112, 130, 140, 181
Keep America Out of War Congress, 18, 19, 22, 94, 101, 106
Knox, Frank, 4, 15, 144
Knoxville, 27–28
Knoxville Peace Council, 27
Kondo Shinichi, 170
Konoye Fumimaro, 96, 141, 144
Korea, 80
Krock, Arthur, 120
Kurusu Saburo, 147, 149, 152

La Follettte, Robert M. Jr., 199

Langdon, William, 121, 134–135, 150, 151, 171
Lattimore, Owen, 36, 67–68

League of Nations, 8, 82, 93
Lend-Lease Act, 4, 17, 22, 23, 25, 40, 71, 86n45, 107, 112, 190
Libby, Frederick J. : and America First, 15; and anti-British views, 15; and antiwar policy, 15; and Armstrong, 14, 16, 129; and China policy, 14–15; and Committee on Pacific Relations, 94, 131, 169, 183; and communism, 15; and Emergency Peace Conference, 18, 19; and Hamilton, Alex, 183; and Japan policy, 15; and Lindbergh, Anne, 16; and Lindbergh, Charles, 16; and National Council for the Prevention of War, 14, 15, 131, 183; and national referendum on peace or war, 15; and Neutrality Act, 15; and No Foreign War Campaign, 19–20; and pro-Japan stance, 128; and Shaw, 179. *See also* Armstrong, Orland Kay
Liberty Magazine, 108, 109, 110, 115n30, 122, 124
Lindbergh, Anne, 16, 26, 164
Lindbergh, Charles A. : and America First, 5, 27–28, 28, 29; and American Jews, 17, 109; and Armstrong, 25, 26, 101; attacked as Nazi and American Hitler by Friends of Democracy, 98; and Emergency Peace Conference, 18; and FBI wiretapping of, 164; and Hearst, William Randolph, 143; and Howard, Roy, 107; and isolationists, 93, 201; and Japan, 5, 6, 10, 101; and Marshall, Verne, 22, 26; and National Council for the Prevention of War, 16; and No Foreign War Campaign, 20, 21, 26; and No Foreign War Committee, 20, 21, 22, 25, 26; and opposition to Roosevelt, 71; and pacifists, 16; and *Scribner's Commentator*, 21, 113; and *Wartime Journals,*, 23, 30
Linebarger, Paul M., 84
Lippmann, Walter, 56, 57, 120
Louisville, 27–28, 28, 44, 123
Louisville *Courier-Journal* , 27, 43
Luce, Henry, 5
Ludlow (Louis L.) Amendment, 48, 100

MacNider, Hanford, 19–20, 32n50

Manchukuo, 44, 47, 55, 71, 74, 96, 152, 173
Manchuria, 2, 8, 80, 82
Marco Polo Bridge Incident, 2
Mariana Islands, 82
Marshall Islands, 82
Marshall, Verne, 21, 21–22, 24, 100, 144
Matsuoka Yosuke, 6, 19, 96
McCarthy, Joseph, 3, 32n50, 37, 73
McCormick, Robert R., 120
McDonald, Barbara, 27, 28
McKim, John Cole, 91–93; and America First, 92; and anti-China views of, 92; and anti-communist views of, 73, 93; and Armstrong, 170–171; and Assistant Attorney General Tom Clark, 169; and Brundage, Avery, 92; and Chiang Kai-shek, 92, 93; and Committee on Pacific Relations, 91, 92, 93, 170–171; criticized by *The Hour* magazine, 145; and *The Decline of Militarism in Japan*, 92; and FBI, 2, 171, 178; and Foreign Agents Registration Act, 169; and isolationism, 92, 93; and *Japanese American Review*, 92, 145, 169; and Japanese Consulate General, 169; and Japanese "Monroe Doctrine", 93; and Japan's invasion of Indochina, 93; and Japan's withdrawal from the League of Nations, 93; and the Kuomintang (Guomindang), 93; and letters to the press, 93; and Manchuria, 93; and *New York Times*, 169; and pro-Japan views of, 91–92, 124, 183n4; and Roosevelt, Franklin, 92; and Stimson, 93; suspected of being foreign agent, 169
McKim, Nellie, 93
Messersmith, George S., 172, 186n54
Methodist Church, 98, 99, 101, 122
Miao, Chester (Miao Ch'iu-sheng), 130, 140
Military Intelligence Division (G-2), War Department, 84, 172
Ministers' No War Committee, 16, 101, 104n54, 156
Missouri Writers Guild, 13
Mitsubishi, 47
Mitsui, 47
Monroe Doctrine, 8, 10

Moore, Frederick, 6, 172
Moore, John Bassett, 39, 49n17
Moore, Norman G., 27, 28
Must We Go to War?, 129

N.Y.K. Line, 173
Nation Magazine, 18
National Antiwar Congress, 101, 106
National Committee for Christian Education in China, 130
National Committee for the War Referendum, 48
National Council for the Prevention of War, 9, 14, 15, 16, 18, 19, 28, 53, 94, 106, 121, 131, 153, 175, 183; and Washington conference, November 1941, 138, 142, 147, 148, 149, 153, 178
National Education Association, 24
National Press Club, 23
National Recovery Administration, 38
Nazi-Soviet Nonaggression Pact. *See* German-Soviet Treaty of Friendship and Alliance
Neutrality Act, 1937, 2, 3, 8–9, 15, 118, 190
New Deal, 24, 27, 37
"New Order" in East Asia, 75
New World, 103n43
New York Association of History Teachers, 24
New York Daily News, 131
New York State Economic Council, 20
New York Sun, 93
New York Times, 14, 24, 48, 63–64, 64, 82, 93, 110, 120, 137, 141, 155
New York World Telegram, 108, 118, 131, 135
Nippon Publishing Company, 169
Nishio, F.M., 170
No Foreign War Campaign, 19, 20, 99
No Foreign War Committee, 21, 25, 100, 144
Nomura Kichisaburo, 6–7, 38, 45, 101, 108, 146, 172; and Committee on Pacific Relations, 131, 146, 166
North China, 75
Nye, Gerald P., 43, 182, 199

Office of Naval Intelligence, 164, 172

Ohashi Chuichi, 111
Ohio State University, 97
Oklahoma City, 29
Olson, Lynne, 2
Oregon University, 6
Oriental Economist, 62, 63
Oursler, Charles Fulton, 108–109, 122

P & S Publishing Company, 21
Pacific Affairs, 36, 55, 61, 63, 65–66, 67–68, 68, 71–72, 79
Page, Kirby, 129
Paris Peace Conference, 82
Patriots of the Republic, 113
Payson, Charles S., 20, 21
Peace Action, 19, 53, 139
Peace Action Council of the Community Church, 63
Peattie, Mark, 84
Peekskill, New York, 169
Peffer, Nathaniel, 64, 94
"People's Campaign against War", 23
People's Platform (radio program), 24
Pepper, Claude, 43
Perry, Matthew, 47
Phelps, G. Sidney, 145
Philippines, 46, 72, 132
"Phony War," 1939-1940, 6, 108
Price, Harry B., 63
Provisional Committee toward a Democratic Peace, 101

Quaker Meeting House conference in Washington, November 1941, 133

Radio Corporation of America (RCA), 46
Rape of Nanjing, 41
Reischauer, Edwin, 107
Reynolds, Robert R., 43
Rivers, William C., 39, 48, 125
Rockefeller Institute of Social and Religious Research, 148
Roosevelt, Franklin D., 15; and Far Eastern dictatorships, 111; isolationists opposition to, 5, 9, 190; and Lend-Lease Act, 4; and opposition to isolationists, 8, 201; and "shoot-on-sight" speech, 122, 158n46; and wiretapping of Committee of Pacific

Relations members, 163–164
Roosevelt, Theodore Jr., 24
Rotarian magazine, 143
Russo-German Mutual Nonaggression Pact. *See* German-Soviet Treaty of Friendship and Alliance

St. Louis, 23, 26, 42, 100
Scripps-Howard newspapers, 107, 108, 131
Schumpeter, Elizabeth Boody : and alienation from Far Eastern studies establishment, 60, 61, 63, 65, 66, 69, 75, 76, 105, 118; and anti-communism of, 73, 77; and Armstrong, 48, 69–70, 75, 119, 121, 125, 141–142; and Baxter, 142; and Bloch, Kurt, 55, 63, 64, 65, 66, 68, 72; charges dismissed by Attorney General Tom Clark, 168; and China views of, 75; and Committee on Pacific Relations, 3, 53, 75, 94, 96; and conservatism (right wing) of, 67, 71, 167; and Criminal Division, Department of Justice, 168; and criticism of U.S. and West's Far Eastern policy, 73, 74, 75–76, 77, 77–78; and doubts about Shaw, 142; and education of, 60; and embargo debate, 73; and "encirclement of Japan" charge, 74; and FBI, 2, 167–168, 178; and Great Depression, 77; and Griswold, 60, 70, 71; and Harvard Economic Service, 69; and Harvard-Radcliffe Bureau of International Research, 60, 69, 71, 73; and Hoover, J. Edgar investigation of, 168; and hostility toward Roosevelt, 71, 121; and *The Industrialization of Japan and Manchukuo, 1930-1940*, 56, 61, 64, 70, 71, 75, 76–81, 167, 168; and Institute of Pacific Relations, 55, 61, 62, 64, 65, 66–67, 69, 73, 79, 169; and Japanese contacts and support of Schumpeter, 76, 80, 167, 168; and Japanese liberals, 74, 76; and Japanese military's behavior, 72, 73, 77; and Japan's "Monroe Doctrine", 77, 82; and Japan's occupation of Korea and Taiwan, 77, 80; and "mad extremists" in Japan, 74; and Manchukuo, 74, 80; and "New Order" in East Asia, 75; and Post Office difficulties, 167; and pro-Japan views of, 71, 74–75, 76, 77, 167, 168; and rejected for job with the Office of Production Management, 168; and reviews of *The Industrialization of Japan and Manchukuo*, 78–81; and Treat, Payson J., 3, 60, 62, 65–66, 67, 68, 70; *Under Cover* omits from pro-Japan charge, 183n4; and U.S. Monroe Doctrine extension to Asia, 78; U.S. Senate, Internal Security Subcommittee, 168; and U.S. Senate Judiciary Committee, 168; and Vandenberg, 62; and Vassar College, 69; and Wheaton College, 69. *See also* Armstrong, Orland Kay; Baxter, William J.; Griswold, A. Whitney; Treat, Payson J.
Schumpeter, Joseph Alois Julius, 54, 56, 60, 64, 72, 73, 76, 119, 167, 168
Scribner's Commentator, 20, 21, 24, 67, 100, 112–113, 113, 124, 131, 143, 144, 166, 179–181, 182
Sears, Roebuck, 164
Selective Service Act, 4, 46, 100, 190
Shaw, Mark R.: and America First, 96, 138, 144; and Armstrong, 21, 94–95, 95, 96, 132, 137–138, 140, 143–144; and Committee on Pacific Relations, 94, 96, 131, 153–155, 170; criticized by *The Hour* magazine, 144; and Institute of Pacific Relations, 132; and Japan domestic political situation, 97; and Japan Society of Boston, 94; and Japanese report on, 131, 146; and Jones, 154; and Kagawa Toyohiko, 95; and the National Council for the Prevention of War, 94, 155; and U.S. Department of State, 96, 151. *See also* Armstrong, Orland Kay
Sherman, William Tecumseh, 29
Shirer, William, 120
Sian Incident, 46
Singapore, 9
Sino-Japanese War, 1937-1945, 47, 68, 72, 109; and isolationists, 9, 92, 93, 130; debate over U.S. policy toward, 2, 3,

48, 73, 77
Sino-Japanese War, 1894-95, 6
Smith, Frederick, 154
Smith, Robert Aura, 155
South Manchurian Railway, 80
Soviet Union, 150
Special Intelligence Service, 115n30
Springfield, Missouri, 13, 17, 18, 19, 28, 29, 30, 42, 125, 147, 165
Spykman, Nicholas John, 60, 61, 65, 69
Steiger, George Nye, 64, 87n53
Stewart, Douglas, 21, 100, 113, 180
Stimson Doctrine, 74, 88n97
Stimson, Henry, 4, 15, 93
Stirling, Yates Jr., 39
Stuart, R. Douglas Jr., 18, 25
Suma Yakichiro, 113

Taft, Robert A., 8, 182
Taiwan, 80
Tansill, Charles C., 121
Terasaki Hidenari, 1, 14, 76, 109, 117–118, 119, 121, 142, 145
Third Naval District, Naval Counter-Intelligence Section, 164
Thomas, Elbert D., 154
Thomas, John, 68
Thomas, Norman, 17, 18, 103n43
Tojo Hideki, 97, 144, 147
Town Hall of the Air (radio program), 22, 113
Townsend, Ralph W., 39, 42, 71; and America First, 112, 171; and *America Has No Enemies in Asia*, 173, 181, 182; arrested in Lake Geneva, 181; and *Asia Answers*, 173; and attacked by Chinese consuls, 174; anti-British views of, 110; and anti-China views of, 108, 110, 111, 112, 113, 176; and anti-communism of, 73, 110, 111, 174; and Berge, Wendell, 173, 175; and Berle, Adolf A. Jr., 173; and Chiang Kai-shek, 110, 111, 112; and Committee on Pacific Relations, 110, 123, 131, 171; and Committee on Trade and Information (Japanese), 176; and Criminal Division, Department of Justice, 176; and criticism of Roosevelt, 111–112; criticized by *The Hour* magazine, 144; and Department of Justice investigation of, 180, 181; and Eggleston on, 179, 182; employed by the State Department, 110, 115n34; and FBI, 171–183; and Foreign Agents Registration Act, 174, 175, 176, 179, 181, 182; and *Friday* magazine charge, 174; and German Consulate General, 173; and grand jury, 177, 179–180, 181; and *The Herald*, 113, 180, 181; and hero to Japanese right wing after war, 183; and *High Cost of Hate*, 171–172, 173, 182; and Hoover, 172, 173, 174–175, 176–177; identified as Japanese agent by Institute for Propaganda Analysis, 179; and imprisonment of, 2, 146, 171, 179, 182; and investigation by the State Department, 153, 171–172, 172, 176, 179; and isolationism, 110; and Japanese Chamber of Commerce, 144, 173, 175, 179; and Japanese Committee on Trade and Information, 110, 182; and Japanese Consulate General, 182; and Lend-Lease Act,, 112, 174; and Libby, 177, 179, 180; and list of isolationists, 180; and Manchukuo, 177; and Manchuria, 174; and McKim, 91, 110, 171; and N.Y.K. Line, 173; and National Council for the Prevention of War, 175; and post office difficulties, 176; and press criticism of, 180; and pro-Japan views, 108, 110, 111, 113, 175, 183n4; and *Propaganda Analysis* report on, 179; and Roosevelt, 171; and *Scribner's Commentator*, 112, 153, 181–182; and *Seeking Foreign Trouble*, 173, 174, 176; and Senator Claude Pepper's call for investigation of, 173; and Sino-Japanese War, 111, 112; suspected of being foreign agent, 169; *There Is No Halfway Neutrality*, 182, 185n53; and travel to Japan, 177; and trial of, 167; and *The Truth about England*, 182; and Wallace, George, 183; and War Department, 174; and *Ways That Are Dark: The Truth about China*, 172–173, 176, 183; and Women's International League for

Peace and Freedom, 175. *See also* Armstrong, Orland Kay
Treat, Payson J., 62, 65, 68, 69; and alienation from Far Eastern establishment, 65–66, 105; and Committee on Pacific Relations, 131. *See also* Schumpeter, Elizabeth Boody
Tripartite Alliance. *See* Tripartite Pact
Tripartite Pact, 7, 9, 37, 76, 106
True, James, 144

Uncensored, 96, 102n22, 137
Under Cover, 113, 182
United Kingdom. *See* Great Britain
United Nations, 201
U.S. Army Air Corps, 13
U.S. Department of State, 134, 169; Division of East European Affairs, 201; Division of Far Eastern Affairs, 121, 144, 151, 153
U.S. House of Representatives: Foreign Relations Committee, 118; Military Affairs Committee, 100; Naval Affairs Committee, 15
U.S.-Japan Trade Treaty. *See* U.S. Treaty of Commerce and Navigation
U.S. Marine Corps, 85
U.S. Navy, 107, 122
U.S. Senate: Foreign Relations Committee, 23, 40, 112; Internal Security Subcommittee, 168; Judiciary Committee, 100, 168; Naval Affairs Committee, 118
U.S. Treasury, 37
U.S. Treaty of Commerce and Navigation (1911), 15, 56, 57, 63, 91
U.S. "War Party", 37, 38
U.S.S. Panay, 112
University of California, Berkeley, 80
University of Chicago, 99
University of Chicago Round Table, 94
University of Florida, 13
University of Missouri, 13, 44, 135
Utley, Freda, 92

Van Zandt, James E., 24
Vandenberg, Arthur H., 86n45
Vichy France, 7
Viereck, George Sylvester, 188n116
Villard, Oswald Garrison, 18

Walsh, David I., 118
Warren, Fletcher, 153
Waseda University, 62
Washington Post, 14, 180
Wesley Foundation, 97
Wheeler, Burton K., 29, 100, 101, 145, 182, 199
White, William Allen, 4, 21
Whitney, Joan, 21
Wilbur, C. Martin, 66, 67, 68, 105
Willkie, Wendell, 38, 71, 148
Wilson, E. Raymond, 153, 161n156
Women's International League for Peace and Freedom, 9, 16, 17, 18, 106, 140, 175
Wood, Robert E., 8, 27–28, 37, 164
Woodstock Hotel, 119, 124–125, 128, 130, 132
World Peace Newsletter, 142
World War I, 3, 13, 21

YMCA, 97, 145, 148
Yale Review, 78
Yap, 82
"Yellow Peril" views, 84
Yoshida Shigeru, 39, 49n17, 55

About the Author

Roger B. Jeans Jr. is Elizabeth Lewis Otey Professor of History Emeritus at Washington and Lee University. His books include *The Letters and Diaries of Colonel John Hart Caughey, 1944–1945: With Wedemeyer in World War II China*; *The CIA and Third Force Movements in China during the Early Cold War: The Great American Dream*; and *Terasaki Hidenari, Pearl Harbor, and Occupied Japan*.

www.ingramcontent.com/pod-product-compliance
Lightning Source LLC
Chambersburg PA
CBHW052036300426
44117CB00012B/1845